No. 1061
$14.95

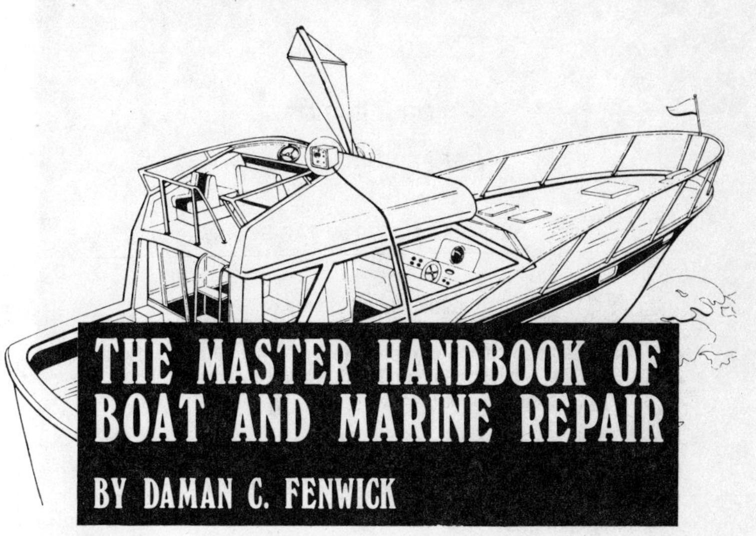

TAB BOOKS

BLUE RIDGE SUMMIT, PA. 17214

FIRST EDITION

FIRST PRINTING—JUNE 1979

Library of Congress Cataloging in Publication Data

Fenwick, Daman C.
The master handbook of boat and marine repair.

Includes index.
1. Boats and boating—Maintenance and repair. 2. Motor-boat engines—Maintenance and repair. I. Title.
VM321.F46   623.82'08   79-12573
ISBN 0-8306-9794-2
ISBN 0-8306-1061-8 pbk.

Contents

Brightwork, the Millionaire's Finish—The New Paints—Drawbacks of the "Hard" Finishes—The "System" Paints—The Epoxy Paints—The Urethanes—The Vinyl and Latex Paints—The Anti-Fouling Bottom Paints—Barnacles, Marine Growths and Bottom Paints—There is a "Maintenance Free" Finish—The New "Miracle" Finishes—How Boats Deteriorate and Depreciate—How to Sell a Bad Boat—How to Protect Your Boat Investment—Sanding and Sandpapers—Sandpaper Selection Guide—Sandpaper Grades—Steel and Bronze Wools—A Boat Paint That Doesn't Have to be Sanded—The Best Cheap Bottom Paint—When Not to Scrub a Boat Bottom—Where to Buy Marine Paints, Sealers, and Anti-Fouling—Determining Paint Needed—Paint Table—A Hammer, Nails and a Sledge on a Boat—The Domestic Type Vacuum Cleaner—The Shop-Type Vacuum Cleaners—The Cordless Power Drill—Fastenings—A Minimum Tool List—Why Carry a Propeller Puller?—Spare Parts and Scuba Divers—The "Adjustable" Wrenches—The Screwdriver—Pliers—Allen Wrenches—C-Clamps—Socket Wrenches—The Combination Box and Open-End Wrench—To Buy or Not to Buy Metric Tools—Varnish Brushes—Paint Brushes—The Paint Roller—Paint Sprayers—The Winter Layup—The Plastic Boathouse.

How Long Will Fiberglass Last?—Can Fiberglass Take Stress?—The Last Test For Fiberglass—The Good Things About Fiberglass—The "Maintenance Free" Myth—Why Fiberglass Boats Don't Leak—More Good Things About Fiberglass—The Hull Thumpers—How to Judge Quality in Fiberglass—Poorly Installed Deck Hardware—Why Stern Cleats Pull Out—The Bad Things About Fiberglass—Getting Fiberglass Boats Repaired—Painting Fiberglass—The "Cure" for Fiberglass Paint Troubles—Getting Ready to Paint—Preparing Fiberglass by the "No Sand" Method—Preparing Fiberglass by the Sanding Method—Power Sanding—Power Sanding Can be Dangerous to Health—Sanding by Hand—Keeping Wives Happy Sanding—A Special Clean Up Tool—How to Make a Tack Rag—Preparing the Bottom—Gel Coat Blisters—The Endless Gel Coat Blister Controversy—The Facts About Warranties—Pettit's Cure for Blisters—Repairing Fiberglass Scratches, Holes—Repairing Deep Holes and Dents—Repairing Major Fiberglass Damage—Tools, Supplies for Major Fiberglass Repairs—The Inside Patch—The Outside Patch—Some Tips on Working With Fiberglass—Fiberglass Repair Kits—Is Waxing Necessary?—Where Not to Wax—Selecting a Color for Your Boat.

Introduction

Who really needs a book like this?

Before 1965, practically nobody.

So why write it?

Things change. People change. Tax laws change.

Fourteen years ago a thick maintenance-repair manual for do-it-yourself boat owners would have been useful mainly as a doorstop or temporary storage place for butterfly specimens. But not today.

Although boat ownership was high years ago, and steadily increasing year after year, the owners of cabin cruisers over 22 feet in length were little interested in learning all the details and fine nuances of maintenance and repair of their boating investments, no matter how small or large. And there was a good reason for this strange lack of interest. It seems that a very generous federal government was actually subsidizing pleasure boat ownership for the rich or affluent few who were in a position to take advantage of a special tax loophole which benefited only a small and privileged minority.

As a result, why should the board chairman of a corporation get his knuckles skinned changing spark plugs on a boat engine? Why should used car dealers, sales executives, and realtors sand dirty boat bottoms and inhale lethal copper dust? Why should neurosurgeons, tax lawyers, and investment counselors get dirty engine grease ground into their fingers while removing head bolts so that exhaust valves can be replaced? Why should this privileged few do this messy work when they could easily hire somebody else to do it, then write off the cost as an income tax deduction?

And how was all this possible?

Years ago when you joined a yacht club, and were taken on a tour by the club's committee chairman in charge of new membership, you were told grandly that, "Our Bill Turner owns the *Egyptian Queen*." "Our George Thompson owns the *Temptress*." "Our Sam Watkins owns the *Snapshot II*."

Later you discovered this was not true at all. The above three men did NOT own the above mentioned yachts. Bill Turner's *Egyptian Queen* was really owned by the Turner Gear and Machine Works, Inc. The *Temptress* was owned by the George Thompson Advertising Agency, Inc. The yacht *Snapshot II* was owned by the Watkins Graphic Arts Supplies, Inc.

This was a tax dodge, perfectly legal and proper, but, unfortunately, available only to the rich who really didn't need a government subsidy to pursue their personal hobbies and pleasures.

Since the three boats mentioned were owned by corporations—ostensibly operated only in the interests of corporate affairs, corporate entertainment, public relations, employee relations, etc.—they were treated like any other capital investment of the corporation. The full cost of purchase, operation, maintenance, repair, and depreciation could be written off as a normal expense of doing business in a competitive world. This cost even included the booze, food and girls for entertainment.

So the Bill Turners, the George Thompsons, and the Sam Watkins who happened to control majority stock in their corporations were able to enjoy all the pleasures of boating without one penny coming out of their own pockets. Even their yacht club dues, dock rentals, tips to dock boys, and subscriptions to boating magazines were deductible—which means they were subsidized by the federal government.

When these men got bored with their toys along about mid-October, they dropped off their keys at some commercial boat yard with the order: "Lay her up!" And that was the last they saw of their boats until the following spring.

The boatyard would send two men over to the club for the boat, relieving the "owner" of the inconvenience of maneuvering that big hull into the slings for haulout. The yard would do all the maintenance chores necessary at layup time. In the spring, yard workers would do all the sanding, cleaning, painting, varnishing, and repairing to ready the yacht for another season. Then they would launch, make shakedown runs for necessary adjustments and tuneups, and deliver the boat back to the yacht club. All the "owner" had to do was pick up the keys at the yard office, along with the bill.

The total cost of this service could run from $5,000 to $25,000. With today's inflation and cheapened dollar, a 50-foot yacht could run up a yard bill of $50,000 over just one winter. Can't you just see the Bill Turners and George Thompsons paying that out of their own pockets? But since the federal government was paying, who cared?

To lesser degree, this was also done by non-corporate boat owners. I realized it one day when an insurance man invited me and my wife aboard his 33-foot cruiser. We ate fried his fried chicken and drank his beer. Then he casually brought up the subject of marine insurance, which we talked about for three minutes.

Before leaving, the insurance man asked us to sign his guest register. As I signed, I noted the names of other guests, or "clients", with the date and precise hour they had been "entertained" on his boat for the purpose of selling them marine insurance.

Because of this device, the insurance man was able to write off the major share of his annual boating expenses as a legitimate business expense. And, before 1965, the Internal Revenue Service (IRS) allowed it. He was even able to deduct his yacht club dues because membership brought him into contact with potential marine insurance buyers.

Before 1965, nine out of ten boats over 26 feet in length were owned by people who were able to avail themselves of this tax relief. All you had to do was show that the boat helped you make a living.

Unfortunately, this tax relief was not available to wage earner types who owned 18-foot cat boats or built 22-foot kit boats in their garages on weekends. Even if you were the assistant manager of a fast food franchise, you could never have convinced the IRS that your 22-foot cruiser helped you sell more pizza.

Somewhere in the vast Internal Revenue Service, an unknown civil servant accidently discovered this tax loophole and brought it to the attention of his superior. Nothing happened.

The civil servant grew angry. He leaked all the details to a syndicated newspaper columnist.

Since there was already a taxpayer clamor for tax reform to plug loopholes for the rich, the IRS moved and did something. They closed the tax loophole for most boatowners and left it only slightly open for the big corporations.

The following years were recovery time in marinas and commercial boatyards as maintenance and repair work dropped sharply. The boatyards depended on maintenance and repair work to keep their highly skilled craftsmen and shipwrights employed on a year round basis. Once these workers left, or were layed off, they could rarely be replaced. New labor coming into the boatyards never quite developed the special skills of oldtime shipwrights, boat painters and varnishers. Painting a boat is just not the same as painting a barn. You don't have to sand a barn, wash it, caulk seams and glaze all nailheads and tiny imperfections in the wood.

Boatyard service deteriorated just as fast as work orders declined. In a few years yards became nothing more then storage areas and graveyards for beached and abandoned boats. The owners couldn't afford to have them serviced and they couldn't do the work themselves. You can still see thousands of these fine old yachts rotting away in marina graveyards all over the country. Tax laws may change, but boats do not. They still have to be washed, sanded, caulked, glazed, painted, varnished, repaired, pampered, and loved. And the last part is the most important because boats are just like women. The more you love them, the better they are.

The real boat lovers never abandoned their boats to weather away on the beach and rot in the sun like dead whales. They rolled with the punches and learned how to care for their boats themselves. I should know. I taught many of them myself.

The change in the tax law, as it affected boaters, also touched and changed my life. I had always been looked upon as the club's resident maverick and malcontent. I complained about the lousy docks that were falling apart. I complained about the dangerous dock wiring that only delivered 95 volts on a 115 volt circuit and burned out electric motors. I complained about the lousy food in the dining room—the tough roast beef and such small portions. I complained about the bar stools in the Pirate's Den. They were too hard.

Since I work for a powerful and influential newspaper, everybody was scared to death of me. They knew I could blow the whistle and get the club into big trouble for misuse of public-owned land, which they leased from the city for one dollar a year.

Everybody avoided me and ran in terror at sight of me. I was unloved. I was lonely. I felt awful.

But this, too, changed. I began to notice club officers smiling at me. I began to notice larger portions on my plate in the dining room. I noticed new padded bar stools in the Pirate's Den, two new boards in my dock, and all the rusty nails hammered down. And the club's two police dogs stopped snarling at me.

I was puzzled for a while. Then I guessed the reason for the warmth and friendliness. Everybody in the club knew that I had built my own cabin cruiser, which I maintained in perfect condition. They knew that I wrote articles for various boating magazines. They obviously had deduced that a man who designs and builds his own cruiser must know something about caring for boats.

My guess was right. Members were slyly picking my brains. They would drop by to compliment me on something I had written for a boating magazine. Then, as if it were an afterthought, they would solicit my advice on what bottom paint to use and how to apply it. They would ask: "How do you stop a leak in the garboard seam? How do you keep varnish from running? How do you keep the radiotelephone tuned? How do you pull a propeller? How do you drain oil out of the engines? How do you keep hull and deck paint from brushing hard and sticky? How do you get potato chip grease marks out of teak?"

The questions never stopped. In fact, I had become the club's resident consultant on boat care and repair, without portfolio or pay. I was loved and needed. I felt wonderful and secure. But I didn't feel so good about having my brains picked without pay.

Then one day somebody asked: "Why don't you write a book?"

"My God!" I said. "Why didn't I think of that?"

That's how I come to write this book.

Daman C. Fenwick

Basic Maintenance
and Repair Tools

If you are one of those rare individuals who derive as much pleasure working on a boat as using it, you are a most fortunate person because no other hobby or recreational sport requires as much maintenance and work as boat ownership. Welcome to the club of blood, sweat, tears and mortgage payments.

As the yacht club drunk said, before falling off a bar stool: "Boating is 50 percent work and 50 percent waiting for good weather. The rest is all fun."

When a successful and prosperous Cleveland auto dealer filed for bankruptcy recently, one of his shocked friends asked: "My God, Harry. What did you *do* with all your money?"

"I'm a boatman."

"Yeah, Harry, I know that, but what did you do with all your money?"

"Well, ah, some of it went for mortgage payments on the boat. Some of it went for yard expenses. Some of it went for paint and sandpaper. Some of it went for club dues and gas. Some of it went for booze. The rest I spent foolishly."

This may sound funny, but there is tragedy and truth in every word. As Voltaire said: "Every man has the right to go to hell in his own fashion." Sometimes owning a boat you get the feeling that you *are* going to hell, driven there by bill collectors.

Why *is* this? Some of it is due, in part, to a myth created by advertising copywriters of "maintenance free" boating. You must understand there is no such thing as a "maintenance free" boat, and there never will be.

New boatbuilding materials, since World War II, have changed the face of boating. They have also made it terribly expensive—but yet, they have changed nothing. As the French journalist, Alphonse Karr, said over a hundred years ago: "The more things change, the more they are the same." So-called "maintenance free" boating falls in the same category as perpetual motion. It is *the* impossible dream.

But, why *is* it impossible? Because of the sea. Boating is a war between man and the sea (Fig. 1-1). And the sea always wins.

The sea is 85 percent oxygen. Man himself is 65 percent. The thin crust of atmosphere surrounding the earth, in which man lives and breathes, is only 23 percent. But the sea, with all its oxygen, is hostile to man. If man submerges his head beneath the surface of the sea for only a few minutes, he will die, even though he is surrounded by oxygen. And when man dies in her element, the sea is cruel to his body, holding it submerged for days, for weeks until it bloats to twice its normal size. Then it slowly rises to the surface where it floats high in the water like those huge animal balloons children play with on bathing beaches.

Then another element, the sun, adds its destructive forces—decomposing swollen tissues, drying out all moisture, returning man to the basic elements of which he is created. When all the water is gone, only a handful of chemical matter is left.

The sea is impersonal. It is not cruel as some have written, even though it can caress you one minute and tear you to pieces the next. The sea just goes relentlessly its own way and everything else must adjust and adapt to it. If you adapt, you survive. If you don't, you die. It's that simple.

On a smaller scale, like inland lakes and rivers, if you do not adapt you may not die, but you will be so miserable you will want to die, like I have so many times on the Great Lakes. Everyone who goes into boating inevitably learns the hard way.

One of the first things a new boatman learns is that things deteriorate rapidly on water. For example, a new cottage built of wood and covered with two coats of paint will look good for years with very little care, other then a fresh-up paint job in about seven years. An automobile gets a good paint job at the factory and is rarely ever painted again. There are millions of automobiles in use today that are 15, 20, even 30 years old and still have their original paint jobs. A boat during that same time span will have been repainted 15, 20 or 30 times.

Fig. 1-1. You live near the sea. You use the sea. But you never own the sea, and any moment it will turn on you and tear you to pieces as it did in this picture, taken many years ago, when it destroyed my home and my boat.

Some years ago I purchased a new 35-foot yacht from a big name builder. It was delivered directly to me from the factory in Baltimore. It was "factory fresh," as the ads say, when the Travel-Lift lowered it into Lake Erie waters that first week in April. It was a gorgeous thing with massive areas of shiny brightwork (that's varnished mahogany to landlubbers), teak, fiberglass cabin top and a huge fiberglass hardtop over the cockpit.

Nothing, absolutely nothing, is as beautiful as new brightwork and teak. Nothing is as depressingly ugly as teak that has weathered for three months. On the forward decks it becomes a dirty gray. In the cockpit it becomes a disaster area. Potato chips, peanuts, pieces of baloney and fried chicken all leave an oily stain. Every time the engines are worked on, dirt and oil get on the teak. Marinas put old engine oil on their dirt roads to keep the dust down. This oil gets into the cracks of boat shoes and leaves an oily design on the teak.

Somebody once said that brightwork was the millionaire's finish. That's because only a millionaire can afford to have hired hands who do nothing all during the boating season but sand and varnish. When they finish at the transom, they start sanding and varnishing again. That's how that famous old J.P. Morgan quote got started. Morgan's yacht, the *Corsair*, was quite a thing in its time, with its entire superstructure finished off in varnished wood. When somebody asked him the upkeep costs on the yacht, Morgan replied: "If you have to ask, you can't afford it."

BRIGHTWORK, THE MILLIONAIRE'S FINISH

It didn't take me long to learn the meaning of those words, "millionaire's finish," because by July 4, while everybody else was having fun, I was sanding and varnishing my new boat—which was less than *three months old!* By mid-August the fiberglass cabin top and hardtop was beginning to chalk and blister. Paint on the hull was cracking and letting moisture get to the wood, which in turn caused the paint to flake off. So there I was in August with a "factory fresh" new yacht costing $20,000, less then four months old—and I was sanding, varnishing, painting and scrubbing teak. To a landlubber, this is unbelieveable. But to anyone who knows the sea it is not. It's just par for the course.

The above is not intended as a criticism of my yacht, because the same thing would have happened regardless of who the builder had been. I know because on the left of me was docked a new Chris Craft, on the right was a Matthews, often called the Cadillac of yachts. The owners of these two boats were doing the same thing.

What happened was the nature of the beast—what happens to *anything* once it enters the corrosive, destructive environment of the sea. It is the reason why the manufacture of boat paints and varnishes is a billion dollar industry with over 30 large companies making nothing else but marine coatings, caulking compounds and bottom anti-fouling paints to protect a boat from the sea.

THE NEW PAINTS

Out of the paint companies' research laboratories have come what to veteran boaters is a confusing and maddening array of new paints, varnishes, sealers, primers, painting systems, caulkers and anti-fouling paints. You don't just paint your boat any more; you put on a "system." It's a whole new world of mumbo-jumbo like phenolic resins, poly vinyl-chloride, alkyds, epoxy, urethane polyester silicone, acrylics, latex rubber, and combinations like alkyd polyurethane and alkyd acrylic.

What does all this mean? I honestly don't know, even after I explain it. The phenolic resin base paints and varnishes have been around the longest. My first contact with them was when they were called by the trade name "Bakelite." I grew to hate them with a passion. My new big name yacht was varnished and painted with this stuff, which produces a surface hard as glass. However, this hard surface added nothing to longevity which, after all, is what every boatowner is looking for, a finish that will *last*.

DRAWBACKS OF THE "HARD" FINISHES

The so-called "hard" finish paints and varnishes have to be repainted just as often as conventional paint and varnish. But that "hard" surface adds to the work of refinishing. You can *not* paint or varnish over an old surface until you thoroughly sand to remove all the gloss. And sanding that hard surface is sheer agony. It takes three times as much sanding materials, effort and time. Who needs *that*?

THE "SYSTEM" PAINTS

With the so-called "system" paints, you often buy a package deal—which can be a bare wood primer undercoater, and the final finish coat. You don't put a "system" paint over an old finish. You take all the old paint off and start from bare wood. One of the "system" paints is the alkyds, which are a synthetic plastic with a modified oil base, whatever that means. They come in one can ready to use, and have their own special thinners and solvents. These paints are unsuited for fiberglass because they are too soft. To overcome this softness, alkyds are now available with silicone added. This is also supposed to make them moisture resistant, which is a meaningless term. After all, everything is "moisture resistant." The important thing is how *long*. In my personal experience, they last no longer then ordinary boat paint. However, these plastic paints are at least reasonably priced and can be applied in almost any temperature. They just take longer to "cure" at temperatures below 70 degrees.

THE EPOXY PAINTS

The epoxy two-container paints are another hard surface finish that are supposed to be long lasting, and have good adhesion to wood, metal and fiberglass. The epoxies too, are supposed to be "moisture resistant." The big drawback to the epoxies is once you mix the two containers together, you have to use the paint all up or throw it away. You can't save half a can of paint for matching color repairs and touch-up work along about the middle of July when the long lasting qualities begin to wear off.

THE URETHANES

The urethanes are a fairly recent "system" paint for marine use which at first didn't catch on too well because of their high price. They are a hard finish again and don't hold color too well. With the reds and the dark blues you have a hellish time with fiberglass repairs trying to match color because the weathered color will have faded. These paints originally came out in a two-part system, but are now available in a one can mixture ready to use.

THE VINYL AND LATEX PAINTS

Of all the new paints with the fancy "new chemistry" names, the vinyls seem to be the best and most widely used. Most latex paints, particularly anti-fouling, are made from poly vinyl-chloride, which has some of the flexibility of rubber and sticks very well to wood, steel and aluminum. The vinyls are not too popular as a topside or interior paint because they don't brush well. Manufacturers spray on the paint. As a bottom paint, vinyl can be slapped on with a brush or roller because appearance on a bottom is not important.

THE ANTI-FOULING BOTTOM PAINTS

The bottom of your boat is out of sight during the boating season, but never out of your mind. In salt water you never stop worrying about your bottom, especially if it's wood, steel, aluminum or fiberglass. Every boat material has one special problem of its own, but all have the same common problem with barnacles, the scourge of the seas.

BARNACLES, MARINE GROWTHS AND BOTTOM PAINTS

If you want to get rich in a hurry, find out how barnacles make their glue. There is absolutely nothing like it on dry land. With man-made glues, after you get past all the fabulous claims and read the directions on the label, you find there are a lot of "ifs" and hedging. You are warned that surfaces to be glued must be absolutely clean and dry. Any dirt, oil or moisture will interfere with adhesion. This point is the glue makers' loop hole when there are complaints about their products. Paint makers, varnish makers, and caulking makers also have a loop hole. All warn you on the label that their product will not stick to a dirty, wet or oily surface.

The barnacle has no such problems. This little beast will stick to *anything*. At the La Que Corrosion Laboratories, where anti-fouling paints are tested, they have found that dirty, greasy test panels placed right next to clean ones will be covered with just as many barnacles, and with the same fantastic adhesive power. You don't *remove* barnacles. You literally disintegrate them to break their hold in little pieces. The only way you can keep the little beasts from sticking to your boat bottom is to repel them with poisons.

For centuries it has been known that copper repels barnacles and other marine creatures. But nobody knows why. If you drop a shiny new penny into a small bowl of goldfish, within minutes they will all jump out of the bowl. You can not put tapwater into a goldfish tank if you have extensive copper plumbing. The fish will start jumping out.

Back in the days when copper was cheap, commercial work-boats were often sheathed on their bottoms with copper plate. This work saved annual painting. Today it is cheaper to use metallic copper paint. On my boat I have installed 24 square feet of sheet copper as a radiotelephone ground plate. The rest of the bottom I paint with copper bronze paint. When I haul, that copper ground plate is the cleanest section on my bottom. It requires no scrubbing to remove slime or moss. It is as smooth and clean as the day I launched. The rest of my bottom will be covered with a green slime.

One gallon of copper bottom paint will often contain 8 pounds of copper in the form of cuprous oxide. That's why it's so expensive, up to $80 a gallon. If you own a small boat, you can escape this expense by hauling your boat on a trailer. You can skip the expensive anti-fouling paints and just use a hard racing finish.

If you must leave your boat *in* the water, welcome to the club of sweat, tears and high-priced bottom paints. I will try to make it a little less expensive for you, but not too much easier because anything you do alone is not easy. The whole idea is you want to *stay* in boating, like my dock partner who owns a Matthews.

You'd think that a man who can afford a Matthews could afford almost anything. That's what I thought, too, until this man came to me one cold day late in April, looking like he wanted to say something but couldn't get started. Finally he blurted out: "Would you show me how to change the oil in my engines?"

"Glad to," I said.

He looked so grateful. I thought he was going to kiss my hand. Later, when he was more relaxed, I asked: "Why do you want to change the oil yourself?"

Again he looked embarrassed. "I got my bill from the yard yesterday. It was over $1800. My God, all they did was paint my bottom and topsides."

"Wait a minute now. You don't just buy some paint and start brushing it on."

"You don't think that was too high?"

"I wouldn't have done the job for twice that much."

His eyes opened wide. "Who painted your boat."

"I did—but I *had* to paint mine. I don't *have* to paint yours, even for money."

"Don't you like money?"

"I love it. I just hate sanding and painting."

"Is it difficult?"

"Very, even the way I do it—and I do everything the easy way."

"Would you show me how?"

"Why do you want to get involved in such miserable work?"

He was embarrassed again. "My tax lawyer told me I wouldn't be able to write off the maintenance and upkeep on my boat as a business expense."

I understood. It sure makes a difference when you have to pay those expenses out of your own pocket. So you buy books like this and paint the bottom yourself—or you give up the sea and boating. It's a painful decision, especially for a desk-bound executive or a neuro-surgeon who has to operate every day and doesn't want to hurt his hands.

I will try to show you how to do the work in the easiest way possible—not always the approved way, not the way experts in boating magazines will tell you. But remember, boating magazine "experts" write for a media that serves the interests of advertisers. These magazines, the high priests of pleasure boating, have helped their advertisers create new markets for products that didn't even exist when I built my first boat after World War II. At that time, the twin-screw pleasure boat was almost unknown, so were depth finders for small boats. The only navigational equipment on these boats was a compass. Large cruisers had one enormous engine with pistons like gallon oil cans. Yet these mastodons only developed 60 horsepower. But they had the torque to swing 30-inch wheels that moved the boats at an economical speed of 12 knots.

Last summer the owner of a new 45-foot boat at the Detroit Yacht Club proudly showed me his electronic and navigational gear—all $30,000 worth! He had just canceled a cruise across Lake St. Clair with his family because the radio direction finder (RDF) wasn't working.

Lake St. Clair is the tiniest of the Great Lakes, hardly much bigger then a fishpond. Yet this yachtman, with all that other gear, was afraid to leave his dock in the Detroit River because the RDF wasn't working.

On the Ohio River at Cincinnati I was aboard a friend's 55-foot houseboat that had as much electronic gear on it as a Navy aircraft carrier. The owner, beaming with pride, said to me: "I'll bet you wish you had this on Lake Erie."

I said: "I couldn't even get this *on* my boat without sinking it."

There's only two ways to go on a river—upstream and downstream. So how do you get lost? Yet this poor man actually thought he *needed* all that stuff. This man did not know that there are commercial fisherman, lobstermen and shrimp boats that go out to sea every day, some for hundreds of miles, and all they have is one engine and a compass. If you read the boating magazines, this is impossible. But these men are too busy making a living to read boating magazines, so they don't know that it is impossible.

THERE IS A "MAINTENANCE FREE" FINISH

When you're not fighting the sea, sun or the weather, you're fighting off someone who wants to make money off of you. Here is something to thwart them—a maintenance free interior finish. This is not the kind of finish the high priests of advertising want you to know about. If you use this, you may never have to refinish the interior of your boat. It is the resin-oil-turp finish.

This wood finishing process goes back thousands of years to Roman galley ships and royal barges of the Pharaohs. All the master's cabins on Yankee Clippers were finished in this manner and so were Spanish galleons.

The resin-oil-turp finish can be used on any open grain wood like oak, mahogany, cherry, walnut and pine—but not teak. The reason for its popularity down through the centuries was it required practically no maintenance and could be easily repaired if damaged.

You must remove all varnish or paint from an existing finish with a paint remover. Clean, sand, and finish off with a fine bronze wool. The wood must be absolutely smooth to begin with because you get no help in this area from the finish material. This is not a film build-up coating like paint or successive coatings of varnish. The final smoothness is in the wood itself and not the finish.

To prepare the finish solution, mix two parts spar varnish, one part linseed oil and three parts turpentine. Let this age for 36 to 48 hours. Putting it on is easy, almost fun. Soak up a rag with the solution and slop it on the wood. Then with your bare hands massage and rub it into the wood until it is thoroughly saturated with the mixture and finally just lays wet on the surface. This may take a half hour.

You now take a clean dry rag and wipe off all the excess. The wood, with all its grain accentuated, is a beautiful thing to behold, satin smooth to touch and permanently finished. If damaged, it can be locally touched up the same way. When dirty, you just wipe it off with a damp cloth. However, this is strictly an inside finish and permanence depends on keeping it away from the sun and salt spray.

THE NEW "MIRACLE" FINISHES

The old finish described above is not a "miracle" finish, which is probably why it has lasted for 3000 years. Poly vinyl-chloride is one of the new "miracles" of paint chemistry. It is also called PVC, which is a dirty word right now with environmentalists. If this scares you off, don't worry about it. There are plenty of other new "miracles" in paint chemistry for your boat with impressive words and descriptions in the brochures you get at the boat shows. There are the "thermosetting plastics." There are the "cross-linking of original substances which produce a molecular change and three-dimensional monomer." There are the phenols, formaldehydes and hydroxyl bearing resins.

All this is very impressive, but who cares? It's like the little old lady at the zoo who was fascinated by two hippopotamuses. Finally she went to a zoo employee and asked: "How can you tell the male from the females?"

The zoo employee replied: "Madam, that is a matter of concern only to another hippopotamus."

I feel the same way about all those new chemistry terms. They are matters of concern only to another organic chemist who works for some paint manufacturer. I don't care if they make boat paint out of sheep dung, just so it doesn't cost too much and stays on my boat. But it doesn't. The sea is still winning the war. In spite of all the new technology, the new "miracle" paints, nothing has changed. You still have to scrub, sand, caulk, paint and varnish every year. Stop doing this just for a short time and your boat will look like the one in the picture.

This boat was launched in April (Fig. 1-2). A week later the owner had a heart attack and died. His widow, too busy with other things, forgot about the boat. So it just floated there in its slip during that long, hot summer and fall.

HOW BOATS DETERIORATE AND DEPRECIATE

The marina hauled the boat in December during an early snow storm and beached it in back of a workshop with no cover or protection. I photographed the boat on a mild day in January. In April this had been a beautiful boat with a showroom gloss and new smell of fresh paint and varnish. In July it started to go. Boat deterioration, once it starts, quickly gets out of control. Like automobiles, boats are financed. In one short season of neglect you can lose your equity if you must sell. You might not get enough from a sale to pay off the bank.

That is what happened to the boat in Fig. 1-2. It originally cost a little over $6,000 (1968 *dollars*). Almost $3,000 was still owed on the mortgage. The widow had a hard time selling it for $1800. It was still a structurally, mechanically sound boat. It just looked bad and needed a cosmetic facelift. The shrewd, experienced boatman who bought it *knew* that he was getting a fantastic bargain in spite of outward appearances.

This is not always so. As the late Bill Harrison, founder of Harrison Marina, told me: "It's almost impossible to sell a boat, even

Fig. 1-2. Neglect your boat just for a short time and it will quickly begin to look like like this. The sea, the wind and the sun took charge of this boat after the owner had a heart attack. This is how it looked when his widow put it up for sale less than a year later.

a very good one, if it has deteriorated in outward appearance. When boat hunting, men always bring their wives and children. Women and children are impressed only by what they *see*. That's why there is so much tinsel, chromium and plastic junk on so many boats. In the world of merchandising, they call this 'flash merchandise.' It is mediocrity and junk jazzed up with eye appeal."

A Harrison Marina salesman told me: "We have four very fine boats in the Yard right now on brokerage, and we can't sell them because they look bad (Fig. 1-3). The husbands are interested, but the wives and children take one look and walk away."

HOW TO SELL A BAD BOAT

"Yet, it's so easy to sell junk," the salesman said. "last week a boatowner sold an old junk heap which he had worked on all winter in one of our storage buildings. He put in a new red rug in the deckhouse, new covers on the couch, new curtains, soft lights. When a buyer and his family came to look, he had a tape recorder playing soft music and coffee was brewing in the galley. That did it. They bought the boat—and never even looked at the engines or in the bilges. Yet that same family, two weeks earlier, had walked away from a far better boat at far less money. The owner had let it deteriorate and it looked bad on the outside."

"Most people don't really buy a boat," Harrison said. "They buy eye appeal. When I tell this to boaters, they think I'm just trying to sell them paint or a big expensive refinishing job."

HOW TO PROTECT YOUR BOAT INVESTMENT

"I don't care where they buy the paint," Harrison said. "I don't care if they buy it someplace else, bring it in here and do the job themselves, just so they do it. But they never do. Then they cry when later they are forced to sell and don't realize enough from the sale to pay off the bank."

This is advice from an old professional with half a century in boating. To protect your equity in that boat you bought with a 10 percent down payment, and have been sweating payments on for three years, you've got to constantly work on it. Relax just for a day or week and things can get away from you. When brightwork starts to go, it can be ruined overnight. Just the night dew seeping into cracks can turn varnished mahogany black. Then you have to wood down and bleach it out with acid. And that is a lot of hard work. Varnishing is easy. It's the preparation that kills you—the *sanding*!

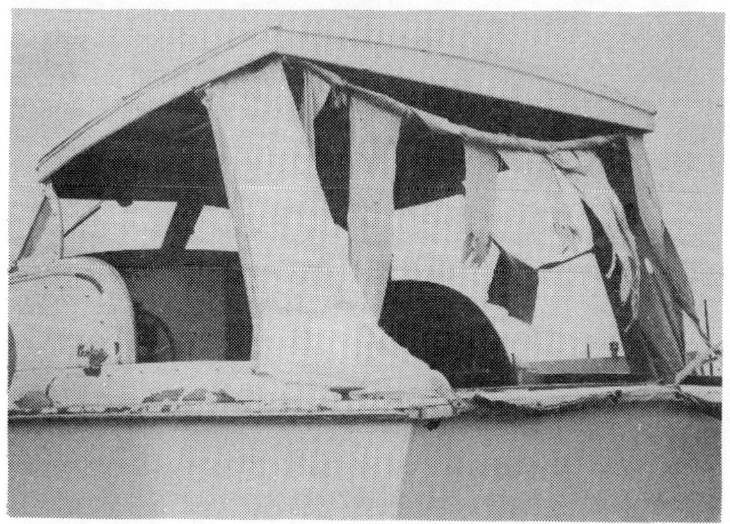

Fig. 1-3. Most people don't really buy a boat. They buy eye appeal. That's why this fine boat just wouldn't sell, even though it is structurally sound. It just looks bad because of neglect, so the owner lost his equity and barely had enough money left over to pay off the bank. Neglect like this hurts only you, not the bank.

SANDING AND SANDPAPERS

Of all boating maintenance chores, sanding is the one most universally and intensely hated by wives who help their husbands in spring fitting. Although there are no statistics on it, sanding has been the cause of many boating divorces. There is only one other boating chore that is more tedius, more messy, and more agonizing than sanding above the waterline, and that is sanding below it—the *bottom* (Fig. 1-4)!

In ancient times, this is a job that was reserved for slaves and criminals in chains. Next to being fed to lions, this was considered the cruelest of punishments. Yet today millions of free Americans, some of them doctors, lawyers, dentists, real estate dealers and insurance brokers, lay on their backs in the spring on still frozen ground to perform this filthy chore. It's unbelieveable. It's one of the reasons why boatmen in the northern part of the United States have more back troubles and arthritis of the spine then any other segment of the population.

No matter how much you grow to hate it, you learn to live with it. Since sanding is so much a part of boating, it is important that you know as much as possible about it and the wide variety of abrasive materials available for your use.

First, there is no "sand" in sandpaper. The word is a misnomer, but continues to be used. Although there are thousands of different kinds of "sanding" materials (abrasives is the right word), as a boater you need to concerned with only the few listed and described below.

SANDPAPER SELECTION GUIDE

Flint. Because it is light yellow in color, this is the paper that looks like it is coated with sand. Actually the abrasive coating is quartz. This paper, available in all hardware stores, is cheap but clogs quickly and wears out fast. It is a poor buy, even if it is cheap.

Garnet. This paper costs a little more, lasts a little longer, but can't be used in power sanders because it wears out too fast. Both flint and garnet are useful mainly for hand sanding on small jobs, like removing paint. They cannot be used wet.

Aluminum Oxide. Now you're working with professionals. Although these papers cost more, they are worth it because they last in either hand or power sanding. They come in both cloth and paper backing, can be used on wood, plastic, metal, and are considered the best abrasive for metal because they can be used with oil as a lubricant.

Silicon Carbide. This is your wet, dry or oil sanding material. It is available under a number of different trade names, is almost always black, and is used in auto body work for fine finish sanding before painting. Although silicon carbide has a paper back, it is waterproof.

Open-Coat Papers. These papers, with only about 50 to 70 percent of their surface covered with abrasive material, are designed to be clog free. With less abrasive, they work slower but last longer.

Crocus Cloth. This comes in only one grade, very fine, and is used to polish metal to a mirror finish. It can also be used to bring back the gloss in gel coats on fiberglass.

Emery Cloth. Use this only on metal, with or without oil. In the coarser grades, some boaters like to use emery cloth on bottoms because it lasts. Personally, I prefer the open-coat papers in extra coarse.

SANDPAPER GRADES

Sandpapers are graded three different ways, but the simplest way to buy it is to just ask for any one of the seven different grades, like extra coarse, very coarse, coarse, medium, fine, extra fine, super fine.

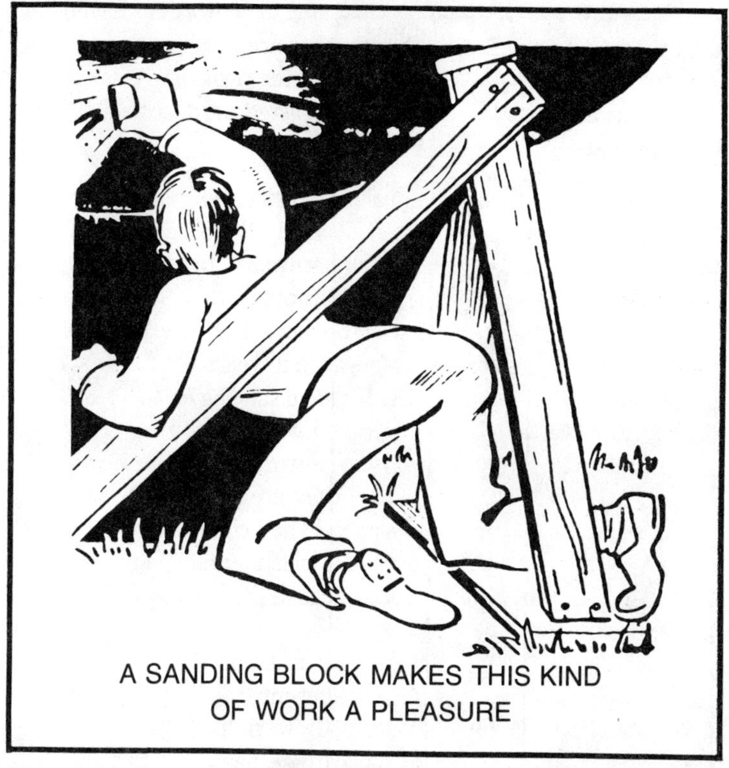

Fig. 1-4. All sorts of devices are available to make sanding easier, but what is easy for one man is agony for another. No matter what you buy to make the job easier, whether manual or power, you will in the end discard all of them and devise your own system.

Fine, extra fine and super fine grades will never get you into any trouble. But if you want to be more precise, there is a numbers system which, theoretically, is more accurate. Maybe it is, but I don't really care. I just like to get the job done and I have always found extra coarse for the bottom, medium for topsides and fine for brightwork helps me do just that with a minimum of palaver. Although I have tried, I could never tell the difference between super fine 600 or 500.

However, if you like to split hairs eight different ways, see Table 1-1.

STEEL AND BRONZE WOOLS

Steel wool has no place on a boat, even for removing rust from engines. Shredded particles fall into the bilges and rust. If you use it

	GRIT	NUMBER
EXTRA COARSE	16	4
	12	4½
VERT COARSE	30	2½
	24	3
	20	3½
COARSE	50	1
	40	1½
	36	2
MEDIUM	80	1/0
	60	½
FINE	150	4/0
	120	3/0
	100	2/0
VERT FINE	240	7/0
	220	6/0
	180	5/0
EXTRA FINE	400	10/0
	360	9/0
	320	8/0
	280	7/0
SUPER FINE	600	
	500	

Table 1-1. Here Is The Numbering System For Sandpaper Grades.

on wood, you can never clean up all the tiny shreds which embed in the paint and wood and later show up as tiny rust spots. Only bronze wool should be used anywhere on a boat.

These metal wool materials have many offbeat uses. For example, steel or bronze wool is used as a sound absorbent material in gun silencers. It makes an excellent air filter when oiled. It can be used to filter paint and varnish by stuffing a wad into a funnel. The wool is useful as a cleaning and sanding tool because it can be held easily to work rounded or sculptured surfaces. It doesn't load up like sandpapers. You just shake it out. You also can use the wool wet or dry. See Table 1-2.

A BOAT PAINT THAT DOESN'T HAVE TO BE SANDED

A great blessing to mankind would be a new boat paint that doesn't have to be sanded. But manufacturers have no time for such a paint because they're too busy turning out super-high gloss white enamels, which have become accepted standards on all fiberglass boats. On a bright sunny day in July, all that glaring white gives you piercing headaches and burning eyeballs. It's almost like being blinded by snow. And all that shiny hard gloss has to be sanded down before repainting. Did you ever see a U.S. Navy vessel painted high gloss white? There is a sound reason why the Navy paints all its ships that flat gray.

Now for the good news. There is a paint you can put on your boat that doesn't have to be sanded down before repainting. You'll never guess what it is, even though it's been around a long time. It has a funny name. It's called *housepaint*.

Did you ever see a professional housepainter sanding? They will sand, scrap only small local areas where the paint is loose and chipped, but not the entire home. Once the loose paint is scraped away, they paint without even washing.

It was while working my way through college in Cleveland that I learned about housepaint. During spring and summer, I worked for a

Table 1-2. The Bronze-Steel Wool Cutting Chart.

GRADE	TYPE	CUTTING ACTION	DRY USE
0000	Super Fine	Extra Light	Buffing waxed fiberglass hulls, gel coats, dulling sheen of varnished and epoxied surfaces, final sanding of wood.
000	Extra Fine	Very Light	Same as above.
00	Very Fine	Light	Cleaning copper before sweat soldering, cleaning aluminum, polish brass.
0	Fine	Medium Light	Intermediate sanding of wood. Removing raised grain on fir plywood.
1	Medium	Moderate	Cleaning all metals for soldering. Removing stains from vinyl. Rough sanding wood, fiberglass.
2	Medium Coarse	Fairly Severe	Removing paint and wax. Cleaning grease from galley stoves. Rough sanding.
3	Coarse	Severe	Rust removal, paint removal. Cleaning paint from glass, pre-sanding of rough wood. Roughing up surfaces prior to gluing.

commercial Lake Erie fisherman who operated a fleet of six wood fishboats. The owner of this fleet was Polish, a man with strong opinions—and he had very strong opinions about paint. His two-story wood frame home was right on the shores of Lake Erie, and he said that any paint that was good enough for his home was good enough for his boats. He wanted nothing to do with over-priced stuff called marine paint.

So all his six boats were painted with charcoal gray housepaint made by Sherwin Williams in Cleveland. In the spring each skipper was given exactly three days to get his boat ready for work. And it was easy. One coat of charcoal gray topside. One coat of Baltimore Red on the bottom.

Housepaint is designed to chalk or wear off. This prevents paint buildup. Surface dirt just keeps washing off. This self-cleaning action keeps the surface surprisingly clean. The only preparatory work I had to do was sweep off cobwebs and leaves. We painted the bottoms with a large roller on a long wooden handle.

During the season, scratches and gouges were easy to fix. They were just filled with a black caulking compound and covered with fresh paint, which quickly blended with the old paint. In spite of this minimal care, the fishboats looked surprisingly good (Fig. 1-5). The charcoal gray, which actually looks like black, didn't show the dirt. The dark color was easy on the eyes.

When I built my first boat years later, I was worried about the canvas-covered decks and cabin top. Paint builds up on canvas because you can't sand it. Eventually the paint becomes so thick and heavy it cracks and alligators. This is a common sight on old boats built before the fiberglass era. There is only one cure for alligatored paint on canvas, and that is complete removal—a horrible job.

Then I remembered the housepaint. I tried it, putting on just one thin coat. The scrubbing and washing down during the season wore off that thin coat. The next season I put on another thin coat. My decks and cabin top always looked as if they had just been newly canvassed.

I later tried housepaint on my topsides, with the same excellent results. However, since I belonged to a snooty yacht club, I always removed the labels from the paint cans. Had it been known what I was using, I quite possibly would have been suspended, even expelled from the club. This particular club, the oldest on western Lake Erie, is predominantly a sailors club, and old rag sailors are intensely serious about the business of boating. They are traditionalists and

Fig. 1-5. Commercial workboats get minimal maintenance care, but look surprisingly good. There is a reason. Fancy, high gloss paints which have to be sanded are not used. Varnish is left to millionaires.

look down on power boat owners. I once heard a new member call a mooring line a rope. Hardly anybody ever spoke to him after that.

I was often asked by some members how I managed to get my boat painted so quickly. I had to do some lying. Using housepaint on a boat is heresy. A few hundred years ago, men were burned at the stake for less. However, these are times of great change. The new breed of boaters today are less concerned about tradition and form. In the Detroit Yacht Club one night last summer, I overheard a group of young sailors talking and one of them said he had trouble "tacking to the right." And nobody scowled or corrected him. I was amazed.

THE BEST CHEAP BOTTOM PAINT

If you want something cheap and easy to work with to go with the housepaint, there's nothing better then Baltimore Red. This anit-fouling bottom paint has been around long before most of us were born, and it is still the biggest selling, mainly because it has withstood the test of time on all types of workboats, fishboats and commercial craft. It has a very distinctive odor. Once you've smelled old Baltimore Red, you never forget it. In April, on the Chesapeake Bay, Long Island Sound and New England coast off the Georgia Banks fishing grounds, you can smell Old Baltimore Red in the air when the wind is right and it makes your heart pound. It has the same effect on some men, including myself, as the bitch in heat scent affects male dogs. You can't keep a dog home when he gets that smell. It's the same with sailors. They want to quit their jobs and head for the boatyard.

Baltimore Red is economical to buy and use. It requires no elaborate preparatory work. It is a dark red, soft coating that keeps wearing off as your hull moves through the water. Any slime that builds up on your bottom during the week washes off with the paint when you take the boat out on weekends. Since it is constantly coming off, even on your hands if you touch it, there is very little left on your bottom by haul out time. Consequently, it never builds up to a heavy coating that will crack, flake off and require a lot of sanding and scraping. You give the bottom a good scrubbing when you haul out, and in the spring it's ready for a new coat with no sanding. That's why the fishboats I worked on could be ready for work in three days—and that included time servicing the engine. Painting is easy. It's the preparation that kills you.

WHEN NOT TO SCRUB A BOAT BOTTOM

While on the subject of scrubbing boat bottoms at haul out, which is highly recommended, there is another form of bottom scrubbing that is not recommended. One of the leading manufacturers of marine paints, Woolsey Marine Industries, warns against the new practice of boaters hiring scuba divers to scrub slime and other growths off their bottoms in mid season (Fig. 1-6). The manufacturer says that the use of stiff brushes, or other mechanical cleaning devices, limits the useful life of anti-fouling paints by accelerating the release of toxicants. This practice has become quite common in tidal waters of the east, west and gulf coasts where scuba diving is popular.

Fig. 1-6. This type of bottom scrubbing is not recommended by boat manufacturers because it limits the useful life of bottom paints. Scuba divers generally use stiff brushes in their bottom scrubbing.

Hard scrubbing removes the toxic paint film, which limits the service life of the coating, Woolsey says. They are warning all their customers that the company cannot stand behind its warranties where this type of bottom cleaning is performed by scuba divers. They add that this does not mean that boat bottoms can not, or should not, be cleaned in mid season. It is perfectly permissible, they say, to remove slime from bottoms if it is done gently with a sponge, chamois or even a very soft brush (Fig. 1-7). But it should not be done with stiff bristled brooms, the kind that are used to sweep concrete driveways and garages.

There is a great deal of status conscious snobbery in boating, which is why you won't see Old Baltimore Red on too many pleasure craft, especially the new all-white, high gloss enamel jobs. When the guests go overboard to swim, red bottom paint must not rub off on them. So these flush deck, doublecabin jobs have their bottoms painted with the new vinyl coatings at up to $100 a gallon, and in new bright colors like blue, green, yellow, red—even white.

WHERE TO BUY MARINE PAINTS, SEALERS, AND ANTI-FOULING

Here is a list of all the paint manufacturers. They also make varnishes, paint removers, sealers, undercoaters, bedding and caulking compounds, teak cleaners, paint additives, non-skid compounds, brushes, painting tools and fiberglass materials. A card from you will bring literature and color charts. If there's a specific item you are interested in, like something to restore the gel coat on your fiberglass boat, mention it. They make so many different things you might wind up with information on everything but what you really want. Manufacturers and addresses are: *Pettit Paint Co., Inc.*, 36 Pine St., Rockaway, N.J. 07866; *Dolphin Paint & Chemical Co.*, 922 Locust, Toledo, Ohio 43603; *Woolsey Marine Industries*, 100 Saw Mill Rd., Danbury, Conn. 06810; *International Paint Co.*, 17 Battery Pl. N., New York N.Y. 10004; *Gloucester Paints Inc.*, 2 Harbor Loop, Gloucester, Mass. 01930; *U.S. Yacht Paint Co.*, Box 96, Roseland, N.J. 07068; *Andrew Brown Div.*, 1900 Koppers Bldg., Pittsburgh, Pa. 15219; *Boat Life Inc.*, 65 Bloomingdale Rd., Hicksville, N.Y. 11801; *Jotun-Baltimore Copper Paint Co.*, 501 Key Hwy., Baltimore, Md. 21230; and *U.S. Marine Coatings, Inc.*, Box 5425, Sarasota, Fla. 33579.

DETERMINING PAINT NEEDED

There are all sorts of mathematical formulas for computing the amount of paint needed for various areas and things to be painted.

Fig. 1-7. Paint manufacturers say it is permissible to scrub bottoms with a sponge, chamois or soft brush. Don't use a stiff or broom like scuba divers use.

Here is one of them: on the topsides you take the height, or freeboard, and multiply this by the length in feet. Then you multiply again by 1.5 and divide by 500 for previously painted boats, by 325 for new wood. I tried this on my calculator and got 55 gallons. That's enough to paint a Navy destroyer.

An old rule of thumb, which doesn't require a calculator, is that one gallon of paint will put one coat on 500 square feet of surface, or 325 square feet of new wood. With varnish, a gallon will cover 750 square feet.

I have never painted anything where I came out even, so I could throw away empty paint cans. One wall of my garage is filled with partially filled paint cans in the colors of every boat I ever built or owned. It doesn't hurt to have a little paint left over because you can use it all during the season for spotting and repair work—unless you are one of those super sailors who never scrapes a dock. I have known only one boatman who never got a scratch on his hull during the season. He did all his cruising on yacht club bar stools.

PAINT TABLE

Table 1-3 will help you get started painting without a calculator. The figures are for two coats over an existing finish. For one coat cut

Table 1-3. Paint Needed For Covering Boat Sections Of Different Sizes.

SIZE	TOPSIDE	BOTTOM	BOOTTOP	DECKS	VARNISH
10′	1 qt.	1 pt.			
14′	2 qts.	1 qt.			
18′	3 pts.	3 qts.	½ pt.	1 qt.	1 qt.
20′	2 qts.	3 qts.	½ pt.	3 qts.	2 qts.
25′	3 qts.	3 qts.	1 pt.	3 qts.	2 qts.
32′	2 gals.	1½ gals.	1 pt.	2 qts.	3 qts.
36′	2½ gals.	2 gal.	1 pt.	1 gal.	1 gal.
40′	3 gals.	2½ gals.	1 pt.	1½ gal.	1 gal.
60′	4 gals.	5 gals.	1 pt.	3½ gals.	2½ gals.

the figures in half. If you put two coats of paint on your topsides, you're crazy. The table below was made up by a paint manufacturer who has a vested interest in selling paint. The biggest headache you get in boating is from over-painting. Remember, the more you put on, the sooner you reach that day of reckoning when it all has to come off with paint removers and blow torches. Then you start all over with the primers and the undercoaters. It's a vicious circle which drives many out of boating.

A HAMMER, NAILS AND A SLEDGE ON A BOAT

"When you go out on big water, always anticipate trouble," an old sailor advised me, "and be ready."

A guest aboard my boat, noting the tools in my engine compartment, asked: "What the devil do you need a hammer, sledge and nails for on a boat?"

Surprisingly, I use them many times during a season. In fact, I would never go cruising without them aboard. As for you, if you just water ski, fish or take boat rides on weekends, then you most certainly do not need these items aboard. But if you are a cruising boatman who likes to tie up in strange, foreign places, and likes to live on his boat for weeks and months at a time, then that is when you need these tools.

Boating today is a booming, crowded sport with almost one fourth of the U.S. population participating. Some experts are predicting that this will double by 1980. That means 100 million Americans involved in boating. You just can't imagine what that means, unless you like to cruise like I do. Even today, marinas and yacht clubs are crowded (Fig. 1-8). In California, Florida and New York

Fig. 1-8. Yacht clubs and marinas are crowded and have waiting lists for dock space. Finding a place to tie up for just one night can be a problem. You often take a dock that normally you wouldn't leave your garbage on.

you get on a long waiting list for docking, and may have to wait for years until someone dies or is lost at sea.

Finding a place to tie up for just one night is always a problem. Often you are forced to take a dock on which normally you wouldn't leave your garbage. What is generously referred to as a dock is often nothing more then four 4×4 pieces of lumber lightly hammered down into soft mud, held together by 2×4s and covered by rough lumber to form a narrow walkway. The whole thing is almost always very loosely held together and wobbles dangerously as you walk on it. The nails are always rusty and often are backing out. Sitting down on these docks is risky because, at the very least, you might tear your clothes (Fig. 1-9).

So you go to the manager/owner and complain because, after all, you're paying 10, 15, and 20 cents a foot for each day that you survive. I tried complaining once in Wallaceburg, Ontario after handing over $7.00 in American money to a dock owner. The man, who looked like actor Walter Brennan, squinted at me for a moment. "You kiddin', mister? If you don't want that dock, you can have your money back. There's a big fleet of boats coming from Detroit today. By six o'clock I can rent this dock twenty times."

Fig. 1-9. This is not a typical downriver dock because it is in good shape and has no rusty nails protruding.

So I shut my big mouth, went back to that crummy dock, took out my hammer, sledge and nails and went to work. A few wacks with the sledge and the 4×4s are a little more firmly in the mud. With the claw hammer all the protruding nails are either pulled out or hammered down. New nails are added where needed and the lousy dock is quickly made serviceable.

This may seem foolish to a non-boater, but it's just rolling with the punches and riding at sea anchor instead of fighting the sea. You adapt and adjust to prevailing conditions in cruising, especially on the nation's rivers and bay areas where you will find many small Mickey Mouse marinas run by farmers who own land with riparian rights on the water. Hammering a few nails is a lot easier then tilting with windmills. And that is why a hammer, sledge and nails should be aboard every cruising boat.

There are certain basic items which should be aboard every boat, even if you just go water skiing or fishing off shore. I wouldn't back my boat 10 feet away from the dock without these basic tools aboard (Fig. 1-10). The larger the boat, the more equipment and electronic gear it has and the more tools you need.

THE DOMESTIC TYPE VACUUM CLEANER

A domestic vacuum cleaner is permanently on my boat. Here is the main reason. On a cruise to Put-In-Bay in Lake Erie, we had tied up at the visitor's dock, put up all cockpit canvas and left the entrance flap open while we went shopping. When we came back a half hour later, the cockpit was covered black with millions of tiny little insects called midges. These insects, which look like overgrown mosquitos, hatch in the bottom of Lake Erie, rise to the surface by the billions, and fly off with the breeze. They are harmless, but messy, especially on teak decks if you step on them. The underside of my hardtop has a white vinyl-like material covering. This was almost black with the insects. If you try to flick them off with a towel, you crush some. This leaves a messy streak which is hard to remove once it dries.

The vacuum cleaner saved our lives. I simply vacuumed them up in about 15 minutes. Then I reversed the hose to the exhaust side and used it as an air blower. The few insects that were on the cabin sides, forward decks and cabin top were easily blown off.

THE SHOP-TYPE VACUUM CLEANERS

This is only one example of the many uses for a small home-type vacuum cleaner aboard even the smallest cruiser. The one illus-

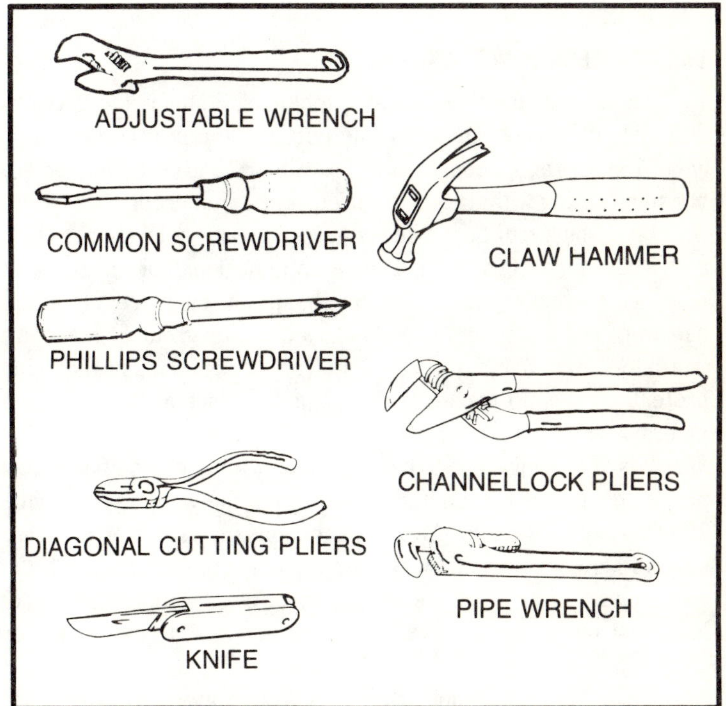

Fig. 1-10. These basic tools are a necessity on even the smallest boat.

trated is easily stowed away even on a 20-footer (Fig. 1-11). The shop-type vacuums are unsuitable because of their awkward size, which makes them difficult to secure. And the so-called "wet/dry" vacuums are even more unsuitable, even though in the advertising brochures they sound wonderful.

Dry dirt is easily disposed of, but you mix dirt and water, which gives you instant cement-like garbage. It is very hard to clean out of that metal container—I know because I had one, and left it in a Buffalo, New York Yacht Club trash can in a fit of temper. My main disenchantment with the shop vacuums is that they quickly lose most of their suction power when that flannel/paper filter over the motor gets covered with dirt, which doesn't take long. The so-called "10-gallon" container is still almost empty and over 50 percent of the suction cleaning power is lost. So what good is that big tank?

The home vacuums use a paper bag to catch the dirt, which also acts as the filter. When you throw away the dirt, you throw away the filter and you have renewed suction power. That is why the home vacs retain almost full cleaning power at all times.

THE CORDLESS POWER DRILL

Another almost indispensable tool aboard ship is the cordless drill. When Black & Decker came out with the first cordless drill about 15 years ago, I bought one. Today it's all battered and scarred, but still working with the same batteries after hundreds of charges.

I have built four boats, and after having once been shocked by a metal-housing electric drill, I have an almost pathological fear of electricity around water. On my boats every piece of metal, hardware and equipment is tied in to a common grounding system, which I will explain in a later chapter on radiotelephones and lightning protection. When I use an electric drill, if I touch any metal, like a mooring bit or stanchion, it's like standing in water.

It is very dangerous to use any older type 2-wire metal-housed power tool because even if the boat isn't in the water, you may be standing on the ground. Metal connections inside power tools are only a fraction of an inch away from the outer metal housing. If the tool is under heavy load, electricity, which always seeks the path of least resistance, can arc over to the metal if it is grounded by your body.

Today all power tools are either 3-wire grounded, or 2-wire with a plastic shock-proof body. I now own four cordless drills and

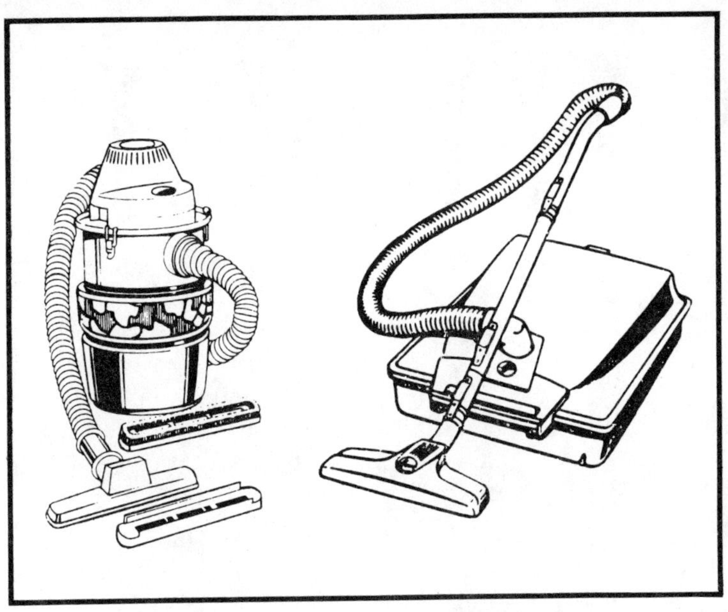

Fig. 1-11. A domestic tank type vacuum cleaner, like the one on the right, is easy to stow on even the smallest cruiser. It will someday save your life on a "buggy" night.

five electric with plastic bodies. I keep one cordless drill and one cordless screwdriver on my boat at all times.

Why so many drills? A wood boat, 30 feet in length, is made up of hundreds of individual pieces of wood, all held together by 11,000 screws and bolts. For every one of those fastenings, a hole had to be drilled—and those holes come in all sizes and shapes. You can go crazy just changing bits.

The first boat I ever built was an 18-foot outboard cruiser. I drilled holes and drove screws manually. My hands would be bleeding every night. On the last boat I built, I used five different electric drills and two power screwdrivers.

The 1/4-inch electric drill is the most used power tool ever made. You cannot drive a screw of any size into anything without first drilling a hole. Aboard ship, regardless of what material they are made of, you are constantly driving screws to install a new compass, a CB radio, an auto pilot, a depth sounder, a bilge pump—it goes on forever. I know a man who has owned the same 32-foot Richardson for 35 years. He's still drilling holes and driving screws. You'd think by now he'd have the thing finished the way he wants it. So remember, until they bury you, your boat is never finished.

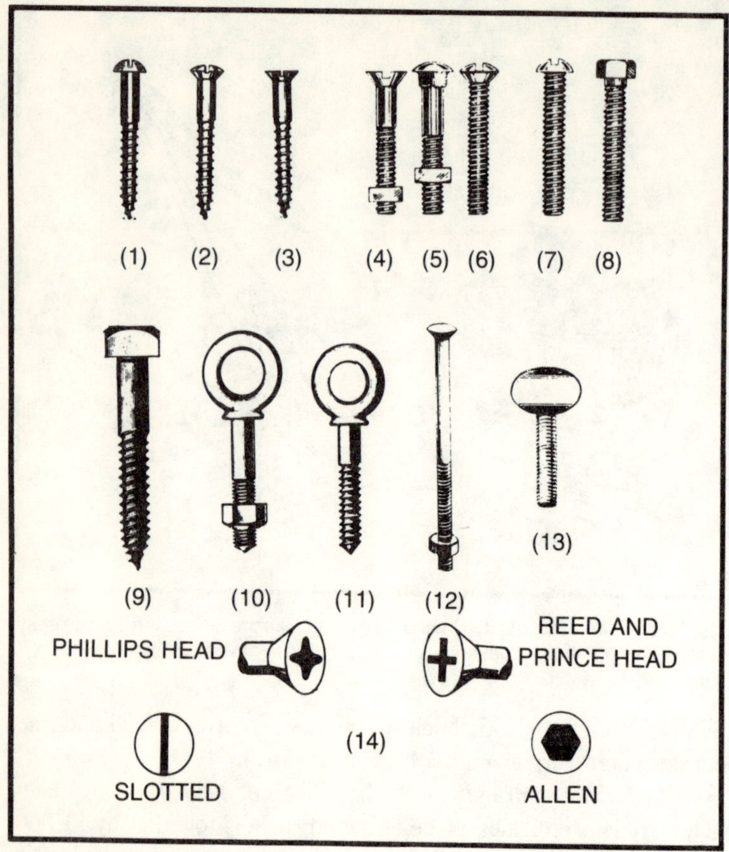

Fig. 1-12. A wood boat is held together by "fasteners." A small cruiser will have over 5,000. You will constantly be buying fasteners. Here's what they're called: (1) round head wood screw, (2) oval head wood screw, (3) flat head wood screw, (4) flat head stove bolt (also called machine screw), (5) carriage bolt, (6) oval head stove bolt, (7) round head stove bolt, (8) hex head machine screw, (9) lag screw, (10) eye bolt, (11) eye screw, (12) strut bolt, (13) thumb screw, (14) Phillips head and prince head, also slot and allen head.

FASTENINGS

The things that hold a boat together are called "fastenings." They are an important part of every boater's life and it is important that you know about them (Fig. 1-12). A fastening can be a bolt, machine screw, wood screw, sheetmetal screw, rivet or nail— anything that holds two things together. In the old days wood boats were fastened with galvanized nails, rivets and long rods, the ends hammered over a washer like a rivet. That's how the *Constitution* was built, and so was the *Mayflower*.

Boat builders today use metals like everdur (bronze), monel (stainless steel) and brass, but not that shiny brass you buy at the local hardware store, which is alloyed with zinc. For dress and finishing up work builders use a marine type brass that is alloyed with tin and chrome plated. These are the most expensive fasteners. I have paid 50 cents for just *one* of these fasteners (Fig. 1-13).

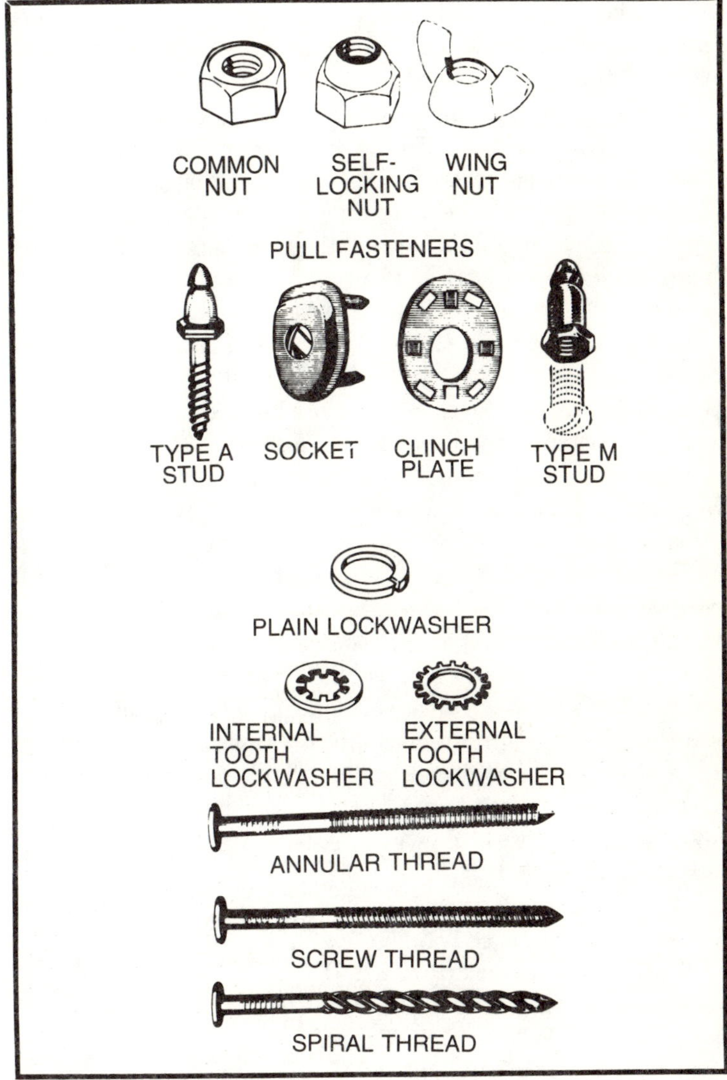

Fig. 1-13. Curtain fasteners, nuts and washers of all types are something of which you never have enough. Keep a supply in your junk box.

Plush marina stores in big cities are the most expensive place to buy fasteners, where they usually have them priced at so much per piece, for the boater who buys a bumper cleat and only needs two screws. Stainless steel, which looks just as good with chrome hardware and fittings, is hard to find in non-marina stores. They are also less expensive if you buy in box lots.

The most common screwhead you will see on a boat is the Reed or Prince head. It looks like a Phillips head and is often mistaken for one. But there is a difference. The Reed/Prince head was designed so that one driver bit would fit all size screws. In high speed production, this saves changing driver bits when working with different size screws. With the Phillips head, you must change bits for each different size in power drive. If you don't, the bit in power drive will jump out of the screwhead and chew it up so badly it can never be removed without making a mess of the wood surface. The Chris Craft Corporation popularized this screw.

These special type heads are important only to the boat builder who uses power drive tools. For the individual boater, the more familiar, and easier to find, slot head will do just as well. For repair work, maintenance and installation of accessories, stainless steel is your best fastener because you can use them for everything. Another very useful fastener is the sheetmetal or tapping screw. This fastener, once used mainly by the sheetmetal industry, is becoming very popular because it is so versatile and can be used on both metal and wood. Also, it has greater holding power in wood when using the short lengths of ¼, ⅜ and ½ inch. For example, if you want to install something on a plywood bulkhead which is only ⅜ inch thick, you must use short screws to avoid coming through on the other side. A ⅜ wood screw has very little thread and holding power, whereas a ⅜ tapping screw is all thread its entire length. Tapping screw threads are also deeper and the screw does not taper to a point like wood screws. This is why they have tremendous holding power in wood. These screws are available in stainless steel and are inexpensive in box lots.

If you can't find stainless fasteners locally, here is a list of sources through the mail: *Yacht Fasteners*, Box 542, Northbrook, IL 60062; *Harper*, Consumer Products Div., 8200 Lehigh Ave., Morton Grove, IL 60053; *Glen-L Marine Designs*, 9152 Rosecrans, Bellflower, CA 90706; *Manhattan Marine & Electric Co.*, 116 Chambers St., New York, NY 10007

The illustrations show the various types of fasteners used by the boating industry. Even though your boat may not be built of wood, it still has fasteners. All of the fasteners illustrated can be bought from the mail sources. The Manhattan Marine catalog costs a buck, and is worth it because it usually has a discount sheet enclosed.

A MINIMUM TOOL LIST

The smallest of boats should have the minimum tool list aboard at all times. For cruising away from home, especially away from the large population centers, I carry tools and equipment over and above what may be considered necessary. For example, I carry spare shafts and propellers. But what good is all this if you can't remove your propellers?

WHY CARRY A PROPELLER PULLER?

After an unhappy experience in Chatham, Ontario one summer, I now carry a propeller puller with me at all times (Figs. 1-14 and 1-15). I hit a floating log, banged up a wheel and bent the starboard

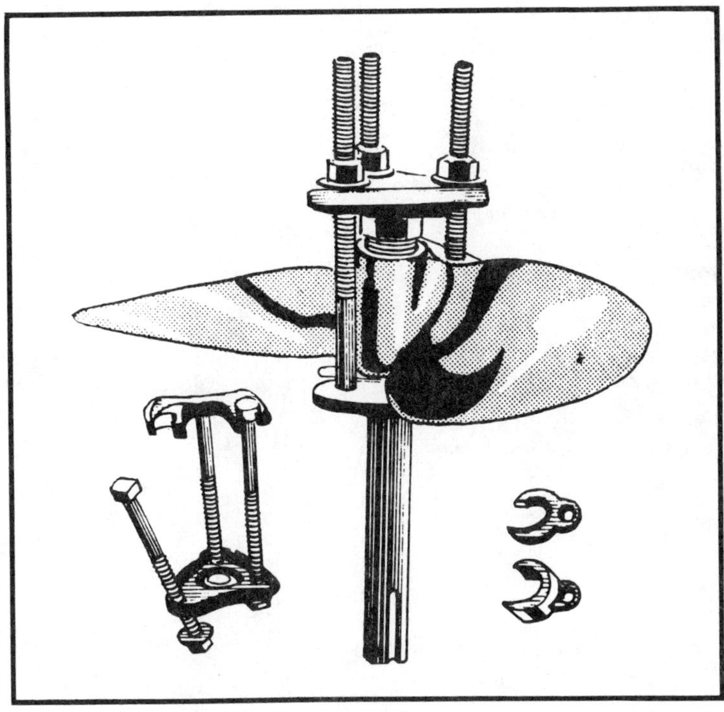

Fig. 1-14. This is something you won't need if you stay close to home. But you better get one if you cruise. Out in the boondocks, propellers are usually removed with a sledge hammer.

shaft. The nearest Travel-Lift was 50 miles away. There was, however, a marine railway run by a farmer 10 miles down the river. It was him or scuba divers. Pulling my shaft with the boat still in the water didn't appeal to me. It is so easy to drop a shaft key, cotter pin or shaft nut. In muddy water, even a scuba diver would have trouble finding anything.

So I limped down river on one engine to the "marine railway." I was pulled out of the river and up a steep hill by an old fashioned tractor with steel wheels and lugs. The old propellers, surprisingly, came off easily. Just as the last cotter pin was being bent over, I noticed that the two new propellers had been installed reversed. The left hand rotation was on the right and vice versa. So they had to be taken off. But this time they wouldn't come off easily. I suggested to the farmer that he use a wheel puller. He said: "What's that?"

I said: "Well, how do you get propellers off?"

He held up a small sledge hammer.

So he banged on my brand new $75 wheels for about ten minutes before they finally broke loose. In the banging, he missed the hib a few times and damaged both blades so badly my wife turned away with tears in her eyes.

Never, never cruise in Canadian waters—any foreign waters—without carrying spare shafts, spare propellers and a propeller puller. I also carry spare shaft nuts, keys and cotter pins, just in case some day I hire a scuba diver.

SPARE PARTS AND SCUBA DIVERS

Amazingly, you can find scuba divers almost anywhere, and they'll come running to help you. If you get into trouble in some out-of-way place, just ask a native. It's unbelieveable! There are no Travel-Lifts when you get away from civilization, but you'll find scuba divers in the darndest places. They are the craziest, most willing helpers you will find anywhere around water. Just one thing, you must be able to show them what to do. And you must have all the necessary tools and equipment.

If you cruise and travel mainly between big cities like Chicago and Milwaukee, Detroit and Toledo, New York and Long Island, Los Angeles and San Diego, you don't need all the tools and equipment I carry because there are plenty of marinas and Travel-Lifts along the way. But the real fun of cruising is getting away from the weekend madness on the Hudson River, East River, Detroit River, in noisy yacht clubs and the over-commercialized marinas. But back in the

Fig. 1-15. You will not get propeller service like this if you cruise very far away from the big cities. Down many rivers and waterways you will find marinas that never heard of a propeller puller.

bush, down the big rivers and up the big bays you will often find mechanics who don't own a complete set of socket wrenches. They're always missing a 9/16 and ½ inch socket, the most used around engines. You will find marina operators who don't own a propeller puller and who will be happy to use yours—and you better have one. A fellow yacht club member had the valves ground on his engine by a mechanic who didn't even own a screwdriver (Fig. 1-16). The mechanic used all his tools and borrowed some from a gas station. Always keep Table 1-4 devices handy.

More on tools later, as various points come up. There is no lumber more versatile and more useful then the 2×4. In 4-foot lengths it is easy to stow in the bilges, and you will find many uses for it when cruising and working on your boat.

THE "ADJUSTABLE" WRENCHES

A further explanation is due on some of the tools listed above. For example, I left out the popular "adjustable" wrench, sometimes

<table>
<tr><td align="center">SPECIAL TOOLS AND ITEMS TO HAVE ABOARD</td></tr>
</table>

Full sets of socket wrenches.
Full sets of combination open/box wrenches.
At least 12 screwdrivers in all sizes and types
Hack saw and extra blades.
Full set of allen wrenches.
Full set of drill bits.
An assortment of pliers.
Set of pipe wrenches (Stillson)
Metal snips
Assortment of files
Hammers, claw and ball-peen
Soldering irons, propane torch
Knife, razor blades
A wide assortment of screws, bolts, lag screws, nails
C-Clamps and spring clamps
Six lengths of 2×4 lumber.

called "knuckle busters." This wrench, along with its first cousin, the monkey wrench, is something you use as a last resort, when nothing else is available. The "adjustable's" jaws only touch two sides of a bolt or nut, which is why it can so easily slip to chew up the corners of the nut and bang your knuckles. Around boats and engines, this wrench is almost useless. It is a handy tool only for career girls who live together in apartments and use it to bang on cold radiators to wake up the janitor.

THE SCREWDRIVER

The world's most used tool, next to the knife and razor blade, is the screwdriver. You never have enough of them, and the bigger your boat, the more sizes you should have aboard. There is nothing more infuriating and frustrating then finding that you can't tighten a loose knob on something because you don't have the right screwdriver. What you have is either too big, too small, too long, too short—or it's the wrong type. I own at least 50 screwdrivers, but I still have this problem.

PLIERS

This is another tool of which you never have enough. You can own as many as 40 different types of pliers, and find a special use for

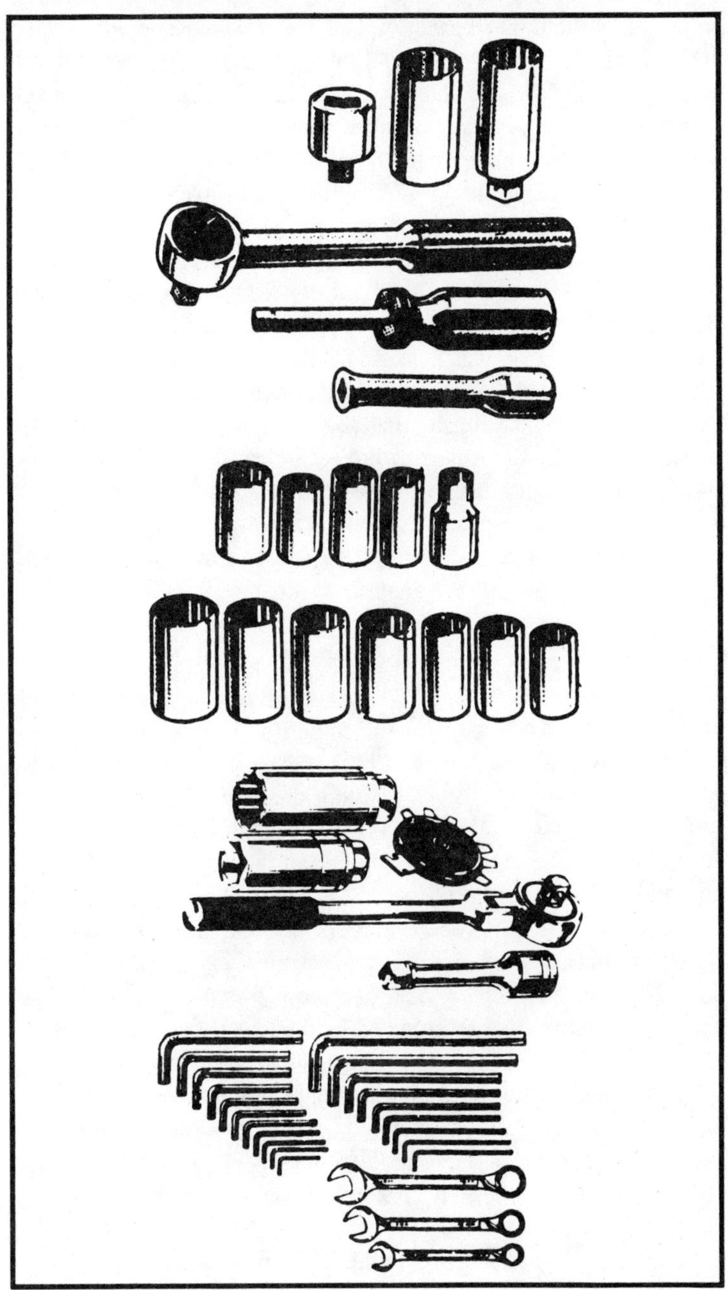

Fig. 1-16. There are mechanics in small towns who don't own any tools. If you hire them on a Sunday, you better have tools like a complete set of socket wrenches, etc.

every one of them on a boat. A useful one is the channel-lock, with jaws like a snake which adjust to swallow a rabbit. You should have two, one with flat jaws and one with round jaws to grab pipe. Vise-grip pliers, which can be locked on both round and flat objects, are also useful in both round and flat jaws. Two different sizes of needle-nose pliers are important aboard larger boats with 120-volt shore wiring and electronic gear. To work with wire, you must have a cutting tool and wire stripper. "Duck-bill" pliers are handy for holding wire while soldering. The list of plier types is endless, just pick your favorites. I neglected to mention that all purpose tool, the common "gas" pliers, which is also called slip-joint pliers because it can be adjusted to two sizes. These pliers come in those plastic case tool kits for household repairs that you buy in drugstores and super-markets. They are the American housewife's favorite tool which she uses to chew up nut heads, remove bottle caps, pick chicken bones out of the garbage disposal, tighten garden hose fittings and crack walnuts. But on a boat I hardly ever use them, except to hold something or to pull off the skin on a catfish I am cleaning.

ALLEN WRENCHES

This is a very important tool, especially if you sail, because you will find allen head screws in all your winches. In power boats you will find them everywhere, hidden in deep holes on shafts, pulleys, radio dials and electronic gear. Not having the right allen wrench can be another one of life's bitter frustrations.

C-CLAMPS

You would be amazed at some of the things you can do with C-clamps, and a first cousin, the spring clamp. I became familiar with them when building boats. You use them to hold things. It's like having two extra arms to help you hold something while you drill, cut, saw, plane or glue. In the spring and fall, when I must transport scaffolding lumber for my winter cover, I carry everything on top of my car, held down with C-clamps. I clamp two long 2×4s on my cartop carrier, then all the other lumber is stacked up between and strapped to them. I transport plywood the same way, with small clamps on the fore and aft ends attached to a rope secured to the bumpers. This holds the plywood ends down against the wind.

When cruising I frequently tie up for lunch or shopping at some dinky little river dock with low 4×4 posts that don't quite reach my sheer rail. They could chew up my topsides. I fix this in a minute by

C-clamping two of my 2×4s to the dock posts, and my sheer rail lays up against them. When I leave, it only takes a minute to remove the clamps and my 2×4s. The C-clamp is a very handy thing to have on a boat.

SOCKET WRENCHES

Socket wrenches are the ultimate tool. Without them the modern automobile engine would never have been designed or manufactured because it could never have been put together. The old Model-T engine could be disassembled and put back together again with just a screwdriver and one adjustable wrench. You need a hundred tools to work on a modern V-8 engine of today, some of them specialized for just one job, like getting at hard-to-reach spark plugs. You can't work on a modern marine engine, inboard or outboard, without socket wrenches and many of the accessories.

The sockets come in graduated sizes of 1/16 inch in ¼, ⅜ and ½ square drive. In ¼ inch drive, the sockets will range in size from 3/16 to ½; in ⅜ inch drive, they go from ⅜ to ⅞ and in ½ inch drive from 7/16 up to 1⅛. There is a larger size available in ¾ inch drive with sockets running up to 2⅜, but this is mainly for heavy equipment.

There are three different type of socket grips (Fig. 1-17). The "6-point" socket fits neatly over a hex nut and bolt, touching all six

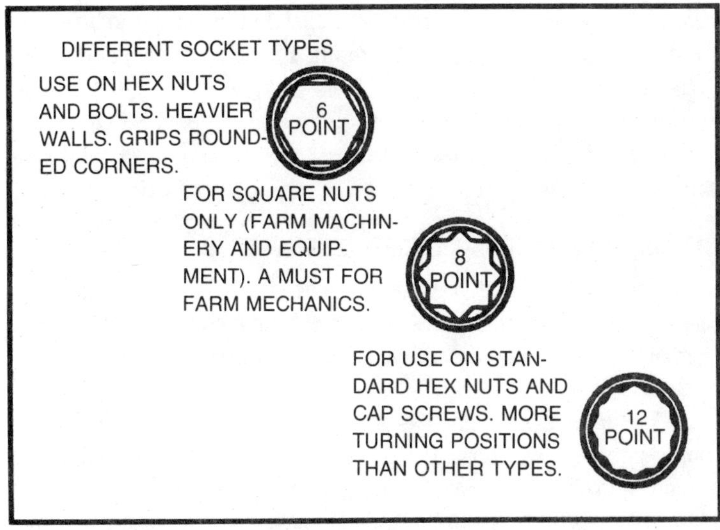

Fig. 1-17. The six-point socket is the best because it will not slip on a hex-head nut. The 12-point is preferred by mechanics because it is a "thin wall" socket that gets into tight places. The eight-point socket is only for square nuts.

sides. Slippage is impossible. The "8-point" grip can only be used on square nuts and is a must for farm machinery mechanics. The "12-point" is the most popular with mechanics because it has more turning positions, and these sockets can be made with thin walls so they can get into tight places. However, the 12-point socket only grips a hex nut on the corners, and sometimes can slip with a frozen bolt or nut. That's why mechanics will have both 6 and 12-point sockets. The 6-point sockets have thicker walls and won't get into tight places like valve covers where the bolts almost touch the metal cover. That's why mechanics prefer the 12-point "Thin-Wall" sockets. They use their 6-point sockets only on frozen bolts.

A whole set of ¼ inch drive sockets and accessories, will fit into a small metal box only six inches long. A full set of ¼ inch and ⅜ inch sockets, with accessories, will handle all the maintenance work on any marine engine because 9/16, ⅝ and 11/16 are the three largest bolts or nuts you will ever work on.

Among the many accessories available are screwdriver bits in both slot and Phillips head. With extension bars and a ratchet handle you can reach into cramped areas in the bilge to drive or back out tough screws. The ratchet handle gives you tremendous leverage—so much, in fact, you must be careful not to break off screws when going into white oak. Incidently, it is virtually impossible to drive an ordinary hardware store brass screw into white oak. I have tried drilling over-size pilot holes, lubricating both the hole and the threads, and still snapped them off. I have even snapped off ⅜ inch galvanized steel lag screws. This will give you an idea of the toughness of white oak, and the power you can develop with a socket ratchet drive. And there will be many times when you will need that muscle desperately.

THE COMBINATION BOX AND OPEN-END WRENCH

Why would you need these wrenches if you have sockets? The reason is there are still things you cannot handle with a socket. For example, how would you remove a flared fitting from a copper water line?

The open end wrench is a necessity when working on the copper plumbing of a boat. It is useful also on big outboard engines. The box and open end of a combination wrench will be the same size. The box end is the safest to use on a tight nut since it will not slip and bang up your knuckles. Then, when the nut is free, you can work faster with the open end side of the wrench.

TO BUY OR NOT TO BUY METRIC TOOLS

Before you go to Sears and Roebuck to buy some metric tools, consider that all American automobiles and marine engines are still being made using the old English system of weights and measurements. The metric wrenches will work, but not too well, because there are no exact match-ups between American and foreign bolt and nut sizes. For example, the American 9/16 is a very common size on auto and marine engines. With metric, the closest you can get is with a 15mm socket or wrench—a very sloppy fit. Two other common sizes are 7/16 and ½ inch, for which you will get loose fits using 11mm and 13mm wrenches. They'll work with 6-point sockets, but not 12-point. If American sockets can slip with a perfect fit, imagine what a metric will do with a loose fit.

The United States is just about the only country left that is not metric. That means all foreign cars, motorcycles and marine engines are metric. If you have a foreign marine engine in your boat, like the Volvo, then you definitely need metric tools. Otherwise, stay American. England, from whom we inherited our system, has gone completely metric. Canada is now in the process of changing over.

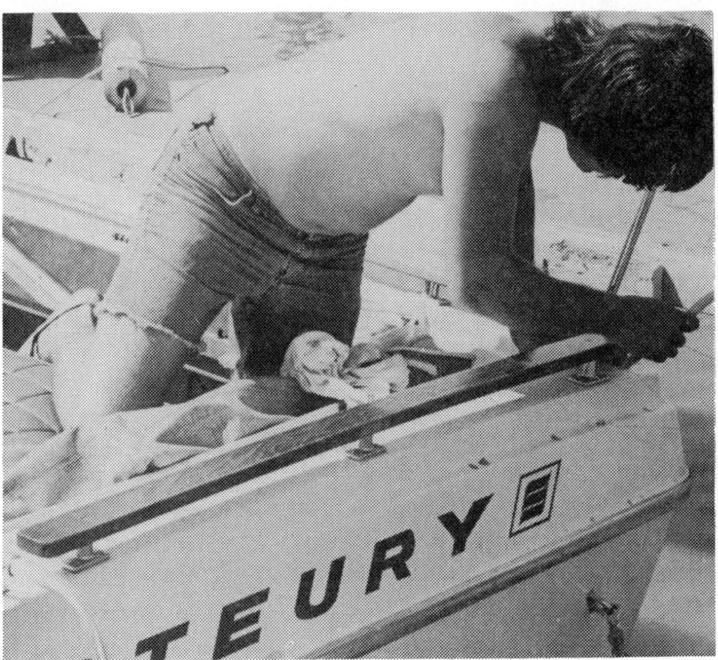

Fig. 1-18. Varnishing is an art and not a craft, which is why professionals use the finest brushes money can buy.

The United States remains an island of square posts surrounded by a world of round holes.

VARNISH BRUSHES

I have watched one of the best professional boat varnishers in action, and I have come to the conclusion that fine varnishing is not a craft but an art requiring almost the talents of a Michelangelo painting God on the ceiling of the Sistine Chapel (Figs. 1-18 and 1-19). This professional that I watched for six weekends was a specialist who did nothing else at a big Detroit boatyard but varnish the yachts of all those "fat cats" from Grosse Pointe and St. Clair Shores.

The yard foreman told me this varnisher was their highest paid employee. When the "fat cats" ordered work to be done on their yachts, they didn't care who worked on their expensive Diesels, who painted their topsides or who painted their bottoms. But they damn well did care who varnished their transoms and brightwork. They all insisted that no one be allowed to touch their brightwork but Ned, the varnish man.

He's a man with a vile disposition and guards his secret well by just grunting when you ask questions. He used only three brushes, all fine camel hair in 1-inch, 2-inch and 3-inch. The foreman told me Ned guarded those brushes like they were emeralds and would snarl at anybody who picked one up.

Fascinated, I watched Ned varnish a transom on a 60-foot Wheeler. He just flowed the varnish with the 3-inch brush in only one direction. He put it on very thick, and amazingly it didn't run. When he finished you could see your reflection in the glass-like finish. It was poetry! It was a symphony in varnish and wood. And it looked so easy.

I tried it on my transom with my brushes. I used the same brand of varnish. I imitated his every move, even spit the way he did. I had a titanic disaster of runs and had to clean the whole mess off with turps.

Ned's transoms are not signed like a Picasso, but everybody knows them. A big yacht will tie up at a gas dock, and somebody will say: "Hey, look! There's a Ned transom." And soon there will be a crowd around the gas dock to look and admire.

I spend one whole summer trying to learn the secret of how he did it, speaking to all the other employees in the boatyard. They just shrugged. Some sneered, obviously with envy. One man, who admitted he disliked Ned, remarked: "The secret's in those damn brushes he uses."

Fig. 1-19. Flat surfaces like this are easy to varnish. There is a tendency to lay the varnish on too heavy. In the sun it will wrinkle.

I am inclined to agree. I have never known a man skilled at painting or varnishing who didn't treat his brushes as if they were priceless treasures out of King Tut's tomb. Good brushes are the secret. Remember this when you shop for varnish brushes and are tempted to buy the cheap throw-away type just so you don't have to clean them. I have done this myself, and always the work I produced with those brushes was something I later wished I could "throw-away" with the brushes.

PAINT BRUSHES

Varnish brushes should only varnish. Paint brushes should only paint. The professionals all agree on this. I still don't know why, if the brushes are thoroughly cleaned. But I never argue with professionals. So I never mix my brushes.

You will rarely see a paint brush larger than 3½ inches being used by a boatyard employee (Fig. 1-20). They use 1-inch for molding and trim, 2-inch for small areas and the 3½ inch for topsides. I had always suspected that the hourly labor charge had something to do with this because it takes longer to paint a hull with a smaller brush. But a foreman told me; "Painting a boat is not quite the same as painting a house. Housepainters always work directly out of a gallon paint bucket. In boat painting you almost always work directly out of a quart can, except, of course, with bottom work. The smaller

Fig. 1-20. These are the brushes suggested by paint manufacturers, but you will never see a professional using a brush over 3½ inches. Painting a boat is not like painting a barn.

brush can more easily be dipped into a quart can without damaging the side bristles.

"Another thing," he continued, "the smaller brush is far less tiring when you paint all day, as a result you don't slow down. With the smaller brush there is less tendency to overpaint, lay it on too thick. This is worse than not painting at all. A heavy coat will crack and alligator."

THE PAINT ROLLER

The short nap roller is the easiest way to bottom paint, and the fastest. It is also the efficient, economical way to spread a coating which can cost up to $100 a gallon. Brushing is wasteful because you are fighting gravity, working up, and losing the heavy-bodied paint as it runs down the brush handle onto your hands and arms. You often get as much paint on yourself as on the boat. Bottom paints are a very heavy material, loaded with metallic compounds which quickly settle to the bottom of the can if not stirred every five minutes.

When you roll it on, you stir the paint every time you refill the tray, and you get it on more uniformly and economically. At $80 to $100 a gallon, you'll do a better job with less paint and save yourself 50 bucks. And there's no clean-up afterwards. You just throw the roller away. If you remembered to line the bottom of the paint tray with heavy aluminum foil, you won't even have to clean it.

The short nap roller is also perfect for final topside painting because it gets the paint on thinner and smoother. That's the whole point, getting it on thin. That's the only way you avoid paint build-up and the problems that go with it.

PAINT SPRAYERS

Bill Harrison of Harrison's Marina used to say: "Paint spraying is like sex; it should be done only in private."

What he meant was that in a crowded marina yard, with other boats and parked cars in close proximity, you should never try to spray paint, even when the wind isn't blowing (Fig. 1-21). I once got some Pettit's Green Mist on my new Chrysler, and it was parked at least 100 feet away from where some clown was spray painting his dinghy.

The spray gun outdoors is a lethal weapon. Commercial boatyards spray paint indoors in a special area that is completely closed off with drape material going up to the ceiling. If your boat is small enough to get in the garage, that is the place to spray paint. Only don't forget to back out your wife's car before you start spraying.

Spray painting outdoors in a crowded boatyard will bring you nothing but troubles, like maybe a broken arm if that Corvette Stingray parked close to you belongs to some young buck who plays defensive tackle in college.

THE WINTER LAYUP

The late Bill Harrison, founder of a well known marina on western Lake Erie, told me: "If it wasn't for winter layups, boats would last forever, or a helluva lot longer than they do propped up on land under dark colored canvas."

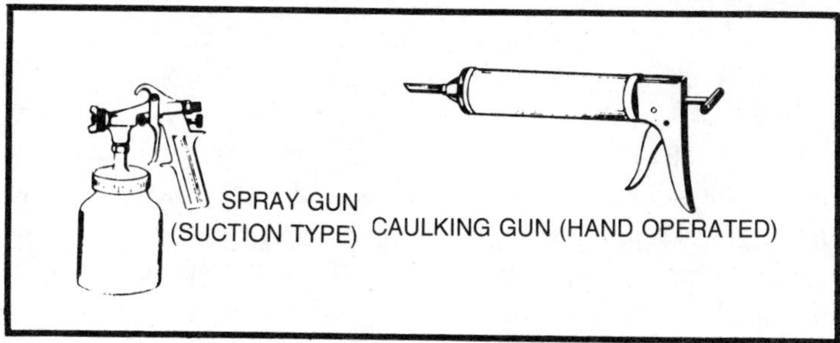

Fig. 1-21. The spray gun will give you nothing but trouble in a crowded boat yard. The slightest air moving will blow paint on other boats and cars.

Fig. 1-22. This is the traditional way of laying up a boat over the winter. It's also a way to lower the life expectancy of a wood boat.

Even the experts agree that most of the damage and rot in wood boats occurs during the winter layup when they are alternately cold and hot. You would not believe how much heat can be generated by the sun under dirty canvas. Harrison told me he once checked the temperature and found a spread of 60 degrees. Outside it was zero; under the canvas on a sunny windless day in January it was a warm, comfortable 60 degrees—that is, the air was 60 degrees. But all surfaces were still ice cold. As a result, warm air condenses on cold surfaces and everything becomes wet as if just washed down with a hose.

On one windless sunny day a 35-foot boat will generate 10 to 15 gallons of fresh sweet water which soaks all the wood, rusts the engines, and corrodes all electrical equipment and switches. The woods in those dark hidden places under decks become so thoroughly saturated with moisture during the winter layup that they never get a chance to really dry out—oh, maybe on the outside, but not inside where fungus likes to feed on wood dampened by sweet fresh water. Remember, fungus will not touch wood that is salty. In salt water boating, your hull below the water line is safe. But you still must guard against rain and condensation above the waterline.

Boatmen are among the most tradition-bound creatures, which is why you will still see boats wintering under wood framework and canvas which are dark green on top to keep off the snow (Fig. 1-22).

THE PLASTIC BOATHOUSE

Boatmen are also among the most resourceful and inventive of men. I have seen wonderful ideas and devices conceived by boaters for their own use which could have been patented and put on the market. Often they do get on the market, but only after somebody else sees and lifts the idea.

A plastic boathouse is one of those ideas. When I first saw this boat under plastic, I laughed, and so did others (Fig. 1-23). It looked so fragile and light, like a box kite waiting for a good wind to lift it up and blow it away. Exactly two weeks after I saw this plastic boathouse, a terrific storm hit the area with winds gusting at over 75-miles-per-hour. Mobiles homes were knocked over, big trucks were blown off the highways, and hundreds of homes and boats were damaged. But, so help me, this plastic boathouse was still standing exactly as you see it.

It was unbelieveable because all around other boats had their canvas ripped off (Fig. 1-24). The plastic looks deceptively flimsy,

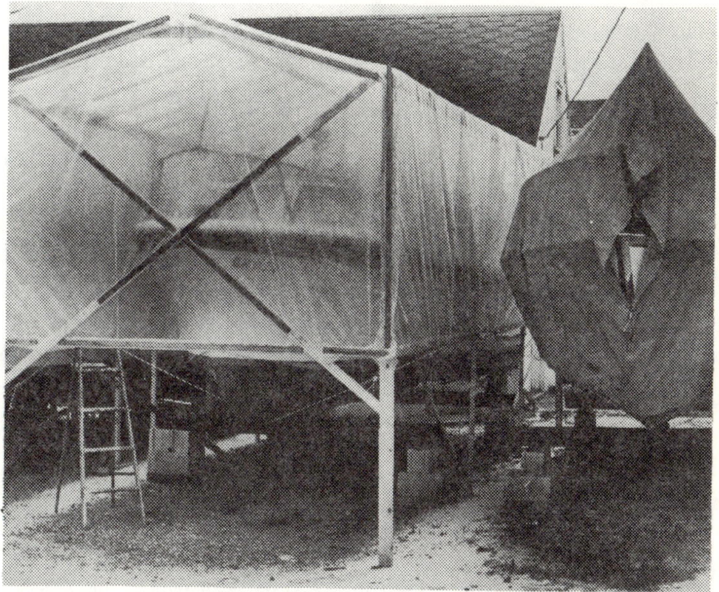

Fig. 1-23. To the right is the old. To the left is the new.

Fig. 1-24. Hundreds of canvas covers were ripped off boats. The only plastic covers that came off were those that were torn or cut by flying debris from neighboring boats, as in this photo.

but it's tougher than an old tire and that plastic wrapped around steaks at the supermarket which you can't remove without cutting and swearing. This is the plastic boathouse's only weakness—you can pierce it, you can cut it. But you can't damage it with sheer muscle power. The framework will break long before the plastic. So remember this fact when building your framework, and don't use cheap lumber with knots like one man did. One of his corner posts had a huge knot, which broke and toppled the whole structure. Once splintered wood pierces the plastic, it will tear and blow all to hell.

The framework for a plastic boathouse is considerably easier to build and costs less then conventional canvas scaffolding. Canvas type frameworks sit directly on the boat itself and usually have a sloping roof angle forward for rain and snow run-off (Fig. 1-25). Also, the framework must be more heavily constructed to support snow loads and wet canvas. It must be endlessly padded to protect both the boat and canvas from chafing. To build such a framework requires more then just simple carpentry skills. For the boatmen who lack these skills, it means turning to the yard for a custom-made job at high hourly labor charges, plus materials.

Fig. 1-25. Conventional canvas framework sits directly on the boat itself. It must be amply padded with rug material to prevent chafing.

The entire framework for a plastic boathouse can be built out of 2×4 stock (Fig. 1-26). Batten material and rafters can be ripped out 2×4s. The batten strips are extremely important because they are used to secure the plastic material to the framework. Nails and

Fig. 1-26. The entire framework can be built out of 2 × 4 stock. Lighter 1×4 lumber can be used for rafters.

Fig. 1-27. In the spring you just rip off the plastic cover and throw it away. But you do save the framework.

staples must not be used directly through plastic. Always use a batten strip or small block of wood over the plastic.

The plastic material, which can be purchased from Sears Roebuck or any lumber yard, comes only in 100-foot lengths, but in many different widths and thicknesses. The most popular size is 24-foot wide and 6 mil thickness. This will cost about $40, but there will be enough for three winter layups because you don't save the plastic. You just rip it off in the spring and throw it away (Fig. 1-27). But you do save the framework.

If you're wondering about that "6 mil" thickness, a "mil" is one thousandth of an inch, or .001. The paper this book is printed on is about 2 mils. The plastic, which is actually polyethylene, comes in degrees of thickness from 1 to 10 mils. When you get over 6 mils, the price really zooms, and you don't really need it that heavy because your plastic boathouse will be only as strong as your framework.

You do not secure the plastic to the roof rafters. You just let it lay loose and the constant fluttering and flapping in the wind keeps the roof amazingly free of snow. This is one of the many fringe benefits that goes with the plastic boathouse, like almost complete freedom from sweating and mildew.

Since the boathouse stands free and away from the boat itself, there is plenty of air movement (Fig. 1-28). In the spring when you want to sand or work on rainy days, you will appreciate that extra workspace around the hull. On windless days with the sun shining, it is only 10 to 15 degrees warmer under the plastic. On windy days, this temperature differential drops to only 5 degrees, and yet it seems much warmer under the plastic because you are protected from the wind.

Fig. 1-28. Plastic boathouse framework sits directly on the ground rather than the boat, and as far away from the hull as the owner wishes.

Fig. 1-29. You will find it sheer joy working under the plastic with plenty of light, air and protection from the weather.

You will find it sheer joy working on your boat in the spring without having to worry about the weather (Fig. 1-29). You will be sanding and painting while others are crying in their beer.

The Fiberglass Boat

It was just 25 years ago that fiberglass entered the world of boating, and hardly anybody noticed. In fact, when it was noticed at all, it brought jeers and questions like: "Who the hell wants a boat made out of glass?" The old traditional boatbuilders wanted nothing to do with fiberglass. They resisted and fought against its acceptance because they could see no future in the new material.

Nobody knows who built the first fiberglass boat back in 1945. Everybody knows who builds them today. When the giants, the old line builders like Chris Craft, Pacemaker and Owens, finally made the switch from traditional wood to fiberglass, there were no more questions like, "Who the hell wants a boat made out of glass?" Everybody did, including the U.S. Navy.

The Navy, in fact, is largely responsible for helping to develop fiberglass as a boatbuilding material for boats larger then dinghies and cartops. The Navy financed the research and development of 28-foot personnel craft which, at the time, was quite a jump from dinghies. That started others into thinking big, new companies like Hatteras and Bertram. Never having worked with wood, these new companies didn't have to re-design their plants or re-tool and re-train workmen.

The Matthews Boat Company of Port Clinton, Ohio, had been the most traditional of builders for over half a century, and their boats were often called the Cadillacs of small yachts. When Matthews went fiberglass, it did something to the industry. It was like reading that Rolls Royce was going to build dune buggies. It was hard to vision those old Matthews craftsmen, who had never worked with anything but steam-bent oak frames and carvel planking, now laying up fiberglass cloth on molds. But they're doing it today as Matthews builds plush yachts in the 50-foot class.

The U.S. Navy is now considering the use of fiberglass in cargo vessels up to 300 feet. The British government is testing 180-foot minesweepers in the 800-ton displacement class. Fishing trawlers in the 85-foot class are already in service, and so are luxury private yachts.

And it all started with a little 8-foot dinghy back in 1945. The only thing holding back fiberglass in big ocean shipbuilding is economics. It is still far cheaper to build an ocean cargo vessel of steel.

HOW LONG WILL FIBERGLASS LAST?

Building with fiberglass is not cheap, as anyone knows who has recently bought a small pleasure craft. When I bought my 35-foot cruiser for $20,000, the same type and size boat in fiberglass was selling around $40,000. When you get into big shipbuilding, you're talking millions. Anything which adds another $50 million to the cost of an oil tanker is going to meet with a lot of resistance, particularly when nobody yet really knows how long a vessel built of fiberglass will last in the hostile sea environment. Fiberglass just hasn't been around long enough to prove anything.

Longevity could be the key that will open the door. Steel vessels in salt water service have a life expectancy of about 20 years—not that they wear out. They corrode out. Galvanic corrosion is the reason why the U.S. Navy de-commissions ships after about 20 years and sells them for scrap. To the eye they still look good, but structurally they have been weakened by both corrosion and stress, which cause cracks in steel plate. That is why old steel vessels sometimes break in half during violent storms.

CAN FIBERGLASS TAKE STRESS?

Fiberglass is immune to galvanic corrosion, which can diminish 1-inch steel hull plates down to a ¼-inch in 20 years. But how will fiberglass withstand the stresses and strains of riding the hills and valleys of mountainous seas, where one moment a ship's bow and propellers are out of the water and the next they are supported by two waves, while amidships the hull is over a deep valley? This puts a tremendous strain on a hull as it is alternately supported, then unsupported amidship. It is like bending a long piece of metal back and forth until it snaps in the middle.

Ocean vessels frequently break apart in the middle as happened to the lake freighter, *Edmund Fitzgerald*, which sank in Lake Superior during a violent storm in the fall of 1975. This always happens to old vessels which are nearing the end of their life expectancy, which is considerably longer in fresh water service where the rate of galvanic corrosion is much slower.

Many freighters working the Great Lakes are over 50 years old. These are the ones lakes sailors fear. One of these sailors told me that he was in the stern section during a Lake Huron storm as they wallowed in heavy beam seas. As he looked down the 900-foot deck, he could see the pilot house listing 15 degrees to port while the stern section was listing 15 degrees to starboard. He was scared to death. Nobody is predicting how an ocean vessel built of fiberglass will hold up under stress like that.

THE LAST TEST FOR FIBERGLASS

Fiberglass hulls, like the Bertrams, have undergone considerable testing in offshore ocean racing and held up well. Boats built of other materials have come unglued and dropped out of the race. But this is a different kind of stress. Small planing hulls slap and pound over the waves. Displacement hulls stay in the water and are twisted and bent rather than hammered on their bottoms. And there's a big difference between a short race from Miami to Bermuda and 20 years of hauling freight and fighting the sea 24 hours a day, seven days a week.

How long fiberglass holds up at sea under these conditions is the question waiting to be answered. If fiberglass passes this test, it will be the end of steel, aluminum and wood as boatbuilding materials.

THE GOOD THINGS ABOUT FIBERGLASS

So, what's good about fiberglass for the pleasure craft buyer?

There are no seams in fiberglass cruisers and sailboats. This eliminates one of boatings most tedious chores, filling in seams that have opened up during winter storage as wood dries out (Fig. 2-1). In the spring, wood boat seams are caulked (Fig. 2-2). The wood swells up after launching and squeezes out all the new seam compounds. Next season you do it all over again.

Fig. 2-1. Fiberglass relieves you of having to look at seams like this every spring.

THE "MAINTENANCE FREE" MYTH

According to all the boatyard foremen I have talked to, fiberglass boats require about 70 to 80 percent as much maintenance as a wood boat of comparable size. The slight savings in the amount of work come mostly in caulking. The well-built fiberglass boat is in one solid unit, (superstructure, decks and hull), with no seams where they come together. In wood construction, these are the chronic trouble spots.

WHY FIBERGLASS BOATS DON'T LEAK

When you eliminate leaks, you have solved one of the biggest annoyances in boating, particularly to wives who just can't understand why a boat leaks every time it rains. They say: "Cars don't leak. So why do boats?"

The "leaks" I refer to are not below the waterline. This area is rarely much of a problem because after a boat has been in the water a few days, the planking swells up and the leaks stop. But the "leaks" from above the waterline never stop. These are the ones that drive women crazy. Men accept them as a fact of life, like an aching back every spring after working on the bottom. It goes with the territory, as they say. But you can never sell leaks to a woman, even after you do succeed in selling them boating. They complain constantly about the bunks being wet, about little puddles of water in the head, in the galley, on the dinette table and in the hanging lockers. You constantly fight leaking on a wood boat and never win. The seamless fiberglass cruiser has eliminated this ancient curse of boating.

MORE GOOD THINGS ABOUT FIBERGLASS

So, what else is good about fiberglass boats? No dry rot! No teredo worms! No galvanic corrosion! No paint flaking off because the wood is moist. No brightwork to sand and varnish during the hot boating season.

All these qualities have made fiberglass the most popular boat building material today. But there are still skeptics, and you will see them at boat shows, thumping on fiberglass hulls with their fists to see if they give a little. This irritates salesmen, for the same reason that used car salesmen are annoyed when they see buyers kick the tires on a car.

THE HULL THUMPERS

Banging on hulls, a salesman told me at a boat show, will tell you absolutely nothing about a boat's quality. In fact, it may even mislead you because a deep, solid thump sound doesn't necessarily indicate a thicker skin or stronger hull. Some very badly built boats feel solid when you thump them, while one of the best fiberglass boats on the market, and most expensive, sounds flimsy and thin.

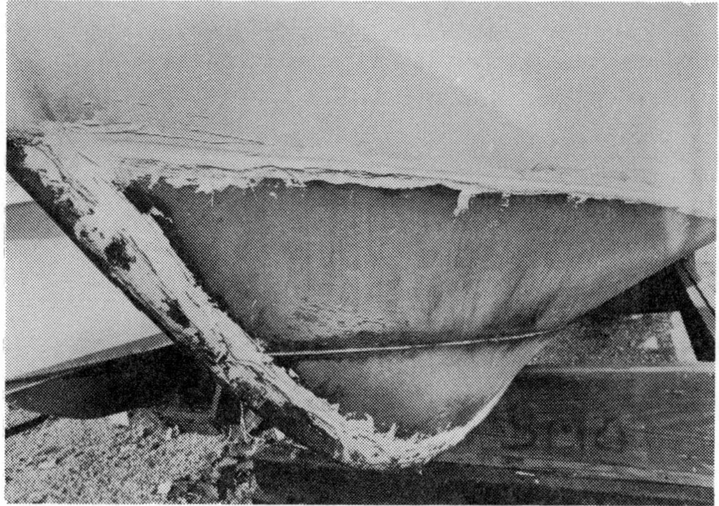
Fig. 2-2. Not even the plywood hulls escape the caulking work in the spring.

HOW TO JUDGE QUALITY IN FIBERGLASS

To judge quality in fiberglass construction, look at the hull the way a professional does. Check to see if the lines are fair. The word "fair" is a boatbuilding term; it means all hull curve lines lay smooth on the frames (Fig. 2-3). If you take a 30-foot rod, or 1-inch square length of wood (called a batten), and bend it into a curve, that curve will be perfectly smooth with no humps or dips. The curve lines of a hull should look the same, natural and not forced. In wood construction, when a long plank is bent around the hull frames, it takes a natural curve. But if one of the frames is a fraction too large or small, when the plank if forced up against that frame, a dip or bump is created, throwing the hull lines out of fair.

The same thing happens in steel, aluminum, and quite often fiberglass hulls that are layed up in metal molds that were not "faired." If you stand back at the transom, and sight along the hull, you will see those little "dips" and "bumps." If you do, beware! These dips are an accurate indication of poor construction. Faired lines are basic in boat building, like plumb walls and level foundations are basic in home construction. When you buy a home, you take it for granted that the builder knows how to plumb the walls. If he doesn't, then he should be building doghouses which don't have to be level or plumb.

It's the same in boat building. Faired lines are a basic must. If the builder can't do this, then he can't build boats—and you should look no further at his product.

Another area where many builders lack know-how, or just don't give a damn, is corners. This is a critical matter! You will find no sharp corners or edges on fiberglass boats built by Chris Craft, Hatteras or Bertram because they know that hard 90-degree turns are a constant source of trouble with fiberglass. The reason is it cracks! So these builders avoid sharp corners and edges. Note this on the next Chris Craft you see. Everything is smoothly rounded off with no sharp or hard turns. This means no hairline cracks or crazing, the bane of fiberglass.

POORLY INSTALLED DECK HARDWARE

Another area where some fiberglass builders cut corners is in the installation of deck hardware. All mooring cleats, bits, etc., should be solidly secured with through bolts and a reinforcing block of wood or metal under the deck. This wood, usually ¾-inch plywood, is also fiberglassed. The skin on some boats under 25 feet

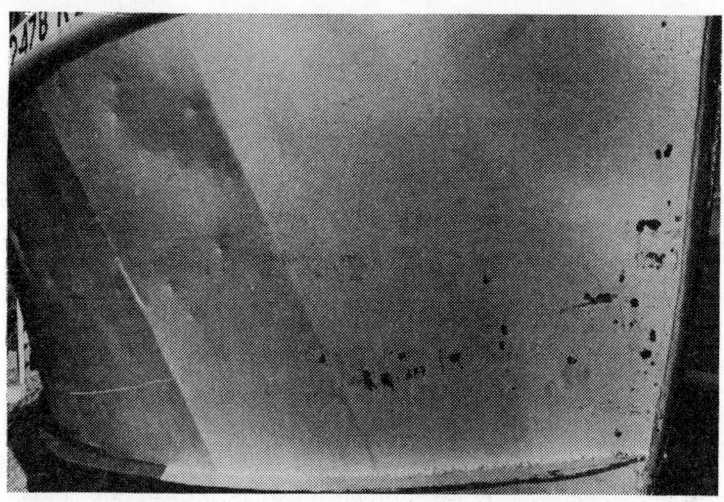

Fig. 2-3. Hull curves should lay smooth on the frames with no humps over the frames.

are sometimes only ⅛ or 3/16 inches thick. Without reinforcing, even bolts can be pulled out. The reason that plywood is frequently used as reinforcing material, also as hull stringers, is that the polyester resins seem to adhere very well to fir plywood, but will not stick to white oak.

I saw stern cleats pulled out of two 30-foot cruisers at a Cleveland yacht club. This club is right on the shores of Lake Erie, protected by a stone breakwall. When the wind is out of any northerly direction, Lake Erie funnels through a narrow entrance channel into the club's basin, where it creates a disastrous surge. Although water in the basin may look smooth and quiet, it is actually surging up and down. Boats are lifted up suddenly and slammed against their lines and docks.

As a visitor to this club, I was surprised to see some of the large yachts tied up with heavy chains and huge spring shock absorbers. I learned why that night when I was knocked out of my bunk. The wind had shifted to the north, and the surge kept me awake all night. I saw this new fiberglass cruiser swinging around loose in its slip. One of its stern cleats had been pulled out. I could still see the screws when I pulled the line up out of the water with the cleat attached.

WHY STERN CLEATS PULL OUT

Stern cleats take the most punishment dockside mainly because so many new boatmen just don't know how to properly tie up their boats. At the stern they use a short line direct to a piling or dock cleat, sometimes no more than 2 feet in length. They keep this line short so the boat won't swing out too far, then swing back and bang against the dock. But they forget something, or often just don't know, that water levels drop and rise! Even on the Great Lakes, where there are no tides, I have seen strong offshore winds make Lake Erie water levels drop 5 feet in one afternoon and leave hundreds of unattended boats hanging on their stern cleats. If the boats are big, decking will sometimes be ripped out.

Maybe putting in stern cleats with wood screws is a good thing for certain types of boatmen, the ones who don't know about tides on coastal waters. When the falling tide drops their boat 5 feet on a 2-foot stern line, the cleat pulls out easily without seriously damaging the boat. Possibly that is why some fiberglass builders still secure all deck hardware with wood screws instead of bolts into reinforcing blocks under the decks to prevent serious structural damage when some dummy fails to tie up his boat properly. Perhaps it is better to have a cleat pull out easily, leaving just two small holes which can be easily repaired. However, I don't think the builders had this in mind when they used wood screws instead of bolts.

THE BAD THINGS ABOUT FIBERGLASS

The stern cleats are first on the list of bad things. A fiberglass hull and cabin, integrated into one solid unit to eliminate seams, is still a thin-skinned structural shell. It must be reinforced throughout, both for strength and stiffness and to provide a solid foundation into which things can be attached. The engines require a solid base. So does the bow pulpit, side rails and stern rails, grab rails, and lifelines as they are called on sailboats. The rigging on sailboats must have a solid base. You don't screw them to a thin fiberglass skin. In the hull bottom, there must be stringers. If wood, they should be completely covered with fiberglass to prevent rot. This is called "encapsulated." In your quality boats, wood is not used. The stringers and girders are molded separately and then bonded to the hull.

The next time you go to a boat show, just try and find out about these things from the salesmen, or that pretty girl on board in the string bikini. All she does is smile, hand out literature and utter phrases like: "Wouldn't you like to come aboard?"

When you say that you would like to look in the bilges, her smile suddenly disappears. She stares at you a moment, like you had two heads, and then she whispers to the salesman. He comes over and says: "I can't show you the bilge right now because all the furniture must be moved and this rug must be rolled up. I can't do that with people coming aboard."

The bikini doll will butt in at this moment. "Can I show you the rotisserie and all-electric galley?"

You interrupt. "I'm not interested in the rotisserie. I just wanna look in the bilge."

"Why?" she asks innocently.

"I wanna see how this boat is built. I wanna see if it will be easy to work on the engines."

You'll get another blank stare, and then she'll turn to greet someone else, who will follow her to look at the rotisserie and the all-electric galley. And the salesman will suddenly become very busy with others coming aboard.

They have a way of rushing you off at the boat shows, so don't go. I don't like them, for the above reasons, and others. They show you only what they want you to see. They give you that garbage about fiberglass being the "maintenance free" boat. All you do is wash and wax them, like your car. And they're so easy to repair. Oh, sure they are.

GETTING FIBERGLASS BOATS REPAIRED

This is another one of the bad things about fiberglass boats— getting them repaired. Commercial boatyards and marinas have been, up until just the past few years, geared to the servicing and repair of wood boats. You'll find this is particularly so in old traditional yards on Chesapeake Bay, Long Island and New England up to Maine. Even today you will still find a few old craftsmen building wood boats right out in the open like it was done for hundreds of years. They even work in the rain. These men have never worked on anything but steamed oak frames and carvel planking. Up in Maine, they even turn up their noses at sawed frames and speak contemptuously of "hard chines" like it was something dirty or evil. For years, Chris Craft was an unmentionable thing that made the locals spit without comment. Chris Craft was one of the pioneers in "hard chine" fast planing hulls.

In this cradle of American boat building, the old boat workmen want nothing to do with fiberglass and refuse to work with it, or even learn how. One of the leading boat magazines, with a vested interest in the sales of fiberglass boats, admitted a few years ago that service know-how was lacking and hurting sales. They said that in many sections of the country it was difficult to get repairs, alterations, or even a simple routine paint job on a fiberglass boat. In boating there is nothing more routine then painting a boat. If you can't get a fiberglass boat painted, what can you get done?

The message is finally getting through to the marinas and old boatyards that fiberglass is here to stay. I, too, have gotten the message. There is an old saying: "Be not the first on whom the new is tried, nor yet the last to lay the old aside."

My present boat is wood. My next boat is going to be fiberglass. I am not going to be "the last to lay the old aside." And I am weary to death of listening to my wife complain about leaks. However, I will be buying a fiberglass boat fully aware of what I am getting into, with no illusions. I am fully aware that when my new fiberglass boat needs service, alterations, repairs and painting, I will have to do it myself. And so will you.

PAINTING FIBERGLASS

A major problem with the early fiberglass boats was painting them. I know because I had some of that early fiberglass as a cabin and hardtop cover, and it nearly drove me crazy. I painted it three times one season, trying to find something that would stay on.

Adhesion was the problem. And that was why boatyards hated to work on fiberglass boats. The good marinas stood behind their work, and when a paint job failed, or didn't satisfy the customer, they did it over and took a loss. You can't stay in business long doing that.

So why did the paint jobs fail? Was it the paint? The paints I used were regular deck and hull paints. But these paints were designed to go on wood. Nobody at the time had developed a paint expressly for fiberglass. Many top quality marine paints gave unsatisfactory results when applied to fiberglass, with such poor adhesion that the paint would peel off in big sheets.

To understand the reason for these paint failures, you have to go back to the actual mold in which a hull is made. These female molds are usually polished metal. The outer skin of a fiberglass boat is called the "gel coat." This is that first layer of heavy, smooth, and shiny polyester resin which is applied directly to the surface of the steel mold. Then layers of both mat and fiberglass cloth material are alternated until the desired hull thickness is built up. In the Hatteras 42 it takes 11 layers of 5 Fab-Mat, and 1 mat to make up a topside thickness of ½-inch. The bottom takes 13 layers to produce a thickness of about ⅝ inch.

Before that first gel coat is applied to the mold, it is first coated with a material called "mold release agent." This stuff keeps the gel coat from sticking to the mold as fiercely as it sticks to the fiberglass material. Some of this "mold release agent" stays with the gel coat, where it is permanently embedded in the outer surface of the boat. These mold release agents are chemicals which are intended to prevent adhesion and they do since not even paint will stick to the gel coat. Even without the mold release agent, the gel coat would be a difficult surface to paint because it is very dense, hard and glossy. Paint must have something to "bite" into before it will stick. Even old paint surfaces must be roughed up with sanding to provide a tooth for new coatings. So, gel coats presented a problem for the marine paint manufacturers.

Another confusion to clear up is that you don't paint "fiberglass." It's there under the gel coat but you never have any contact with it, any more so then you do with the steel mesh which reinforces concrete in highways. When you drive on the highway, you only contact the concrete. When you touch a fiberglass hull, you only contact a layer of polyester resin which is the gel coat.

This polyester resin is another reason why boatyards have disliked working on fiberglass boats. There is no uniformity in gel coats. There is a wide variation in physical and chemical properties of the polyester resin used by different boat manufacturers. Finding a paint system that would work on all gel coats would only add to an already confusing situation because new paint "systems" would work on one manufacturer's boats and fail miserably on others.

These problems were pretty well known in the boating service industry, which has its own trade publications, and us early fiberglass owners got lousy service and treatment in many yards and marinas. And you can't really blame them. As a marina manager in Port Clinton, Ohio told me: "I have enough headaches without taking on somebody else's. Painting fiberglass is a big headache. Let the builders and paint manufacturers find the cure."

And they have.

THE "CURE" FOR FIBERGLASS PAINT TROUBLES

All of the marine paint manufacturers have come up with their "cure" for fiberglass paint problems. Most of these cures are "system" paints. That means you start from scratch using a special primer, an undercoater, and then a final paint job, which is usually one of the new paints based on polyurethane resins, or one of the epoxy paints. You lay the paints on with a brush and they level out and look as if they were sprayed.

For below the waterline, there are "system" paints also, with a final anti-fouling coating and a vinyl base. It is a foolish mistake to believe that barnacles don't like gel coats. As a matter of fact, barnacles just love gel coats because they stick to it as if they were made out of polyester resin. And when you scrape them off, they leave pits in your bottom sometimes ⅛ inch deep.

All of the paint manufacturers now make a full line of new paints, new putties, polypoxy caulking compounds, surfacing and repair materials, fiberglass cloths and mat materials, polyester resins and gel coat repair kits. With all these wonderful new materials available, the boatyards and marinas will welcome your patronage—if you can afford them. If you can't, welcome to the club of sweat, blood and sanding.

GETTING READY TO PAINT

You will not like sanding! You just can't get away from sandpaper—and nobody has tried harder then I. Some years ago there was a new product on the market called something like liquid sand or maybe it was no sand. It may still be around under a different name. The product was a liquid that you spread over any painted or varnished surface with a rag. It was supposed to chemically "soften" the old coating, remove the gloss, and make it "tacky" so that the new paint would get a good "bite" on the old surface. It sounded convincing. Naturally, I tried it on my brightwork. Two weeks later I wanted to slash my wrists. My brightwork was one big mass of big ugly blisters. It looked horrible. My boat was the conversation piece in all the yacht club bars that summer. They were saying things like: "That guy will do anything to get out of sanding." And they were right.

I had to rent inside work space so I could wood down and re-varnish. It cost me $300. I learned later that the liquid sand was supposed to be used only on conventional spar varnishes and paints. It would not work on the new hard varnishes, like "Bakelite," or the new hard paints.

PREPARING FIBERGLASS BY THE "NO SAND" METHOD

If, after reading what happened to me with "no sanding" methods, you want to try it for yourself, the Baltimore Copper Paint Company, who make the regatta line of marine products, have their own "no sand" product. It is called 3351 No-Sand Primer. Basically, it's the same thing I used. Although they call it a primer, it's a very thin material and is intended more as a surface treatment than a usual coat of paint.

Before you do the above, however, you must use their regatta 3840 Fiberglass Pre-prime Wash to remove all surface dirt and residual mold release agent. With saturated rags you wash down the hull. Follow this by drying with clean rags.

The "no sand" primer is supposed to form an effective bond between the gel coat and the polyurethane paint that you put on next. If you want to try this method, lots of luck.

Sanding is still the best way to prepare a gel coat for refinishing.

PREPARING FIBERGLASS BY THE SANDING METHOD

On topsides use a 80-120 grit paper to remove the gloss. This paper is pretty coarse and will leave some scratches, so follow up lightly with 240-320 grit paper until the scratches are gone. On the bottom you don't need to remove the scratches because the barnacles don't mind. When you finish sanding, clean off all the dust in your favorite manner, vacuum or brush, then thoroughly clean the hull with a pre-prime wash, like regatta's 3840. Other paint manufacturers have basically the same products by different names. It doesn't really matter which you use, but when you select one, stick with that line from beginning to end.

POWER SANDING

I've tried all types of power sanding, even with dust catcher bags and hose hook-ups to power vacuum. And it's still tedious, messy work. If you manually hand sand, you get dust mostly on your hands. If you power sand, you get dust in your eyes, your hair, your mouth, your nose, your ears and your navel if bare-waisted. Motors in all power tools have a fan blade on them whose purpose is to dissipate heat and keep out dust. On a power sander, this blower just scatters the dust around over a wider area.

POWER SANDING CAN BE DANGEROUS TO HEALTH

A friend of mine became quite ill after power sanding his bottom. Don't ever do this! Copper bottom paints are a deadly poison and the dust from sanding is highly toxic. In fact, even the sanding dust from gel coat might be toxic. So many new substances, like PVC for example, are suddenly declared hostile to humans and the environment. Maybe tomorrow polyester resin is next. I wouldn't take any chances with power sanding. Wet sand and keep the dust down, both topside and the bottom. Use a bucket of water and a sponge to keep the work area wet as you hand-sand. When you finish, use a hose and a car-wash brush to clean up. You can paint the next day.

SANDING BY HAND

Handsanding is still the best. Hand-hold sandpaper only when working on rounded and curved surfaces. On flat surfaces hand-holding sandpaper is inefficient and wastes sandpaper. You can buy one of the devices for holding sandpaper

KEEPING WIVES HAPPY SANDING

If your wife helps you with the sanding, do not let her sand down one entire side of a hull before cleaning up. There is a good reason. Always when you clean up after sanding, you will find out that there is still some gloss left in the paint surface and you must go back and do it all over. And your wife will shriek: "Oh, my God! You mean I've got to go back and do it all over? No, I'm getting a divorce!"

To avoid mutiny, or legal problems such as divorce, instruct your wife to sand only a small 3-foot square area at a time. When she demands to know why, tell her that you read in a boating magazine about a scientific study made on sanding of paint finishes, and this way was found most efficient. This will satisfy her. You must use Freudian devices like this if you want to stay in boating, stay married, and run a tight ship without mutiny.

In chapter one all the many grades of sandpaper are listed, but you really only need three—coarse for bottoms, medium for topsides, and fine for varnish. If you're a finishing freak, you will ignore the above and do it your own way. But don't try to wet sand with a dry paper.

Always wear cotton or rubber gloves, when sanding and the oldest clothes you've got. As a boater, you should never throw old clothes away. Save your worst clothes for bottom work. When you finish on the bottom, put those old clothes in your dock box and save them for disasters.

A SPECIAL CLEAN UP TOOL

Many boaters may not care for this special clean-up tool, the portable type ½ horsepower air compressor, but it is my favorite. I bought one on sale for $65 and wouldn't part with it for ten times that amount if it were irreplaceable. With an air gun attachment, compressed air at 100 pounds per square inch is great for cleaning up after sanding and blowing out old caulking. Dirt and sanding dust collect in corners and the vacuum just won't suck it up. Sandpaper works so much better after you blow off the accumulated dust.

In winter lay-up, compressed air is useful in many ways. Break a fitting on your plumbing; then blow out all the water. I blow off my engines. I do the same with all my water hoses, both at home and on the boat. If you use a power sander, compressed air will keep the sandpaper clean. The power sander itself needs cleaning when you finish. One blast of air and it's clean as new. Do the same with your person, clothes and hair. I even blow dust out of my fingernails. Have you tried to get your automobile tires checked at a gas station

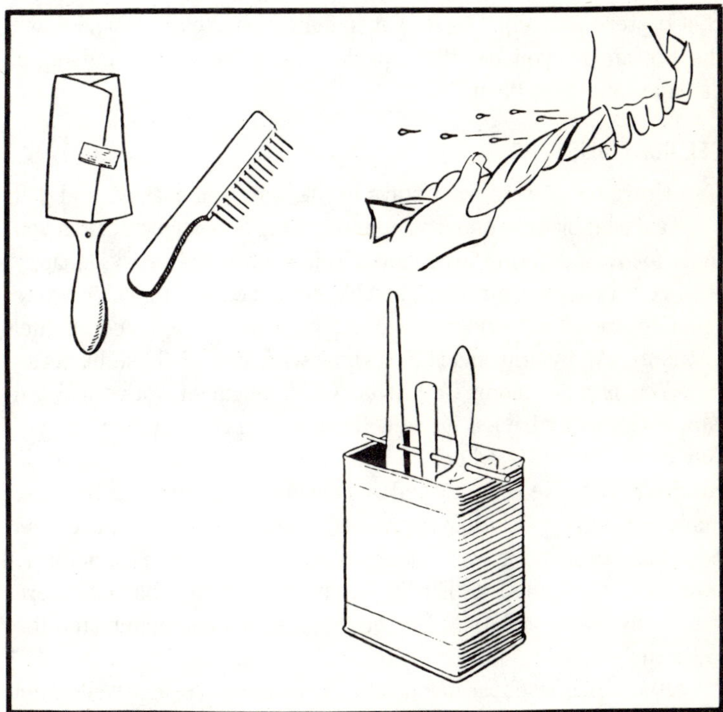

Fig. 2-4. Useful items are a tack rag, "keeping can," comb, brush and brush cover.

recently? With a compressor, you can do this at home when your tires are cold, which is the best time to check tire pressure.

HOW TO MAKE A TACK RAG

After sanding, whether you vacuum, blow or brush off the dust, there is still some dust that can only be removed with a tack rag (Fig. 2-4). You can buy them, or you can make your own. Take a large rag, like an old T-shirt, and soak in hot water. Wring it out. Sprinkle it with turpentine and knead it thoroughly into the rag. Now do the same with some varnish (Fig. 2-5). You now have a tack rag, which you can't beat for removing that last vestige of sanding dust. Always keep old tack rags in an old coffee can.

PREPARING THE BOTTOM

If your boat is a trailerable type which is not left in the water long enough to require anti-fouling paint, then your bottom work will not vary too much from what you have been doing topsides. And since trailered boats don't experience too many problems with gel coat blisters, you don't have that to fight with. You just sand down the bottom as you did the topsides, fill in scratches and other damage, and then paint.

GEL COAT BLISTERS

However, if your boat stays in the water all season, and you have gel coat blisters under your anti-fouling bottom paint, then you must follow a different procedure. You are probably very unhappy with your boat's performance and blame those blisters which broke open to cause a very rough bottom. This robbed you of fuel economy. And you would like to know what causes those blisters.

You are not alone. A Huron, Ohio, engineer with the Ford Motor Company hauled his new 31-foot fiberglass cruiser in mid-August to change a wheel he had banged up running aground in Sandusky Bay. He was shocked to find his bottom a mass of blisters, many of them broken, leaving ragged scars. He had purchased the boat that April and it was still under warranty. The manufacturer, however, disclaimed all liability, charging that the blisters were caused by water pollution. Bacterial organisms had penetrated the gel coat.

Another houseboat manufacturer, in almost a similar situation with a Toledo owner, also disclaimed liability, charging it was a well known fact that Lake Erie was the most polluted body of water in the

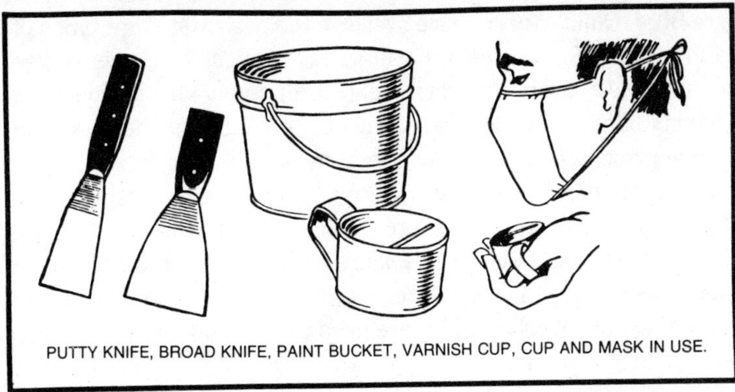

Fig. 2-5. The old-fashioned varnish cup is still around, but you'll see it only where professionals work.

world, and nothing more then a filthy sewer. Then the builder even quoted a much publicized statement by Prince Philip of England who told a conservation conference in France: "It is said of Lake Erie that if anybody falls into it, they don't drown, they just decay."

If this is true, then I should be dead because the same year Prince Philip made that statement, I anchored off Cedar Point every day for a week to go swimming in that "filthy sewer.' While playing water polo, I swallowed some of that "polluted" water. I didn't even get sick.

THE ENDLESS GEL COAT BLISTER CONTROVERSY

Nobody, to date, has been able to pin down exactly what causes the blisters, and who is at fault. Hordes of "experts" in both the manufacturing and service industries have been offering their opinions. They all agree the trouble occurs between the gel coat and that first layer of laminate, which can be fiberglass cloth or mat. Voids in this area become air or gas pockets. Later they admit water and burst.

Some blame sloppy workmanship. The gel coat is sprayed on, usually to a thickness of 15 to 20 mils. If the spray nozzles are improperly set, foaming will result. Foaming means bubbles, and bubbles mean air. The result is a porous gel that will later absorb water.

Boatbuilding is a seasonal business, with frequent layoffs. New hands are hired who lack experience in the manual operation of rolling out the laminate with grooved metal rollers to force out all the air bubbles.

Boat manufacturers have available today two different types of resin material for gel coats. Orthothalic, which costs the least, has been around a long time. In fact, new entrepreneurs by the hundreds back in the fifties would buy a drum of resin, a roll of fiberglass and with very little know-how set themselves up in business.

A fairly new gel coat resin, isothalic, is more expensive and is supposed to be tougher and more water resistant. But it blisters just like the first type, and nobody knows why. One reason might be there are many variables in the way it is used to produce that gel coat. Many chemical additives are used to control density, viscosity and the rate of cure.

The gel coat mystifies the fiberglass boat owner. He hears so much about it. What is it? Why does it cause so much trouble?

The gel coat is that nice shiny outer skin on all fiberglass boats which is put on for three reasons: to hide the coarse fiberglass materials and resins which combine to make up the real fiberglass underneath, to make the hull surface look pretty, and to make it easy to remove the hull from the female mold.

In other words, the gel coat is strictly a cosmetic thing which in no way adds or diminishes the hull's structural strength or integrity. Chemically, the gel coat is a thermo-setting polyester resin. However, the gel coat, and fiberglass underneath, are distinctively different and separate. For example, the gel coat is pigmented with paint colors and, after curing, remains resilient and self supporting. The fiberglass has no paint pigments added, is transparent so you can see the laminate, and cures to a very hard surface. Fiberglass boat hulls actually could get along without the gel coat. They just wouldn't look very nice.

In 1972 one of the boating magazines made an exhaustive study of the gel coat blister problem. All of the giants in fiberglass boat building were getting flack from buyers. So this problem is not limited to the small builder who works in a garage with one drum of resin and a roll of fiberglass, and who lacks know-how. Who has more know-how and experience then Hatteras, Bertram, Chris Craft, Century, Penn Yan, and Glasspar?

Every one of the major manufacturers has an explanation or theory. Some blame the suppliers of gel coat materials, saying that porosity in the formula is the villain. However, Glidden-Durkee, a leading producer of gel coat material, states there is no "porosity" whatsoever in the formula and there are no raw materials in the gel composition that could cause it to 'vary" from batch to batch. They claim the gel is easier to spray at some gun settings, and this could create the illusion that one batch was different from another. They also claim that an improper gun setting could mix too much air with the gel. This could cause pinholes and blistering.

Another gel supplier blames the mat, the blanket of chopped fiberglass strands which is widely used as the first layer in the mold next to the gel coat. They say that binder used to hold the glass strands together is the culprit. When this binder is put in badly, it creates large granules. Later, when the resins polymerize, the granules form a gas, which creates a void, or blister. The Bertram Yacht Company seems to agree with this because they returned 25,000 pounds of mat material to a supplier because they felt it had too much binder.

If you have wondered why fiberglass boats are always painted white, here is the reason. Chris Craft claims that in warm climates and temperatures of 90 degrees plus, dark coatings can absorb heat from the sun and reach internal temperatures of 150 degrees. Dark reds and blacks can reach temperatures of 160 degrees. This is close to the temperature at which many polyester resins begin to soften.

The Hatteras Boat Company reports that all their complaints of blistered hulls come from a warm tropical climate. What do they do about the complaints? Hatteras tells the owner to have the bottom coarse disk sanded to remove the blisters, then re-painted.

THE FACTS ABOUT WARRANTIES

The gel coat is excluded from all boat warranties. When a gel coat blisters, Chris Craft says there is nothing structurally wrong with the boat. They simply advise the owner to sand down hard to the fiberglass, prime with an epoxy paint, and re-coat with a urethane paint, which in many cases will look better then the original gel coat.

Bertram's warranty also excludes the gel coat. When a buyer complains, they advise him not to worry about the "cosmetic" appearance since blistering does not affect the boat's strength. If he persists, they advise him to fill in with fiberglass auto-repair putty which he can buy in any auto supply store, sand down and paint with gel coat or epoxy paint.

In summation, nobody really knows WHY fiberglass blisters. No boat manufacturer will guarantee that a boat you buy will not blister. If your boat does blister, it will not sink or fall apart. You should not worry about the blisters; you should just ignore them.

PETTIT'S CURE FOR BLISTERS

The Pettit Paint Company, which was making bottom paint for the U.S. Navy over 100 years ago (and considered one of the best in the world at the time), has made their own studies on the great gel coat mystery. They say that just sanding and re-painting will not eliminate the blister problem. Here are the corrective procedures they recommend for a permanent cure. Remove all the old anti-fouling paint from your bottom, either by sanding or with an inflammable type paint remover. With all the old paint removed, and broken blisters scrapped off clean, these areas should then be glazed with Pettit's 7050-7055 Polypoxy Underwater Patching Compound, which comes in both a can and tube. The patched areas must be left to dry overnight.

The following day, sand down the entire bottom with a heavy grit paper to get a dull, frosty finish. Then wash down with Pettit's 15095 Fiberglass Dewaxer. This very potent chemical removes any mold release agent left in your gel coat. It also slightly etches the gel surface to provide good adhesion for the undercoaters to follow.

When your bottom is chemically cleaned with the dewaxer, it should be painted within two hours with Pettit's 4169 Polypoxy Undercoater, which comes in two cans. You mix two parts of "A" to one part Polypoxy 4027 Hardener. Let this stand for an hour, give it another good stirring, then apply with a short nap roller. Drying time for this first coat is about two hours. Then you apply a second coat the same way. If the mix has gotten a little too stiff for rolling, thin it with Polypoxy Thinner.

When the second undercoater is dry, usually in about two hours if the temperature is around 60 to 70 degrees, you are ready for two coats of Unepoxy Anti-fouling paint. You can put this on with a roller, brush or spray. Bottom painting is always best done with a roller on a long handle, the longer the better. You can't get far enough away from that poisonous stuff. If you put it on with a brush, your back will ache all summer and you won't have much fun. If you put it on with spray, all your neighbors in the yard will sign a petition to have you committed to an institution for the insane. I will repeat again and again that bottom anti-fouling paints are poisonous, toxic substances. Even brushing is not recommended, because in tight areas under a boat you can't avoid inhaling the fumes with the stuff slopping all over you. I love the smell of some bottom paints—but only at a distance of at least 200 yards.

You can apply the second coat of anti-fouling after the first coat has become tack free, or you can wait until you are ready to launch, but no longer then 16 hours.

The above "system" paint for blistered fiberglass hulls is Pettit's. It is not necessarily the best or the only system, but was used only as an illustration. Every major paint manufacturer has a "system" of their own. Whichever one you use, stick with it from beginning to end. Don't put one manufacturer's paint over another's primer or undercoater.

REPAIRING FIBERGLASS SCRATCHES, HOLES

Small holes and minor scratches are easily repaired with fiberglass "putties" which you an buy in any auto supply store. However, if you are status conscious, using the auto repair stuff puts you on the same social level as us slobs who put housepaint on boats. If you belong to a yacht club, you should always remove the labels from the cans. Then if anybody asks where you got that "gray stuff," you can say you picked it up in a quaint little marina up in the Georgian Bay last summer. That will raise you one notch in the club pecking order.

The exclusively marine type products, like Pettit's Polyester Mender, are fast-setting extra-white compounds which look better on a white gel surface than the auto type grays. They also cost more. Below the waterline, color is of no importance; but topside it is better to use something that matches. The marine product dries hard in about 30 minutes and is ready to sand, file and paint.

REPAIRING DEEP HOLES AND DENTS

If you ran into a gas dock last summer and have some deep dents, mix some resin filler with polyester resin. This stuff is packaged with a catalyst, and you mix just enough for each repair job. Also, there are eight resin colorants available so you can match your gel coat color. You fill the bottom of the gashes and holes first, then you finish off with the colored resin. If your hull is white, you can finish off with the Polyester Mender which will give you a perfect match-up. To restore the finished repair patch so it matches the gloss of the surrounding gel coat, sand smooth with grit 400 paper, wet or dry. Then polish with compound and a rotary buffing wheel, which you can rent.

Another reason why white is the almost standard color for fiberglass boats is that when making repairs, white presents no color matching problems. With deep colors, such as red and blue, it is almost impossible to get an exact match because of aging. When making extensive and numerous repairs, you may wind up with spots that don't match, and if you're fussy, it may bother you like an itch you can't reach. If it does, the only solution is to sand down the entire topsides to a "frosty" appearance, re-wash and re-paint. That's the only solution. Remember this with your next boat. Stick with white, even if you hate it like I do.

REPAIRING MAJOR FIBERGLASS DAMAGE

With large structural damage, you will be working with fiberglass cloth and mat material. This stuff comes in rolls and tapes of various widths. It is also available in package deals of various sizes for small repairs. There are various weights and weaves for small boats under 20 feet. A "Woven Roving" cloth is used for repairs to heavier boats over 20 feet.

Polyester resin is the most common all-purpose formula used for both layout and finishing because 65 percent of all boats in the United States are under sixteen feet in length, 30 percent are 16 to 26 feet, and less then four percent are over 26 feet. In the larger boats with higher stress factors, the epoxy resins are used. The major difference is adhesion, cure time and cost.

TOOLS, SUPPLIES FOR MAJOR FIBERGLASS REPAIRS

Here is a list of tools and supplies you should have on hand before you go to work. Don't attempt to do a major fiberglass repair job until you are ready. Remember, once you get started there is no time to go looking for things.

1. Sander, disc or oscillating. You'll need a drill, preferably high speed ¼-inch, and a small grinder bit to be used in cutting away damaged material.
2. Silicone carbide sandpaper for dry sanding and aluminum oxide for wet sanding in both rough and fine grits.
3. Selection of tools to cut fiberglass material clean and smooth. Metal cutting tools like hacksaw blades, keyhole saws with fine teeth, and files are fine. Bring everything you've got that might prove useful, even a knife, razor blades and scissors.
4. Something to use for separating material. This can be heavy cellophane, polyethylene, polyvinyl, Saran but not wax paper.

5. Some cheap throw-away paint brushes. If you use good brushes, be sure to have plenty of Acetone on hand for cleaning up, and rags.

6. Backing material in pieces larger then the area to be repaired. This can be clean cardboard, heavy aluminum foil, screening material, aluminum or copper flashing material.

7. Several large coffee cans.

8. Strong detergent for cleaning up hands and tools before resin hardens.

9. Plenty of pressure tape in extra wide size.

10. If working in temperatures below 60 degrees, heat lamps will be needed to speed up hardening.

11. If you are health conscious, you might want to use a respirator to avoid inhaling glass powder. Personally, I prefer to use a big fan off to one side which blows all the dust away from me.

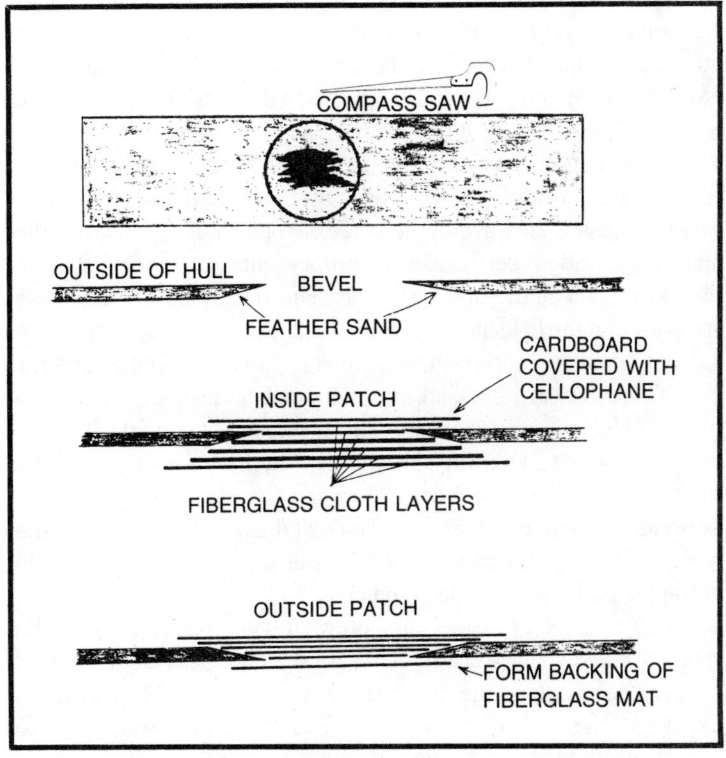

Fig. 2-6. On an inside patch you bevel from the inside. On an outside patch you reverse the bevels and cloth laying procedure.

Trim away all the damaged material, or just cut a round hole around it. When possible, it is best to patch from the inside (Fig. 2-6). This avoids that heavy build-up of material on the outside. However, there are many areas on a boat where you just can't work from the inside. When necessary, the repair can be made from the outside. It just will require more sanding and finishing up.

THE INSIDE PATCH

We will take the inside repair patch first. On the inside of that hole you just cut, file down, and chamfer the edge to at least a 45 degree angle. This provides a larger surface area to which the cloth can adhere.

Before you do anything else, all your fiberglass and mat material must be cut to size and ready at hand. You will have little time for this later because polyester resin allows a work time of about 15-30 minutes before it hardens.

The inside pieces should be cut 6 inches larger than the hole. You will need from 6 to 10 layers, depending on the thickness of your hull at this point, because the repair fill must match the hull thickness. You will need one additional layer on the outside, but this need by only 4 inches larger than the hole.

Now, before you start laying fiberglass mat or cloth into the hole from the inside, you must back up that hole from the outside. The expression they use in the trade is "build a bridge" across the hole. This "bridge" serves as a temporary foundation and must be on the same level as the outer gel coat skin. If the outside and inside areas around the hole have been thoroughly sanded down to provide a good "tooth" for the resin, we are ready to lay down the bridge.

The cardboard back-up material must be protected from the resin. This is where we use the separating material. Cut the cardboard about two inches larger then the fiberglass that is to be laid over the hole on the outside. For position guidelines, temporarily press the cardboard on the hull so that it exactly centers over the hole. Make pencil marks on all four sides. This will guide you in getting it back up there again quickly.

Lay a sheet of cellophane, or whatever you have, over the cardboard and you are ready. Saturate the fiberglass cloth, or mat with the resin, using the brush to work out any bubbles. Lay this directly in the center of that back-up cardboard covered with the cellophane. Now press this over the hole, using the pencil marks as a guide. The pressure tape, which you previously cut to proper length and have available close at hand, is used to hold the cardboard in place. Use plenty of tape because the back-up board must follow any hull curves and lay hard and flush against the work area.

You are now ready to fill in the hole from the inside. Whether you use cloth or mat material depends on the thickness of your hull. Mat is quicker. Cloth takes more layers and more time. A hull thickness of less than 3/16 inch can be handled in one cure cycle. For a thicker hull, plan on two cycles to avoid overheating and blisters.

Working now on the inside, saturate the cloth with resin, press it into the hole, and brush out the bubbles. Alternate layers of cloth should have been pre-cut so they fit into the hole, gradually increasing in size to fill out the scalloped area. When the hole is finally filled to the same thickness as the hull, you lay one or two more of the larger pieces of pre-cut cloth which extend 6 inches beyond the hole. On the last piece, brush out carefully to remove any air pockets.

THE OUTSIDE PATCH

For damage to your hull that is not accessible from the inside, you just do the entire job from the outside. When the hole is cut around the damaged area, you chamfer the edges on the outside. Cardboard can not be used for a "bridge" on the inside, so we use a different technique to build one on the outside.

Cut a piece of cloth just slightly larger then the hole, about an inch. Saturate this with resin, lay it over the chamfered hole, let it set a few minutes to stiffen, then gently push it into the hole to form a slight concavity, but no deeper then the thickness of the hull. As you push it in, the edges of the cloth should just reach and cover the chamfered bevel. When this sets hard, you have a "bridge" across the hole on which to build, to fill up the hole layer by layer as you did on the inside patch. You finish up the same way, with one or two layers of the cloth which were cut to extend 4 inches beyond the hole.

If temperatures are below 60 degrees, you can use a heat lamp for an hour or two, but this is not really necessary unless you're in a big hurry to get launched in the spring and want to "post-cure" the repair job. If you do use heat lamps, don't put them any closer than 8 inches to the repaired area, and don't use bulbs stronger than 300 watts.

When thoroughly cured, the surface can be trimmed, sanded and faired down. Any slight imperfections or flaws can be taken care of with polyester mender. The finished job should be perfectly smooth to touch and to the eye. It should be almost impossible to detect. You can match the old gel coat by mixing some resin with Polyester Colorant. Sand this down with 400 grit paper, then polish with compound and a buffing wheel.

SOME TIPS ON WORKING WITH FIBERGLASS

In some parts of the United States, moisture in the air, or humidity, can be quite high during some periods of the year. This tends to slow down and inhibit the resin from curing. Temperature also is a factor in working time and speed of cure (Fig. 2-7). In cold weather, below 70 degrees Fahrenheit, you can speed up the cure time by adding more hardener, and in hot weather, above 85 degrees, you can slow it down by using less. However, never use less than ½ hardener per quart of resin, or more than double the amount in cold weather. If you try to sand before the repair job has thoroughly cured, your sandpaper will just fill up.

A good place to work is very important when working with fiberglass because the sun and wind will have a direct affect on your results. Direct sun causes the resin to gel and harden very fast—so fast that you just don't have any time to work. A direct wind blowing on your work can cause an "orange peel" or very rough finish that will give you fits. Try to have a place to work that is protected from the weather. If you have a trailerable boat, this can be a carport, garage or barn. Many marinas will rent you inside working space by the day. I have done this many times. In a later chapter, I will show you a method of winter lay-up that will automatically provide you with winter cover, and a well sheltered work space in the spring.

FIBERGLASS REPAIR KITS

All marine stores now sell various types of fiberglass repair "kits" for everything from minor gel coat touching up of scratches to more extensive damage requiring cloth material and mat. The "gel kits" are popular with owners of small boats that are trailered because most of the damage to them is minor—the inevitable knicks and scuffs that come with frequent launching and hauling out.

For gouges and structural damage, the repair "kits" are useful mainly because they instruct you how to do the job. The kits, however, never have enough of one or two items needed, which is the reason why some boatmen prefer to buy what they need separately. Everything you need is available item by item. The only

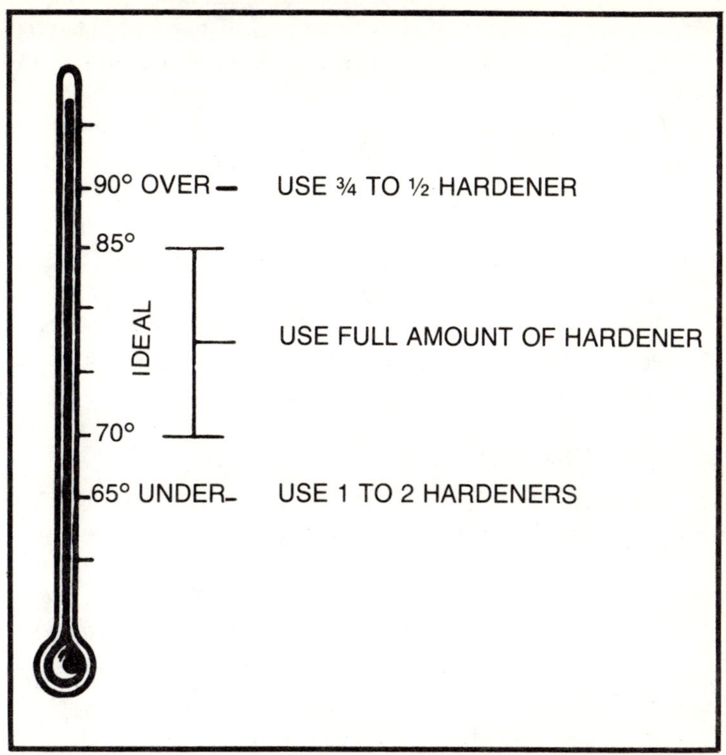

Fig. 2-7. Temperature is an important factor when working with fiberglass.

trouble with this more practical method is that you don't get those "instructions" that come with the kits.

The companies listed sell everything for the most minor gel repairs and for practically rebuilding a fiberglass boat. Some of them, like Pettit, even provide brochures and guides to fiberglass covering and repair. Companies include:

Kristal Kraft Inc., 900 Fourth St., Palmetto, Fla., 33561 (resins, cloth materials, rollers, brushes, instructions);

Lan-O-Sheen Inc., 1 West Water St., St. Paul, Min. 55107 (fiberglass cloth, mat, resins, hardeners, colorants, reinforcing putties with chopped glass, regular putty);

Pettit Paint Co., Inc., 36 Pine St., Rockaway, N.J. 07866 (all fiberglass cloths, tapes, mats, putties, resins, brushes, rollers, instructions);

Defender Industries, 255 Main St., New Rochelle, N.Y. 10801 (all fiberglass repair materials, resins, catalog available for $1);

Baltek Corp., Box 195, Northvale, N.J. 07647 (core material for repair, reinforcing decks, transoms, hulls, also for boat building);

Eastman Machine Co., 779 Washington St., Buffalo, N.Y. 14203 (this makes portable power tools for cutting fiberglass cloth and mat.)

Glen-L Marine Designs, 9152 Rosecrans, Bellflower, Calif. 90706 (all fiberglass boatbuilding and repair supplies, catalog available for $1.)

Fibre Glass-Evercoat Co., Inc., 6600 Cornell Rd., Cincinnati, Ohio 45242 (all fiberglass cloth and mat materials in rolls or pre-cut packages).

IS WAXING NECESSARY?

Waxing is a personal thing, like preferences in underarm deodorant. Some people wax everything they own. Some people don't wax anything, and still manage to survive. I once had two neighbors who bought new cars of the same make and color. One of them was a wax freak. The other hated the stuff and wouldn't go to car washes because whether you paid for it or not, you got wax on your windshield. The wax freak kept his car in the garage all the time, where he was constantly washing and waxing it. The other man kept his car outside because the garage was used for more important things, like storing his boat. Both men kept those automobiles 10 years. And, so help me, you couldn't tell them apart unless you checked the license plates. The finish on both cars looked the same, and each had the same amount of rust in exactly the same places.

The only answer to the question of waxing is that the physical effort of applying it to your boat is healthful. It's wonderful exercise, burns hundreds of calories and is better then jogging along expressways and inhaling all those poisonous car fumes. And some day when you are ready to paint your boat, the physical effort of removing all that wax will also be good for you. Remember, you can't paint over wax.

WHERE NOT TO WAX

If your boat is large enough to walk on, like a cruiser, do not wax the decks. Gel coats are slippery enough without wax. As a boatowner you should never forget that the instant any guest puts a foot on your boat, you are legally responsible for the guest's welfare and safety. If you don't care about your own neck, or your family's, think about your guests, your liability insurance premiums, and all those "contingency fee" lawyers just waiting to sue you. The boating season is also the happy hunting season for hungry lawyers. They know that boaters in the cruiser class have liability insurance and that landlubber guests are always having "accidents" after going through a couple of six-packs.

SELECTING A COLOR FOR YOUR BOAT

If you hate glossy white like I do, you may want to consider some other color. You will read, or you will be warned, that black, red and blue deteriorate in the sun and don't hold up long. Since all paints and colors deteriorate, how "long" is relative. It's like the 92-year-old woman being warned by her doctor that if she didn't give up smoking five packs a day, she wouldn't live long. And he was right. She refused to give up smoking. She died two years later.

When you're talking about a life expectancy in paint of 5 or 10 years, then color would be important. But the life expectancy of a boat paint, regardless of color, is just one short season. In this respect, all boat colors last just as "long"—one season.

You will also be warned against painting your topsides white, and the cabin, decks and flying bridge some darker color. This will make your boat hot inside. They tell you the same thing about automobiles, the white ones are "cooler" than the black ones, they

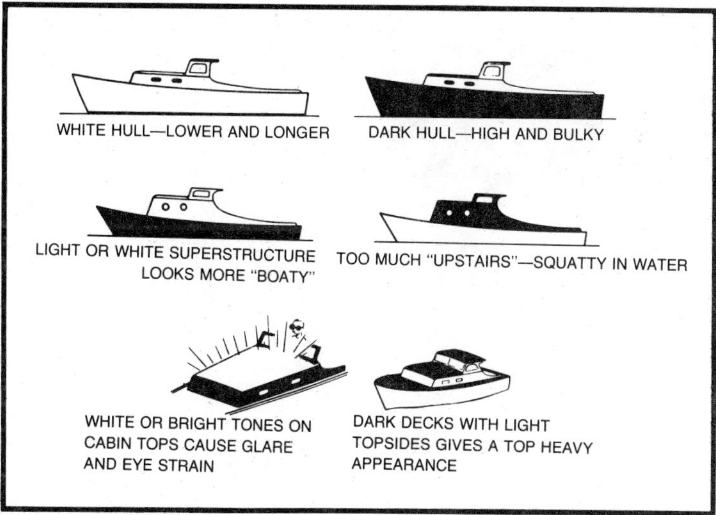

Fig. 2-8. This is what the experts say about hull color combinations.

say. But, without air conditioning, you roll up those windows in July and they're all hot inside. It is the same with all boats—they are unbearably hot inside. The degree of "hotness" or "coolness" is something for people to quibble and argue about. As for you, the difference is something you will never be able to detect.

You will also hear the specious argument that a dark color, above a white hull, will make your boat look top heavy (Fig. 2-8). All white is supposed to make your boat look long and sleek like an Italian cruise ship on the Mediterranean. If you use more then two colors on the exterior, everybody at the marina will think you're getting ready to have a Polish wedding aboard.

I don't believe that and neither do the marine paint manufacturers who make deck and hull paint in all those tantalizing colors. One of the most beautiful boats I have ever seen in my life was a Chris Craft Seaskiff painted black, green, yellow and white. It was really sexy. The mortgage at the bank says it's your boat, so paint it any damn color you please.

The Wood Boat

Wood boats are easy to work on. Wood boats are hard to work on. Both statements are true.

Wood is the oldest building material known to man. As a result, man has accumulated much knowledge and skill in working with wood. He made his first tools and his first weapons of wood. Stone was next. Scholars and historians are still trying to learn how the Egyptians built the great pyramids, since they had no knowledge of leverage and no block and tackle. How did they lift those huge stones weighing hundreds of tons?

The Persians and Phoenicians were building complex merchant ships of wood over 5000 years ago. The Pharaoh Snefru, who ruled Egypt in the twenty-sixth century, tells in his annals about "bringing 40 ships filled with cedar logs from Phoenicia. These people also knew nothing about leverage, yet they were building ships with huge steam-bent ribs of hard wood. Some of those timbers were 12-inches square, 50 feet long and weighed tons. They had to be steamed, or boiled, for at least 12 hours, manually lifted out of the steam vats, carried to a bending form and then bent into a curve that would conform to the hull shape. You can't really appreciate the enormity of this task unless you have worked with steamed timbers. I once helped a friend steam-bend frames into a 30-foot hull he was building. The white oak framing wood was only 1-inch square, but it took the muscle of four men to bend it into place. In later shipbuilding, a system of block and tackle was used to do this. But how did the ancients do it? How did Noah build the Ark? He had only the help of his three sons, Shem, Ham and Japheth, to build that huge vessel of "gopher wood" that would carry as passengers all the animals of the world. How did they lift, steam and bend those massive timbers that had to weigh tons or a vessel big enough to carry all those animals?

THE TOUGHNESS OF WHITE OAK

That is why working with wood is both easy and hard. Man has done things with wood that today boggles the mind. The *U.S.S. Constitution* has oak planking that was strong enough to repel cannonballs. At a range of 100 yards, they bounced off the hull like tennis balls off a brick wall. White oak was the first armored plating for ships of war, and it was far more effective then steel plating armor against torpedoes in World War I. Warships of the era of John Paul Jones and Lord Nelson were destroyed most often by fire rather then cannonballs hitting the hull. In fact, gunners directed their fire above the hull using grape-shot to create the most damage on personnel, and to start fires that would burn all the sails and leave a ship helpless in the water.

Boats built of wood, if cared for, will last forever. A wood boat was found in King Tut's tomb, in perfect condition, ready for the water. Commodore Perry's flagship, the *U.S.S. Niagara,* can be seen today in Erie, Pennsylvania, permanently beached downtown on the waterfront, neglected and exposed to the weather of all seasons. I saw it a few years ago and, although it was 164 years old, the wood was in surprisingly good condition.

When a wood boat dies, it is from neglect and abandonment, like the hulls you see buried on beach sands. If protected from its natural enemies, a wood boat will last forever because there is no discernible aging or breakdown of the fibers. But wood can be quickly destroyed by the termites and fungi that feed on it.

A NATURAL SAFETY FEATURE OF WOOD

A boat built of wood has a natural safety feature that you will find in no other boat. Wood is buoyant in itself. For example, if you take 100 pounds of solid steel, aluminum, cement or fiberglass and throw it in the water, what happens? It immediately sinks, of course. Now, take 100 pounds of solid wood and throw it in the water. What happens? It floats! In fact, it will still float with two men sitting on it. A boat built of wood has this extra margin of safety which has saved many lives down through the centuries, but which is hardly ever noted in new stories.

A few years ago, two cabin cruisers collided head-on in the Sandusky, Ohio ship channel. One was a plywood-planked single screw 24-footer, the other was twin-engine 29-foot steel. Both hulls were severely damaged, holed, and filled with water rapidly. The steel boat sank in less then a minute. The wood boat sank slowly to the windows of its trunk cabin, then just lay there in the water. The four occupants climbed out of the cockpit and sat on the trunk cabin, with only their feet getting wet.

The two occupants of the steel boat swam over to the wood boat and climbed aboard. When the Coast Guard arrived, all six were sitting on the trunk cabin top and arguing fiercely about rules of the road. The Coast Guard later cited the wood boat owner for only having two lifejackets aboard. None of his passengers could swim, but since his boat was wood, nobody drowned. But this was not mentioned in the news reports. It hardly ever is.

There are no statistics that show how many lives have been saved by the fact that a boat was built of wood, just as there are no statistics that show how many lives were lost because panic-stricken sailors gave up, left their boats, and swam for shore. They rarely make it, and days later their boats will be found, awash in the sea but still floating. A wood boat will not sink, completely, that is. Even with heavy engines, there is still enough reserve buoyancy to keep it from going completely under.

WHY WOOD SAILBOATS SINK

Deep keel sailboats have iron, lead or cement weighing up to 12 or more tons bolted to their keels for stability. They also will have a few tons of pig iron ingots distributed around in the bilges for trim purposes. With all this additional weight, the wood sailboat loses its reserve buoyancy. Once they lose their watertight integrity, they sink like any metal boat.

A SAILBOAT THAT WILL NOT SINK

There is, however, a sailboat that will not sink. It has a center-board instead of a deep and weighted keel. This board, or fin, is raised or lowered as conditions demand. The centerboard is popular in shoal waters, but it is not too often seen on long ocean passages because it can too easily be flipped over on its beams. But if it is, the centerboard won't sink. The deep weighted keel boat is rarely flipped over. It is a more stable craft, a better sea boat. But if it is ever flipped over, it goes down.

WOOD BOATS ARE EASILY REPAIRED

A wood boat can be repaired anywhere in the world—in the most primitive places with the most primitive tools, with some local species of exotic wood that you never heard of, like the "gopher wood" in Noah's Ark. You can hop-skip from island to island in the Caribbean for the rest of your life and never be out of touch or too remote for repair services on a wood boat. On the most isolated islands you'll see somebody building a boat on the beach. It is the one universal language that all boatmen understand. Pull into a strange port and all you have to do is point to the banged in sheer rail or broken wood spar, wave some money around, and everybody will smile and nod. Ten minutes later six guys will be on your boat taking measurements. But you point to the banged up topsides on a fiberglass or aluminum boat, and they just stand dumb and stare at you. I know because I've been there and seen this happen.

For the do-it-yourselfer, the wood boat is the easiest to fix, to maintain, the cheapest to initially buy—and you have an unlimited choice of used boats to pick from. Don't let old age frighten you, even up to 50 years. Some of the most charming, most livable boats you will ever find or see were built before World War II. I fell madly in love with a 60-footer at the Buffalo Yacht Club and tried desperately to buy it. But the lawyer who was excutor for the deceased owner's estate was in no hurry to sell. He just wanted to drink the booze I was buying and talk.

This boat would have kept me busy at least two years fixing it up, but it was a floating palace and worth all the time and effort. When I heard a few months later that it finally sold for $7,500 to settle the estate, I wanted to kill myself. Cosmetically it looked terrible, which is why it sold for so little. But it was structurally and mechanically sound, like so many old boats are. After overhauling and refinishing, I could today easily sell that fine old yacht for about $50,000. With wood boats, age is relative. Don't let numbers frighten you and don't be too cautious about that problem that seems to terrify so many boaters, dry rot!

DRY ROT

There is a tendency with new boaters to over-react to dry rot. In fact, dry rot, like cancer and syphilis a few years ago, is a dirty,

Fig. 3-1. This is dry rot in its most advanced form.

unmentionable word in some posh boating fraternities (Fig. 3-1). Nice people just don't have dry rot for the same reason they don't have body lice. As a result many boaters become what I call wood hypochondriacs. They are forever peering down into the bilges and sniffing. If they see a little puddle of water, they quickly soak it up with a sponge, then wipe the area dry with paper towels. If they see the slightest drip from a shaft log, they tighten it another turn. Then they have to buy new shafts every year because the packing is finally too tight, which scores the shafts and makes them leak more.

First, water in the bilge will not cause dry rot. In fact, it will actually prevent rot. To understand why you must understand what dry rot is. One thing dry rot is not "dry." It got that name because of the powdery appearance of decayed wood. This "decay" of seasoned wood is caused by the attacks of living organisms called saprophytic fungi who feed on wood fiber. These organisms cannot live in water because they require oxygen. That is why water in the bilges will prevent rot. The fungi also cannot feed on dry wood. They require a small amount of moisture in the wood. It must be just slightly damp. It must be warm, 70 degrees or above. It must be dark, with little or no air movement. These are the conditions that invite an attack by these organisms. Mopping up the water in your bilge only invites rot because you are keeping the wood in your inner keel, floors and frames merely moist, when they would be far safer thoroughly wet.

The fungus will not touch wood that is permeated with salt. In salt water your hull below the water line is safe from dry rot—in fact, even above the waterline to a diminishing degree because topside wood will absorb some salt in time. The areas where your boat is vulnerable is under all the decks, in corners, and at the sheer where frames and decks beams end. Here it is dark, hot and frequently moist from rain water leaks or condensation. Condensation provides most of the moisture in just the right amounts for dry rot.

HOW TO PREVENT DRY ROT

To prevent dry rot, keep the wood in your boat dry. If that is impossible, then keep it thoroughly wet and soaked. Keep it salty. It's as simple as that. Wood that is kept dry will last forever. There are today samples of wood used by the ancient Romans that are still in perfect condition, but, like the boy king Tutankhamen's boat, a combination of circumstances protected them from attack by wood's natural enemies—fungus, termites and insects. The wood in your boat need be protected only from fungus.

So how do you keep the wood dry? The best way is during actual construction by not leaving an inch of wood in critical areas unprotected by paint, bedding compound or caulking. Where ever two pieces of wood join, touch or connect, the surface between them must be buttered with a soft "bedding" compound, preferably the type with a fungicide added. All end grains of exposed wood must be either painted or sealed with the fungicide compound.

It is almost always where two pieces of wood touch or connect that dry rot starts—and most often in the end grain of a frame, deck beam or butt block on upper planking near the sheer. Either from rain water leaks or condensation, water seeps in between two pieces of wood, where it will not evaporate. The areas under decks and the corners around the sheer, the transom, and the stem are always dark and hot, which along with the right amount of moisture provides ideal conditions for fungus infestation.

WHY FACTORY BUILT BOATS ROT

It is only when you build a boat yourself that all wood surfaces can be protected. You will take the time. The cost-conscious man-ufacturer will not. There is no time on assembly lines to hold up production while two pieces of wood are buttered with bedding compound before being bolted or screwed together. The delays would double labor costs and the price of boats. Manufacturers first build the entire boat, then they paint it. But by this time there are hundreds of connecting wood surfaces that cannot be reached by the paint brush or spray. And that is where dry rot gets started.

Don't waste time looking for dry rot in the middle of a painted frame, rib, deck beam or in the bilges of salt water boats, or even fresh water boats that are kept permanently wet. Remember, the fungus cannot live in water. Stop fighting that water in the bilge. Salt is the cheapest, most effective of fungicides. Let the sea water slosh around in your bilges and get everything salty.

In factory built boats, the upper end grain of frames, ribs and deck beams are unpainted. The rope locker is a difficult place to paint, even for a midget. The stem is often neglected for this reason. Since your boat is already built, what can you do now? You can do three things:

- find and stop the fresh water leaks (more on this later).
- stop condensation when away from the boat by using an exhaust ventilating fan similar to the turbine type which was once standard equipment on all Matthews boats.
- in the fall, during lay-up work, squirt fungicide into all those vulnerable areas with a long-spout pressure oil can (This will soak in over the winter and dispel some of the odor. More on this later.

IF YOU ALREADY HAVE DRY ROT

Don't panic if you find dry rot on your boat. It is not going to fall apart or sink just because you found a "soft" butt block. This actually happened to me, and I was so ashamed I hung a tarp over the side of my hull so nobody could see what I was doing. I sold the boat that summer because I was convinced it would soon fall apart. That was 20 years ago. I saw this old 1932 Richardson last summer and recognized it immediately—you always do. It looked wonderful. I couldn't even find the plank I had replaced. Old boats never die, only the owners.

The only rotted wood that should cause you concern is the stem at the chine in a fresh water boat. Plank fastenings into the chine will loosen as the wood softens. Since the planks here are sharply bent and under a strain, they tend to pull away from the stem. There are frequent instances where a plank has sprung free of the stem, leaving quite a gap for water to enter. Every spring on the Great Lakes brings its almost routine Coast Guard rescue story. A boat with ten kids aboard suddenly "springs a big leak" and takes on water. And always this "big leak" turns out to be a plank pulled away from the stem at the chine. When these boats are stopped dead in the water, they usually stop leaking because the pulled plank is almost always considerably above the waterline. It is only when they plow into a wave that they take on water. As a former member of the Coast Guard Auxiliary, I have helped on many of these rescue missions and never knew one to sink with loss of life.

HOW TO REPAIR A ROTTED STEM

Repairing a rotted stem area is a major project and beyond the capabilities of most boat owners. If you have the money, let the yard do it. If not, you can still do it yourself by using an easier way that doesn't require boatbuilding skills. There is a patented Rx cure for dry rot owned by Boatlife, Inc., 65 Bloomingdale Rd., Hicksville, New York 11801. Their product is called "Git" rot. You apply this into the rotted wood. "Git" rot makes it possible to "repair" rotted wood without removing the infected area. In stems and keel sections, this can be like a reprieve from an income tax audit. But how do keels, which are always in the water, get infected? They don't get infected while in the water. It's out of the water, on the beach in winter storage, where over 90 percent of fungus infestations originally occur. Look in any boatyard and you will see dozens of boats still under their winter covers in July, some for years. It's hot under those covers, rain and snow blow in, and water settles in the bilge. That's how keel sections rot.

I have never used "Git' rot myself, but I have seen a similar product used on a keel, stem and butt block. It was originally introduced by the late Mr. Callahan of "Chilled Varnish" fame, and it worked amazingly well. "Git" rot is basically the same thing, is used in the same manner, and produces the same final results. It transforms a soft, powdery mass of rotted wood into a rock-hard substance that clunks when you tap it.

Before you treat your stem, you must back out all the screws on the planking ends, at least one plank above and below the infected area. As the manufacturer says: "Applying 'Git' rot is like a blood transfusion." It penetrates and soaks into every fiber of the wood by "capilliary action," as Callahan used to explain in his ads. It is best to apply it from above the infected area so you have gravity working for you along with "capilliary action."

To get into the infected wood, you drill a staggered series of holes ⅛ to ¼ inch in diameter at a downward angle, if possible. The best means of introducing "Git" rot into the rotted stem is with the longest, thinnest spout pressure oil can you find available. The longer the spout the better because you will be working in tight hard-to-reach areas. You may not be able to get a drill into some of these areas. So use a long, sharp-pointed ice pick. It will work even better then a drill because the rotted wood is very soft. After penetration with the ice pick, work it around to enlarge the hole in a tapered funnel shape. Only the top holes should be enlarged this way. The bottom holes are for venting purposes, to release trapped air as "Git" rot works into the fibers. It will do this very slowly, so don't get discouraged like my friend did. The stem on his 40-year-old boat was quite a heavy piece of oak and it took three days to get complete penetration. The tapered holes that you make at the top are the access "reservoirs" for "Git" rot, and you must keep them filled from the long-spout oil can. It's a long slow process, so you must be patient.

In cold weather, if you do this during the winter, the treated area will feel tacky for days, even weeks. Don't worry about this because eventually it will cure to a very hard mass. When finished, you mix "Git" rot half and half with sawdust. Use this to fill up all those holes you drilled. In rotted wood, which has crumpled and broken off in junks, you use the same sawdust mixture to build up, patch and re-shape the rotted section to its original state.

When your stem is completely cured and patched up, you are ready to re-fasten the planking. If the screws you backed out were No. 8, you will replace them with the next size larger, No. 10. But first you must re-thread those screwholes in the stem, which is not easy. Did you ever try to drive a screw into lead? It will be the same with your new stem. Do not use brass replacement screws because they will snap off on the second turn. Use Everdur or stainless and don't try to drive them in without stopping. Work them in slowly, in and out, in and out, and ease in a little on each turn to cut a new deeper thread. Be patient with this because there is nothing so infuriating as breaking a screw on that last quarter turn.

With all the holes re-threaded and your planks screwed back in place, you are finished and decidedly better off financially. If your boat is a cruiser in the 30-foot class, you have saved yourself about $1000 in high-priced labor costs. Boatyard personnel these days are skilled mainly in operating Travel-Lifts, tractors, hosing down bottoms and pumping gas. The few old craftsmen around who can repair wood boats don't come cheap.

BOATBUILDING WOODS

If you plan on doing any alterations or repairs, you will need to know something about wood—and I don't mean that stuff you buy down at the lumberyard. There are only two basic types of lumber, softwoods and hardwoods. Wood from broad-leaved trees are called hardwood and wood from coniferous trees are called softwood, even though this is not always true. There are many softwood trees with wood that is actually harder. The terms are merely old labels that have stuck, even though inaccurate. The softwoods, in general, contain considerable resin. The hardwoods do not. Most lumber produced in the United States is from softwood trees. Lumber from the hardwoods goes mostly into furniture and other high-grade premium uses.

Two of the toughest, strongest U.S. woods, next to northern white oak, are hickory and ash, which were used in wagon spokes, baseball bats and axe handles. Hickory, which is stiffer then ash, is used for golf club handles. Northern white oak, of which there is very little left, was the traditional structural and framing wood of boatbuilders because of its great strength, hard-as-iron toughness, ability to hold fastenings and resistance to rot.

If you're just going to add a room on to your home, most of this information about trees is of no use to you, but in the environment of the sea, you must know which woods are resistant to marine borers like the Terrible Terredo worm, and to fungus infections because in this respect all woods are not created equal. For reasons nobody understands, marine borers don't like teak or greenheart. It is suspected that an abrasive silica in these two woods is distasteful to them. For this reason teak and greenheart are often used for underwater construction of wharves. Some foreign boatbuilders, who sell in the United States, are using teak to build entire boats from keel up.

It is important that you understand the difference between sapwood and heartwood. Sapwood is that first layer of wood behind the bark which is alive and composed of living cells filled with vital fluids. This is the lifeline of a tree through which it gets nourishment and moisture. Heartwood is the center portion of the trunk which dies completely as the tree grows and the ducts become plugged. The living protoplasm in the cells are replaced by gums, resins, or just air. The living sapwood of all trees has low resistance to rot. The dead heartwood, on the other hand, is resistant to rot and some woods, like walnut, cedar, redwood, mahogany, cypress and teak, are extremely resistant to rot. In the building of boats, or repair, especially in vital areas like the stem, inner keel and outer keel, you always specify heartwood when you buy wood. The vital areas of a boat are difficult and costly things to repair, and the people who specialize in the selling of boat woods know this. It is reflected in their prices.

Freshly cut wood contains much water, from ⅓ to ½ its total weight. Before it can be fabricated, it must be "seasoned," which means the water must be removed. This is always done at the source because getting rid of the water reduces shipping costs. Dry wood is resistant to rot and easy to work with. Also, fresh wood changes shape during the drying out, so it is better for this to happen before it is used for fabricating.

THE "SEASONING" OF WOOD

There are two ways to "season" wood, by kiln drying which removes all the moisture in a few days, or air drying to a moisture content of from 12 to 15 percent, which takes months. In air drying the wood must be watched and periodically re-stacked to new positions to prevent warping and checking. This is laborious, time-consuming and is why air dried wood is so expensive.

This fact is the big difference between lumberyard wood and boat wood. And since boat wood is so expensive, you will rarely ever find it available in a conventional lumberyard in non-boating areas of the country. They consider it a specialty item with low volume and something of a nuisance because it must be periodically re-stacked. For this reason, many large marinas will have their own little private lumberyard of boat woods, and will even sell it to you as needed, even cut and milled to exact size. Cutting and milling, incidently, costs extra.

HOW TO DETERMINE COST OF BOAT WOOD

All lumber measurements are in the rough, before the wood has been finished off, and lumber is sold by the board foot, which is a piece of wood 1-inch thick and 12-inches square, or 12×12×1. In milling, a ¼ inch is lost, so your common 1×6 lumber will finish off as ¾×5¾ inches. Suppose you need planking wood exactly one-inch thick. Lumber thicknesses are measured in quarters. Four quarters wood is 1 inch; five quarters is 1¼ inches. To get 1-inch planking wood, you must buy and pay for five quarters wood, then have it planed down to your exact size.

This adds to the high cost of boat lumber because often to get a specific size wood for frames, ribs or planking, you must pay for larger stock. For example, if you need oak frames which will measure exactly 1×3, you will never split four of these out of 1×12 stock. You must buy a larger size and pay for the waste as it is cut and planed down.

WHERE TO BUY BOAT LUMBER

Here are your best sources of supply for boat lumber:

M. L. Condon Co., 258 Ferris Avenue, White Plains, N.Y. 10603 (Oak, White Cedar, Teak, Cypress, Long Leaf Yellow Pine, Sitka Spruce, mast and spar grade, Phillipine Mahogany, Honduras Mahogany, Western Red Cedar, African Mahogany, plywood in all types, grades, sizes. Ripping and planing to order); *H. H. Monteath Co.*, 2500 Park Ave., Bronx, N.Y. 10451 (Sitka Spruce, Mahogany, White Oak, Teak. All types of marine plywood in exotic woods); *Harbor Sales Co., Inc.*, 1401 Russell St., Baltimore, MD 21230 (Their own special brands of marine plywood, Aircraft plywood, Rangoon Teak, and other woods for boatbuilding and repair).

WHERE YOU CAN USE KILN-DRIED LUMBER

Wood from your local lumberyard can be used in a boat, but not for planking, framing or structural timbers. Since it is so dry, it could in some instances swell up, split and even seriously damage your boat. It can be safely used as long as you keep it out of the basic hull and cabin structure. I have used it in the bilges for all sorts of alterations and conveniences like boxes for my tools and batteries or a floor for my generator. I have even used it for bunk framing, door jams, cabin sole supporting posts—almost anything on the inside of your boat which does affect the hull shape. Another cost-saver which can be taken advantage of on inside work are cadmium plated lag screws with hex heads and washers. With a socket wrench, they're easy to work with and never loosen. I use them only where their exposed heads are out of sight under bunks, etc. Slap some paint on them and they'll last forever.

There is a vast selection of boat woods available to you, and you don't necessarily have to use one or the other. For example, white oak is traditional for framing, ribs, stringers, chines, etc., but you don't have to use oak. Personally, I hate it. I still occasionally have an ache in my back, put there by white oak. A board foot of white oak weighs almost 4 pounds, which may not register anything with you.

But look again at that oak after it becomes the outer keel and skeg on a large cruiser. It is 4 inches thick and 18 inches deep at the skeg, which raises the weight to 24 pounds a foot. The keel on a 30-foot boat can weigh close to a quarter ton.

Think about that when you order boat lumber. White oak is one of the heaviest of woods, next to teak, which is handled mainly by elephants because it is so heavy. There are substitutes for oak which are just as strong, with less weight. One of them is fir, which weighs 2.8 pounds per board foot. Weight is important with racing hulls. Here you want great strength, without the weight.

IMPORTANT BOATING WOODS

Douglas fir is a popular domestic wood, largely used to fabricate the most common type of plywood. It is a hard, strong wood which is often substituted for oak. For framing and longitudinals, buy only the vertical grain wood.

Tangile has a more common name, Philippine Mahogany. It was popularized by the boating industry, particularly during the "kit boat" era of the fifties when one major manufacturer used it even for all the structural members like the keel, stem and frames. Since the light red variety of this wood is extremely soft, it presented no problems to amateur boat builders in driving all those brass screws that were supplied with the kits. This wood is not a mahogany, but actually a tropical cedar with certain mahogany-like characteristics. Other importers of true mahogany complained and sued until the Federal Trade Commission finally settled the dispute by ordering the wood to be designated by the prefix "Philippine" Mahogany. Previously, mahogany was just called mahogany. However, now even the true mahoganies are somtimes labeled with a prefix, like Honduras Mahogany. The Philippine wood is fairly rot resistant and finishes off nicely when stained red.

Khaya is another wood that passes for mahogany and is called "African" Mahogany. It is hard, highly rot resistant and can be used anywhere on a boat, if you can afford it.

Mahogany is the real "mahogany" and it grows in Central America, Mexico, the West Indies, and southern Florida. This wood is sometimes called Honduras Mahogany. It is just as heavy as oak and just as strong, hard and dense. Because of its beautiful grain, it finishes beautifully and is used in furniture. It is highly resistant to rot and can be used anywhere on a boat, but since it is so expensive, you will find it only on the most expensive yachts.

White Oak is one of only 11 oak varieties that are used in boat building, with the Northern White Oak once the most popular. It is a heavy wood, weighing 47 pounds per cubic foot. Its worst feature is a tendency to check, split and crack in large timbers like keels and skegs. It is the best wood for ribs that must be steam-bent.

Red Oak is not recommended for structural hull members because it rots too easily. Use it only for interior trim, molding, etc., where it looks very nice with a natural oil finish.

Lignumvitae is the hardest, heaviest wood known and is imported from the West Indies and Central America. Because the wood is naturally oily, and unbelieveably hard, it is used in the tropics for propeller shaft bearings, and for sheer and gunwales because it is resistant to abrasion. It holds up under rough use and is ideal for workboats that are not pampered.

Greenheart is a favorite wood with European builders because it is extremely rot resistant and also repels marine borers like the Teredo Worm. Most of it is imported from British Guiana, but it also grows in South American and the West Indies. It is used in hull planking.

Ironbark is important if you like to use your boat in the winter and want to protect the hull from ice damage. Sheath or double plank it with this wood. That's what it is mainly used for, ice sheathing on tugs and workboats. It is imported from Australia, is resistant to marine borers, and is very heavy and hard.

Black Locust is another hard, heavy wood with certain specialty uses on a boat. Because it is highly shock-resistant, use it for support knees, braces, engine mounts, etc., on race boats. Although rot resistant, it is vulnerable to crustacean forms of marine life.

Teak is one of the most popular of the imported woods, so much so that you can even buy it in plywood. It is strong and not too heavy. Although originally used mainly for decking and handrails, it is now being used more extensively in boatbuilding because of its resistance to rot and worms. Teak looks good unpainted, but requires much maintenance and care, so much so that it almost becomes a nuisance and burden. If you hate work, stay away from teak decking.

Longleaf Yellow Pine is another domestic wood that can be used as a substitute when you can't get white oak. It is just as strong and durable and weighs about a ½ pound less per board foot. It is just slightly less rot resistant then white oak.

Cypress (bald) is an American wood from the southern states and literally grows in water, which may be the reason why it holds up so well in boats and around water. It was once a favorite wood for making photographic darkroom sinks in many newspaper photo departments. However, it is soft, has poor screw holding power and should not be used where strength is a factor. It is sometimes used for planking on workboats, but a cypress planked boat will absorb almost its weight in water, and lose much speed.

Redwood is immune to fungus infestation and ideal for replacing rotted cabin framing and deck beams. It is light, average in strength, and a pleasure to work. It can also be used for planking.

Sitka Spruce is the wood to use where weight and strength are important, as in small trailerable boats, and particularly racing hulls. It weighs only 2¼ pounds per board foot, is easy to work with and can be used to build an entire boat from keel to planking. Before aluminum took over, it was also used for spars and masts, in fact, it still is.

Cedar (*Port Orford*) the most preferred of the four cedars used in boatbuilding because it is the strongest. It has its own very distinctive odor. On small boats you can use this wood for framing, stringers, deck beams, planking, chines and sheers. All the cedars are extremely resistant to fungus infections.

Cedar (*Alaska*) is almost the equal in quality to Port Orford and can be used anywhere on small boats. On larger craft it is used mainly for planking.

Cedar (*Atlantic White*) should never be used for anything but planking because it is soft, brittle and splits easily when you drive large screws through holes that are too small. Just be sure that the holes are the same size as the screw.

Cedar (*Northern White*) is another soft, weak, brittle wood, and is suitable only for boat planking.

Pine (*Eastern White*) is a common lumberyard wood and is sometimes used by some small boatbuilders for decking and planking. However it is weak, has poor screw holding power, and its dimensions are severely affected when it gets wet.

THE WONDER OF PLYWOOD

I have purposely left plywood for the last because it is so important—in fact, from an environmental viewpoint, the invention of plywood is the worst thing that ever happened to trees because it opened up new uses for wood and new reasons to denude our forests. Plywood has been used to build everything from the world's largest airplane, like Howard Hughes's "Spruce Goose," to some of the largest pleasure yachts, which normally would have been built of steel. Plywood made it possible to achieve the strength of steel without the weight because pound for pound, plywood is stronger then steel.

Some of the bad things about wood are shrinking, swelling, cupping, warping, checking, splitting—and just plain breaking under stress. Plywood eliminates all those bad things because it is a totally engineered product, like an automobile, where a living thing, wood, is reduced to almost inert functional matter, making it even superior to steel because all metals expand with heat and contract with cold. As one engineer said: "Plywood just lays there, never expands, contracts, warps, checks, cups or splits—or develop stress cracks like steel."

All this makes plywood a remarkable product and as a boater you should know more about it because there is more to plywood then just picking up a few 4×8 sheets at Bargain City and tying them down on top of your car. The manufacturing of plywood is an enormous and complex thing, as is the grading, classification and selling. To completely cover the subject would take a book of this type with over 900 pages. However, your interest in plywood is limited to the specific grades and classifications suitable for marine use—and this eliminates most of those 900 pages. But it doesn't eliminate all of the complexities.

You probably have noticed that sometimes plywood will have three layers, sometimes five, or even more, and you probably wondered why. And you probably wondered how they cut that wood so thin.

When the logs come into the mill, the bark is removed, then the log is lifted into a huge lathe where it is turned against a long cutting blade that peels off a layer of wood the way you would peel the skin off an apple. This long unbroken layer of wood is then kiln dried and cut to size. Then the sheets are laid one over the other with grain running in different directions, generally perpendicular to one another, so that the finished sheet of wood will be equally strong in all directions. The layers are bonded together with glue or synthetic resins under hydraulic pressure, with the glue line being stronger then the wood itself.

It is these cross laminations of layer upon layer that eliminate all the bad features of wood. Splitting is impossible in any direction and so is shrinking, swelling, warping and checking. The amount of stiffness and bending strength is determined by the number of plies. The more plies, the more you can bend. This is an important consideration in plywood selected for planking, especially in the bow sections. It is not important for plywood that will lay flat, like transoms, cockpit floors, or even planking in the stern sections of semi-V hulls which are almost flat.

There are basically two types of plywood, interior and exterior.

SELECTING THE RIGHT PLYWOOD

Interior plywoods are bonded with ordinary glue, which in the presence of any moisture or dampness will soften, causing the plies to separate. There is nothing sadder looking than a piece of plywood with the plies coming apart. You should never use interior plywood anywhere on a boat, even if it is to be fiberglass covered—and *especially* if it is to be fiberglass because big bubbles and cupped areas are also a very sad sight.

The exterior grade plywoods are bonded together with more expensive 100 percent waterproof glues, which is why exterior costs more, and is worth it. Any exterior grade is suitable for use in boats, with some even more suitable, like the premium grade "Marine Exterior," which is the best and the only grade you should use for hull planking.

The inner plies in regular exterior grade are made up of random and odd sizes, and they do not always butt up tight against each other. In fact, they often have gaps of an inch between them. This leaves an inner void which you can often see on the edge grain of a cut piece of plywood. These voids cause all sorts of agonies when planking a boat because you will often hit a void when drilling and countersinking for screw holes. There will be nothing but the thin outer veneer to hold the screwhead and subsequent wood dough filling. Also in bending, these voids will sometimes crack. Regular exterior is alright for flat bulkhead panels—for any flat piece that will not require any fastenings through the center. Marine Exterior, as you have already guessed, is very expensive.

Large sheet plywood cannot be bent into a compound curve. That means bending in two directions at once. This is why boats built with plywood are designed expressly for plywood. And this is why some older plywood boats often looked boxy, with straight lines up forward.

Conventionally planked hulls will have inwardly curved, con-cave V-sections up forward. This presents two curves in different directions. With small strips of wood, compound curves can be developed in the forward V-sections, but not with a large sheet of plywood. Try this for yourself with a sheet of letterhead paper. Try bending it in two directions at the same time. The paper will bend smoothly in only one direction.

Exterior grade plywoods can be identified by the industry's grade trade mark, which will be either "EXT—APA" or "EXT—DFPA." Those last letters are the quality standards control body, like the Douglas Fir Plywood Association, or the American Plywood Association (Fig. 3-2).

The type and grade of plywood you buy should be no more than suits your needs for the specific application at hand because you pay for everything, so why pay for something you don't need, like two perfect surfaces when one of them will be facing the bilges.

Plywood surfaces are graded N, A, B, C, D, with "N" being the best surface grade available, with no patches. With "A"-faced plywood, although perfectly smooth, you will still have patches, but no larger then 1-inch in diameter, and edge-glued by DFPA specifications so that if the panel is bent outwardly, the patches won't pop out.

The "B"-faced plywood will have larger oval and round patches up to 2 inches in diameter, and they will not be edge-glued. See what I mean when I said you pay for everything when you buy plywood? The "B" surface grades should not be used for hull planking where there is bending because the patches could pop out.

The "C"-faced plywood is not patched and the knot holes and pitch pockets are left uncovered in all their glaring ugliness. Another thing to remember when you buy exterior is these knot holes and pitch pockets will also be all through the inner plies, along with all those gaps where the butts don't quite touch.

You can buy plywood in any combination of surfaces, like N-N, A-A, A-B, or N-A. The "N-N" would give you two perfect veneer surfaces, the ultimate in plywood. You can also buy one surface, or both, veneered with various fine finishing woods like mahogany or teak or oak. If both surfaces are visible, like on a cabin bulkhead facing two ways, have both surfaces in mahogany or teak, which wouldn't have to be painted. Some kit boats, like one by Sears Roebuck a few years ago, supplied planking panels veneered in mahogany.

There is currently another grade of plywood available with a special resin-impregnated surface which is supposed to give you a

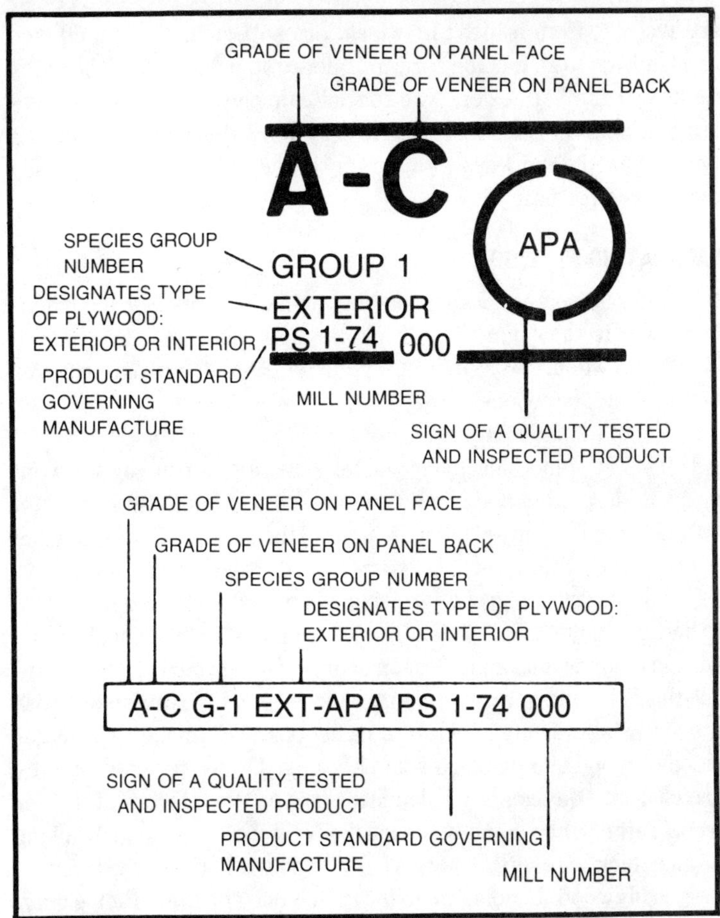

Fig. 3-2. Plywood panels will be stamped on both the face and edge.

head start on painting. This over-lay is available in various densities and degrees of hardness and slickness. I would recommend this finish only for interior work like decks, cabin floor, bulkheads, etc. I would not try to use it for planking because it is difficult to plug the screw holes, and sand them down later without cutting through the finish. And the plywood, with this surface, does not take to bending too well.

PLYWOOD SIZES

The most popular and common plywood size is those 4×8 foot sheets which will just fit into a full size station wagon. Thicknesses are available from ⅛ inch to 1⅛ inch. Sizes 24-inch, 30-inch, 60-inch wide, and up to 20 feet long are considered standard and will be stock items with lumber dealers who specialize in plywood. Longer sheets are available on special order. Any plywood sheet over 8 feet is a beast to handle and work with, so why bother when you can so easily make a simple butt joint.

LAMINATING PLYWOOD

Curious boaters always looked stunned and unbelieving when, in answer to their questions, I told them my boat was planked with ¾-inch plywood. "My God!" they would gasp. "How did you ever bend ¾-inch plywood?"

I didn't. I laminated.

This is something many boaters overlook. You can do wondrous things with wood when you stop fighting it and laminate. Not only did I laminate my planking, I also did the same with the inner and outer chines, the sheer, the stem and the keel.

Large timbers, properly seasoned for keels and stems, are hard to find. And I don't like the way these big pieces of wood check after a season in the water, and a season of drying on the beach. The way to lick this is to glue or screw together three layers of 1-inch wood with the grains all running in different directions. This makes a stronger piece of wood and eliminates all checking. Chine and sheer curves are easier to develop if you laminate two or three layers of thinner wood rather then fight with one heavy piece. Plywood planking ¾-inch thick, or even thicker, is easy if you work with three layers of ¼-inch plywood, bending them into place one at a time, then gluing. Also, laminating eliminates the need for butt joints because you stagger each layer at the ends so you can make a scarf-joint. In fact, that's the way longer lengths of plywood are made at the factory. They just scarf-joint shorter pieces together.

THE CARVEL PLANKED HULL

When Noah built the Ark, he carvel planked it. This is the oldest, simplest, and the easiest way to plank a boat hull (Fig. 3-3). In fact, it was the only way up until the last 50 years when the first V-shaped hull with hard chines made its appearance in racing hulls and speed boats.

In carvel planking, man made use of one of the inherent weaknesses of wood, expanding when it got wet. It is this very characteristic of wood that makes boats dry and wine and water casks

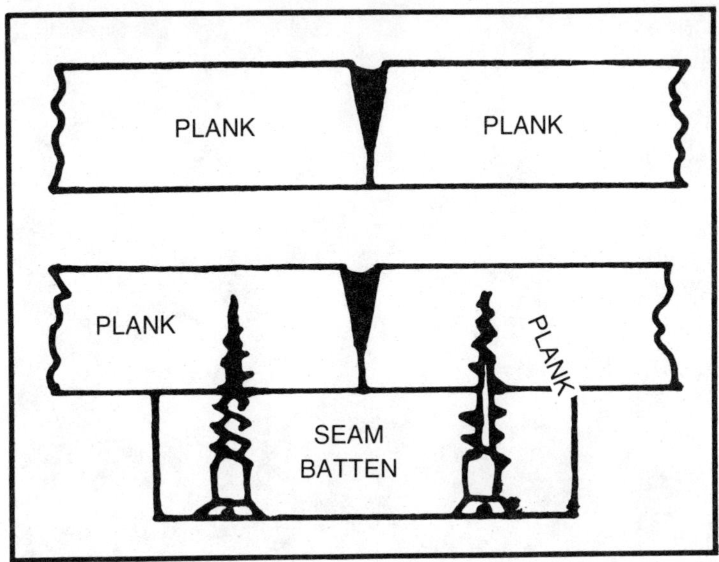

Fig. 3-3. The top drawing is carvel planking; the bottom is batten seam planking.

leak-proof. In a wood barrel, each stave presses against the next stave in a complete circle. When the staves are wet, they expand tighter and tighter against each other to make a completely leak-proof seal.

This is the principal of carvel planking. However, when carvel planked boats are hauled out for the winter, another inherent weakness in wood occurs: the hull planking shrinks as it dries out, leaving large gaps between the planks. In the spring you can see daylight between each plank, which is very disconcerting to a new boat owner. If you launched such a boat, it would sink in minutes because it takes at least 48 hours for the planking to swell up enough to stop the leaking. So this is why a special type of cotton is hammered into the seams, followed by a soft caulking compound. These are merely stop-gap devices put in the seams to hold back the water and give the wood a chance to expand. As the planks expand, they push out all the new soft compound, and the ritual of caulking is performed over and over each spring.

Carvel planked boats are round-bottomed with steam-bent oak ribs. From a manufacturing standpoint, these are the easiest boats to build because each hull is started on a mold over which the ribs are steam-bent, and then planked. For production building this is fast and easy, but impractical for the amateur who must go through all the extra work of building a mold for just one boat. And steaming oak ribs

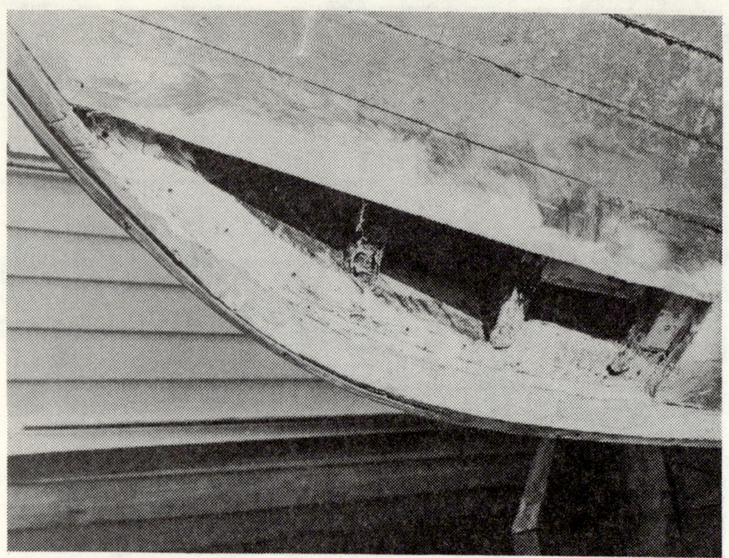

Fig. 3-4. This carvel plank was removed starting at the butt, which can be clearly seen. You just back out the screws and out comes the plank.

requires special equipment which also will be used only once. Amateurs usually stay away from carvel-planked boats for these reasons, even though they are easier to build. Carvel hulls are also the easiest to repair. I have removed a damaged carvel plank, replaced it and had it primed for painting in less than two hours. You could never do this with any other type of planking. It is something to consider with today's high labor costs because used boats with carvel planking are often the cheapest and the best buys, and the most plentiful because they've been around a long, long time.

REPAIRING A CARVEL PLANKED HULL

It requires no mechanical or woodworking skills to replace a damaged carvel plank. Even your mother can do it. You start at a butt, which you can clearly see because the paint line is almost always broken (Fig. 3-4). With a screwdriver or ice pick, dig out the wood dough filling or wood plug covering the screwheads. Back out all the screws, save one for size identification, and throw the rest into the lagoon or trash barrel. Why not save them? You shouldn't because the heads are always chewed up when you back them out and there isn't anything that will give you chest pains faster then fasteners with bad heads. Be kind to your heart and throw them away.

Make a straight pencil line where you will cut. This will be between two ribs. Drill a small hole just big enough to accept whatever type of sawing tool you will use, a keyhole saw or sabre saw (Fig. 3-5). An electric sabre saw is best (Fig. 3-6). Make a clean straight cut and pull out the damaged plank. If stuck, tap it from the inside. If you can't get inside, drive two long over-size screws part way into two of the holes and use them as handles to pull on the plank.

The plank that you have removed will serve as a pattern for the new replacement plank. This is important to remember in boat

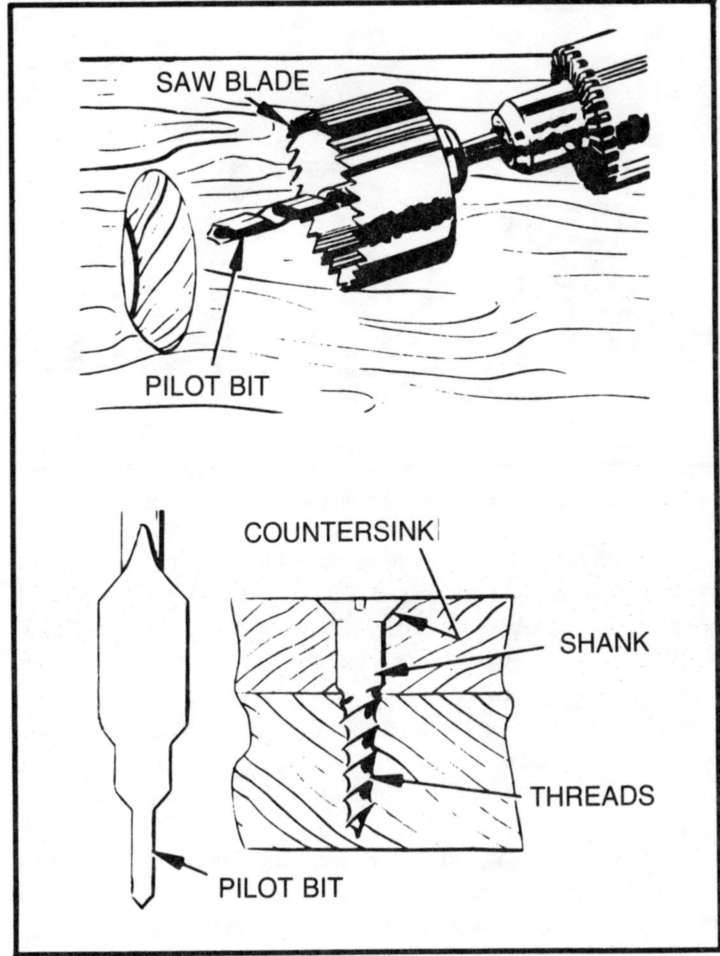

Fig. 3-5. A big hole is necessary to get the saber saw started. Screw holes in planking must be drilled with a pilot bit for either countersinking or plugging.

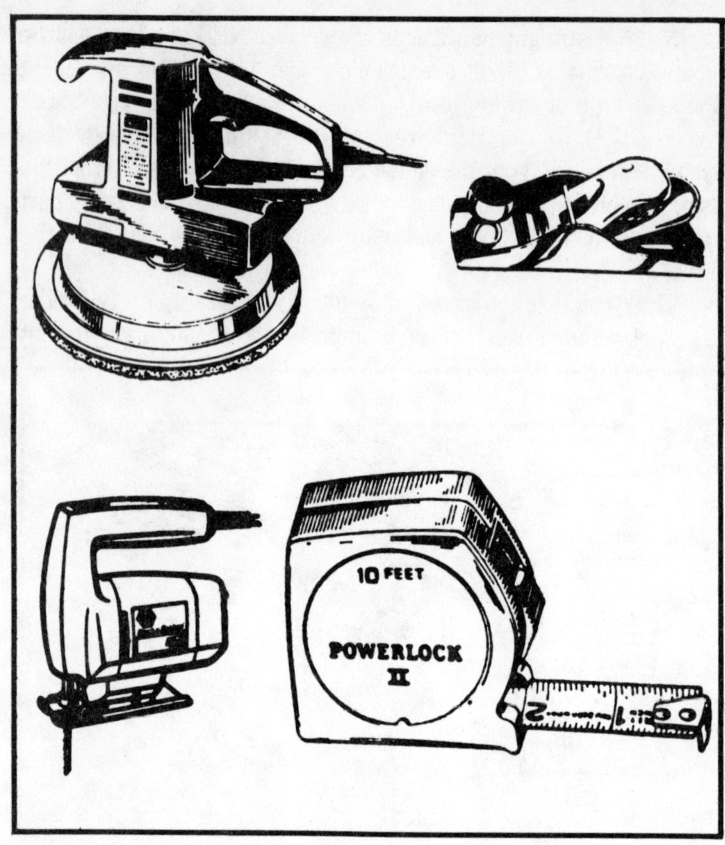

Fig. 3-6. You will need these tools when making hull repairs on carvel planking.

repair. Always be careful in removing anything that you are replacing because it will be your pattern. It simplifies work which has already been done by somebody else. All you have to do is take that damaged plank or whatever else you are repairing, to the yard woodworking shop and ask them to mill you an exact duplicate.

The cost of having the yard mill you a new carvel plank is small compared to the labor charges of having them do the entire job. It's the labor charges, about $20 an hour, that kill you. So how long does it take?

I replaced a plank in two hours. But I don't have prostate trouble. I don't have to stop working every half hour and walk clear across the yard to the men's room. This usually takes 15 minutes. So figure it out. At 20 bucks an hour, the carpenter's prostate gland is costing you 5 bucks every time he takes that walk.

I don't know why it is, maybe it's an occupational hazard, but I have never known a good boat millwright or carpenter who didn't have prostate trouble. Back in the old days, before women got involved in boat maintenance, a boatowner or carpenter could answer a call of nature right on the ground without moving from the boat. But today with women all over the place sanding and painting, you just can't do that. You have to take that long walk—and that is what adds to the labor costs. And that is why you are removing that plank yourself (Fig. 3-7).

The yard woodworking shop will mill you a nice new plank out of white cedar or mahogany and even drill the screwholes in the precisely the same positions. This new plank will be, or should be, an exact duplicate of what you removed. You should have no difficulties in putting it back and driving in nice new screws (Fig. 3-8). Now plug the screwheads with wood dough. Sand down in a couple of hours and you're ready to prime paint.

PRIMERS AND UNDERCOATERS

Have you ever wondered what the difference was between a primer and an undercoater? Primers are very thin and the cans feel light in weight. Undercoaters are very thick and the cans feel like they are filled with lead. Primers are intended to soak into the wood and not just lay on top. The wood, after priming, looks rough with all

Fig. 3-7. Five carvel planks are removed in this manner. Note how the cuts are staggered.

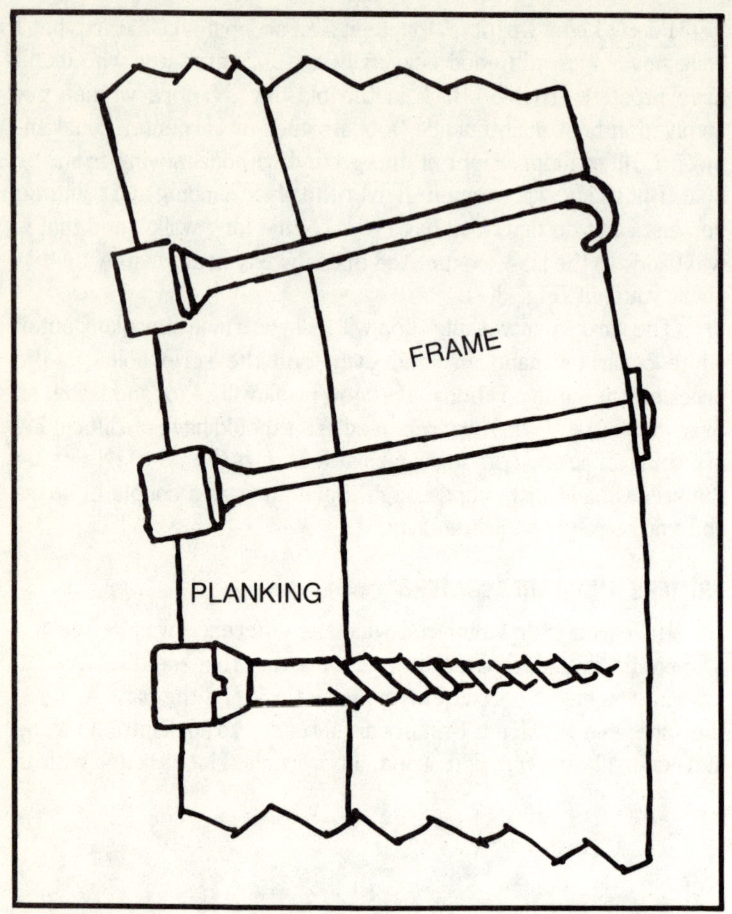

Fig. 3-8. These are the three types of fastenings used on small boats.

the grain visible and is a disappointment to the inexperienced boat owner who can't understand what went wrong. He figures maybe he didn't put on enough primer. Perhaps he should go back and do the job over.

Primers are supposed to look like that. They are merely the base, the "tooth" to which succeeding coats adhere. It's the undercoater that covers up the grain patterns and smooths over the roughness. That's why it's so thick, to give you a fast paint build-up. Don't put on any more undercoater then necessary to smooth out the roughness and cover the grain.

Undercoaters smudge and dirty easily. You must be careful not to touch them with soiled hands. After the undercoat is painted with a finish coat of full gloss or semi-gloss, you can wash off dirt. It is the fashion at this time to super-gloss everything with rock-hard paints. You will curse them later. That old fashioned stuff called paint, in semi gloss, is still the best. When you get indigestion or heartburn, you will understand why I keep saying this.

If you have primed that new carvel plank, you are ready to caulk the seam. It is always better to prime the seams before caulking. I don't know why, but the experts say the raw wood draws all the oils out of the caulking, causing it to dry out. But since the caulking is in the seam such a short time, I could never understand what difference it makes. In carvel planking, as with barrel staves, it is better if nothing is put in the seams. When bare wood planks swell together they form a perfect water-tight seal. But something has to be put in the seam to temporarily hold back the flood until the wood swells. You can skip the cotton. Just fill the seam with anything that's soft, and don't worry about longevity or quality because next spring you will be doing it all over again. Why waste money on expensive seam compounds that are supposed to last forever? "Forever" on a carvel planked bottom is about 48 hours.

REPLACING STEAM-BENT RIBS

It is rarely necessary to replace a rib, or ribs, in a saltwater boat, or even a freshwater boat that is regularly in use and moderately maintained. But a boat that has been abandoned or left up on the beach a few years under hot canvas will most likely have a rotted rib or two—and more. If you are ever tempted to buy such a boat—and you will find dozens in every boatyard—take into consideration that you will be buying much work and you will need much

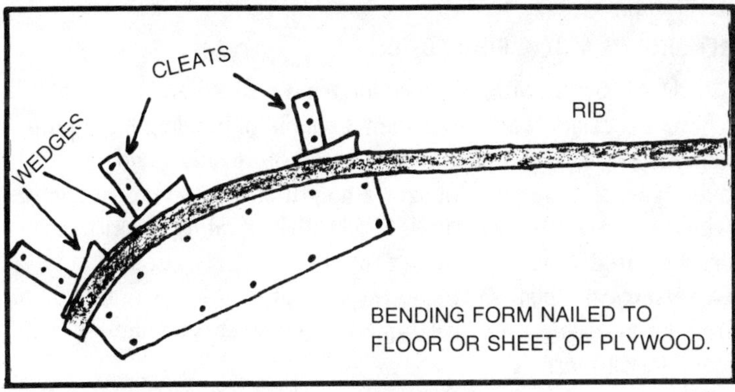

Fig. 3-9. Rig up some type of bending form as illustrated here. Always overbend because it's easier to unbend if you have too much.

Fig. 3-10. Once the rib is pre-bent, it's easy to work it into place.

money and free time. So don't pay out too much money for some-body else's neglect. Before you buy such a boat, try to get an estimate on what it would cost for a professional overhaul and refinishing job. Then deduct that from the asking price.

If just the end of a rib is infected, you don't have to remove the entire rib. You can treat the infected portion with "Git" Rot, or cut only a short section and then butt another length of new rib right alongside. If the rotted section is at the turn of the bilge, then you have some bending to do.

BENDING IN A NEW RIB SECTION

Don't be frightened; you don't have to steam to bend oak. There are easier ways. I've seen a bundle of bending oak tied to a cement block, lowered into the water off a dock, and left there overnight. Another way utilizes a length of house-type rain gutter with the ends sealed off. This is filled with hot water. The rib, or ribs, are weighted down in the water and the gutter is stretched out over two electric hot plates. The hotter the water, the less time it takes. An hour in boiling water will tame the toughest oak. Just hot water will take all morning.

Don't try to bend the rib in the boat (Fig. 3-9). Do the prelimi-nary bending outside over any round surface—over the outside of

the hull itself. One end of the rib can be wedged with a 2×4 up under
the hull against the keel; then bend up with leverage helping you.
Secure the end to a cleat until the wood sets a little.

Once you get some bend into the rib, it's easier to get that long
piece of wood into the bilges, where you can horse it in further with
C-clamps (Fig. 3-10). This is why I don't like to replace an entire rib
because that long piece of wood is a beast to work with in cramped
quarters. It is so much easier to use the short-length-butt system
(Fig. 3-11).

REMOVING OLD PAINT

If you bought one of those abandoned derelicts that have been
sitting in the boatyard a few years, then you have a lot of old paint to
remove. Don't try to save it—take it off (Fig. 3-12)! There are three
ways to do this: with a blowtorch, a commercial type disc sander, or
with paint removers. Professionals prefer the blowtorch. For them
it's easy and fast. But they have the experience. You don't. By the
time you finish removing all the paint on your boat, you will also have
the experience. You will also have a boat covered with scorched

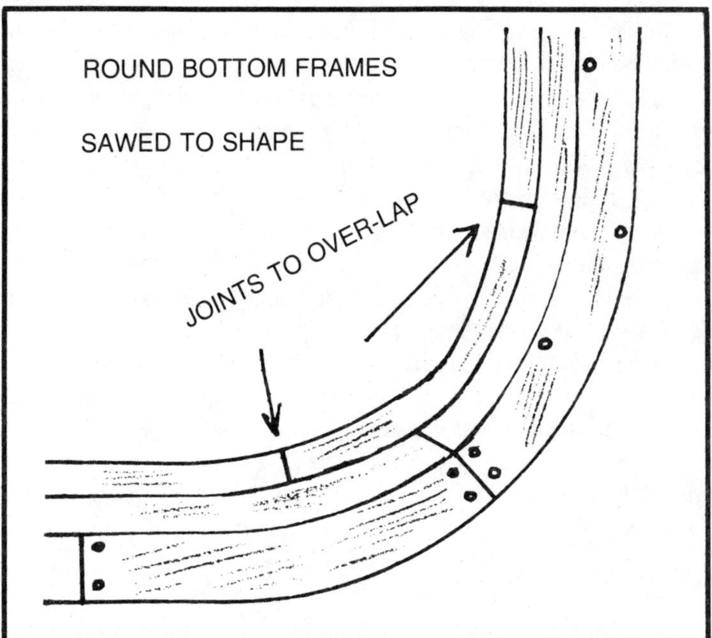

Fig. 3-11. An easier way to replace a steamed rib is to saw one to shape. Note the
rotted transom in Fig. 3-7.

Fig. 3-12. Don't try to save this paint job. Take it off.

wood. It is the price you must pay for on-the-job training. So forget about blowtorches (Fig. 3-13). Forget about propane paint removers. They work, but you'll go broke buying propane fuel cylinders.

Your next best bet is to rent a big professional type disc sander, if you don't mind the dust. If you do, then you better go with the paint removers. They work, if you let them. Don't expect instant results. They just don't work that way. There is a soak/wait time element involved. Like with the blowtorch, you need on-the-job training, but at least with the paint removers, while you're getting this training you aren't hurting anything. You're just wasting a lot of paint remover by not giving it time to work.

You have noted that the paint on your decks and trunk cabintop is alligatored. The same is true with the side and forward decks. Under that paint there is canvas, which was pretty much the accepted way of covering decks before fiberglass. There was also an evil practice of over-painting those canvas-covered decks, which is why they alligatored. This is why the paint must be removed.

FIBERGLASSING OLD DECKS

When you remove the paint off the old canvas-covered decks, etc., you will find bad spots where the canvas is cracked and separated from the wood. What to do? Well, you can re-canvas, or fiberglass. Fiberglass is better because it will be easier and less work. To re-canvas you must remove much wood. On the trunk cabintop, for example, the canvas lays under the windshield. On the side and forward decks it lays under molding and under the sheer. All that wood has to be removed before you can lay new canvas. If you fiberglass, you cover everything. This will save you much labor, and at the same time eliminate many old annoying leaks.

After all the paint and old canvas are removed, if you find any rotted wood, just clean it out. If a section of molding is bad, do the same with it. With a dry fiberglass filler, which you mix with polyester or epoxy resin, you can fill in and mold a replacement for any wood that you remove. Screw holes, cracks and small gouges are filled in with fiberglass repair putty. Remember, any wood surface to be covered with fiberglass must first be repaired with compatible materials such as the above. Any screwheads previously filled with wood dough must be cleaned out and refilled with fiberglass putty. The resins will not adhere to any oil-based seam compounds or wood doughs.

This may scare you off from fiberglassing the hull as well, when you consider all those screwheads and seams that will have to be cleaned out and refilled. Any of the fiberglass suppliers previously listed will send you prices and data on ordering resins, putties, cloths, etc., with step-by-step instructions. Also, "Git" Rot for repairing fungus-infected wood is only one of many similar products available under different trade names. In some areas you may want to "cure" rather than cut out and remold with fiberglass. If a section

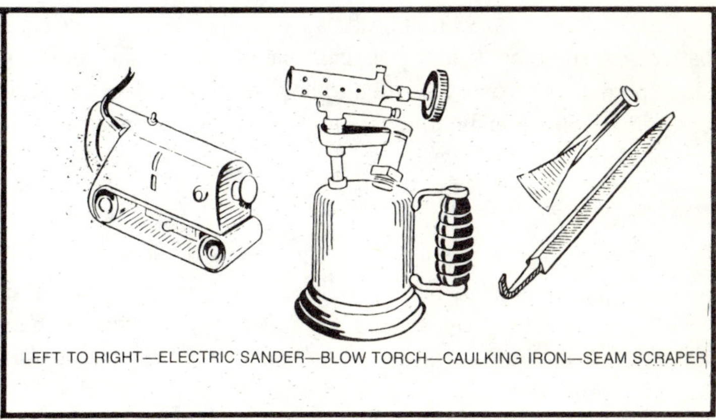

Fig. 3-13. Professionals prefer the blowtorch for paint removal. For the amateur, paint removers and power sanders are less damaging.

of molding is just soft, but still all there, then cure it. But if it has started to crumple and fall away, then dig it all out and fill in with the heavy fiberglass repair material. With the wonderful new repair materials available today, you can patch, "cure," and repair just about anything on a wood boat without involving yourself in carpentry work.

THE "HARD CHINE" HULL

The expansion principle utilized in barrels and carvel-planked boat hulls just doesn't work in the V-shaped type of hull with its hard chine. The "chine" is that sharp point where the bottom and sides of a hull meet (Fig. 3-14). In a carvel-planked hull there is no "chine," and each plank butts against another plank in a continuous line, like in a barrel. In a V-hull, the bottom ends at the chine. It is the chine that destroys the barrel-stave principle of expansion. The bottom planks in a V-hull expand all right, but they don't close up tight. They just push the next plank away because there is nothing at the chine to stop all the expansion and pushing. As a result, when all the swelling and pushing ends, the bottom seams are still open.

Incredible as it may seem, there was a company some years ago that actually built a V-bottom hard chine cruiser with carvel planking. These boats were disasters and never stopped leaking. One boat sank at its dock one summer when the battery ran down and two bilge pumps stopped working. This company is no longer in the business of building boats. They're building mobile homes now. They leak, too.

There are many different ways to achieve water-tight integrity in a hard chine hull, and Chris Craft has used all of them. There is the batten seam method, double planking, clinker or lapstrake, and large sheet plywood planking. Each of the above methods achieves instant and permanent water-tightness without waiting for wood to expand, as you do in the carvel method.

BATTEN SEAMS

In batten seams, the planks are put on in much the same manner as carvel planks except that they all come together over a batten (see Fig. 3-3). A "batten" is just a longitudinal stringer that has been notched into the frames and spaced so that they back up all the plank seams. With every seam backed up this way, and caulked with an elastic sealer, they never leak.

All those longitudinal stringers also strengthen the hull because there is double wood thickness in the planking over the battens. For

Fig. 3-14. The planing hull is almost always of semi-V hard chine construction. The spray rails actually cover the chine where bottom and topside planks meet.

example, if the planks are ¾-inch thick, then over the battens there will be 1½-inches of wood thickness. This makes a very strong hull with less weight topside.

Although an entire hull can be batten seamed, builders rarely plank bottoms this way because you can never pump all the water out of the bilges. It collects between the battens and promotes rot.

DOUBLE PLANKING

Chris Craft double planks the bottoms of their top line boats. The first layer of planks will run at a diagonal into the keel and chine. The second layer will go on in the usual way (Fig. 3-15). Between the two layers of planking will be canvas, buttered both sides with some type of permanently elastic bedding.

I have owned two cruisers that were double planked both topside and bottom. I like this method and I don't. On the plus side the hulls are water-tight, solid, heavy and you get a Cadillac ride in short choppy seas. On the bad side, they are mean to repair. If you own a double planked hull, don't ever run aground in rocky shoals or hit a cement dock like I did.

When I was still in college, I bought a used car for $95. It had no brakes. When I went back and asked the dealer: "What'll I do if I have to stop real quick?" He said: "Look for something inexpensive to run into."

That's what happened to me at Cedar Point one summer when winds were gusting at 40-miles-an-hour and all I could see were rows of big expensive yachts, and no place to go. I looked for something "inexpensive." All I could see was the end of a long concrete dock. So I hit it. I had to haul out and it took me a week to repair the damage. With carvel planking, I could have repaired the same damage in one afternoon without hauling out.

A badly holed double plank hull can be a major construction project when that inside diagonal lay of planking is involved. To replace one inside plank you must remove all the outside planks. That, of course, is ridiculous. There is an easier way.

First you remove the outside plank, or planks, that have been damaged. This wood is usually a ½-inch thick. You cannot use a saw of any kind. Personally, I use a router with a ⅛-inch bit set at ½-inch routing depth. One end of the plank will be at a butt joint, so it doesn't have to be cut. It's the other end where you rout a straight cut just deep enough to barely touch the canvas. If you must remove more then one plank to get at the inside damage, stagger the outside cuts so they don't all end together. It looks bad and people will stare at your boat and whisper.

With the inside damage exposed, you can proceed to repair this as if it were a sheet of plywood. With a sabre saw, cut out a neat square or rectangular hole around the damaged wood. The inside layer of planking is also ½-inch wood, unless your yacht is in the 60-foot class, in which case you won't be doing this. One of your slaves will. If your inside planking really is ½-inch (sometimes it's a trifle less), you're lucky because then you can fill that hole easily with ½-inch plywood. This fill wood that goes in the hole must be exactly the same thickness as the inner layer of planking because it is actually going to be sandwiched between another larger sheet of ¼-inch plywood inside, and the finish planks on the outside.

The inside ¼-inch cover plywood should be about 2 inches larger than the hole piece, screwed in all around four sides, and through the center into the fill wood. Chamfer or bevel the edges for a nice appearance. If the inside of your hull in this area is varnished, use mahogany plywood. If it is painted, use fir. You can even make it a conversation piece. Tell your guests that's how you brought back grass on that last cruise to Acapulco.

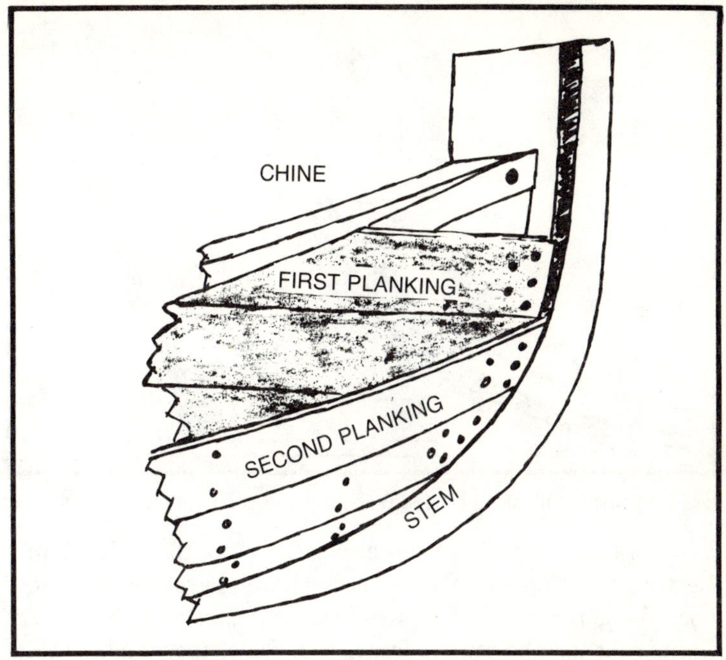

Fig. 3-15. Double-planked hulls are the strongest, the most watertight, and the most difficult to repair.

On the outside you must replace that layer of canvas that you cut out, or your outside planks wont be level with the rest of the hull. Butter this canvas on both sides with bedding and it will stick in there by itself. Now you can replace the outside planks. This part is so easy your mother can do it.

THE LAPSTRAKE HULL

Clinker planking, as labstrake hulls are sometimes called, is another method of achieving the added strength of double thickness in planking without actually having a double thickness (Fig. 3-16). You get that double strength in the overlaps, and you get it without double weight. Those overlaps in the planks also make the lapstrake hull both a "dryer" and a softer riding boat. What is meant by "dryer" is that as the bow rises and falls in heavy seas, less water runs up the sides to blow back on the windshield. Each one of those overlapping steps acts as an individual spray rail to deflect and throw away water. They also provide a cushioning effect as the bow comes down into a sea. Cruisers with this type of planking became popular during the fifties and sixties. They were called "Sea Skiffs" or just "Skiffs." I

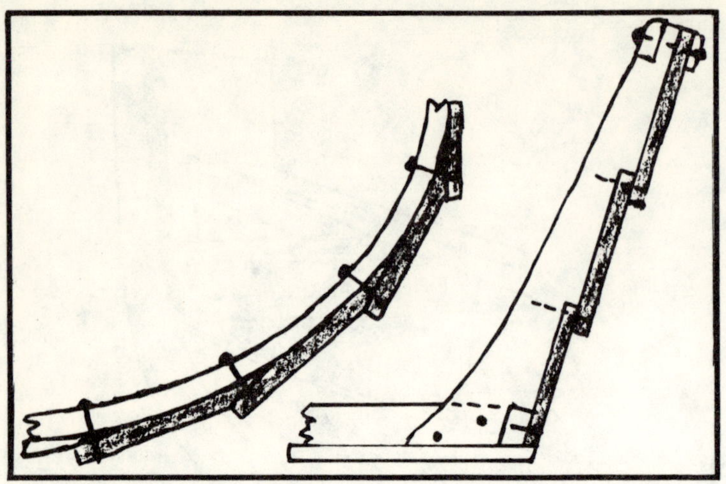

Fig. 3-16. Clinker planking is used on both round and hard chined hulls.

have on many occasions seen convincing proof that "skiffs" with lapstrake planking are "dryer" running boats. In convoy with other boats on club cruises, I could see how much water all the boats were taking over their bows, and always the "skiffs" took the least (Fig. 3-17). I always envied them because my windshield wipers were running constantly and theirs weren't even on.

The windshield wiper is an extremely important piece of navigation equipment on any boat that cruises the Great Lakes because the least bit of wind will bring a chop, and this brings spray and solid water over your bow. I have in one season burned out two wiper motors, even the so-called "heavy duty" ones. A boat windshield is intermittently wet and dry. You hit a wave, get water on your glass, and then run dry then get wet. This is hard on windshield wiper motors, and they overheat and burn out.

Everybody dreams of someday owning a "dry" boat—and this is why skiffs became so popular (Fig. 3-18). Chris Craft built a 40-foot "Sea Skiff" in the sixties that was absolutely the driest boat I ever handled. I ran this boat into 20-mile winds and never saw a drop of water hit the glass. The owner, a dentist and new to boating, remarked to me, "I have no need for a windshield wiper because I never go out when it rains."

SANDING AND PAINTING LAPSTRAKE PLANKING

Lapstrake planking is easy to sand and paint. Since you are working on a smaller surface area, power sanders get a better "bite" and you can start at the bow. Finish one strake at a time and do the same with painting. You can finish one strake and knock off for lunch (Fig. 3-19). You can't do this with a flat smooth surface. Once you start painting, you stay with it until finished.

The wood in lapstrake planking can be either plywood, cedar, mahogany or even cypress. You can get into endless arguments on the merits of solid wood versus plywood in this type of hull. The plywood strakes are stronger and will not check, split, expand or dry out. The boat weight remains constant because plywood does not soak up water.

Solid wood strakes absorb water, and with cypress this can be considerable. No sealer is used on the plank overlaps because expansion takes care of the leaks. With plywood strakes a permanently flexible sealer must be used on the overlaps to make them

Fig. 3-17. This smooth fiberglass hull is a very "wet" boat in even a small chop. As that forward V comes down into a wave, water runs up the smooth sides and then gets blown back on the windshield, over the hardtop and into the cockpit. All smooth hulls of this type are wet running in even the smallest waves.

Fig. 3-18. This is a dry running boat in rough water because every one of those overlaps in the planking acts as a spray deflector to throw water away from the hull. As a result, very little water gets up high enough to be blown back on the windshield or into the cockpit. So clinker hulls are definitely much "dryer" boats.

leakproof. You never have to re-caulk because there is no drying out or shrinking of the wood. Solid wood strakes dry out and leave big gaps in the overlaps. These boats will leak badly on launching and take longer than a carvel planked hull to swell up tight.

This is why companies like Lyman, one of the oldest lapstrake (clinker) boat builders, use plywood. Size for size, plywood is stronger, which means thinner strakes can be used, resulting in a lighter boat. Less power will be needed for propulsion. A cypress planked hull, when water soaked, will outweigh the plywood hull many times and require considerably more horsepower and gasoline. Back in the days of slow displacement hulls and cheap gasoline, nobody considered this important. But people are beginning to realize that weight, in boats and automobiles, takes power to move. Reduce weight and you reduce operating costs.

Plywood strakes are not only easier to paint, but they stay painted longer. The chief cause for paint failure is moisture. Nobody yet has been able to produce a paint that will stick to wet wood. The solid woods used in conventional planking soak up much water, especially cypress, which is almost like a sponge. And this is why you paint every year. I have seen plywood clinker hulls go two and three years without a new paint job. That outer veneer on plywood is very thin and with penetrating prime coat sealers to waterproof them, they soak up no water. The waterproof glue line prevents penetration of moisture to the inner plies, so plywood never gets water soaked. And paint stays on for that reason.

I have seen plywood hulls badly damaged after collisions, but I have never seen one holed. However, fir plywood is easily gouged and chewed up by rubbing and banging against docks. Nothing looks worse then a lacerated plywood hull that has been left unattended for long periods to bang against a dock. And this is how most hull damage occurs. Collisions at sea are rarities, except on the Detroit River, the busiest waterway in the world (Fig. 3-20). Spectators will crowd the Belle Isle bridge on a Sunday afternoon just to watch the crazy boaters trying to kill each other.

If you are a dentist or obstetrician who is handier with forceps then wood tools, it might be better if you left hull repairs to the professionals because lapstrake planking is tough to work on. This is not to imply a dentist can't do the job. You can.

REPAIRING LAPSTRAKE HULLS

Removing damaged lapstrake planks is slow work, especially if they are riveted with copper nails hammered over burrs, which look

Fig. 3-19. Lapstrake hulls are a joy to paint. You can finish one strake and knock off for a beer or lunch.

133

Fig. 3-20. More hull repair work is done in the Detroit area than anywhere else in the world. Detroit is the busiest boating community.

like small washers. Use a ¼-inch drill and abrasive wheel to grind off the nail ends over the burrs. With a nail set, you can hit the nail end through the burr hole and push it out far enough to reach with pliers on the other side. When you re-fasten new planks, use bolts and nuts.

Use a sabre saw to remove all the damaged wood between the top and bottom overlaps. This will give you working room and a place to use a C-clamp to hold a block of wood which will serve as both a guide and protection for one side of the cutting edge as you cut with a keyhole saw. This is the hard part, cutting that inch of wood on the overlaps. And that is the reason for that block of wood, to give you a straight edge against which to lay the keyhole saw as you cut parallel with the plank surface very carefully so you don't cut through and damage the wood underneath. Just take it slow and easy.

The recommended way to remove a damaged lapstrake plank is to make your cut right up against the inside edge of a rib, leaving the good portion of the plank still fastened on the rib. When you put in new wood, you are supposed to make what is called a scarf joint (Fig. 3-21). Look at the illustration. If you can do this, hooray for you! I have designed boats. I have built boats. I have repaired boats and I still can't make a decent scarf joint. So don't be ashamed to chicken out and do it the coward's way, the butt block way (Fig. 3-22). A butt block doesn't look as neat from the inside, but I can promise that none of your boating guests will ever notice, or even complain about it if they do notice. In my experience, the only things boating guests notice or complain about later is if your beer is warm or your wife's fried chicken is cold. Nobody notices butt blocks or scarf joints but "experts" who write for boating magazines, and how often do you have one of them as a guest? So the hell with scarf joints. Do it the easy way and have fun boating instead of going crazy trying to do something the so-called right way.

Incidently, when you remove the damaged plank, or planks, you will see that they are slightly beveled on the overlapping edges. Use the damaged plank that you removed as a pattern to guide you in duplicating that same bevel in the new planks. That's the whole secret of boat repair—using the old as a model for the new. Getting the bevel is easy with a small hand plane or wood rasps.

Butter down both edges liberally with a flexible sealer, of which the marine stores have an endless variety for just that very purpose.

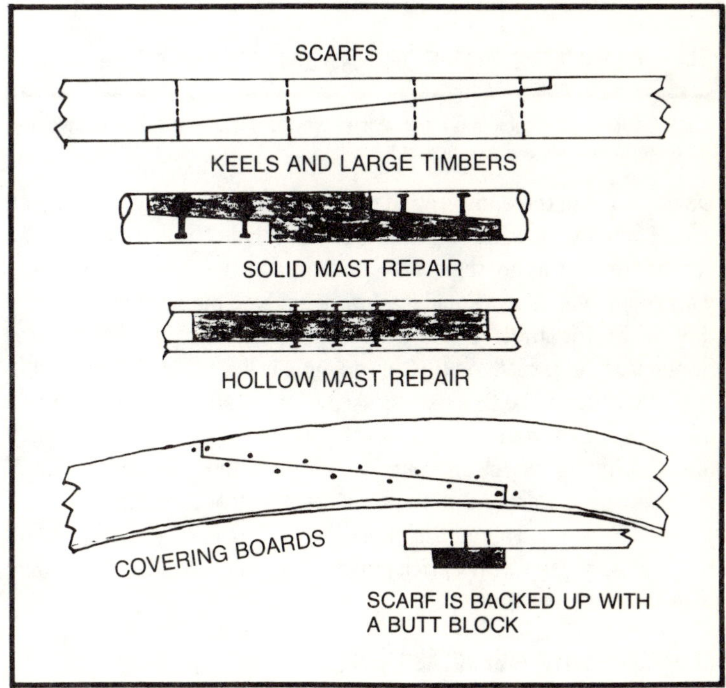

Fig. 3-21. Making a scarf joint on a large piece of wood is much easier than doing it on ⅜ or ½-inch plywood.

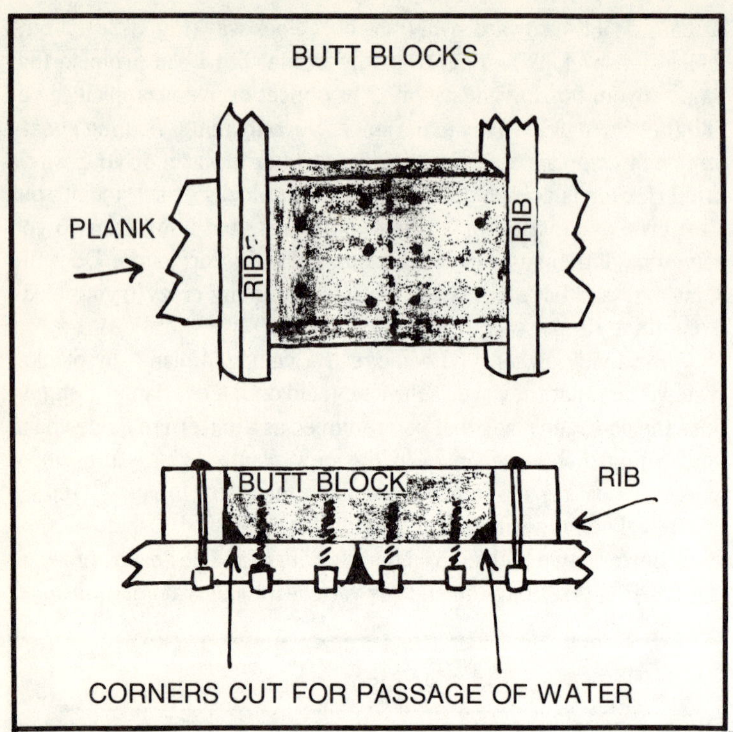

Fig. 3-22. The butt block is a much easier way to back up joints in planks and requires no special skills or power tools.

Do the same in the ends around the butt blocks. When you re-fasten with flathead machine screws, drill the holes undersize so the screws must thread their way through the wood. This makes a watertight seal. Use a small washer behind the nuts so you can draw the planks together. Don't worry about the nuts working loose. Some paint or varnish on the thread ends will act as a lock washer.

If you don't like that excess screw length sticking out to scratch a leg or stick on your clothes, saw them off and smooth down with a file or grinding wheel on your ¼-inch drill. Liberal applications of paint or varnish around the nut will keep it from working loose. If you're still worried about the nuts working loose, give the sawed off bolt end a hard tap with a prick punch. This will expand it slightly and help keep it from turning.

REPAIRING WITH FIBERGLASS

In abrasion damages, scuffs and gouges an alternative to lapstrake plank removal and replacement is to repair and patch up with fiberglass. You can do a remarkably good job on even the most severe outside hull damage. Clean damaged plywood, which will be rough and splintered, presents a perfect foundation for the heavy fiberglass repair putties that you can build up and mold to any shape. The splintered wood is just what you need for good adhesion and you can repair any damage excepting, of course, a Detroit River Sunday afternoon hull smasher. In this case, some insurance company will be involved and they will be paying the bills, so why bother? Any repair work that you do will be minor, the type on which you don't file insurance claims because of that $100 deductible. This type of repair is best done by you, and with fiberglass.

COVERING LAPSTRAKE HULLS WITH FIBERGLASS

You can fiberglass a lapstrake hull, but if the planks are plywood, it isn't necessary or worth the effort. The main reason for covering a lapstrake hull with fiberglass is to stop leaking, which can be considerable on boats planked with cedar, mahogany or cypress. But leaking is hardly ever a problem with the plywood-straked hulls. The same is true with painting. They are the easiest boats to keep painted. So why bother?

Lapstrake hulls with solid wood strakes are a different can of worms. There is plenty of justification and argument for fiberglassing these hulls, and I know many who did. Some are happy. Some are not. The happy ones had small outboards, which could be turned over and worked on in a garage.

The unhappy ones had cruisers lapstraked with solid wood, the kind that most needs fiberglassing. You just don't turn a cruiser upside down, you work from the bottom up. And right there is where the ballgame is lost because it's almost impossible to do a proper fiberglass job working against gravity.

A manufacturer in Jacksonville, Florida, who builds 60 and 75-foot yachts of wood, then fiberglasses them, does it with the hulls turned upside down. This builder obviously found out that you can't do the job any other way, and do it right. Why else would they design and build special equipment for turning over those huge hulls?

So, if you have a lapstrake cruiser and plan on fiberglassing the entire hull, turn it upside down or forget it. Don't take on a private little war with gravity because you are doomed to lose. Remember, we are thinking in terms of covering an entire hull with cloth and mat material. Making small repairs on bottoms is a different matter, and entirely workable. For this you only need two hands. To layup large sheets of cloth you need more arms then a centipede. Since you most certainly are not going to turn your cruiser upside down, we can skip any further discussion of fiberglassing lapstrake cruisers. If you have an outboard which you plan to cover, you will get all the information and instructions you need when you buy the materials for the job. It's sort of a package deal.

THE SHEET PLYWOOD HULL

Kit boats of the fifties and sixties were all designed to be planked with large sheets of plywood on the bottom and topside, with no seams between the keel and chine, or the sheer and chine (Fig. 3-23). There is a vertical break lengthwise where two sheets join, but this is always over another large piece of wood called a butt. This makes plywood boats virtually leakproof because the seams are always over something, like the inner keel and the inner chine. These seams never expand or contract. They always remain watertight. They need never be caulked—in fact, you couldn't even if you tried because flexible sealers are applied during building and are always between two pieces of wood where you can't reach anyway.

The early kit boats were planked with ¼, $^5/_{16}$ and ⅜ plywood, the last being the thickest that could be bent and handled by the home builder. I built one with ⅜ plywood and I vowed I would never do it again. That bend and twisting on the forward bottom sections was brutal agony and I once seriously considered slashing my wrists with a sharp chisel.

In my later boats I always laminated with layers of ¼-inch plywood, which is easy to bend and glue together in any shape you want. Remember that. You can do anything with plywood if you laminate. After all, what is plywood? It's just layer upon layer glued together. When you laminate, you are just continuing the process with more layers and more waterproof glue.

The early plywood hulls that were used on the Great Lakes got a lot of people into boating, and quite a few out of boating. They looked good on paper, as the expression goes, but on choppy water they were terrible things to be in, especially for girlfriends and wives who grew to hate boats because of them.

The lightly-planked V-bottom hardchined kit boats, and those built by name manufacturers, all had one major flaw. They were too buoyant and floated high in the water like a cork. Some had no keels or skegs. To understand the importance of a skeg, think of it as a canoe paddle you are pushing back and forth in the water. There is

Fig. 3-23. Boats built with plywood are designed especially for use of this material because there can be no compound curves in the forward sections. The forward "V" in a plywood hull is straight and not concave as with conventional planking. Early plywood boats were boxy and very wet running because that concave "V" deflected water away from the boat.

tremendous water pressure on that paddle, slowing its movement through the water.

The skeg (stern end of the keel) is affected in the same manner when a boat rolls. It performs the same function a shock absorber does on an automobile, which resists up and down movement. The skeg resists side movement. It also acts as a stabilizing fin to keep a boat on a straight line when moving, and not be blown sideways.

Plywood hulls all had small 4 or 6-inch skegs, if they had any. Some only drawed 6-inches of water. One 22-foot cruiser only had 12-inches of hull in the water. With 95 percent of the boat out of the water, they were at the mercy of wind and every little ripple of water. Like a bowl of jello, they never stopped moving and quivering. Life for those aboard was very exhausting, which is why wives grew to hate boating. After a day on the water they would be tired, cranky and have sore buttocks from the constant pounding.

A keel and skeg doesn't stop boat roll; it merely slows it down to where you can live with it and not have your head snapped off. The long, easy, slow roll of a 6-foot-deep-keeled sailboat is restful and puts you to sleep once you overcome seasickness.

These bad points of early plywood hulls is why I kept building new ones, trying to correct the flaws of the previous one. I kept going to heavier structural framing and planking. With extra-thick white oak framing and ¾-inch planking I finally got a soft Cadillac ride on Lake Erie. This lake is very shallow, which makes it just about the most miserable body of water in the world for boating. When you have a large area mass of water and shallow depths, you get steep seas spaced just close enough together to make life sheer hell for anyone in a boat under 50 feet.

Owners of plywood boats are constantly modifying and rebuilding them in an endless search for ways to correct their bad points.

IMPROVING A PLYWOOD HULL

One man who owned a 30-foot express cruiser planked with ⅜ plywood was so unhappy with the way his bottom planking fluttered at planing speeds, he copper-sheathed the whole bottom. This man is a photo-engraver. Through his employer, a commercial engraving establishment, he was able to buy five cases of 16-gauge copper engraving metal in sheet sizes of 24×36 inches. This metal is 1/16-inch thick and very heavy. It was an effort for me to even lift one out of the box when I helped him.

These plates were bolted to the bottom plywood, the stringers and to L-shaped brackets on the inside bolted to the sides of all frames. The reason for this is that screw fastenings into the frames were loosening and backing out. He added two additional longitudinal stringers of white oak, running only between the frames rather then being notched through them. On the ends he fastened them to the frames with those L-shaped brackets, which he made himself out of that engraver's copper plate. Then he added additional intermediate bottom framing. All this was to stiffen the bottom.

He built up the keel and skeg, adding 10 more inches of wood, and copper-plating the sides to help hold it all together. Finally, he doubled the surface area of his rudder, brazing more metal to it.

Although I was skeptical of all this in the beginning, to my surprise, and everybody else in the yard, it worked. The improvements that resulted really justified all that work. The copper plate added almost a half ton of weight on the bottom and increased the draft about 6 inches. This ballast-like weight, plus the deeper skeg, slowed and softened the roll. The larger rudder area, and the new skeg, vastly improved handling and docking. The ride in choppy water was soft and easy, with no more bottom plank flutter.

Two additional bonus features of all that copper is that this boatowner will no longer need to copper paint his bottom. And he has the best radiotelephone grounding system on the Great Lakes. This man is finally happy with his plywood-planked cruiser, if you can still call it that.

This is just what one unhappy boatowner did to overcome the bad effects of an over-light hull which cruises in big water. Copper sheathing a boat bottom is not new, or even unusual—but doing it with heavy 16-gauge copper engraving metal is, I am certain, a first in pleasure craft boating. In retrospect, it was a brilliant idea because this man achieved everything he wanted, like double-plank strength, without putting on another layer of plywood, and ballast weight for stability.

A light plywood planked boat, used on rivers and small inland lakes, will never encounter any of the conditions which make boating on the Great Lakes, especially Lake Erie, so miserably painful at times. The modifications and improvements are of no interest to a river boatman. He wants a light, buoyant hull, quick to get up on plane because when planing, his boat produces the smallest wake.

Big wakes at slow speeds erode river shorelines and bring down the fury of river property owners (Fig. 3-24). A heavy, deep-draft hull at slow speeds will drag behind an enormous wave that can swamp those little fishing johnboats along the shore. River boatmen have no problems with roll, so they have no need for keels or deep skegs. With the price of river gas going up, they want less bottom resistance and weight to push around.

WEDGES, SHINGLES AND HOOKS

On big water, experienced boaters actually prefer to run with the bows high and their sterns buried deep. In heavy weather, this is the best way to go. Only mental cases try to "plane" a boat in 3-foot seas. Moving slowly with the bow up high, you have better control and you get less solid water smashing against your windshield.

However, it was the fashion, and still is, to bring those bows down with all sorts of devices and do-it-yourself with wood "shingles" or "wedges." These are 15 and 18-inch lengths of cedar or mahogany, about 5 inches wide and ¾-inch thick at one end and tapering down to about ¼-inch or less. They actually look like old-fashioned wood shingles, which is how they got the name.

Running across the entire bottom at the stern, water pressure against the "wedge" provided a lift which, in turn, brought down the bow. They worked fine. The trouble is they worked all the time, even when you didn't want them to, like in a following sea when they were downright dangerous. With a single screw, they could cause you to lose control and broach. This is one of the most feared and most terrifying things that could happen to you. It happened to me five times in one afternoon, and I still haven't recovered. That's why I have no use for "shingles," "wedges" or "hooks."

THE PLANING "HOOK"

I unintentionally installed a "hook" on my boat, and it almost caused a fatal disaster. The edge grain of the plywood lays exposed where the bottom planking is fastened to the transom, protected only by paint. For some reason that always bothered me. So I covered it one year with a length of seam batten wood, approximately 1 inch by 2 inches. The transom was at an angle. This created a slight "hook" on the trailing bottom edge. It looked harmless to me because "shingles" installed in this area were usually 18 inches long, and I couldn't see how that little 1-inch of wood could affect my hull's performance. I learned something I will never forget. It's the "little" things that kill you.

At first I was delighted with my boat's sudden improved performance, the way the bow dropped down quickly and I ran level with a smooth wake behind me. It was amazing, I thought, how that little piece of wood could make such a difference. Then, as they say, came the dawn.

I got caught in a heavy following sea running from Erie to Dunkirk. The eastern end of Lake Erie is deep, which makes a different wave pattern, mostly bigger and meaner. My boat took on a strange new character, going from Dr. Jekyl to Mr. Hyde. I could no longer control it at the helm. It seemed to have a mind of its own and did whatever it wanted. Going downhill on a big swell, it would suddenly veer hard to port. Once it started that swing, nothing could stop it. At the bottom of the trough I would be almost flipped over on my beams.

Fig. 3-24. Big deep-draft hulls like this drag such big wakes at slow speeds that they cause much shore erosion. Property owners on two Canadian rivers leading to Wallaceburg and Chatham, Ontario put up signs on their shorelines reading: "Go home, Yank!" The owner of this boat is turning around and preparing to do that.

In sea talk this is called "broaching." In plain talk this is called "disaster." If the following sea is big enough, it will flip you over like a pancake in a skillet.

A law of the sea says never lose control of your ship in a following sea, or a breaking sea when approaching an inlet. A breaking sea has the power of a hundred cement mixers, and you'll think you're in one of them if you ever lose control.

"Wedges," "shingles," and "hooks" all cause a hull to behave erratically in a following sea and, so help me, I don't know why. I'm sure there is a scientific paper buried in Washington archives explaining this just as there is another paper explaining why I scratch and dig at my armpits like a monkey every time I read a scientific paper.

So please accept the proven, established fact (through trial and error) that permanent type "shingle" installations are not for you if you boat on big water. On rivers, however, they can't hurt you, so go ahead and put them on. How thick a wedge is a matter of trial and error. Just remember, a little goes a long way. I would recommend ½-inch tapering down to ⅛ inch as a good starting point. The longer the wedge, the less erratic a hull will behave in following seas.

Fig. 3-25. The mechanically controlled "Trim Tabs" are the safest on single screw inboards with just one small rudder, such as this one.

MECHANICAL TRIM TABS

For the big water boatman who wants trim control of his hull, there is only one good solution. Get the mechanical types that can be controlled, either manually at the transom, or by electro-hydraulic power and push button convenience at the helm (Fig. 3-25). They are called *Trim Planes, Boat Levelers, Trim-Selvs, Step-N-Trim* and *Flex-A-Trim*. The least expensive run $17.50 a pair and are nothing more than shingles in plastic rather then wood. The electro-hydraulic types, the most expensive, run from $300 up to $600 (Fig. 3-26).

Push button control at the helm is the best, if you can bite the cost bullet, because you can fine tune to precisely the right amount of lift at all speeds and, most important, you can turn the thing off, as it were, in a following sea. That is what you must have—control (FIg. 3-27)! Here is a list of manufacturers and a source of further information: *L. Saraga Inc.*, 87 Engineers Drive, Hicksville, N.Y. 11801; *Bennett Marine Inc.*, 20400 Nine Mile Rd., St. Clair Shores, Mich. 48080; *Sky-Way Communications*, 10833 E. Jefferson, Detroit, Mich. 48214; *Diversified Products Co.*, 1136 Venice Blvd., Los Angeles, Calif. 90015; *Boat Levelers Mfg. Co.*, 7305 Natural Bridge,

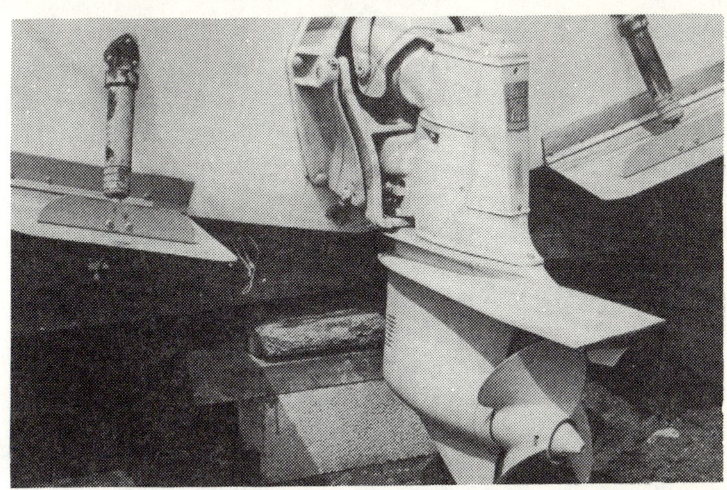
Fig. 3-26. Smaller versions of "Trim Tabs" are available even for outboard drive hulls.

St. Louis, Mo. 63121; *Scott Molding Co.*, Box 2958, Sarasota, Fla. 33578; *Kashoh U.S.A. Inc.*, 15 Roosevelt Ave., Larchmont, N.Y. 10538; *Olson Ind. Inc.*, Box 2520, Sarasota, Fla. 33578.

REPAIRING PLYWOOD PLANKED HULLS

The sheet planked plywood hull is the easiest to repair and paint, another reason for its great popularity. You will rarely find a

Fig. 3-27. Boatmen are resourceful and inventive. This man designed and made his own. It is adjusted manually on the inside.

hull planked with a greater thickness then ⅜, even in boats up to 30 feet. However, Chris Craft did build a 35-foot double cabin cruiser in their Cavalier line which was planked with ⅝ on the bottom and ½ topside. I'm not certain how they bent that ⅝ bottom planking at the bow, but since they already have steaming equipment for bending oak ribs in their Sea Skiff line, I suspect that is how they tamed the plywood. With dry steam you can bend anything.

If backed up with close framing and three or four longitudinal stringers, both bottom and topside, ⅜-inch plywood is adequate up to 24 feet. Beyond that it makes for too light a boat and, with just one engine as ballast it will bounce around like a cork in choppy water, as previously mentioned. In rivers it doesn't matter how light a hull is—in fact, it's even desirable because it cuts down on gas consumption.

Plywood in ¼ and ⅜ inches is easily available anywhere in the United States. I once bought some odd pieces in a drug store. It may not be cheap anymore but you can get your hands on it in a hurry if necessary.

With gouged, holed plywood, you just cut around the damaged area, preferably with a sabre saw and fine tooth blade. A neat square or rectangular cut is best. Don't fool around with round holes. The only place on a hull for round holes is for screws.

MAKING A PLYWOOD REPAIR PLUG

Using the square or rectangular opening as a guide, mark out a piece of new plywood to fit tightly into that opening. Now mark out another piece of plywood about 2 inches larger. Glue these two pieces together with Elmer's waterproof glue. You now have a single sheet of plywood, but with two different thicknesses. In short, you have made a sheet plywood plug that will cover and fill that opening you made in your hull.

There are two ways to secure that "plug" in the hull planking. You can glue it in. Or you can bolt it in with brass machine screws. Personally, I prefer the glue method because this produces a perfect finish job that will be invisible to the eye. I repaired a plywood boat in this manner 10 years ago and you still can't see where the repair was made.

With machine screws you have all those screwheads that must be countersunk, filled with wood dough and sanded down. And the plugged screwheads do become visible, no matter how good a job

146

you do. And if the screwheads are visible, they wave a red flag to any potential buyer that your boat was damaged and repaired.

When you glue that "plug" to the planking, it becomes an integral part of your hull, rather then just something that has been fastened to it with screws. After all, what is plywood? It's just multiple layers of wood glued together, and nothing else. When you glue that "plug" to your planking, you are just adding a few more layers of lamination, using the same type of glue they use at the mill.

I needed some 1-inch plywood once in a hurry. It was unavailable, so I made my own. Two sheets of ½-inch plywood glued together makes one sheet of 1-inch plywood. The possibilities are endless.

Topside the glue method makes a totally invisible finish job on small repairs. Below the waterline, use the machine screw method, but with bronze or Everdur. On bottoms quality is unimportant. I have never seen a boat buyer crawling around on the ground under a boat looking for visible screwheads. But topside they squint and run their hands over the hull, giving it a thump like a used car buyer kicking a tire.

Before gluing you must, of course, remove the paint on 2 inches of wood inside the opening. You must also be able to put a little weight or pressure on the "plug" until the glue sets. This is not too difficult. One of my favorite gluing weights is a cement footing block, which is solid and quite heavy. On a vertical surface, rig up a temporary stand for the block, then lean it against what you are gluing. A long piece of wood can be wedged against something, the opposite side of the hull for example. It doesn't take much. Improvise something.

With your 2-part Elmer's glue mixed, prepare another mixture half-and-half with sawdust. You apply the regular mix to the flat wood surfaces. The sawdust mix goes as a fill in the outside crack. It will sand down to a smooth permanent finish. Fit the "plug" into the opening carefully and put pressure on the inside. Then with a putty knife, push back the sawdust glue mix that has oozed out. Press it in firmly all around, leaving a slight build-up. This will look messy at first, but when sanded down there will be nothing left but a thin dark line. When you later repaint the entire hull, the repaired area will be impossible for anyone but you to locate, except, of course, from the inside. And that inside piece, with the four edges chamfered, will look so much neater without all those protruding nuts and washers. In fact, the wood will look like it belonged there.

I know many seafaring men who are intensely distrustful of anything on a boat that is glued, nailed or stapled. They would never patch with just glue as a fastener. They trust nothing but bolts and nuts. If you are one of these men, okay, forget about the glue. Just use flexible seam or bedding compound on the patch and secure it with about 12 bolts. What kind? If you go to a hardware store and ask for flat head bolts, machine screws or stove bolts, you will always get the same thing. Brass you can get anywhere, even in drugstores. Don't use shiny hardware store brass on the bottom.

If you like the idea of no screwheads to putty on the outside, but still want more than glue holding that patch, put in a dozen wood screws from the inside for insurance. If you're going through two thicknesses of ⅜ plywood, then ¾-inch No. 14 sheetmetal screws will give maximum holding power. Why sheetmetal screws? At short lengths, they have deeper threads than wood screws. Why from the inside? The main purpose of the glue method is to get away from all those tell-tale puttied screwheads on the smooth outside planking. Sure, you can hide them for a while, but eventually the paint cracks around the wood dough and the whole world can see where you damaged your hull last summer when you miscalculated wind drift and hit the yacht club pile driver. I know because I did it.

# The Metal Boats

You cannot go into the subject of metal boats without also going into the subject of metals because there is a relationship between all metals. For example, stainless steel is just ordinary steel with a small amount of chromium added. Brass is just copper with zinc added in various amounts to produce Admiralty brass, cartridge brass, naval brass and just ordinary hardware store brass. There is even a brass with aluminum added for extra strength.

And since metals are used with other metals, it is important to understand how they react to each other, how they help each other and how they often destroy each other. If you own a metal boat, you must understand this when you go to fasten a piece of metal to your boat with another piece of metal. Will they be compatible, or will they fight each other? If they do, one of them always loses. Do you know who the loser will be?

Ordinary steel stains and rusts quickly, but in company with chromium it is rustless. In fact, stainless steel was originally called "rustless iron." Why it is "rustless" was learned entirely by accident when a French scrap iron dealer, inspecting the remains of some old World War I cannon, noticed that one particular cannon barrel was still shiny and bright, unaffected by time and weather, while all the others were badly rusted. He investigated this strange phenomenon and learned that during manufacture, this particular cannon had through some error been "contaminated" with chromium. It had slipped by all the inspectors.

WHY THERE ARE NO STAINLESS STEEL BOATS

At the Cleveland Boat Show there was much interest in a stainless steel hardware display and one man remarked: "If boat hardware, fasteners, shafts and propellers can be made out of stainless steel, then why not the whole boat? If everything was the same metal, then everything would be compatible and there would be no problems with galvanic corrosion."

I thought of that myself many times. Why don't they build boats with stainless steel? Yes, I know it would be very expensive, but so what? There is a great deal of money in this country and a great many Americans have that money, as all custom boat manufacturers very well know.

Henry Burger up in Manitowoc, Wisconsin, is the leading builder in this country of all-metal customized luxury yachts for people who are so rich that, when it comes to cost, they don't have to ask. They just tell Henry Burger what they want, like solid gold faucets in the bathrooms, and he installs it for them.

Now, if one of these buyers decide that they want a Burger yacht built entirely of stainless steel, and with the solid gold water faucets, the cost will be the last thing that might influence them to change their mind. When you have a million shares of Blue Chip stock in your portfolio (you would be amazed at how many Americans do) and you receive annually about 10 dollars a share in dividends, you are not going to be overly concerned about an extra 100 grand added to the cost of your new yacht just because you want stainless steel instead of aluminum. So why hasn't somebody gone to Henry Burger and ordered one of his 80-footers built entirely of stainless? If cost didn't influence their decision, what did? I wondered about his. So I investigated.

The most repeated answer to my question was: "The cost of a stainless steel yacht would be prohibitive."

So what else is new? Is there any other reason? There definitely is.

Although there are many different types of stainless steel, only a few are suitable for marine service, such as hardware, fasteners and propeller shafts. But they would not be suitable for a boat hull because in the salt water environment they pit and corrode. Immersed totally in salt water, the pitting could be disastrous.

The "straight-chrome" stainless steel, also called the "400 series," is highly magnetic, the least expensive, and the least suited for any marine application. This is the type that winds up in razor blades, cutlery, valve seats, pumps and engine components. The "chromium-nickel" stainless steel, called the "300 series," is non-magnetic. This is the type that winds up on your boat in cleats and bow rails because the "nickel" gives it resistance to pitting and corrosion.

Your best marine stainless steel, and most expensive, are the 316 and 317 types which have molybdenum added, an alloy which further increases resistance to pitting. But no stainless is completely free of corrosion and pitting. They are just "resistant" to increasing degree, which is almost a meaningless term.

How bad is the "pitting?"

It will average about 6 to 7 thousandths of an inch per year (.006 or .007), but there have been instances in quiet seawater, where a hull lay moored and unused for long periods, where the depth of pitting reached an alarming 80 thousandths of an inch (.080). This exceeds the thickness of 14-gauge metal, which is .078. Thirty-foot cabin cruisers in ordinary steel are plated with 16-gauge metal, which is .062, or 1/16 of an inch thick. A stainless steel hull, even plated with 14-gauge metal, could in a year's time look like your wife's colander which she uses to drain spaghetti.

Why does stainless steel pit? The reason is called crevice corrosion due to lack of oxygen. It will not pit or corrode on decks where it is exposed to air and sun, but under a fitting that has been poorly bedded down and where water has seeped they will corrode. Painting is no solution because under the coating there is no oxygen. It is the same below the waterline with fastenings and shafts. Barnacles love stainless steel and will cluster all over propeller shafts that remain idle long. And under the barnacles corrosion will accelerate until the metal literally wastes away.

As you can see, stainless steel is not quite the miracle metal you had imagined—not when it is used entirely by itself. However, stainless steel is compatible and holds up better when used with other metals, like a rub rail or propeller shaft on an aluminum or ordinary steel boat. Stainless steel bolts hold up very well in aluminum outdrives, but the same bolts in a stainless steel hull immersed in salt water will waste away. It is very confusing. It is also why nobody is building stainless steel luxury yachts.

Because of an accident and inspection goof, we today have stainless steel, the one metal you can safely use with other metals with no fear of serious galvanic action. That is the reason why stainless steel is used extensively for gears, shafts and bolts in aluminum outdrives and outboard motors. With bronze, the aluminum housing would be eaten away in a short time. Even copper type anti-fouling paints on an outdrive will ruin it in a short time if left immersed in warm salt water.

GALVANIC CORROSION

The chemistry between two dissimilar metals which causes one of them to waste away is called "electro-chemical corrosion," "electrolytic corrosion," "electrolysis," or "galvanic corrosion." They all mean the same thing—that if you place two dissimilar metals in an electrolyte (saltwater, sulphuric acid, etc.), you create an energy cell identical to those little dry batteries you put in flashlights, cameras and wristwatches. The battery in your car is nothing more then lead and zinc, two dissimilar metals immersed in sulphuric acid, the electrolyte. The zinc is connected to the negative (−) pole, the lead is connected to the positive (+) pole. Put a volt meter across those two poles and you will read an energy potential of about 13 volts.

You can test this out for yourself if you own a OVM (Ohms-Volt-Meter). Take a strip of copper and another strip of zinc, magnesium or aluminum, whichever is available. Immerse both strips of metal in a jar of seawater, if available. If not, just put some table salt in ordinary tap water. Connect the terminals of your OVM to the metal strips, the red positive (+) to the copper, the black negative (+) to the zinc. Set your OVM on the lowest scale and it will read about 0.3 volts. You have just created a wet cell battery like the one in your car. If you leave those metal strips in the salt water long enough, the zinc, magnesium or aluminum will completely disappear.

ALUMINUM RADIOTELEPHONE GROUND PLATES

This is exactly what happened to a boater who installed an aluminum ground plate for his new radiotelephone before launching in spring. He had heard that aluminum was a good electrical conductor and was sometimes used in place of copper as, for instance, in battery jumper cables. So he bought two sheets of Reynolds Aluminum, which is readily available in hardware stores, and all the aluminum screws they had.

He put his usual two coats of metallic copper anti-fouling paint on his bottom, then screwed on the two aluminum ground plates, using ½-inch bronze bolts and washers through the hull for electrical connection to his radiotelephone.

He launched the same day I did, the first Sunday in May. The first Sunday in August he heard a strange thumping on his bottom then a vibration as something hit his propeller. He figured it was a small piece of floating debris. But the thumping persisted so he hauled out. Half of one ground plate was gone. It had ripped off and fouled in his propeller. The rest of the aluminum on both sides was just changing, held by the bronze bolts. Almost all the aluminum screws were gone. And this happened in fresh water. In salt water that aluminum would have been gone in days, even hours.

Cold fresh water, like what you find in Lake Superior, is not a good conductor and damage will be minimal and stretched out over years. But this is not so with warm, brackish and highly polluted water with industrial wastes. This makes even "fresh" water a good electrolyte. So don't get careless just because you boat only in fresh water.

What happened to the aluminum also happens to brass screws (zinc copper) below the waterline. The zinc part disappears and the remaining copper is so loose it falls out itself or you can pick it out with an icepick. It will also happen topside and on decks if you use brass to fasten down hardware. These screws are exposed to

Fig. 4-1. Atmospheric corrosion is often overlooked because it is not too well understood. This all-steel boat is a good example. The corrosion here is blamed on "rust."

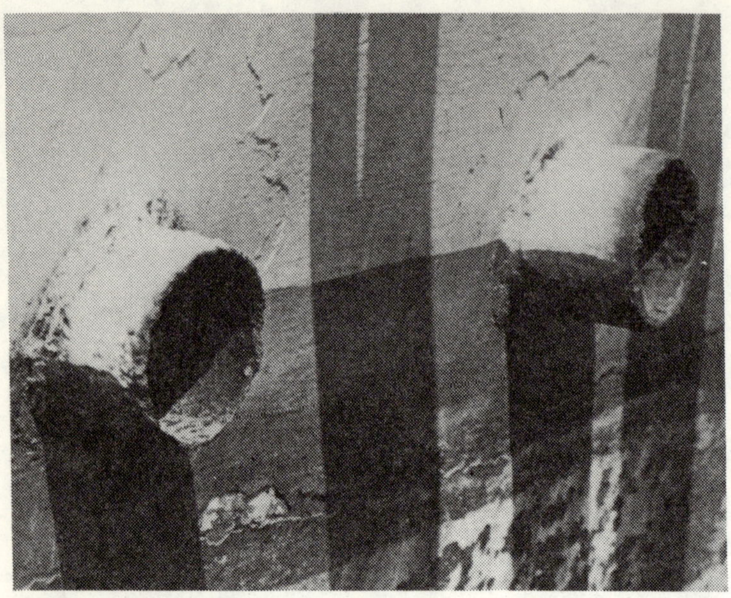

Fig. 4-2. This steel boat used raw saltwater as an engine coolant, which, of course, gets blown out the exhasut pipes. These galvanized exhaust pipes were badly corroded.

saltwater spray and, if you neglect to hose down with fresh water when you come in from sea, they will be attacked.

There is another form of marine corrosion often overlooked because it is not too well understood. This is atmospheric corrosion caused by oxygen, carbon dioxide, sulphur and chlorine compounds in the air—even hundreds of miles out at sea (Fig. 4-1). These four elements cause pitting in metal hulls and hardware (Fig. 4-2).

THE GALVANIC SCALE

The amount of electrical energy produced by two dissimilar metals depends on their position in the Galvanic Scale, the strength of the electrolyte and the size of the two metals (Fig. 4-3). For example, in an auto battery if you want more capacity you get a truck or Diesel battery, or special marine types which weigh almost 200 pounds. They have bigger and thicker plates and consequently produce more energy.

The metals that are low in Table 4-1 are also called "less noble." They are the anodes, the negative (−) end of the electrical circuit. The metals high on the scale are called "most noble." They are the cathodes, the positive (+) pole in the battery.

The difference in electrical potential between two metals depends on their position in the galvanic scale. Your greatest potential, and your most powerful battery, would be one made with platinum/magnesium or gold/zinc. There is hardly a need to explain why this will never be done.

THE SACRIFICIAL ZINC ANODE

Zinc, with its high negative potential, is often used to protect other metals (Fig. 4-4). When electrically connected to another metal, it becomes the "sacrificial" anode. In marine stores they sell zinc for this purpose in all shapes and forms and call them "electrolysis eliminators" (Fig. 4-5). In newspaper engraving plants they use magnesium metal. I have a newspaper friend who owns a 27-foot Inland Seas steel boat and every spring he fastens two strips of this metal to his skeg (Fig. 4-6). He swears it works.

Aluminum is close to the bottom of the galvanic scale. If you own a boat of this metal, you must be extra careful at all times, even when just tying up alongside those high steel bulkheads you find in many river towns. During the Port Huron to Mackinac Race, I have

Fig. 4-3. This rudder had an extension both welded and bolted on the lower end. The brasses, brackets and bolts were all different alloys of brass. The brackets contained zinc and were almost completely eaten away.

GALVANIC SCALE
CATHODES (will not corrode)
Platinum
Gold
Graphite
Titanium
Silver
Stainless steel (passive)
Nickel
Silver solder
Monel
Copper-nickel alloys
Bronzes
Copper
Brasses
Tin
Lead
Lead-tin solders
Stainless steel (active)
Cast iron
Steel or iron
Cadmium
Aluminum
Zinc
Magnesium
ANODES (will corrode)

Table 4-1. This Table Shows Rankings Of Metals On The Galvanic Scale.

seen sailors in aluminum boats tie up to the city's steel bulkheads with anchor chains and steel cables. This makes an electrical connection between two huge masses of dissimilar metal in an electrolyte of brackish polluted water to become one huge battery. In warm Florida salt water, the effects would be instant with paint on the aluminum hull showing blistered bulges in a matter of hours. When you scrape the bulges, there will be white powder underneath.

Although this sounds scary, it's really not all that bad because how often do you tie your little outboard up to a steel bulkhead with steel cables or an anchor chain? This was mentioned only to illustrate how serious electrolytic action can be. All you need remember, if you have an aluminum hull, is don't mix metals when you make alterations, repairs or installations of equipment. Aluminum deck hardware, cleats, bits and chocks are readily available and so are aluminum screws and bolts.

HOW TO IDENTIFY METALS

If you can't get aluminum fastenings, use Monel or stainless steel of the passive type. How can you tell if it's the "passive" type?

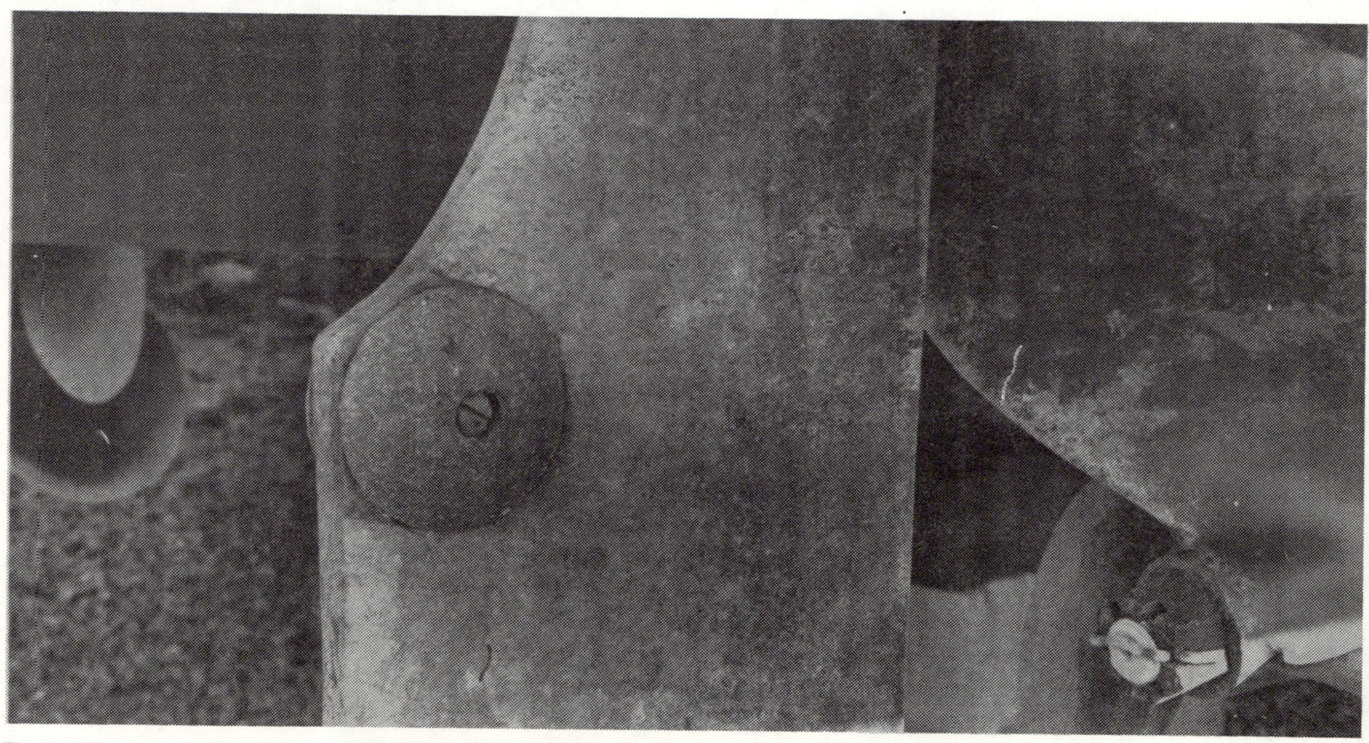

Fig. 4-4. The round object bolted to this rudder is a zinc "sacrificial" anode.

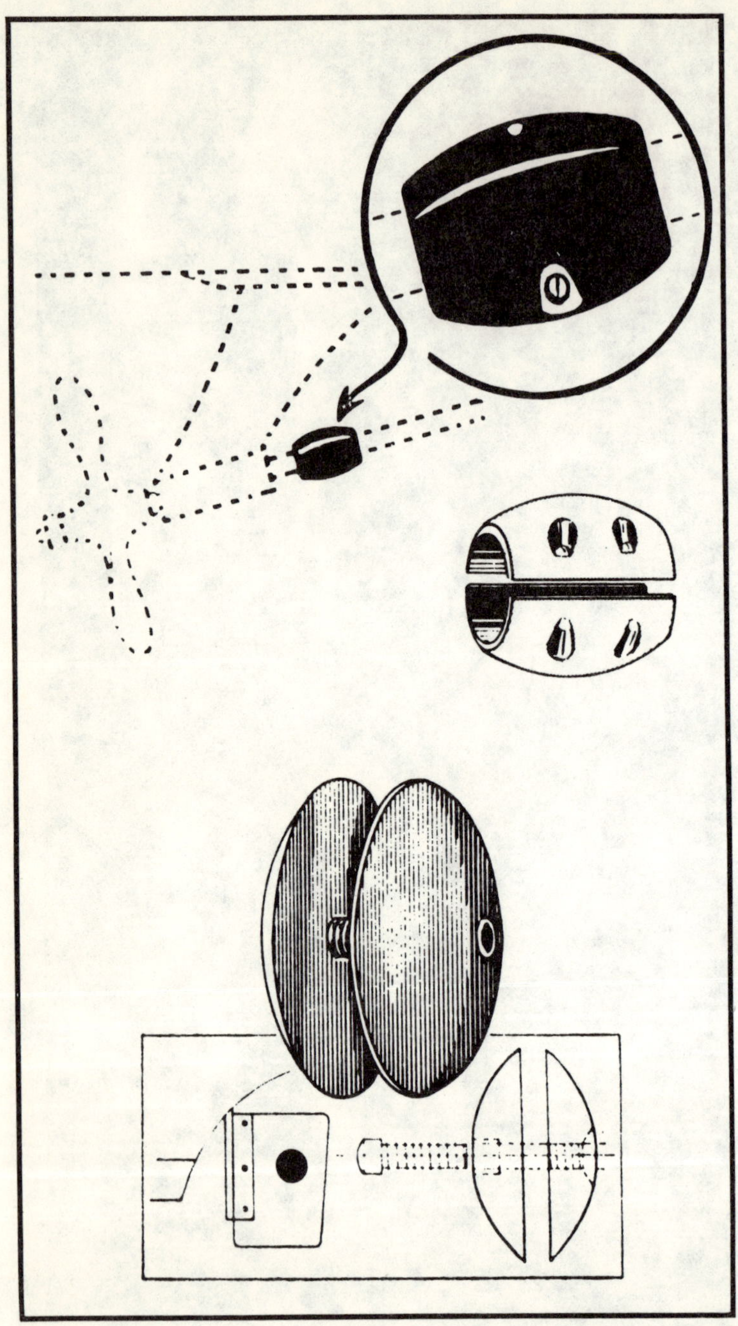

Fig. 4-5. "Sacrificial" anodes are available to fit on propeller shafts, ruders, keels and hulls.

Easy. Use a magnet. The "active" type stainless, the 400 series, is highly magnetic. That means a magnet will pick up the screws. The "passive" types are non-magnetic and will not adhere to the magnet.

A small magnet is a mighty handy thing to have around and will help you identify metals as ferrous or non-ferrous. Fasteners made of aluminum, stainless steel, zinc-coated steel and cadmium-plated steel all look alike when mixed together in a cigar box of assorted screws and bolts, but not to a magnet. A magnet will help you quickly separate the sheep from the goats.

Bronze hardware on aluminum means trouble, unless you use a gasket as a dielectric (insulator) under the fitting (Fig. 4-7). The dielectric material can be a few coats of paint, phenolic bakelite, plastic or a heavy type seam material like Bedlast.

TBTO BOTTOM PAINTS FOR METAL HULLS

There is no "copper" in the tributyltin (TBTO) bottom anti-fouling paints, and this has eliminated the biggest source of corrosion

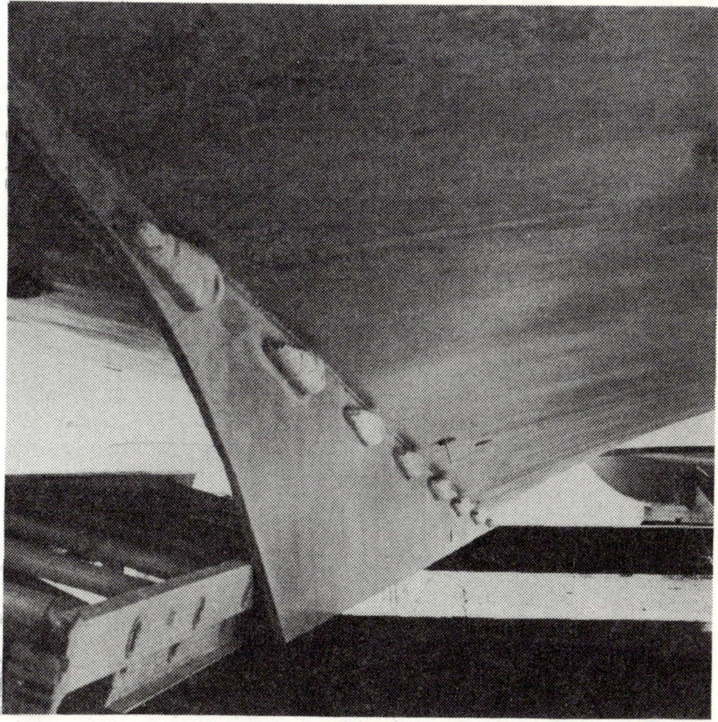

Fig. 4-6. This steel boat owner has gone to unusual lengths to protect his investment with 16 large zinc anodes bolted to his keel, eight on each side.

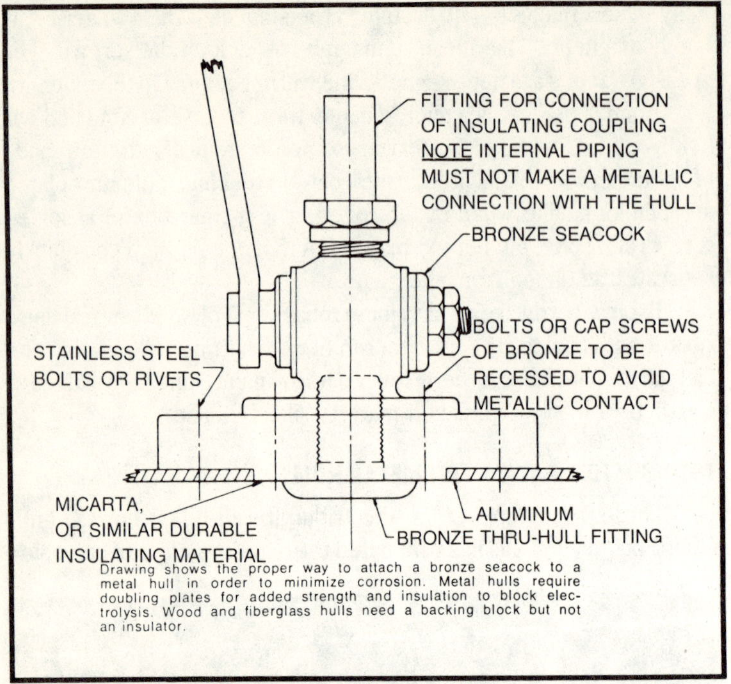

Fig. 4-7. Bronze hardware fastened to aluminum boats must be isolated with some form of dielectric or insulator.

problems with metal hulls. Before TBTO, steel and aluminum bottoms had to be specially washed, primed and undercoated with numerous "barrier" layers of paint to act as a dielectric (insulator) between the copper bearing paint and metal hull. This worked, to a degree, but everytime you scraped off some paint on your bottom, you cut through the protective "barrier" and copper would attack the steel or aluminum. On a small 25-foot boat, it doesn't take long to penetrate 16-gauge metal.

I have never known, met or talked to a metal boatowner who had anything good to say about anti-fouling bottom paints. I often ask them for alternatives.

A frequent answer I get: "Buy the cheapest. I tried one of them damn new paints that don't have copper in them. They're no better. They just cost more."

Another complaint was that to make the switch from copper to TBTO, you had to buy another "system" deal. This meant you had to sandblast down to shiny bare metal and start from there with endless coats of "compatible" products like washes, primers, undercoaters, and then two or three coats of anti-fouling. This can be very expensive, even with a small boat.

With the copper-bearing bottom paints, you must apply endless washes, primers and undercoaters to build up a protective "barrier" between the hull metal and copper. The main advantage of the TBTO paints is that when the bottom is scraped down to bare metal, the TBTO anti-fouling won't attack the exposed metal and present you with some pinhole leaks. All manufactured metal boats today, aluminum and steel, come from the factories with TBTO paints on their bottoms.

BOATER IGNORANCE ABOUT ANTI-FOULING PAINTS

No other product in their line brings marine paint manufacturers as many customer complaints as anti-fouling paints. No other product in their line is as little understood. In the first place, it is not a paint. It is a coating, a vehicle to hold in suspension and a poisonous toxicant that will repel the 600 odd forms of plants and 1300 living organisms in fresh and salt water that are looking for a place to set up housekeeping and raise a big family (Fig. 4-8).

Hundreds of years ago somebody observed that copper stayed clean when immersed in the sea, whereas everything else got covered with growth and barnacles. To this day nobody can explain why, and it is still one of the great mysteries of marine biology.

Wood sailing vessels, and even workboats today, were often sheathed with coppper metal. It worked, but created problems

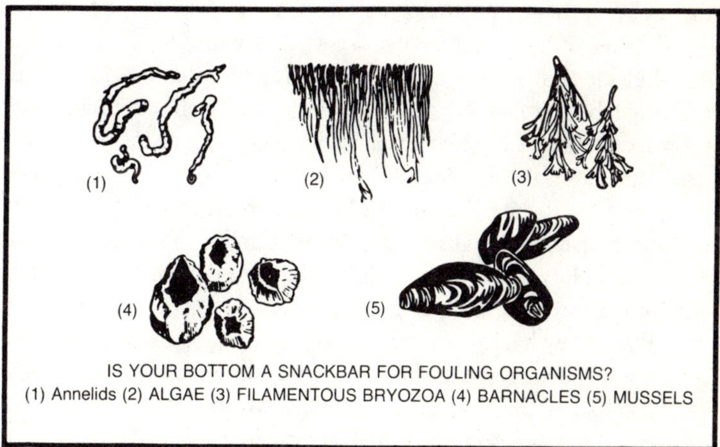

Fig. 4-8. These are a few of the more common organisms that attach themselves to boat bottoms.

because the thin copper sheets were always ripping off, mainly because little was known about galvanic corrosion. The galvanized nails that were used as fasteners would waste away in a short time. Nobody understood why hot-dipped galvanized bolts and screws seemingly lasted forever when used to hold wood to wood, but disintegrated when used to hold copper to wood. But then copper, like women, has always mystified men of the sea.

Eventually someone came up with the idea of putting metallic copper substances into a fluid holding vehicle, and then brushing it on a boat bottom instead of hammering it on with boat nails. And it worked! And it still does.

WHY ANTI-FOULING PAINTS FAIL

Then why is there so much dissatisfaction with copper anti-fouling paints? Copper is copper. Aspirin is aspirin. Nylon is nylon. Only the labels are different.

In this case, something is different—the vehicle that HOLDS the copper. There are soft "vehicles" for slow boats, hard ones for fast boats, and endless others for variations of fouling conditions. You can have different fouling conditions in the same marina. This is how some of the most bitter, violent confrontations come about between boat owners, paint sellers and paint manufacturers. I have had some direct confrontations with the Dolphin Paint Company who put out a very superior bottom paint. And I've written some nasty letters to International, Pettit and Baltimore Copper. I confess now that none of these fine companies were in any way responsible for my failures with bottom paints. So what is wrong?

Let's look at a vintage 35-foot steel Roamer that was hauled out early last September because the owner had noticed an alarming drop in engine RPM's (revolutions per minute) and an increase in his gas/hour rate. In late May when he had launched, the engines peaked at their rated 3800 RPM. He cruised at 2800 RPM and burned 20 gallons of gas an hour. In September the engines would not wind up beyond 2800 and he was burning 33 gallons an hour at wide open throttle, and going nowhere.

When they hauled him out, moss was hanging 6 inches thick on his bottom. Just before his boat had gone into the Travel-lift slings, they had hauled the marina's steel-hulled workboat, and didn't even bother to hose or scrub the bottom because it was clean (Fig. 4-9). They just set it up on two oil drums and a block of wood. The owner of the Roamer walked around that workboat, staring in utter disbe-

Fig. 4-9. This steel workboat was in the water six months and came out clean with no moss or grass on the bottom.

lief at the clean red bottom. Then he looked at his own bottom, with four boys hacking away with brushes and water. Then his face and neck started to get red. When he walked into the marina offices, he was shaking with anger and could hardly speak. This man was convinced he had been conned, cheated and robbed.

Like so many are today, this man was new to boating. He had originally wanted a summer cottage on the water somewhere, but waterfront property is scarce and priced out of reach for even a prosperous used car dealer. So he settled for a boat instead and used it most of the summer as a floating summer cottage.

But the salesman who sold him the used boat didn't know that. Neither did the marina shop foreman who advised him to have the bottom sandblasted and completely refinished with a TBTO system to "eliminate electrolysis." Confused, and a little frightened by all the talk about electrolysis, he let the marina refinish his bottom. The bill for almost $500 upset him, but when they explained to him all the things that had to be done, he paid it.

Then when he saw the clean bottom on the marina's workboat, with "just 20 dollars worth of paint," and the mess on his own boat, "with a 500 dollar paint job," his anger could be understood.

How could this be? Two boats were docked in the same marina and the same fouling conditions; yet one comes out clean, and one comes out with a green shag rug on the bottom. It's hard for a new boater to understand this. No amount of explaining will ever convince the man with the Roamer that he had not been taken and had not been sold something he didn't need.

This man was not taken. He was not overcharged. I know because I was there in the same water. I had the same "crap," as he called it, on my bottom, only I didn't spend $500. I did it myself. But I wouldn't sandblast and refinish somebody else's bottom for three times $500 because it's just too much work. The Roamer job was fairly priced; it was well done because I saw it done.

So what went wrong?

Nothing went wrong. As Jimmy Durante used to say, "and dem's the conditions that prevail."

Let's look at the "conditions that prevail" in every boating area in the country.

There is a saying in India, "You never look at the same river twice." A river is constantly on the move, and so is the sea. The river you saw a moment ago is gone and you are looking at a new river.

The water under your boat is constantly changing. Look at a hundred boats lined up in a marina and the fouling conditions will be different under every hull. Paint every one with the same antifouling, and you will still see a big difference in bottom appearance when they are hauled. Some will be clean like the workboat. Some will be crusted with barnacles. Some will have shag rugs.

Anybody who scuba dives knows that the undersea world, like the world we live in, has a varying topography, plantlife and fishlife. When you drive in the country, you will see thick vegetation and trees one moment, then a barren wasteland the next moment. That's the way it is in the sea. I have tied up in marinas where the water would be 12-feet deep in my slip and thick plantlife would foul in my wheels and water intakes. Yet in the next slip there would be no plantlife growing and I could see the beer cans on the bottom.

Water that is fouled with derelicts and rotting logs offers more food for organisms then a sandy or muddy bottom in a slip just 20 feet away. That's the way it is. Nothing is uniform or predictable just because water all looks the same from up above. It isn't the same, foot-by-foot, gallon-by-gallon. It isn't the same from one day, one season, one year to the next.

As in farming and wine making, there are good years and bad years. For example, 1962 was a very bad year for fouling because we had low water and boats would frequently sit on the mud over beer cans and rocks. Some of the paint got scrapped off. This provides a foothold for some organisms, like barnacles. Then other organisms pile on top and they spread like a cancer. Also, low water in many harbors causes all boats to lay in the mud at their moorings during low tide. This mud in many industrial areas has enough pollutants and chemicals in it to neutralize anti-fouling toxicants and coat the bottoms to prevent any further leaching of the toxicants.

Saltwater anti-fouling is designed expressly for salt water. Salt water is slightly alkaline, but chemicals and other industrial contaminants can increase this alkaline condition to a point where it will stop the leaching of the toxicant, even seal it off. If there are industrial acid wastes in the water, they were quickly deplete the toxicant, leaving the anti-fouling paint virtually dead.

WHY SALT WATER ANTI-FOULING PAINTS FAIL

Other things that screw up salt water anti-fouling paints are heavy rains and floods which bring in silt, dirt and a temporary lowering of the salinity. Salt water paints are designed to leach in a saline solution. Less salinity slows down leaching of toxicant from the paint. Then silt and dirt feed the organisms that are taking hold on your bottom. Weather conditions can also affect slime accumulations. Once your bottom is covered with slime, toxicant release is slowed and even stopped.

Here again there is no uniformity. You can have a great deal of flooding silt, debris and mud in one end of a cove where a stream empties, and practically none at the other end. So all boats would not be equally affected.

HOW ELECTRICITY AFFECTS ANTI-FOULING PAINTS

This is something that would never occur to most boatmen today, that electrical gear was neutralizing their bottom protection. But it is according to the Pettit Paint Company who say: "With the many electrical components put on boats these days, improper grounding procedures occur. Loose electricity in the area around a boat can neutralize the anti-fouling paints on many boats right in the area with rapid fouling conditions. All electrical work should be done properly and checked out thoroughly." This subject will be covered at length in another chapter.

Getting back to the Roamer, this boat was docked in a quiet and remote corner of the marina, almost totally cut off from an influx of fresh water and exposed to very little traffic. The water here was shallow, warm and infested with growth and lily pads. The Roamer spent most of the declining days of a hot summer in its slip, hosting beer parties. These are all ideal conditions for bottom fouling.

The marina workboat, on the other hand, was tied up at the marina gas dock, which was practically in the entrance channel from the lake. This is deep water and an area with as much boat traffic as the Detroit River on a Sunday afternoon. The water here is constantly being churned up by propellers and the wash of passing boats. There are no vegetation or lily pads here.

The workboat also was in daily use, its bottom kept clean by water action with dirt and slime being removed with the soft type bottom paint. This explains why the workboat had a clean bottom and why the Roamer was badly fouled. You just can't make snap judgements at haul-out time on the basis of what you see until you know all the facts. And "dem's the conditions that prevail" wherever you have boats.

If you boat in excessively polluted waters, it might be cheaper to just skip the anti-fouling and use ordinary hard racing type bottom paint. Try this just once, though, and you'll never do it again.

First, there is little to be saved, mere pennies. Second, when ordinary paint gets fouled, it takes a hammer and chisel to get the gook off. The biggest argument for continued use of anti-fouling is that bottoms are easy to clean while still wet. In some marinas all they use for bottom cleaning is a high presure jet water spray. If you have barnacles or thick moss, they tell you to hack it off yourself. They refuse to tie up the Travel-lift too long, so they dump you temporarily somewhere in the yard so you can work on it yourself, but by that time the gook on your bottom has dried and is harder than cement.

HOW TO BUY THE RIGHT ANTI-FOULING

There is no universal anti-fouling paint, or one for all seasons as some boat advertising would have you believe. A Gulf Of Mexico paint is no good up in Martha's Vineyard. A Great Lakes paint will not work in Florida or in the Mississippi River, especially the Delta area below New Orleans. If your bottom was painted in Milwaukee and you plan on cruising down the Mississippi to New Orleans, or down the Intercoastal Waterway to Florida, don't stay too long in one place along the way or you'll collect a lot of new friends on your bottom.

When you get to Miami or New Orleans, haul out and repaint—and before you do, check with local boatmen. Every local-

Fig. 4-10. This boat is never left in the water more than three days at a time. Note how clean the bottom is. If your boat is used like this, you do not need expensive anti-fouling bottom protection.

ity has one special paint which works well in their waters. Always respect the judgement of local boatmen who have learned what works best for them through countless years of trial and error and ignore the bottom paint advertising in boat magazines. Copywriters and ad men do most of their boating and cruising sitting on yacht club bar stools.

WHEN NOT TO USE ANTI-FOULING

There is no need for anti-fouling on your bottom if your boat is trailered and just dropped in the water over weekends (Fig. 4-10). Even a few weeks vacation on some lake won't foul you much because you will be using the boat every day. There are special hard bottom paints especially designed to take the scuffing of in and out launchings and trailering. There are hard, extra smooth bottom paints that reduce surface friction for racing hulls.

HOW OFTEN TO PAINT METAL BOATS

A question often asked by new owners of metal boats is "why do I have to paint every year (Fig. 4-11)? I don't paint my car every year."

If there is no excessive electrolytic action, you don't really have to paint a steel or aluminum boat every year. It's a cosmetic thing mostly. There are no seams in a metal boat. That eliminates paint film cracks. This is the biggest headache with wood, and the reason why many switch to metal—to get away from the annual chore of repairing all those cracks in the paint film over seams.

The boat owners who paint every year, even when they don't have to, are the ones with a fetish about "gloss." They are the same people who wax their cars every month and install seat covers the same day they buy a new car. If you like that glistening eyeball piercing shine on your boat, then paint every year. If you can live without the gloss, then skip the painting for two, three, four years—assuming, of course, that you don't use old tires for bumpers on your dock. If you do, you will spend so much time with SOS pads cleaning black rubber off your topsides, you won't have any gloss at the end of the season.

The determining factor on how often you paint is how often do you scrub down with rough abrasive cleaners to remove those unsightly streaks you get when rainwater washes down all the dirt from the cabin and decks. This has to be the most tenacious dirt in the world to wash away. I can understand why you never see any TV

Fig. 4-11. The big headache with copper bottom paint on wood boats is it cracks, blisters and peels off. You won't see this on a steel bottom.

commercials using boats to demonstrate how a certain brand of detergent removes dirt better then Brand-X.

I have tried every known detergent, including many industrial types, but I have never found anything that you put in a bucket of water that will remove dirt streaks from a white hull with one swipe, like they show you in those TV commercials. You get the dirt off with Ajax and muscle. If you use old tires for bumpers, it takes Ajax and SOS pads plus muscle.

All this scrubbing with abrasive cleaners every weekend is hard on paint gloss. And that is why you paint metal boats every year—to restore the gloss, not because you need more paint.

If you are a gloss freak, paint it every year. If you are not, skip the painting for as many years as you wish, that is, if your aluminum has not been converted into a battery by the metal-to-metal contact between your hull and the copper gasoline lines from your tank to the engine. In that case, you will KNOW when to paint.

TOPSIDE PAINTING OF STEEL HULLS

The mere freshing up of the gloss on a metal hull is easy. You just wash off the dirt, sand down and paint with a brush or roller. To avoid paint build up, the roller is best. It's when you get down to a complete refinish job from bare metal up that it becomes complicated.

All finish paints are water permeable. That means water can get through the paint film. With steel that means rust. With aluminum it means oxidation, sometimes called "white rust." To prevent this, "barrier" coats must be applied. All of the major paint manufacturers have their "systems" for protecting metal bottoms and topsides. Just using Baltimore Copper Paint Co. as an example, not a recommendation, here is their "system" for "bright" metal that has been thoroughly cleaned with emery cloth or sandblasting equipment:

A. 1 coat REGATTA Vinyltex Wash Primer;
B. 2 coats REGATTA Epoxydur Black Mastic;
C. 1 coat REGATTA Vinyltex 3750 Tie-Coat;
D. 2 coats any deck or hull paint.

The epoxy "mastic" is a very tough waterproof coating, which is put up a wall between the water and the metal. A basic rule to remember is always put at least four coats between steel and the weather.

REFINISHING PAINTED TOPSIDE STEEL

If your topsides are in good condition, wire brush all the rust spots, clean thoroughly, and then spot prime with 2 coats of Regatta 3300 Quick Dry Red Lead, or 3302 Zinc Chromate. If you have dents or distortions in the weld areas, you can fair these spots with Regatta Epoxydur Fairing Compound.

REFINISHING PAINTED STEEL BOTTOMS

If your bottom paint is in good condition, with just a few bare rust spots, wire brush the whole bottom, clean thoroughly and then spot prime the bare metal with two coats of 3300 Quick Dry Red Lead. If the bottom is in fair condition, make that 3 coats of Red Lead before you apply the final 2 coats of anti-fouling.

PAINTING ALUMINUM

Refinishing aluminum from bare metal up is a more involved operation than with steel, particularly hulls with welded joints. The big problem with aluminum is getting good adhesion with the larger boats that have complex electrical systems and electronic gear.

REFINISHING BARE ALUMINUM BOTTOMS

Aluminum is a smooth non-porous metal and paint just will not stick to it until you rough it up by sanding with emery cloth or 100 grit sandpaper. If sandblasting equipment is available, use 80 mesh white silica sand.

If you dislike sanding, and want no part of sandblasting, there is another way. The Woolsey Paint Company has a system for aluminum that eliminates the sanding. They use "etching" instead of sanding. They have a pretreatment called a Bare Metal Primecoat which both primes and etches in one operation to provide an ideal "anchor coat" for their paints.

The Woolsey "system" consists of

1 coat Bare Metal Primecoat,
1 coat Barrier Coat,
1 coat Anti-Galvanic "Guardcoat,"
2nd coat Barrier coat,
2nd coat Anti-Galvanic "Guardcoat,"
3rd coat Barrier Coat,
2 coats anti-fouling paint.

The Woolsey "Anti-Galvanic Guardcoat" is a vinyl mastic material basically similar to Regatta's Black Mastic, which prevents moisture penetration and chemical deterioration. When the listed coatings are applied in the prescribed manner, you should end up with a film thickness of 10 to 12 mils (thousandths of an inch), which will also insulate against electrolytic action. The "system," which provides an extra margin of protection for aluminum bottoms against the copper in anti-fouling paints, can also be used for topsides.

In the Regatta line, there are four "systems" for aluminum boats, the "All-Vinyl System," "The Epoxydur Mastic System," the "Vinyl Anti-Fouling System," and the "Simplified System" for small outboard boats having no welded joints and used in fresh water.

THE EPOXYDUR MASTIC SYSTEM FOR ALUMINUM

This one is the easiest to apply, but you must put on multiple coats to achieve a minimum thickness of 10 mils, with 12 being better. This goes over bare metal, which has been prepared with sanding and cleaning.

A. Use 1 coat Regatta Vinyltex Wash to achieve a thickness of 5 mils. (To prepare the above, mix #50 Vinyltex Wash Primer Base with #51 Activator according to directions on container. One gallon will cover 200 square foot.)

B. Use 2 coats Regatta Epoxydur Black Mastic for a thickness of 12 to 16 mils. (For the above you mix #3630

Epoxydur Black Mastic Base with #3631 Epoxydur Mastic Converter according to directions on containers. Apply with a roller).

C. Use 2 coats Regatta Vinyltex Anti-Fouling with TBTO on bottoms. On topsides, apply 2 coats of any deck or hull paint.

THE ALL VINYL SYSTEM FOR ALUMINUM

A. You need 1 coat Regatta Vinyltex Wash Primer for a thickness of 5 mils. (Mix #50 Vinyltex Wash Primer Base with #51 Activator according to directions on containers. (One gallon will cover approximately 200 sq. ft.)

B. Use 4 coats of Regatta Vinyltex #53 Zinc Chromate Anti-Corrosive, 6 mils minimum. Apply with roller.

C. Use 2 coats Regatta Vinyltex Anti-Fouling with TBTO, 4 mils.

VINYL ANTI-CORROSIVE TOPSIDE SYSTEM

A. Needed is 1 coat Vinyltex Wash primer. Mix and apply as in directions for bottom paints. Allow 1 hour to dry.

B. Use 2 coats Vinyltex #53 Zinc Chromate Anti-Corrosive. Allow 1 hour drying between coats.

C. Use 1 or 2 finish coats of deck or hull paint.

CONVENTIONAL ZINC CHROMATE TOPSIDE SYSTEM

"A" is same as above. In "B" you use #3302 Zinc Chromate. Apply two coats and allow 3 to 4 hours between coats. "C" is same as above.

Small Aluminum Boat Topside System

"A" is same as above. In "B" you apply 1 coat of 3204 Undercoat White; allow an over-night dry. In "C" you apply 1 finish coat of any hull paint.

Simplified Bottom System For Small Aluminum Boats

A. Use 1 coat Vinyltex Wash Primer—5 mils.

B. Use 2 coats Vinyltex Anto-fouling with TBTO.

WELDING

Before World War II it was considered impractical to build pleasure craft in steel less than 60 feet long. At that length, the plating would be at least 3-gauge steel, which is ¼ inch (0.250). This was the thinnest steel that could be welded without excessive warping or buckling. Smaller boats were built of thinner metal, but they were strictly commercial types, workboats and barges where faired hull lines were considered unimportant.

The only small steel boats in the private pleasure craft field were converted steel lifeboats which were riveted and bolted. There were companies that specialized in converting lifeboats, building up from the double-ender hull with decking, cabins and 25 h.p. Gray Lugger engines. They were hideous looking things, contemptuously referred to as "rusty barrels." I helped a friend with a valve job on his engine and I got seasick while we worked tied up in his slip. It was Sunday and the wash from passing boats kept us rolling constantly.

Better welding techniques developed during the war made it possible to successfully weld steel down to 18 gauge, which is slightly less then 1/16 of an inch. This opened up the pleasureboat field to steel. Aluminum was slower developing because this metal

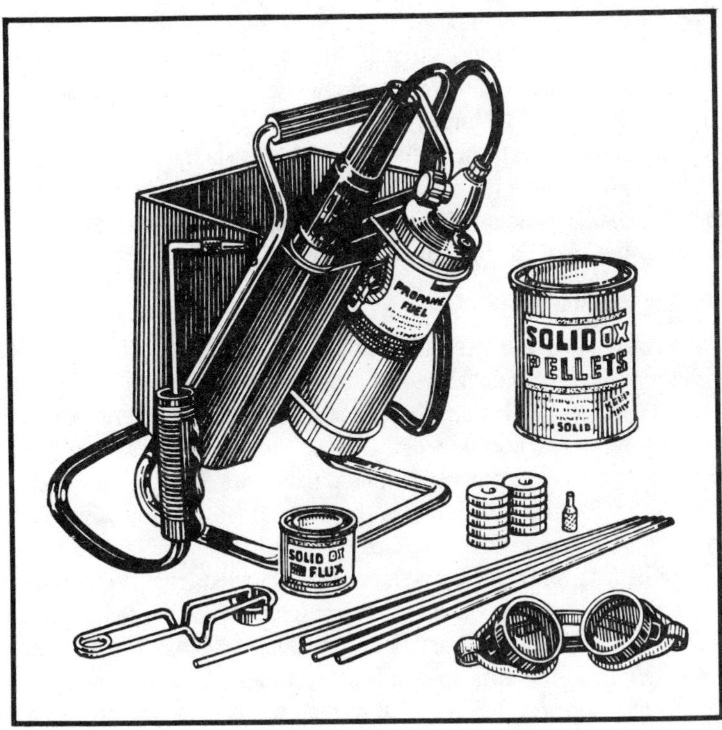

Fig. 4-12. Oxygen-gas and arc welding has become a do-it-yourself thing with all the new mini-welders suddenly available.

has always been, and still is, tough to weld. For this reason, all early aluminum boats, mainly small outboard, were riveted.

After the war, aluminum alloys that were totally unsuited for marine use were being picked up cheap on the war surplus market and used to build boats. Aircraft aluminum and rivets just didn't work out in the marine environment and, as a result, aluminum got a bad reputation.

New alloys and new welding techniques also developed in aluminum. Today, because of the energy situation, aluminum and fiberglass are squeezing out wood and steel as the leading building materials for big pleasure yachts and smaller boats for weekend yachtsmen.

Welding is a subject rarely even mentioned in boating magazines and books because until just recently, few boaters knew anything about welding, or even wanted to. But today there is a proliferation of new mini home-type oxygen/gas welders that you can buy at Sears, Wards or Penny's for $29.95. They use oxygen in dry pellet form; the gas is propane (Fig. 4-12). Electric arc home shop welders have been around for years and now they're getting smaller, cheaper and more attractive for the do-it-yourselfer. Sears and Ward's now have a 50-amp model that works on a 115-volt house circuit fused for 15-20 amps.

If you own a metal boat, inevitably there is going to come a day when you will need a weld job. So, for the first time welding is going to be touched on at length in a boating manual—not to teach you how to weld, but how to stay out of trouble.

Welding Aluminum

Professional welders call aluminum a "dirty" metal. Contact with the atmosphere defiles it and makes it difficult to weld because oxygen and nitrogen instantly combine with the molten metal, which causes a weak and porous weld. It wasn't until a way was found to protect and isolate the weld zone from the atmosphere that aluminum welds became good as the metal itself. This new way of welding aluminum is called TIG or "heliarc" welding.

In heliarc welding, the weld zone is shielded from the atmosphere by an inert gas which is fed through the welding torch (Fig. 4-13). This gas is either helium or argon. Because of this 100 percent protection from the atmosphere, heliarc welds are stronger, more ductile and more corrosion-resistant than welds made by any other process. If you own an aluminum boat, all the welds were made by this process—at least I hope they were, for your sake.

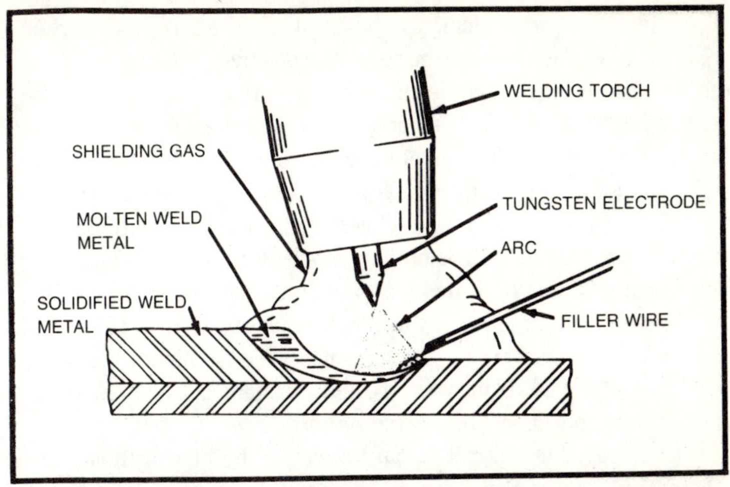

Fig. 4-13. Heliarc welding of aluminum is not for the weekend do-it-yourselfer because the smallest heliarc outfit costs about $2,000.

Do-It-Yourself Aluminum Welding

Although aluminum is today highly weldable, it is still beyond the capabilities of most do-it-yourselfers. I tell you this mainly to protect you, the poor American male, from all those assaults on your manhood in advertising coming at you from all directions. There's that one with the gorgeous thing in a string bikini standing beside a 295-amp arc welder. Her I can understand, but I can't understand why I bought a 295-amp arc welder because I never use it.

The instruction manual that comes with my welder makes it sound so easy to weld aluminum. It says: "Welding aluminum is not difficult, but does require more care then welding other material." The man who wrote that never welded anything together but baloney and bread with butter.

The manual continues: "The materials needed are a carbon arc torch to heat the aluminum to a molten state, and a special flux-coated aluminum welding rod which is used to add metal to the work being welded when it reaches the molten state."

In brazing operations, and welding aluminum, you work with a carbon arc torch, which to me has always been the easiest way to weld because this is just high heat soldering. With a simple soldering iron you have very little heat and work with 600-degree solder. With a propane torch you have more heat, but still not enough to braze. With the carbon arc torch you go up to 10,000 degrees which will melt just about anything, even a banker's heart.

The carbon arc welding torch is basically the same as a carbon arc light. There are two carbon rods, one positive, one negative, and the tips are brought together until voltage arcs, producing intense heat and light. This light is so bright that, like the sun, it can cause serious eye damage if you don't have the right type of dark lenses in your protective helmet or goggles. It can also cause severe skin burns. So you must also wear gloves and protective clothing.

The carbon arc torch is nothing more then a very hot soldering iron which you hold over the work area until the metal and welding rod melt and fuse together, as in simple soldering (Fig. 4-14). If you can solder, you can braze. You can also weld aluminum the same way. It won't be as strong or corrosion-resistant as the other welds in your boat, but it will be a weld of sorts.

I will say that aluminum can be welded by one of those mini 50-amp welders at Sears and Ward's, but if you're looking for an excuse to buy one, read further. I have welded aluminum many times, but always in a workshop under the best control conditions.

The Critical Moment in Welding Aluminum

As in Fig. 4-14, you hold the carbon arc in one hand, the aluminum filler rod in the other. You heat the work area until you notice a slight rise on the surface. This means it is melting underneath, the critical moment, the moment of truth, as it were, in welding aluminum.

The aluminum filler rod, which has been held close to the heat, is now pushed under the surface where it will melt and fuse with the molten aluminum out of the atmosphere. You can not fuse the two metals on the surface as you do with soldering. This is the whole secret of welding aluminum—getting away from the contaminating atmosphere. At that critical moment when the surface starts to buckle and rise, you push the filler rod through and under the surface where it melts and fuses, protected from the atmosphere. This is precisely what heliarc welding does, but in a more elaborate and expensive way. The cheapest heliarc outfit will cost about $2000.

If you understand what I have just explained, you can weld aluminum. If you don't, forget it.

The fact that you now know how to weld aluminum still doesn't mean that you can pick up a 50-amp arc welder at Sears, rush out to the boatyard, plug into a 115-volt outlet and start repairing some damage to your hull from last summer. The welds that I was referring to were made on aluminum bars and angles that were ¼-inch

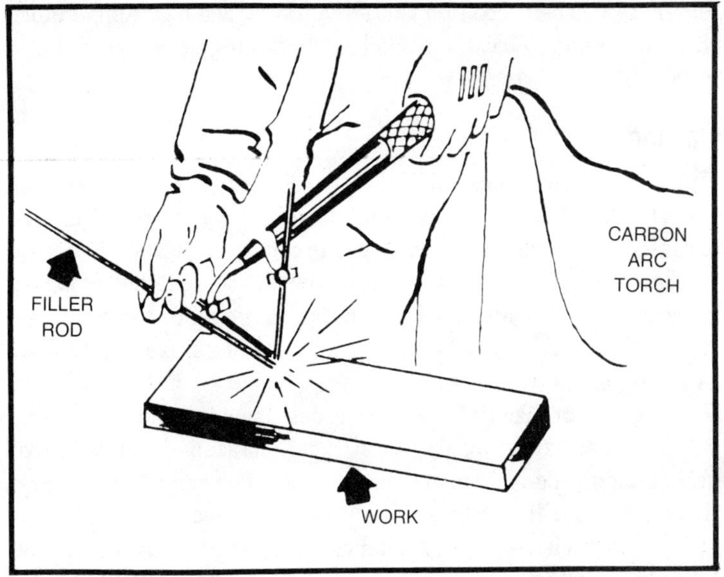

Fig. 4-14. The carbon arc welding torch is just a very high-heat soldering iron that will melt anything.

thick. Now consider what would happen if you heated up two pieces of 18-gauge aluminum (less then 1/16 inch), and then at the critical moment, pushed the filler under the buckling surface. Can you guess? You would push a hole right through the thin molten metal.

When working with thin gauge metals, such as you find in small boats, you just don't have enough thickness to push through to get under, and you can't work on the surface in the atmosphere. Your metal thickness must be at least ¼-inch. You just don't find aluminum boats with hulls that thick until you get up to about 50 feet.

Thin gauge aluminum can only be welded by heliarc, which is how your boat was built. This is true also of other thin metals, especially paper-thin automobile bodies. It is impossible to weld auto bodies by conventional methods because the metal is so thin; you just burn holes. Any welding that you might do on an aluminum boat will be limited to heavy structural pieces and castings, like hardware and outdrives. With thin aluminum, like the hull plating on small boat hulls, forget about welding.

Welding Steel

You may not be able to weld thin steel, but you can braze it, which in many cases is even better then welding. There is no limit to

the things you can repair on a boat by brazing and high temperature
silver soldering. You can join different metals together, like cast iron
to brass, iron to steel.

BRAZING

Brazing is a process of joining two different metals together by
use of a third metal. In brazing, lower temperatures are used
because the metals are not brought to a fluid or plastic state as in
welding. Carbon arc brazing is still the best known method of joining
galvanized iron because the lower temperature tends to protect the
zinc coating on galvanized iron. The strength of a brazed joint is only
as strong as the third metal used.

Copper, bronze and brass are easily brazed. Almost any metal
on your boat, excepting aluminum, can be brazed—even with that
mini 50-amp welder. Many electrical connections on a boat are best
silver soldered. If you have ever seen electronic gear after it has
gone through a winter lay-up under canvas, you will understand why.
Everything will be corroded and stuck. Electrical switch connections
will have excessively high resistance; some won't even work. Converted iceboxes with compressors in the bilge have long copper lines
and fittings to be brazed. I used sweat solder on these fittings once
and they didn't last a week.

If you can solder, you can braze. Using the carbon arc as a
soldering iron, you heat the work until it becomes a dull red. Then
you hold the filler rod under the flame where it will melt and fall on the
work area. That's all there is to it.

There are two methods of brazing. One is called the "fusion"
method. The other is called the "bonding" method. The difference
between them is temperature. In fusion, the work and filler rod are
both heated to the same temperature. In binding, the work is heated
to a considerably higher temperature than the filler rod so that when
it is finally added, it flows into the porous surface of the work. For
this reason a bonded braze joint is stronger then a fused joint. Where
you want maximum strength, use the bonding method. Where
strength is not important, and where you do not want to overheat the
materials being repaired, use the fusion method.

THE 50-AMP ARC WELDERS

The main attraction of those mini 50-amp welders is that you
can plug them into an ordinary home circuit. You should consider
them as nothing more then high temperature carbon arc soldering

irons for silver soldering, brazing small items like the fittings on
½-inch copper tubing. But when it comes to cutting and welding, that
is a different story.

In cutting steel with a welding torch, you work at the highest
heat setting. Fifty amps will just barely cut you a hole in an automobile fender. But you can do that with a steak knife or can
opener. In fact, two juveniles were arrested in Pontiac, Michigan,
for mutilating cars with a can opener.

I recently drilled two ⅛-inch holes in a car body with a slow
speed cordless drill. It took exactly one second per hole to go
through that thin metal. I helped a friend install an antenna mount on
the side decking of a 27-foot steel cruiser. Using a high speed drill
and a new ⅛ carbon steel bit, it took him 20 minutes to drill two
holes. On that kind of steel a 50-amp welder would be useless.

THE SOLID OXYGEN MINI-WELDERS

When I asked a highly skilled industrial welder at American
Shipbuilding in Lorain, Ohio, which he liked to work with best, arc or
gas, I got a pained look and a shrug. When I persisted, he said: "I like
'em both."

"But if you had to make a choice," I said.

Again I got a pained look. "In shipbuilding we gotta use both.
There's no other way.

"But for your own personal use. If you could only have one,
which would you take?"

He scowled, pondered a moment. "I guess I'd take the arc."

"Why?"

"You can do more things with arc. Of course, it don't cut worth a
damn, but it welds faster and better. I can weld a ¾-inch hull plate in
less than an hour. With gas it would take half a day—and the welds
wouldn't be as good. But, man, for cutting you can't beat gas."

I tried one more question. "What do you think of those new
mini-hometype welders that use propane, gas and oxygen in dry
pellet form?"

He stared at me in open disgust, turned abruptly and walked
away without answering.

Boatowners who have bought one of these "welders" all have
the same complaint: "Just when you've got enough oxygen to braze a
broken winch handle, you run out of oxygen."

And that tells you everything there is to know about the 29
dollar solid-oxygen gas "welder."

If you are seriously thinking of doing your own boat welding, wait for sales at Sears and Ward's. At this writing, you could buy Ward's 295-amp for $149. It is listed in the catalog at $209. With this welder you can even build a steel boat.

STEEL HULL REPAIRS WITHOUT WELDING

You are not going to hole a steel hull too easily, but you can sure dent and buckle them without even trying. The easy, professional way steel boats are repaired in commercial yards is to neatly cut out mangled metal with oxygen-gas torches, weld in new metal, grind down the outside hull welds, prime and paint. Everything looks like new.

Aboard all Navy ships there are a damage control crew and a complete inventory of steel plates and girders in all types and sizes, and the best welding equipment for instant at-sea repairs. That's the nice thing about steel, it's so easily repaired on big ships.

On small ships it can be just as easily repaired, but rarely is unless some insurance company is paying the bills. But when you've got $100 deductible, and you hit a red buoy in the channel some dark night, it's embarrassing to explain that red paint on your hull. So you fix it yourself.

Hammering out dents and buckles in hull plates is no different than hammering out dents and buckles in auto fenders. You just hammer much harder, you sweat much harder and you swear much harder because there is nothing between here and Tupelo, Mississippi, that is hotter then a steel boat in July and August.

Automobile bump-out dollies can be bought at any auto parts store, but they're not too useful because it is difficult to coordinate the work of two men, one hammering on the inside, one on the outside with a dolly.

The most useful tools for hammering out dents from the inside are ¾-inch steel rods in various lengths up to 36 inches. The long length is useful for getting at dents in those hard-to-reach places like back under the galley sink. You just lay the flat end of that 36-inch rod up against the dent and hammer until you've pushed it all out.

Final finish bumping is done on the outside. But you need solid back-up support on the inside. The best thing is the steel plate on the end of those steel screw-jack posts which are used in home basements to support sagging floors. They come in three sizes, adjusting 20 to 36 inches, 36 to 56 inches and 56 to 93 inches. You'll find them in the Sears and Ward's catalogs at 9 to 15 dollars. By bracing this screw post against the opposite side of your hull, you can push out really large dents. The flat plate on the end of the post gives you a good dolly surface on which to bump from the outside of the hull. You can do a credibly good job this way. Deep scrapes, gouges in the metal, and other imperfections can be taken care of with auto body repair compounds.

REPAIRING A HOLED STEEL HULL

If you have actually holed your steel hull, rare as this is, and you are not equipped to weld, you can repair a small hole with fiberglass—that is, after you have done all the preliminary bumping out and have a reasonably smooth surface to work with. The *Fibre Glass Evercoat Co., Inc.*, 6600 Cornell Road, Cincinnati, Ohio 45242 has a line of special repair kits for metal boats, steel and aluminum. They also have specialty items, like "Fix-a-dent," to take care of scratches, dents and rusted out areas in steel boats. Their repair kits come with complete step-by-step instructions.

If your damage is extensive, then you better go with welding. A good welder can oxygen/gas remove damaged metal so neatly it will look like it has been cut with a hacksaw. Then he will arc-weld new metal to your boat and grind down the welds. After it is painted, you will never know where the damage was. That's the beauty of steel; it's so easy to repair with welding.

REPAIRING ALUMINUM HULLS WITHOUT WELDING

You bump out dents and buckles in aluminum hulls in the same manner as explained for steel, only it's much easier. With small outboard hulls you can work with the hand dollies. On larger hulls, and larger dents, you will have to resort to basement screw-jack steel posts to muscle out the buckled area. If you hole an aluminum hull, you have the same options as with steel. You can fiberglass the damage yourself or you can have it heliarc welded by a professional. Either way you'll be traveling first class.

The Sailboat

There has never been any lack of interest in sailing, but now with the energy crisis, even "stinkpotters," (power boatmen) are switching over and becoming "rag boaters." There is also new interest in that old hybrid, the motor sailor. However, it takes more then a checkbook to make a sailor. They are a very special breed (Fig. 5-1).

I know not one power boater who made the switch and liked it. They feel pretty much about sailing as the late newspaperman Daman Runyan who wrote, after covering the America's Cup Race, "it's like watching grass grow." The man in the power boat wants to go someplace, he wants to move, and he always has a destination in mind. A sailor, however, has arrived at his destination the moment he steps aboard his boat. That's why sailors care nothing about going someplace. They say to you, "Where is there to go when you're already there?"

So every weekend you see them on rivers and lakes, sailing back and forth, and looking so serenely contented and happy when they tack across your bow and you have to slow down because they have the right of way. Sailors have more fun than people. They are the only truly happy boaters (Fig. 5-2).

Most power boaters hate maintenance. Painting and sanding interferes with cruising, like from one yacht club bar to the next. Sailors love to sand and paint because they love their boats. Rarely will you find a power man who really loves his boat. He's always thinking about the next boat he's going to buy that will have a bigger

Fig. 5-1. Here is one old power boat man who switched because of the energy crisis. He and his family are taking their first sail with the dealer.

AC generator so he can have air conditioning. The "rag" boater already has air conditioning—the wind in his sails.

A WARNING TO POWER BOATERS

For power boaters who are seriously thinking of switching to sail, be sure you have the right temperament for sailing. If you hated maintenance on power boats, you'll hate it even more on sail because there's more of it. You can survive and get by being a dummy in a powerboat, as you can see any weekend. But no dummy survives very long in a sailboat. It takes brains to sail. It takes brains to care for a sailboat because there is so much to take care of, so much to understand. You don't just turn a key and shove off with a sailboat.

As a former powerboater ruefully remarked at the club bar, after his third Scotch double: "When you crank that rag up that stick, funny things start to happen."

Yeah, and it gets even funnier when you forget to drop the centerboard on a hard reach.

THE CLASS BOATS

If you are still determined to make the switch, then you are probably wondering what all that talk is about "class boats." There are three: "one design," "open class," and "development class."

The purpose of "one design" construction is to make for complete uniformity in racing. If you own a "one design" hull, you can take that boat anywhere in the world and the boats you compete with will be exactly the same as yours. That makes for a fair race because all things being equal, the skipper with the most savy always wins. There is no such thing as luck here. It's all brains. The only leeway you have in giving yourself a little edge is in how you slick up your bottom with super smooth, friction-free racing finishes. And what makes you think the competition isn't doing the same thing on their bottoms? Other than this, everything else is equal. It's brains against brains and if you're a powerboat dummy, one design is not for you.

In your "open class" and "development class" there is no uniformity in hull length, beam and sail area as long as the boat measures up to a specific design limit, like 12 meters for example, which takes into account all such variables as length, beam, sail area, etc. You can experiment all you wish, increasing or decreasing the length, beam and sail area. But when you run it all through a computer, it must add up to exactly 12 meters. In other words, you can change anything you wish, just so everything averages out.

The famous America's Cup Races are a 12-meter class. Countless millions have already been spent building and designing new boats for that race, on the American side to keep the famous cup, on the British side to win it back. All the boats are different in size,

Fig. 5-2. Sailors are the only truly happy boatmen.

shape and appearance, but they all average out as 12 meters, which makes them equal in that respect. And that is the purpose of "open design," to encourage experimentation and development of new ideas and designs.

Class boats are to sailing what the Grand Prix and Indianapolis Speedway are to automobiles. The tires you drive on today were developed on "class" cars that tear up dirt tracks on raceways all over the country. New winches, spinnakers, Dacron sails and lines were first tested on class boats. The same is true with new scuff-resistant paints and racing finishes. Class boats are trailered and shipped all over the world.

The people who sail these boats are in the top level of intelligence, even kids in their damn little snipes (Fig. 5-3). All my life I've been dodging them in narrow channels. They are so smart they frighten me, like that snotty-nosed boy who tacked close to my transom and yelled back: "Hey, mister, your port engine is running rich. Black smoke's comin' out the exhaust."

And he was right. That's what made me so mad.

There's something about sailing that attracts only the best. If you decide to switch from power to sail, you will be joining the elite. If you buy a used boat, you will be working harder on maintenance chores then ever before because there is so much more to do, so much more to check out.

The most important thing on a sail boat is the rigging. The most important part of that rigging is that tall stick in the center which is called a mast. A lot of things happen on that piece of wood. It holds up the sail, it has tracks and fittings for stays and shrouds and it has sheaves for halyards, cleats, electric wire and lights, spreaders for the shrouds, wind-speed-direction indicators and radio-phone antennas. The mast is the crankshaft and pistons of your boat's engine.

THE MAIN MAST

How many masts your boat has depends on how it is rigged. If it has one, it is probably a sloop. If it has two, it is probably a ketch or yawl, depending on the position of that shorter mizzen mast in the rear. If it's aft of the helm, your boat is a yawl. If it's forward of the helm, your boat is a ketch.

If your main sail comes to a point at the top of the mast, you are Marconi rigged. If it is fastened, instead, to another spar at the top, you are gaff rigged. This type rigging can get by with a shorter mast, which can be an advantage. Still, the Marconi rigged sloop is the

Fig. 5-3. The kids who sail the One Designs are the brightest youngsters you'll find anywhere. Sailing seems to attract brains.

most popular around today because it is the simplest and easiest for one person to handle alone. You can raise, lower and reef without leaving the wheel.

For the junior executive, nursing his first ulcer, there is no more soothing balm or cure for fingernail biting than an afternoon of sailing in the peace you get only when wind alone moves you through the water. The silence is almost hypnotic. This is why sailing has such an appeal for smart, ambitious men—men like John F. Kennedy, who was an ardent sailor. There are times when a man just has to get off by himself to see if his head is screwed on right. The fiberglass sloop, in the 20 to 30-foot size, is today the most popular and fastest selling boat around. In the long run, a sloop is cheaper than full time therapy with an analyst.

THE WOOD MAST

If the used boat you bought is more than 10 years old, the mast is probably wood also. Wood masts are relatively easy to maintain and easy to check because they are always varnished. You can see if anything is wrong. That is the reason why you never paint a wood mast. Paint only conceals defects like cracks, rot and loose fastenings. If everything is in good shape, you sand down and then varnish with at least two coats. Three is better.

WHY HARDWARE IS NEVER REMOVED

You always varnish around all hardware attached to the mast, like cleats, tracks, etc. As an old power boat man, you are accustomed to removing all hardware before painting and varnishing because it is neater. But that annual in-and-out with the fastenings enlarges and eventually strips the threads in the wood. You have a loose piece of hardware on your mast, which you can get along without, believe me.

In sailing, the failure of one little item, like a broken turnbuckle or a sheave pulling out, can start a chain reaction that will have you carrying on two-way conversations with yourself. People down at the office will start shaking their heads and whispering behind your back.

If everything on your mast is tight, leave it that way. When I say "tight" I refer to fastenings. I do not say you should go around giving every screwhead another quarter turn. This is the worst thing you can do because it inevitably strips the wood threads.

Fastenings don't back out by themselves. If they're loose, there has to be a reason, like soft wood. And soft wood means rot. If it is rot, don't over-react and get drunk. Refer back to the chapter on dry rot, fix the soft section with "Git-Rot" and re-thread with larger screws.

THE MAST HEAD

The best time to check and work on a mast head is before it is stepped (put back in the boat) and not after in a bosun's chair. The bosun's chair is strictly for kids and jockeys who weigh 95 pounds and is not for anyone who has to consult a calorie counter every day before ordering lunch. And besides, it isn't everybody who feels comfortable perched on top of a high pole replacing stuck sheaves.

The mast head is subject to great stress and strain, and this is one place where you don't want anything working loose (Fig. 5-4).

Fig. 5-4. Much depends on smooth action and trouble-free operation of the sheaves. So check out the mast head before you step the mast.

Check everything for tightness and corrosion. Check welds for cracks. Be sure all bolts have lock washers or self-locking nuts and all clevis pins are secured with cotter pins in good shape (Fig. 5-5).

There is nothing more aggravating than a sticky sheave on the mast head. Few men realize the wear and tear to which it is subject. That wheel in the sheave is small and every time you hoist and lower sail, it turns many revolutions—and sometimes at tremendous speed. It's like the man who bought a boat trailer with very small wheels and then couldn't understand why the tires blow on the first fishing trip. He didn't realize that when his car was moving at 60 mph, the small trailer wheels were rolling along twice as fast at 120 mph.

When you drop sail hurriedly, the little sheave wheel is traveling at great speed. Don't be surprised to find excessive wear. If you do, replace it. The top of that pole is one place where you don't want anything less then 100 percent because it's a long ride up there in a lousy bosun's chair on a hot day in July.

You've heard that old saying about "for want of a nail a battle was lost," etc. A lot more "battles" have been lost on sailing ships for want of a cotter pin. This simple little device, costing pennies, can sometimes mean life or death when it breaks or drops out of a clevis pin. The cotter pin is always attached to some critical component or hardware on which so much depends. Turnbuckles are just one example. Shackles and sheaves are another. The shackle is a device used to secure anchors to chain, then to line (rode). The shackle clevis pin is secured with a cotter pin. If that pin falls out, goodbye anchor, goodbye ship. There are countless tales of boats losing their anchors at a critical time, drifting up on a rocky shore or reef to be battered to pieces.

According to a recent news story out of Groton, Connecticut, even the U.S. Navy has this problem. America's newest attack submarine dropped its anchor and lost it. The USS Philadelphia, completing its second trial run, dropped anchor outside New London harbor because the Thames River near the Navy's submarine base was foggy. The anchor was dropped, its chain slid free and followed the anchor to the bottom of Long Island Sound.

This news item, I'm sure, wound up on the bulletin boards of every yacht club in the country because only us dumb pleasure boaters do things like that. The other end of the anchor rode is supposed to be secured with a shackle to an eyebolt in the stem. The Navy doesn't say, but either the shackle was not secured, or the clevis pin fell out.

There are hundreds of things on a sailing vessel, even power boats, that will not function very long without that ridiculous little thing called a cotter pin. Yet there is nothing on a boat that is more taken for granted. Two cans of assorted cotter pins is standard equipment on my boat. If I have to remove a cotter pin for any

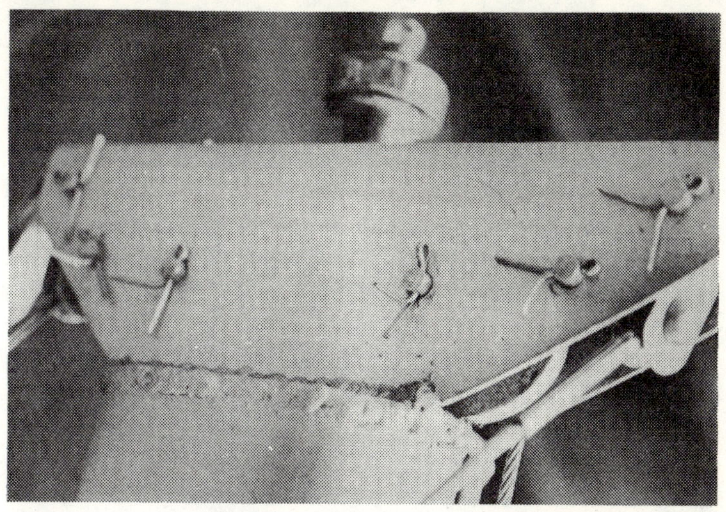

Fig. 5-5. Be sure all the cotter pins are in good shape. Also, check the welds for cracks and the sheave clevis pins and the sheaves themselves for smooth action.

reason, I never use it again. I throw it overboard and install a new one.

The wind indicator is a delicate and sensitive device, overly affected by corrosion. Usually all it needs is a good cleaning with brass wool and some light oil. The light and antenna connections are also subject to corrosion and should be cleaned to cut down losses through resistance. If you have light connections on the crosstrees, check them also.

THE SAIL TRACK

The sail track is another taken for granted device, until it causes trouble. One of life's great aggravations to a sailor is to get the mast stepped, the rigging tuned, and then discover that the sail slides stick half way up the mast. If you hate bosun's chairs like I do, it means you hire some kid to go up in the chair and clean out the track.

Cleaning out the sail track should be the last thing you do before stepping the mast. No matter how careful you are when painting or varnishing, drippings off the brush will get into the sail track, where it dries hard and gives you fits. Another problem with sail tracks is moths. They like to spin those little fur balls in tight corners, and they always do this about half way up the mast. Run a spare slide up and down the track to make sure it runs smooth and doesn't stick on paint, varnish, cocoons, metal burrs or protruding screwheads.

THE MAST STEP

If your mast is wood, check the mast step for rot. Water is always running down the mast and keeping this area wet. For this reason, it should be liberally "poisoned" every year with a fungicide. When the mast is stepped, it should fit snug and tight with absolutely no play. If there is movement (there always is), use wood wedges to snug it down tight. Also, swab down the wedges with fungicide.

If your mast is aluminum, the step should also be aluminum, and bolted down with stainless steel, not bronze. Because of the proximity of bronze keel bolts, there could be galvanic action here. If there is, the metal must be protected with paint just as aluminum hulls are protected from copper bottom paints.

REPAIRING A BROKEN MAST

A broken wood mast can be repaired, and many boating books go into great detail on how to go about doing this. I will not. And for a good reason. The smart people who sail are too smart to waste time repairing a broken wood mast when it is so easily replaced with aluminum. Most sailors with wood masts have been just waiting for an excuse anyway to buy a new metal mast. They are in no mood to patch up an old wood one that has probably been giving them trouble with cracks and dry rot in the step. Twenty or thirty years ago I would say yes, fix it up, but not in today's throwaway economy.

I know very well how to repair a broken mast. Even with my boatbuilding skills and experience, though, I would not care to patch up a sick old spruce mast with glue, bolts and scarf joints. I don't think I could make a good scarf joint. And if I can't do it, neither can you or all the other accountants, pediatricians, dentists and tax lawyers. And you are all too smart to try.

THE ALUMINUM MAST

The aluminum mast is light and doesn't require ten men to carry to the storage area in the fall. It doesn't have to rest absolutely level to avoid taking a permanent set. If anodized, it need not be painted. If not, it should be painted. Refer to the previous chapter on painting aluminum boats.

Paint is necessary to protect the aluminum mast, both from atmospheric corrosion and galvanic attack from hardware attached to it. Bronze winches should be isolated with a block of wood, or other insulating material like nylon, plastic, teflon, mica, etc., and fastened to the mast with stainless steel screws (Fig. 5-6). The

Fig. 5-6. Bronze halyard winches must be isolated from the aluminum mast. Remove the drum and check around the base for corrosion.

same is true with all the other hardware like cleats, sail tracks and sheaves. Don't try to use aluminum fasteners. It takes quite a bit of torque to drive a sheetmetal screw into metal, and the aluminum fasteners break too easily.

THE MAST COLLAR

Mast collars are a chronic trouble spot on all sail boats. They always leak and keep the mast step wet. They also keep the hot decking, an area prone to rot, permanently moist. Checking the collar once in the spring is not enough. Movement of the mast is always opening up new leaks—and the mast should not move. If you see cracks in the collar, that means the mast is working. This is bad for reasons other than leaking. It can damage the surrounding deck.

Check those wedges in the step—in fact, check them often during the season, after every sail. When loose, just give them another wack with a hammer.

THE KEEL

There are two basic hull types in sailing vessels. One has a deep, weighted keel and the other has a centerboard. Without either, plus a rudder, a sailboat will not sail. Water pressure on the keel, plus an opposite air pressure on the sails, moves the hull through the water. To illustrate, hold a piece of soap between two fingers and squeeze. What happens? The soap squirts out from between your fingers. That is exactly what happens with a sailboat. Water pressure on the keel is one finger. Air pressure on the sail is the other finger. The hull is the soap. Squeeze and the hull moves. The rudder is vital to sailing in that it maintains pressure by adjusting to different wind directions and sail angles.

The deep, weighted keel also serves to stabilize the hull and keep it from turning over. The hull with a weighted keel behaves like those toy dolls with rounded bottoms that always return upright after being pushed over on their sides. Keel boats have been flipped over on their beams, sails awash in the sea, and yet, like the doll, have returned upright. So long as all hatches remained closed and their watertight integrity is not violated to destroy buoyancy, the keel boat will remain afloat and keep swinging back up. This is why the keel boat is considered the most seaworthy of all craft. They are almost unsinkable, until holed to admit the sea. Then they sink like a rock.

The keel, made of lead, cast iron or concrete, can weigh many tons and is bolted to the hull bottom with long keel bolts. The nuts are visible on the inner keel. These keel bolts should be carefully inspected every three years for corrosion because you don't really know, with an old boat, what type of metal was used. There are bronzes and there are bronzes. The same is true with stainless steel. Then there is hot-dipped galvanized iron, much used in the past on the Great Lakes.

In fresh water, galvanized keel bolts will last forever. But they will not in salt water. Check the nuts with a magnet. If they stick to the metal, your keel bolts are either galvanized iron or stainless steel, the highly magnetic type which will not hold up when sealed off from the atmosphere, as keel bolts do. This type of stainless steel will corrode and waste away, even faster in some instances then old fashioned hot-dip galvanized.

REPLACING KEEL BOLTS

Replacing keel bolts is a job best left to the commercial yard because they will have to be hammered out from the inside. It's quite a job and requires raising the hull high enough to insert new bolts from below. They can be over 6 feet long. These are not really "bolts." They are solid bronze rods, cut to exact length, and threaded on both ends to take a nut and washer. Sometimes the nut and washer on the bottom end is brazed to the rod. Then with the hull lifted up high in the Travel-lift slings, the rods are pushed and hammered up from below. This is a job the yards will undertake only in the winter off season because it will tie up the Travel-lift for days, even weeks. They don't just lift you up in the air 8 feet and replace those bolts in a half hour. Since you don't own a Travel-lift, this is not a do-it-yourself job.

THE CENTERBOARD HULL

The centerboard hull type's chief advantage is shallow draft. With the board up the hull will float on "a heavy dew," as they say in Chesapeake Bay country. Except for an occasional few bars of pig iron in the bilges for trim purposes, the centerboard hull has no permanent or fixed keel. When under sail, it drops down a "board" which serves the same purpose as a keel—a surface on which water can apply pressure.

When not in use, the "board," usually a plate of steel or bronze, is swung up into a narrow compartment right in the center of the main cabin. All sorts of devices are used to conceal the identity of ths obstruction, like making it look like a dinette table. This is the biggest objection to the centerboard hull, that annoying centerboard trunk in the cabin.

On a Lightning, the centerboard is easily handled by manually pulling on a short line secured to a cleat. On a big ocean cruising ketch, there will be two centerboards, each weighing half a ton and raised and lowered by special electric power winches with controls at the helm. When making long passages under engine power through canals and innercoastal waterways, the centerboards can be used as an anchor by just dropping them down into the mud.

The centerboard hull is also less stable. Any sudden or unexpected gust of wind will flip the hull over on its beams, as very frequently happens during races. However, since the centerboard hull is not weighed down with heavy ballast, it remains afloat and nobody gets hurt, just wet. Two men, a boy and a girl, using the centerboard for leverage, can raise the boat easily and bail it out with a bucket. I've done this many times. It's crazy, but it keeps the kids off the streets.

The centerboard plate rides on a pin. Both the plate and pin wear away, which makes for a loose, sloppy and noisy connection. Since you can't make a hole smaller, you make the pin larger.

PAINTING INSIDE THE CENTERBOARD TRUNK

The centerboard itself, depending on what metal it is made of, should be painted accordingly. If it is copper (my favorite centerboard metal), you can skip painting. If it is steel, refer to the chapter on painting steel hulls.

The inside of the centerboard trunk is so difficult to paint that many don't even bother. This is a mistake because it can get so covered with barnacles you can't move the centerboard, or even clean it out without dynamite.

Painting inside is easier then you think. Get a strip of ⅜-inch plywood about 4 inches wide and 48 inches long. On one end, tack a strip of carpeting material so it runs over the end and covers both sides. Soak this in anti-fouling paint and just slop it around. Be sure to wear gloves because you will also be slopping paint on that length of plywood, which will run down on your hands and up your arms. You will waste a lot of paint and money. But you'll get the job done—and I didn't say it would be cheap. I just said it would be easy.

THE RUDDER

On a single screw powerboat, the rudder is sometimes useless, like when moving astern when the propeller and rudder exert opposite forces and literally fight each other. In twin screw you can ignore the rudder and steer with just the engines alone.

In a sailboat, however, you can't do anything without the rudder because it is an integral part of the power train itself (Figs. 5-7 and 5-8). Without the rudder there is no power, and you just lay in the water with your sails flapping.

The rudder holds a sailboat in a certain postion rather than "steers" it. You don't really "steer" a sailboat as you do with power—in a straight line from A to B—because the wind isn't always blowing in the direction you want to go. Most of the time a sailboat

Fig. 5-7. Here are the inboard rudder and deep keel.

travels in a zigzag manner. This is called "tacking" back and forth until you eventually arrive at your destination.

The rudder holds the boat in those tacking positions to get the best wind angle on the sails and the best water pressure on the keel or centerboard. The instant you release the wheel, the rudder will swing dead ahead and you will lose the wind and lay dead in the water.

Laying "dead in the water" is also called "heaving to." Sailboats do this in a storm. The wheel is lashed to keep it from swinging. All sail is dropped, except the mizzen, which is shortened to act as a weather vane and keep the bow into the seas. The ketch and yawl, with the mizzen, is popular with ocean sailors. You can heave to with the mizzen and ride out a storm. If you're away from the shipping lanes, where you can get run over at night, you can batten down the hatches, go below, lash yourself to a bunk and sleep for a week.

The keeled sailboat, in any length, is the safest vessel in long ocean passages—safer then many oil tankers and freighters. On a sailboat, damage to the rudder means total loss of power. At sea this can mean disaster, unless you've got plenty of food and water. I hope

Fig. 5-8. Shown is the outboard rudder.

by now you are properly impressed with the importance of your rudder and give it the attention it deserves.

The sailboat rudder takes a terrible beating because it is under constant pressure and strain—not only on the external rudder itself, but all the mechanical control gear back to the helmsman's wheel. The simplest, strongest, and most foolproof steering hook-up is through worm gear at the helm and steel wire on big pulleys to a quadrant tiller (Fig. 5-9). There are special hot-dipped, galvanized, heavy-duty block and cheek pulleys for this type of steering along with ⅜-inch flexible steel wire and huge galvanized turnbuckles with locknuts.

These items are minimum requirements for anything over 25 feet that goes to sea. In a recent Admiral's Cup Race, one of the entrants was named Kiss, taken from the first letters in the unwrit-

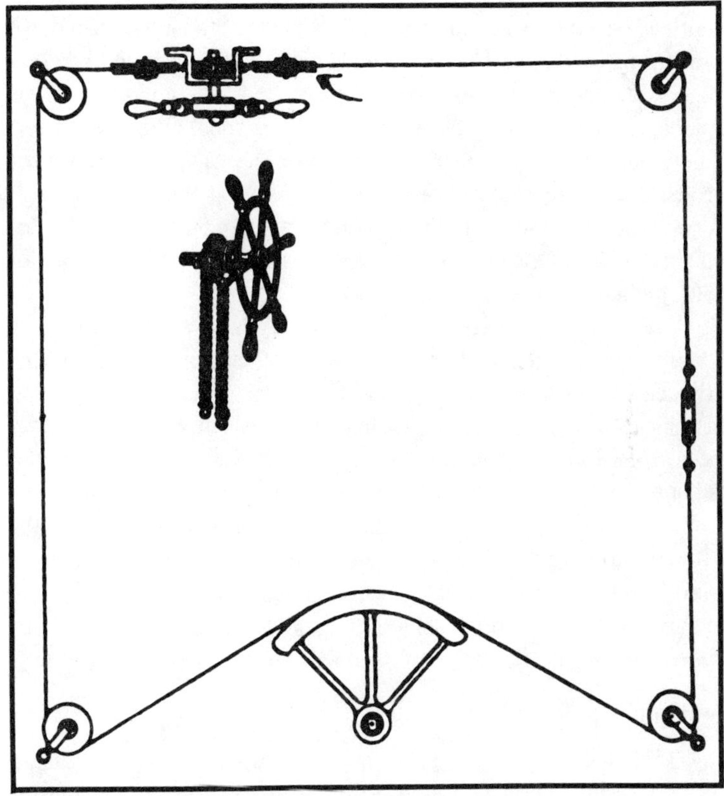

Fig. 5-9. This is the oldest and simplest steering hookup that will never break down.

ten code of the sea "keep it simple, stupid." That could be amended to say "keep it strong, stupid."

Where your life and safety are concerned, always remember Kiss. The type of steering hook-up described is very simple, very strong and very foolproof. The only thing that ever goes wrong is the wire will loosen up if the turnbuckle locknut is not tightened.

There are many new types of steering hook-ups to a helm wheel, which are just fine for controlling twin inboard rudders, outboard drives and outboard motors. But I would never trust my life to them out in the Gulf Stream between Miami and Bimini. The Gulf Stream terrifies me. When I go out there in a sailboat, it will not have a rudder controlled by a lot of complicated plumbing, hydraulic fluid and rubber tubing that I can't easily service with tools I have on board.

I cannot tell you what to do with your particular rudder control system. I can only suggest that you set aside one afternoon to doing nothing else but examining your rudder and everything attached to it and from it, whether it be a simple tiller arm or a helmsman's wheel.

Rudders in old wood boats will also be made of wood, not one piece, but many and held together with long rods. Over the winter, the wood dries out and shrinks. Through the gaps you can see the rods. Note if they are shrinking in diameter. If there are splits or checks in the wood, you can fix them by fastening metal cheek plates on both sides of the split. On smaller boats, check the bronze pintles and gudgeons for wear (Fig. 5-10).

After you have carefully checked everything, ask yourself if you would feel comfortable taking your wife and kids on a sail from, say, the Yacht Basin in Newport Bay, California, to Catalina out in the Pacific on a hazy day when you can't see the island. If you can answer yes, then I guess your rudder is, for your peace of mind, in good shape and doesn't need any attention. And for this you are entitled to an insignia of membership in the International Association of Rescued Mariners, which is a solid gold four-leaf clover pin affixed to a simulated fur rabbit's foot. It will, hopefully, bring you lots of luck because anybody who absolutely trusts his rudder will also trust a used car dealer. Such a man needs all the luck he can get.

STANDING RIGGING

There are two kinds of rigging on a sailboat. One type runs. The other just lays there. So long as your rigging stays that way, you are in good shape, an international Lightning champion once told me. But

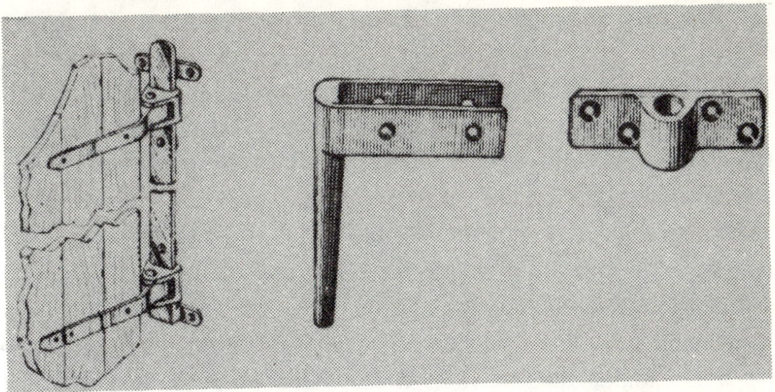

Fig. 5-10. Nobody ever thinks about pintles and gudgeons until their rudders just lift up and float off by themselves. They do have the self-locking type.

when the running rigging starts to stand, and the standing rigging starts to run, you are in trouble.

Translated, that means that running rigging should always be free to run, move, and not get hung up or jammed in a block because of a kink. When the running rigging will not "run," you can lose control of your ship, be unable to jibe at a critical time and collide with other vessels.

Standing rigging is supposed to do just that, stand! When it moves, it's because something has gone wrong. Something has let go; perhaps a turnbuckle has snapped or a shroud has parted. Then a revolting sequence of developments will occur—you will get hit in the head by a falling mast and buried under a mass of wire. If you don't get killed, consider yourself lucky and start immediately going to church regularly. The next time you may not be so lucky.

MANILA RIGGING

Except in places like Hong Kong Harbor, you will very rarely see rigging, either standing or running, of manila rope. When you do see it, you will also see bamboo hoops insted of mast tracks and slides, and a little old lady cooking over a charcoal fire. The only users of manila rope today are ocean freighters and the U.S. Coast Guard fleet of cutters. They use manila for hausers—monstrous things up to 4 inches in diameter. They are so big and heavy that they have to be payed out in stages. An ocean freighter, tied up for loading, will have three of these docking lines at the bow, four amidships for spring lines, and three off the stern. That adds up to a fantastic amount of rope. If those 4-inch hausers were nylon, they would probably cost a million dollars.

Manila is absolutely verboten for rigging in an American sailing vessel, and is rarely used today even for dock lines because it has the habit of shrinking when wet. This makes it extremely difficult to set dock lines with just the right amount of slack, yet not so loose you swing and bang into your neighbor. Marinas and yacht clubs are getting downright hostile with boatowners who don't tie up their boats properly. It's almost impossible to do this with manila. Manila is being squeezed out of the pleasure boat market by synthetics like nylon, dacron and polyolefin.

Nylon is best for anchor rodes and docking lines because it stretches under tension (Fig. 5-11). This is highly desirable in docking lines and helps to reduce shock when a boat tosses and pitches in its slip when some clown forgets to reduce speed and drags a big wash. Stretch is also desirable when riding at anchor in rough water because it reduces the strain on mooring bits.

However, stretch is not desirable in running rigging because you could never get your sails set properly. Dacron, which does not stretch, is the favorite running rigging in small sail boats. Dacron is expensive, but will last for years if properly cared for—and this few sailors know how to do.

SOME FACTS ABOUT SYNTHETIC ROPES

Although everybody in boating uses rope, nobody really understands them. They just assume that a rope with a tensile strength of 2500 pounds is like, wow, what more do you need? Figures on tensile strength are very misleading—in fact, they're downright deceptive. There is a safety figure to be considered, which they don't tell you about. To determine the safe working strength of rope, you use the figure five. Multiply your load by this figure. For example, if your load is 500 pounds, multiplied by five, your rope must have "tensile" strength of 2500 pounds.

We are talking about new, fresh rope right off the store reel. Kinks and knots change everything. New rope has an almost fiendish way of kinking on you. If you're in a hurry, or just careless, putting a strain on those kinks, or running them through a block, will weaken the fibers of the strands. The rope will deteriorate rapidly and fail you someday at a critical moment when you jibe suddenly to miss some clown in an outboard who never read rules of the road.

Concerning those knots you learned to tie at Power Squadron classes last winter, did anybody tell you that knots reduce the tensile

Fig. 5-11. Nylon is best for anchor rodes and docking lines because it stretches under tension and acts as a shock absorber.

strength of a rope almost 50 percent? The much used clove hitch and bowline reduce the strength 60 percent.

So what happened to that "2500 pounds" you started off with? You're down to a safe working strength of only 300 pounds, and you can get that much of a load on a Snipe mainsheet if you reach hard in a stiff wind. Why do you suppose they have all those expensive winches on a sailboat? Winches handle the terrific loads on running rigging. Without winches to do all the hard work, it would take the muscle of a big crew to handle the running rigging on even the smallest boats. The average boater, easily cranking the handle on a deck winch, or halyard, just doesn't appreciate the load on the rope itself, until one day it parts and all sorts of strange things start to happen.

LENGTHENING THE LIFE OF RIGGING ROPE

There are some basic rules you must follow to lengthen the life of your running rigging if it is dacron.

203

■ **Kinks**. When unpacking new rope for re-rigging, handle very carefully and put no strain on it. Pull slowly through the blocks until all the twist has been worked out. This causes kinks—twist in the rope that occurs when you just pull it out of the coil. Pulling a kink through a block will drastically shorten the life of the rope.

■ **Avoid small blocks**. If you re-rig with larger rope, then go to larger blocks as well or you will have excessive wear from increased internal friction when the larger diameter runs through too small a block. There is also external friction where the rope chafes against the sides, or cheeks, or the blocks. Rigging rope should match the blocks through which they run. The block shell should be 3 inches for ⅜-inch rope; 4 inches for ½-inch; 5 inches for ⅝-inch; 6 inches for ¾-inch; 8 inches for ⅞-inch; 9 inches for 1 inch; and 12 inches for 1¼-inch rope.

■ **Don't overload.** If you ever exceed 75 percent of a rope's tensile strength, you will permanently damage it. To continue using a damaged rope could be downright dangerous because it might fail on you at a critical time.

■ **Guard against slipping.** It is bad practice to let rope slip on the drum of a winch and then suddenly snub it. The sudden jerk as it is snubbed weakens the fibers. It's even worse to let the rope lay against the revolving drum of a winch because enough heat can be generated by friction to melt the outer layers of synthetic fiber.

■ **Equalize the wear.** Halyards take a lot of wear on one end. You can equalize this wear by turning the rope end-for-end. A small section of rope that is repeatedly stretched around a cleat will not run smooth through a block. Most of the wear and tear on running rigging is going through blocks and sheaves that are not properly aligned. This causes the rope to chafe against the sides or cheeks of a block.

HOW TO SELECT NEW BLOCKS

There is a natural tendency among sailors to buy stainless steel hardware on the mistaken belief that it will last forever. This is a fallacy because there is some stainless steel that won't last a year in a semi-tropical saltwater environment. So don't be oversold on stainless, especially when buying new blocks. Blocks made of soft synthetic material will cause no damage to your boat when they are dropped or banged, as so frequently happens during a hard day of sailing. Deck blocks for mainsheets and jibsheets do a lot of flopping around and banging on decks, especially when the sails are luffing.

On metal blocks, the cheeks will be thin and the edges sharper. On soft synthetic material, the cheeks will be thick and the edges will be rounded to cause less chafe damage.

Why Blocks Fail

When will a block fail? According to Murphy's Law, a block will fail on you precisely at the moment it can cause you the most embarrassment and discomfiture. How do you prevent that? By not sending a boy to do a man's job.

The Right Size Blocks

For a small day sailer or cruiser, you should have blocks that will handle ⅜-inch rope and have a load capacity of 1,000 pounds. A medium-size sailboat will require blocks to handle ½-inch rope or ⅛-inch wire. The large boats (35 feet and over), should have ⅝-inch rope or 3/16-inch wire with a working load on the blocks of from 2,000 to 2500 pounds.

When you get up to blocks for ⅝-inch rope, they are quite large and cause damage when they hit the boat. For this reason a soft impact material is best. If the boat is used in salt water, blocks with openings in the cheeks and sheaves are desirable for easy flushing out with fresh water.

If your boat is used for both racing and cruising, you should consider blocks with grooves in the sheaves to handle both rope and wire. In racing, wire is preferred for running and solid steel rods are best for standing to cut down on wind resistance. However, the rod is very expensive and you will rarely see it on cruising family boats.

The toughest test for rope, blocks and wire is at the masthead or jibhead. The halyards at this point must make a 180 degree turn and are under constant load. These sheaves, at the very least, should be grooved for wire. You can get by with rope sheaves in the other blocks, but if you run a wire halyard through a rope sheave on the masthead, both the wire and sheave will be damaged.

SOME FACTS ABOUT WIRE ROPE

Wire rope, also called cable, is used for everything on sailboats from raising and lowering the centerboard to holding up the masts with rigging called shrouds, headstays, backstays and bobstays. The rope is also used for rigging which runs and is called halyards, topping lifts, furling lines, jib sheets, main sheets, mizzen sheets and outhauls. It is also used for lifelines, steering cables, lanyards, slings for tenders, trailers and winch cables. It is very strong and ⅛-inch wire will do the work of ½-inch rope. It is corrosion-resistant, never needs any special maintenance and is easily available in any size, stiff or flexible, to suit your special needs. And because it is so strong and trouble free, nobody thinks too much about the rigging until it breaks. Then they want to know why.

Why Wire Rope Fails

When wire rope fails, it is for three reasons: it has been exposed to excessive chafing; it has been run through blocks designed for larger size synthetic rope; and it is the wrong wire rope for the job.

Wire rope chafes excessively sliding through frozen blocks and when permitted to slip on winches before snubbing. It chafes when rubbing on fairleads, reaching struts and spinnaker poles.

When the wrong type of wire (like super flexible 6×42) is run through a block without wire grooves, under load it tends to flatten out like a garden hose that has been stepped on. This causes friction and rubbing between the fine strands and they break, setting into motion a chain reaction which breaks other strands.

A wrong type of rope would be super flexible 6×42 for halyards. This rope has maximum flexiblity and minimum strength and resistance to chafing because of the fine wire strands and center core of fiber. A far better wire rope for halyards is 7×19, with a flexibility rating of 6×37 IWRC and a core of metal rather then fiber. The "IWRC" designation means "independent wire rope core." That center core of metal prevents flattening out under load when running through a small sheave.

The Two Types of Wire Rope

Wire rope is manufactured in two types for marine applications, preformed and non-preformed. Although it may not seem like much, and hardly worth the extra cost, this difference is very imporant in sailing. Preformed wire rope lays easily in coils, whereas the non-preformed has to be forced into a coil and will spring out straight again when you let one end go. This force that you use on non-preformed rope—bending it into a coil—sets up internal stress as it resists the bending. There is additional stress on non-preformed as it makes that 180 degree turn in a masthead sheave. Preformed rope, on the other hand, easily makes that bend without resisting. Since it is free of this internal stress, preformed wire rope will give much longer service and will not break on you unexpectedly some-day as you tack repeatedly in a narrow ship channel.

When to Replace Galvanized Rope

Galvanized wire rope is the strongest, has the greatest fatigue resistance and is also the cheapest to buy. A main halyard in 3/16-inch galvanized, 80-foot long, will cost about $30. That same halyard in stainless steel will cost over $80. However, over the long pull, it all evens out because the galvanized rope will be replaced more often. It may even cost more if you consider yard costs for rerigging.

Galvanized rope doesn't wear out, it rusts out literally from the inside out. The constant inner friction in inner strands as they run through blocks wears off the galvanizing. Then they start to rust. You will begin to see this brown discoloration first on your hands. Galvanized rope will also streak with a white chalky powder of oxidized zinc.

When you see these first signs of zinc deterioration, it means the end is near for your galvanized rope and, if it's mid-season, you can start saving for next year. By the end of the season, the inner strands will rust, break and their sharp ends will work out to the surface to form "hooks" or "whiskers." You can tell by wiping the rope with a soft cloth. If it sticks, it is time to rerig.

Wire Rope Metals

There are three different types of stainless steel used for yacht rigging. Type 302, the most common, has good corrosion resistance in salt water and is strong. Type 304 has a tendency to become brittle and does not resist fatigue as well as 302. Type 316 has the best resistance to salt water corrosion of all stainless steels, and costs three times as much. It has to be specially ordered and you may wait six months to a year for delivery. Monel has the best resistance to salt water corrosion, but only half the strength of stainless steel. This means you must use a heavier wire to get equal load capacity and blocks with the right size grooves for that wire. All things considered, this makes switching to Monel very expensive.

Phosphor bronze is another metal which must be used in larger diameters to match the strength of the stainless steels. This bronze is used only where a non-magnetic, non-sparking material is important, or where you want to eliminate the radio interference caused by steering cables working through blocks and a rudder quadrant.

The Three Most Used Wire Rope Strands

The three most popular wire ropes used on production boats today are 1×19, 7×7 and 7×19. Wire rope types are designated by these numbers, and there are an endless variety of others, but only these three, plus also 6×42, are of any interest to you (Fig. 5-12). These numbers indicate wire strands per rope times the number of wire per strand. In 1×19 wire, for example, there is just one large gauge wire per strand, and 19 strands of a single wire. In 7×7 rope, there are 7 strands with 7 wires in each strand.

The 1×19 wire size is a standard for standing rigging because it has minimum stretch and gives the best support for masts under all sorts of loads. The 7×7 rope in sizes 3/64, 1/16 and 3/32 is flexible enough to go through the blocks of smaller boats. In some sailors and cruisers it is too stiff and is used mainly for vinyl-coated cables and lifelines on deck rails.

The 7×19 rope, also designated 6×37 IWRC, is the standard for running rigging, or for any function where the rope must move through pulleys, sheaves and around the drums of winches on boats and trailers.

With 6×42 rope you get maximum flexibility, minimum strength and wear resistance. It also stretches like a rubber band. It is used for halyards and steering cables that control rudders. In steering cables the stretch can be taken up with turnbuckles. In halyards it is a nuisance. Before you consider using 6×42 rope for halyards, read further.

The Stretch Factor in Wire Rope

Galvanized rope in 1×19 strands will stretch ¼ inch per 100 feet; 7×7 will stretch ¾ inch; 7×19 will stretch 3 inches; 6×42 will stretch 4 inches.

Stainless steel rope in 1/19 will stretch 5/32 inch per 100 feet; 7×7 will stretch ⅞ inch; 7×19 will stretch 4 inches; and 6×42 will stretch 6 inches.

This explains why 1/19-inch wire rope is the accepted standard for standing rigging.

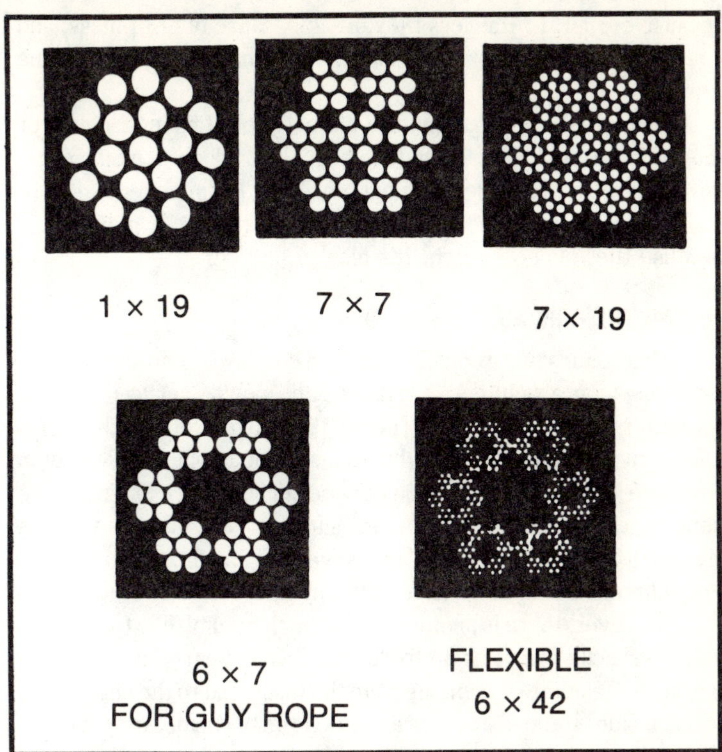

Fig. 5-12. The five most used wire rope types in sailing.

Strength of Wire Rope

As with manila and synthetic ropes, the manufacturer's figures of wire rope strength should be considered with the same suspicion as the mileage figures on a used car odometer. Always divide the manufacturer's figures by five. If the manufacturer says his ¼-inch 1×19 stainless wire rope has a strength of 8,200 pounds, divide this by five. You get a safe working strength of 1,640 pounds. This gives you a safety margin to allow for variables like shock loads, corrosion, rust, stress fatigue, wear and tear and stupidity. As Mark Twain once said: "Everybody's stupid on certain subjects." So you must allow for the fact that, like me, you might be "stupid" on rigging.

WHEN TO REPLACE STAINLESS RIGGING

Running rigging works much harder then standing, so it has to be checked constantly for wear and weaknesses. Some stainless becomes brittle and cracks. In galvanized rope, inner strands break because of rust. In stainless they break because of brittleness, and you get the same "whiskers" and "hooks." That is the sign it is time to rerig.

Solid steel rod rigging is the ultimate for standing rigging for those who are rich and demand the best. You will get top efficiency, low wind resistance, great strength and long life in either Monel or stainless steel 316. And once you tune rod rigging, it stays tuned because there is no stretch. It's nice to be rich.

TUNING THE RIGGING

This sounds more complicated then it really is. It just means the mast must be absolutely straight up and down, vertical or, as a carpenter would say, "plumb" (Fig. 5-13). A plumb bob on the end of a line run up the mast on the halyard shackle is one simple way of doing the job, if your slip is in quiet water. This is a job that has to be done on a windless day. If your slip is in an area where the water is always disturbed by currents and waves coming in a channel, then the plumb bob cannot be used with any success.

However, there is another way. Attach a plumb line to the main halyard shackle, run this up to the masthead sheave, and then use this line to take measurements from the masthead to the chainplates on each side. If the distance is longer on the port side, for example, then the mast is leaning to starboard. You just make adjustments on the upper and lower shrouds until the plumb line is the same measurement on both sides.

Do the same with the fore and aft stays. The tension on all stays and shrouds should be the same, tight, but not too tight. Remember, you're not tuning a bass fiddle. If you tighten too much, you can drive the mast right through the deck, even through the hull bottom on a small centerboard. Some yards have a tension tool which you can rent, or even buy if you're rich and can afford rod rigging. So why play it by ear? If you err, do it on the loose side because a slight slackness in the stays and shrouds will be taken up by the mast as it bends. Of course, this working of the mast also plays hell with the mast collar. If you don't get it right the first time, you can always check the tension again and again and make minor adjustments. Nobody's perfect.

RERIGGING

Don't try to do this after the mast is stepped. Oh, it can be done if you can find a nut who will go up the mast in a bosun's chair.

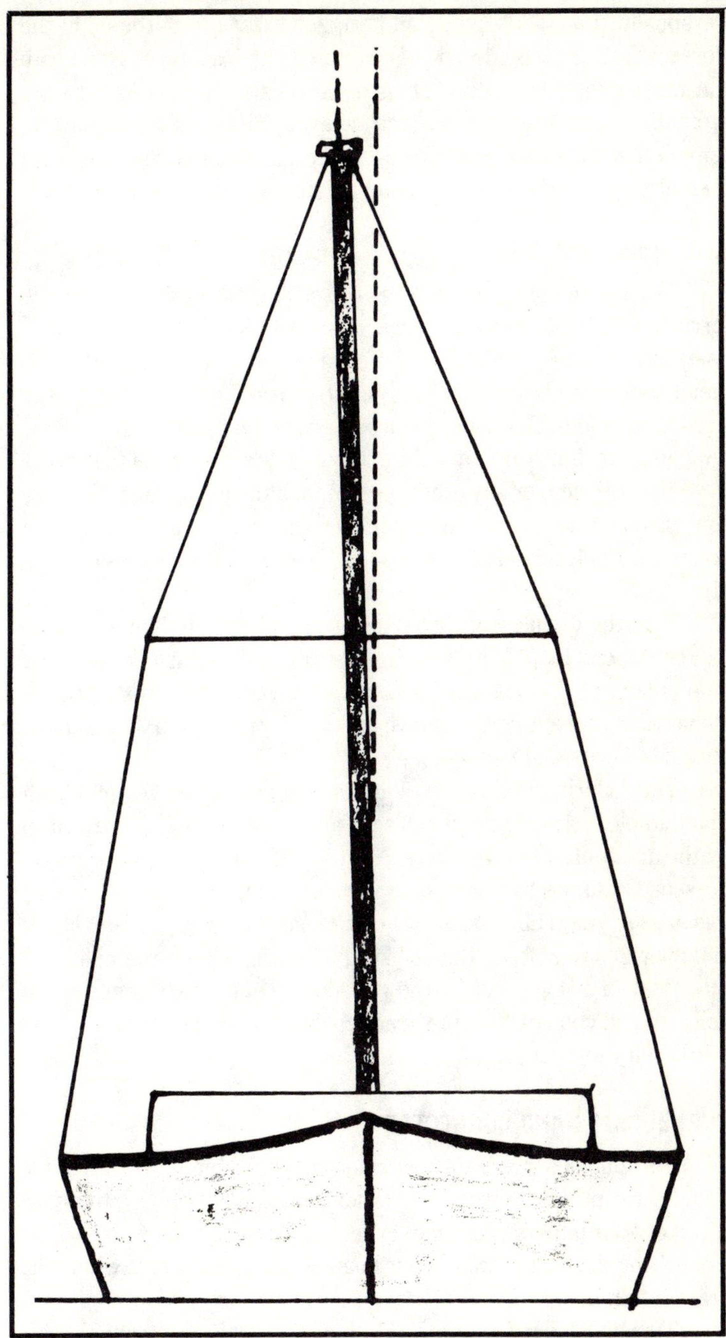

Fig. 5-13. Tuning the rigging simply means that the mast be plumb.

Personally, I wouldn't go up an unrigged mast for all the oil in the Persian Gulf. So why do you have to do it the hard way? Even with the mast unstepped and resting on horses nice and close to the ground, it is still a tedious job because every piece of rigging must be removed and carefully measured. A new piece is made, spliced and then attached before you proceed to the next piece.

WIRE ROPE SPLICING

The two most used methods of splicing wire are swaging and ferrules (Fig. 5-14). Both require a special tool similar to the ones used to compress connectors on electric wire. The ferrule tool is inexpensive and is used by most do-it-yourself sailors. The swage tool is very expensive, but can be rented in many yards and marinas. Suppliers for these items will be listed at the end of this chapter.

The ferrules, or any other type connector, must match the wire rope size and be the proper metal. For stainless steel rope you use copper; for galvanized rope you use a special alloy which is compatible.

With the ferrules you must also use a matching thimble, which makes the end loop. With swaging, this is unnecessary because the loop is part of the connector. You have a very neat, more professional and more manufactured look. All production boats have swaged splices and connectors.

The Talurit ferrules don't look as neat and are more bulky with that thimble loop on the end, but they are less likely to be screwed up by the amateur. With the swage, if you don't get precisely the right pressure, you will have cause for concern. You will always worry as this nags at your subconscious like an unpaid bill from your bookie. If you are sensitive about things like this, but still want the manufactured look of swage, then let the yard do it. Then if the swaged splice pulls out and you get hit in the head, you've got somebody to sue who has liability insurance.

TURNBUCKLES AND CONNECTORS

Turnbuckles are those wonderfully efficient screw-leverage devices for putting tension on standing rigging. With just the easy effort of your fingers you can exert enough pressure on your mast to blast through the bottom of your boat. So remember that when you start turning.

Turnbuckles for marine use come in galvanized, stainless steel and silicon bronze. You will rarely see galvanized anymore, except

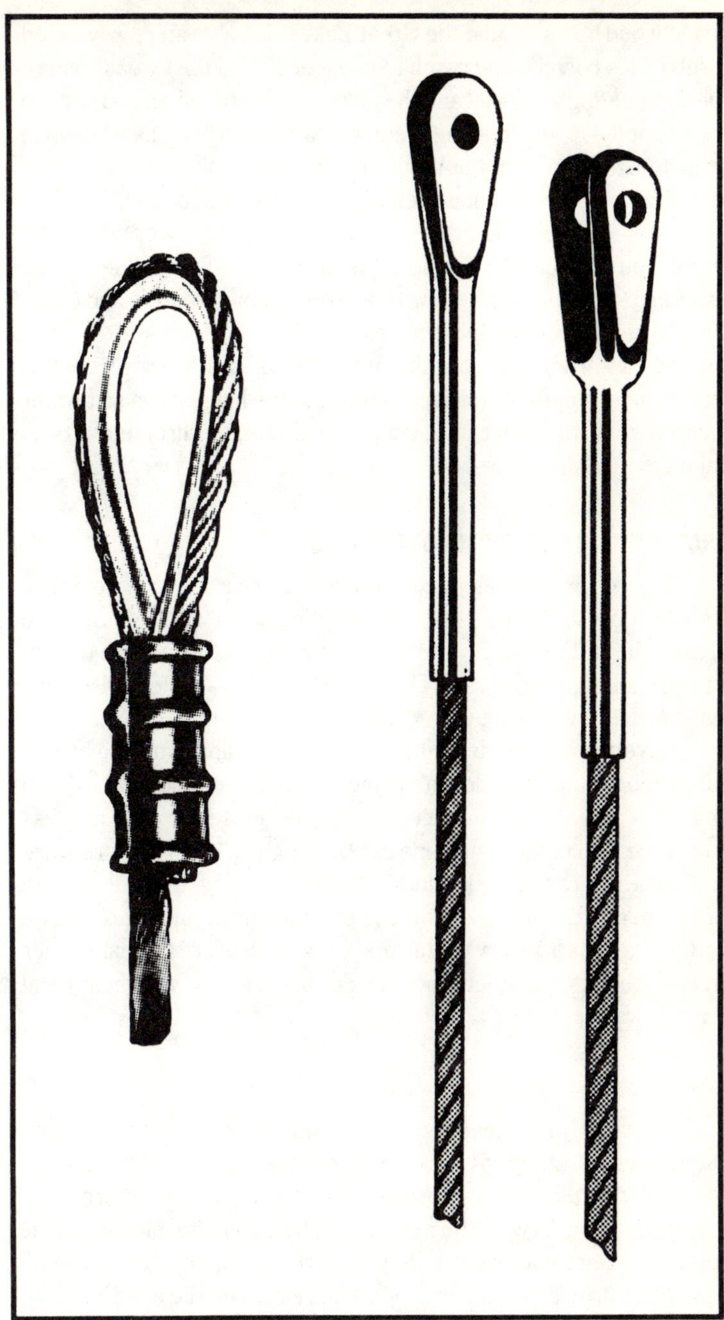

Fig. 5-14. Here are the two most common types of rope splicing, the ferrule and the swage.

on old wood boats around the Great Lakes. In salt water, galvanized turnbuckles corrode and rust badly, especially on the threads where the zinc coating wears off and they freeze up tight. Then you have to soak in penetrating oil, bang them with a wrench and talk to them in profane language. On a hot day this can be revolting.

Stainless steel turnbuckles are strongest when new, but they age just like people. They develop aches and pains, get brittle and crack. You just periodically check the turnbuckles for hairline cracks, especially at the chainplates where stress is the greatest and exposure to salt water the most severe.

Silicon bronze turnbuckles must be used in a size larger to match the strength of stainless. They last the longest in a salt water environment, but don't look very nice when the chrome starts to flake off. It always does.

PROTECTING SAILS FROM COTTER PINS

The cotter pins in shroud turnbuckles are a constant source of trouble because the mainsail, when running down wind, will rub hard against them (Fig. 5-15). The sharp ends of a cotter pin can quickly damage an expensive sail. The jib, when close hauled, also rubs against the lower shrouds.

Cover the cotter pins with aluminum duct tape. This is a heavy, satin-smooth tape that doesn't come unglued after dousings in fresh and salt water. Its aluminum color matches perfectly with stainless and galvanized metal. Duct tape can be bought in any hardware store and comes only in 2-inch width. It is very easily ripped down the middle to make 1-inch width for easier wrapping around a turnbuckle cotter pin. This is a very useful tape to have on board for many other chafe problems and emergency repairs because it is very heavy and strong.

SPREADERS

Spreaders are those crosspieces up the mast that spread out the shrouds so they give the mast support along its length (Fig. 5-16). Without spreaders it would be necessary to have more stays and shrouds; otherwise the mast would buckle in the middle. On tall television antenna towers they call this support "guy wires." Spreaders provide the same support and eliminate the need for more stays half way up the mast, which would only be in the way when you shift sail, as in tacking.

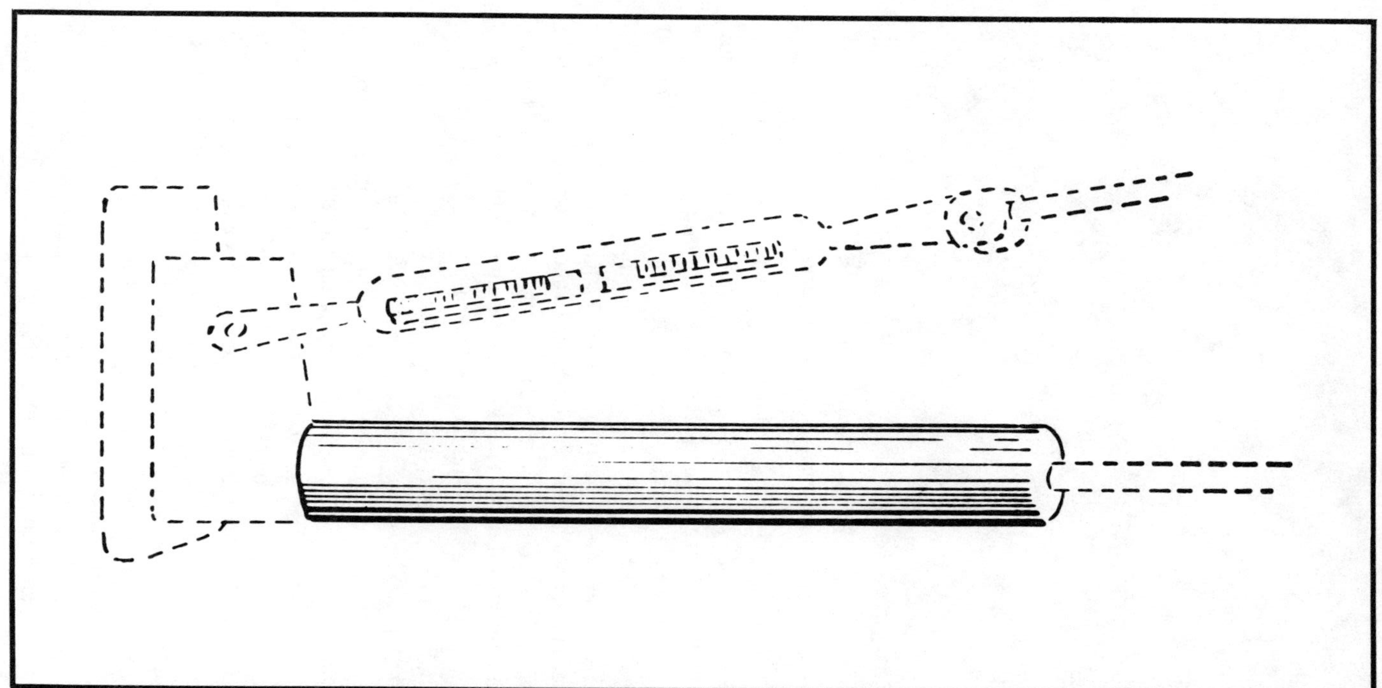

Fig. 5-15. Here's how to protect sails from cotter pins.

Fig. 5-16. Shown are spreaders and chafe protectors.

These spreaders are under great stress. If one of them ever breaks under sail, you could be dismasted. This is very distressing and humiliating because in yacht club classes for new sailors they will be discussing and analyzing what happened to you for the next 50 years. You will become a legend in your time.

I know because it happened to me. I backed a big single screw cruiser out of a yacht club slip and failed to allow for a strong current and wind. I lost control, smashed into a steel piledriver, and then hit three expensive boats. The insurance claims went over $10,000. That was 27 years ago and they still discuss and analyze what I did wrong in Power Squadron classes. Like Miranda, I'm famous for being stupid. This is the kind of fame you don't need.

So check those spreaders before you step the mast so you can get your nose down close for a thorough inspection. In a bosun's chair you are too busy doing other things like gawking at the scenery, showing off and clowning.

With all the distractions, you accomplish nothing up in a bosun's chair except reasserting your youthful virility by proving you can do it. And besides, if you did find something, how would you fix it swinging around in that dumb chair? A stepped mast 50 feet up in the air is no place to make repairs.

The main thing to check is the many different fasteners used to secure the spreader to the mast (Fig. 5-17). Check for galvanic

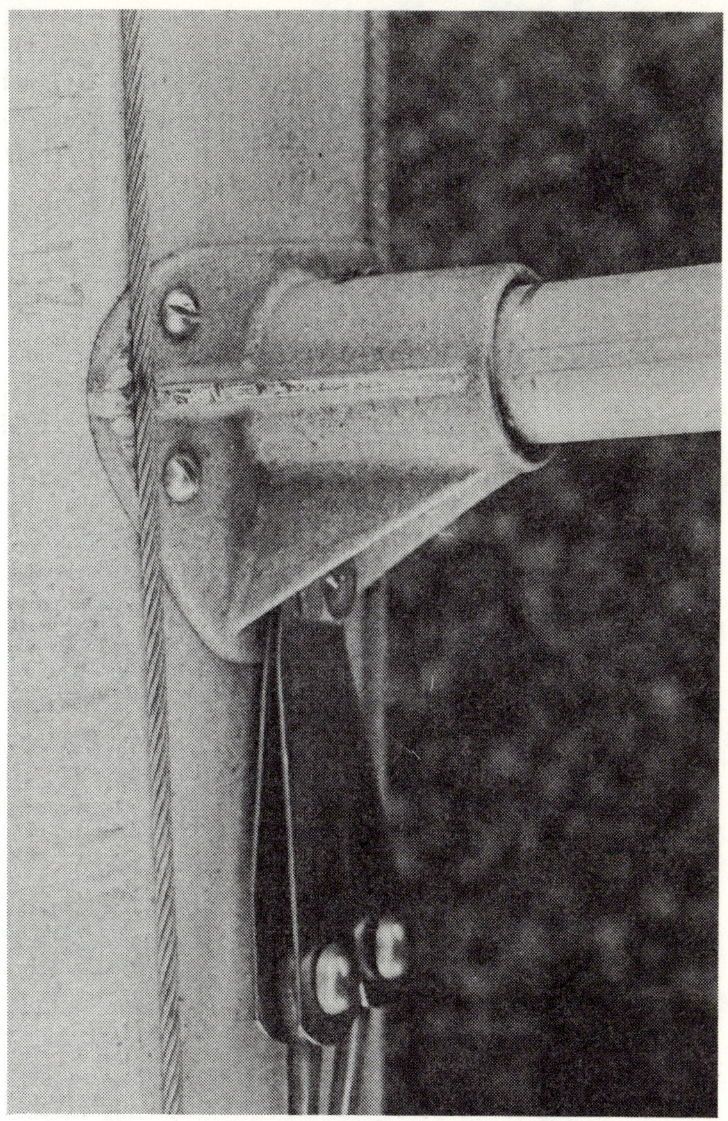

Fig. 5-17. Attach spreader fastenings to the mast.

corrosion and stress damage. If anything is loose, find out why it is loose. Screws into wood don't back out like tapping screws into metal. If wood screws feel loose, it's because the wood is moist. This can mean trouble.

In metal, when tapping screws get loose, they back out and drop off. If your mast is aluminum, look for open screw holes.

Fig. 5-18. From left to right are a centerboard winch, halyard winch and winch handle case.

Tapping screws will fall out wherever there is movement and stress. The hole enlarges, loosens the screw and it backs out. This means you must replace with a larger screw and a lock washer. The lock washer must be stainless steel.

WINCHES

Like turnbuckles, winches are marvelous mechanical devices. I often wonder how the Egyptians built the pyramids without them. I wonder how they sailed without them (Fig. 5-18).

Winches are either easy or hard to disassemble. It's all a matter of relativity. If, as a boy, you took pleasure in disassembling alarm clocks and putting them back together again, you will have no trouble with a winch. If, as a man, you find it painful to replace the fuel cell in a Timex electronic watch, a winch will drive you up the mast. Shun them but you can't ignore them completely because every boat that sails today has from three to eight winches, and occasionally one of them must be serviced.

If you look at the exploded drawing of a Barient sheet winch, you will note that it looks like the guts of an alarm clock (Figs. 5-19 and 5-20). It's those little things that wear out and have to be replaced—the endless "pawls," "roller bearings" and "pawl springs."

Overhauling Winches

In this respect, winches are like starters, alternators, and the carburetor in your car. They must periodically be removed and

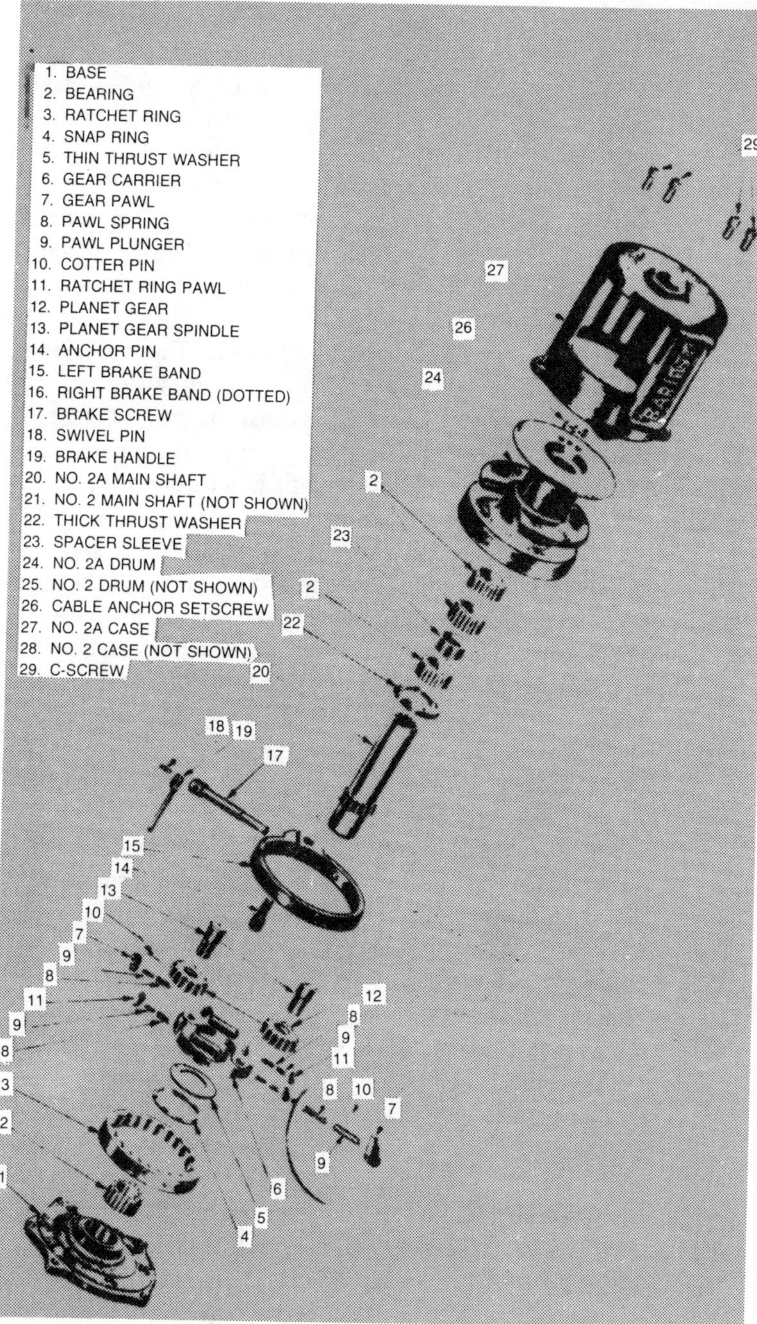

Fig. 5-19. This is a barient sheet winch.

overhauled, or "rebuilt," whatever that means. You might remove the winch, take it to the yard or marina head mechanic and tell him you want a complete overhaul. Now here is where we get to that "rebuilt"business. Yards hate these little jobs just as gas station mechanics hate little carburetor overhauls. As a result, a whole new industry has been born in this country which specializes in little jobs like overhauling automobile starters, alternators, carburetors, transmissions, etc. Only they don't call them overhauls. Everything has to be upgraded, so overhauls are euphemistically called "factory rebuilts." But they don't "factory rebuild" your carburetor. You get somebody else's and they take yours in "exchange." The attraction of all this is you don't have to wait, and it's cheaper then buying new.

Today you can do this with winches because marinas in California, Florida and Long Island are so busy servicing the expensive boats they sell that they haven't time for little jobs that bring in little revenue and tie up their $8-an-hour mechanics.

Winches are very expensive little devices and you just don't lightly consider the purchase of a new one without first having long discussions with your banker, your lawyer, your investment counselor and your analyst. There are winches that cost more than a new car. There are winches on the America's Cup boats that cost more than my boat. You can understand, therefore, my awe and deep respect for winches.

You might also overhaul the damn thing yourself and say to hell with somebody else's so-called "rebuilt."

There are service and repair "kits" available for practically all Barient winches. They provide everything you need for a complete "rebuild" job. Before you get started, or even remove your winch, order one of these "A" or "B" kits, either through the marina or direct. There is no point in disassembling the winch ahead of time and then waiting two weeks for the parts. There are two reasons: you will forget in two weeks how you took it apart and will have trouble getting it back together; if you disassemble in the cabin (which you should), and have everything spread out on paper over the dinette table (which you should) what happens when your family comes aboard over the weekend? I'll tell you what happens—you will find pieces of baloney, potato chips and chicken breading mixed in with pawl springs and snap rings—if you can find them.

Never, never start a winch repair job unless you can finish it in one sitting while everything is fresh in your mind and you can remember how you took it apart. If you do this on a weekend, plan

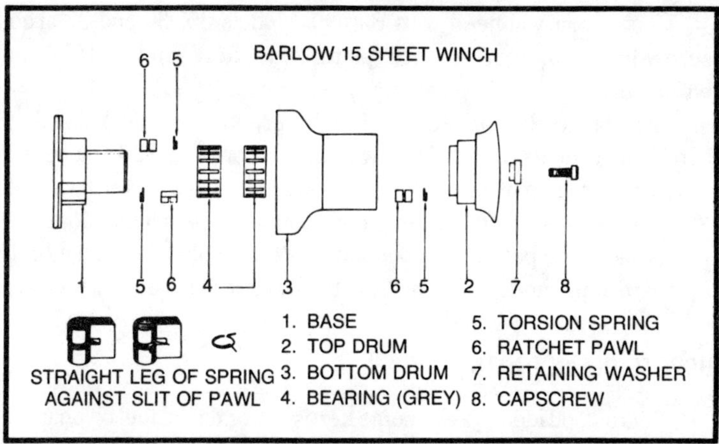

Fig. 5-20. Shown is a barlow sheet winch.

some ruse to get rid of the wife and kids. Send them over to MacDonald's for cheeseburgers and malts on you.

As you disassemble, lay the parts out on paper in proper order left-to-right just as you do with words when writing a letter. Everything goes back together in reverse sequence, right-to-left. This way you don't try to put on the franistan before the jigston.

The beautiful thing about the Barient "kits" is they include a full set of exploded drawings which identify every part and where it goes. A typical "Kit A" will include: one bearing, four snap rings, six pawl springs and two pawls, plus a tube of Barlube grease.

Don't try to use ordinary lubricants, like that white stuff called Lubriplate, because it gums up in sea atmosphere. Also, never use detergent oil on any brass or bronze because it will cause corrosion. Always use non-detergent oil, such as the oil used in outboard motors.

"Kit B" also includes a full set of exploded drawings, a tube of Barlube grease, one bearing, four snap rings, six pawl springs, two pawls, one drum nut, two plungers, two pawls, two springs, two roller bearings and one red cloth.

Tools Needed to Service Winches

There are some Barient winches, like the Models 3, 3-A, 10, 10-H, and 16, which can be fixed with that old fashioned woman's hairpin. This is literally true because all you need is a screwdriver or a "small pointed object." Other models require little more than a few Allen wrenches and one box wrench.

221

Tools you will need with Barient Models 35, 30 and 32 are a screwdriver, universal deck plate key, 5/16 and 3/16 Allen wrenches, and a 7/16 box wrench.

For Model 28 you need a screwdriver, universal deckplate key and ¼-inch and 3/16-inch Allen wrenches. For Model 26 you need a screwdriver or small pointed object and a ½ inch box wrench. Model 22 requires a screwdriver or small pointed object and Model 20 needs the same plus a 3/16 pin punch. You should have these tools on board at all times, plus one "Kit B" in reserve for emergencies.

HOW TO CLEAN PARTS

It is a good idea to keep some kerosene or diesel fuel on board in a plastic container. This is wonderful stuff for many cleaning chores aboard ship when working around machinery, repairing things that are dirty and greasy, and cleaning all the internal parts in your winches. Never use gasoline to clean anything on a boat. Don't even use it off your boat because it just ruins your hands. Gasoline is good for only one thing, fuel for internal combustion engines. I fear and hate the stuff because once you get gasoline on a boat, there is no place for the fumes to go but down. That means the fumes wind up in the lowest part of your bilge where they can lay for days waiting for a spark. The fumes from just one cup of gasoline has the explosive power of three sticks of dynamite.

Kerosene and diesel fuel are relatively safe fuels because the fumes are not explosive. I even use kerosene to clean my paint brushes because there is just enough oil in this fuel to keep paint brushes soft, not dried out and hard, as happens when you clean with turpentine or paint thinner. I learned this from professional house painters. Kerosene is just diesel fuel refined one step further until it is water clear. In hill and mountain country they call it "coal oil."

Everything in a winch removes and comes apart easily, unless it is held by something like a fastener, C-ring or snap ring. So if something won't come apart, don't get impatient and try to force it because it is probably held by one of these things.

Don't dump all the small parts into a bucket of kerosene for cleaning. You're not mixing cement. Clean each part individually with a toothbrush. Dry with a rag and lay on your paper in proper order. When everything is out, cleaned and on the paper, then you inspect for wear and damage. Springs and gears don't wear out, but pawls do and you can't see the wear on a pawl. So replace all the pawls.

Here is how a Barient halyard winch comes apart. Back out the four Allen screws in the case and lift it straight off gently. If it sticks, jiggle until it comes off. Don't hit it with a hammer or anything else. Remove the bearings one at a time, clean, dry and lay them out on your paper. I always like to do this down on the deck. If I drop a bearing, it only has a few inches to fall. You drop a bearing off the dinette table and it will almost certainly be damaged.

The brake band assembly comes out next, but first remove the handle by turning counterclockwise. There is no need to remove the swivel pin screw that holds the handle.

Remove the winch drum and the planet gear assembly. It all comes out together and need not be disassembled unless a gear must be replaced. This rarely is necessary. Wash the whole assembly, dry carefully and inspect. The two gear pawls are what usually have to be replaced. Although they look alike, they are not the same. Each pawl is shaped to fit a specific gear. So be careful when you replace them. Get them back in proper position or they won't work. The two gears are pressed into place by spindles and can not be easily removed. So don't try.

With everything cleaned and all the pawls replaced, you now lubricate with a light machine oil—not auto engine oil. Grease all the gear teeth and bearings. Do not lubricate the brake drum. You are now ready to reassemble, which you do in reverse order.

This is a typical example of approximately what you will do with almost any winch, regardless of type or make. To go into this thoroughly, covering all makes and all types, would fill a book as thick as the Sears catalog with nothing else but winches. As I said, if you had no trouble with alarm clocks, you will have none with winches. There are thousands of different clock movements, but basically they are all the same. It is the same with winches. If you can fix one, you can fix them all.

SAILS

There are four kinds of sail: cotton, canvas, nylon and Dacron. There are three kinds of sailors: cruising, Sunday and racing.

Although to the unpracticed eye they may all look alike, they are as different as onions and garlic to a French chef. This is particularly true with sailors and their boats, who even speak different languages. In boating clubs and yacht clubs, cruising sailors talk only to cruising sailors; Sunday sailors talk only to Sunday sailors; racing sailors talk only to God and the International Rules Committee.

There is such as vast array of sophisticated gadgets and complex mechanical devices on racing boats to control the sails that I long ago gave up trying to even understand them, let alone trying to write about them. A racing boats jibs, for example, comes in an endless variety of sizes, shapes, weights and configurations. Those picturesque spinnakers and sweeping genoas blow my mind when I consider the skills and money involved.

The cruising sailor lives in a different world. To him it's a big day when he gets up two head sails and talks about it for weeks. Sunday sailors, of which I am one, rarely get up more than the main. We like our sailing easy and simple because we're not going any place. We just want to relax, break open a six pack and take catnaps between tacks. That's the way we sail, and always on Sunday. That's why we Sunday sailors hit more channel buoys then any other breed of boaters. We're asleep at the tiller.

Cruising sailors are always going someplace. They prefer to spend their money on direction-finders, depth finders and radio-telephones rather then spinnakers, expensive winches and racing sails. The Sunday sailor likes economy and simplicity, like old fashioned cotton sails. The racing sailor doesn't care about cost and will spend anything to get a slight edge on his competition. He has special plastic windows installed in the luffs of jibs just so he can see yarn telltales and know precisely how to trim sail for maximum speed. We Sunday sailors get bored with all the finer points. If we move without the sails flapping too much, we're satisfied with the trim. For this reason, it is almost impossible to write about sailing for all sailors when you speak only one language, like: "Let's get the rag up and blow."

The making of sails is a vast industry, and for racing it is a fine art and science. Contrary to what most non-sailors may think, you can't just hang up a bedsheet on a pole and go sailing. A sail is designed to act as an airfoil, except when running down wind, and then you could get by with a bedsheet. It's when you come about and head into the wind that funny things start to happen. Races are not won by sailing in one wind direction.

Cotton and canvas sails are rarely seen anymore, but are still available just as manila rope is still available and used by many old sailors and nostalgia freaks. Production boats today all come from the factories with Dacron sails and new sailors are conditioned early in life, during the years at the yacht clubs, to believe that there are no other sails but the synthetics. Nobody bothers to tell them how

Britannia swept the Seven Seas or how Yankee Clippers broke all speed records with plain old canvas.

Cotton and Canvas Sails

New sailors are told that cotton fibers break down under exposure to sun and air, are weak, lose their shape and have a short life expectancy. Cotton is attacked by mildew and stains easily.

True. Yet sailing vessels for centuries survived without Dacron which, incidently, only came into existence within the lifetimes of many new Snipe sailors. It was not canvas sails that eventually put the tall Ships out of business. It was the steam engine, plus also another ingenious invention, the screw propeller.

I know of Egyptian cotton sails that are still in regular use today after 20 years of hard sailing. I know of others that have been used 30 and 40 years. Of course, these sails were given tender and loving care. Not even Dacron or nylon will last without some tender, loving care.

Cotton and canvas are easy to maintain in fresh water service. If wet, you hoist them up the mast and let the wind and sun dry them. In salt water use, they must be hosed down with fresh water. This can be done as they are being hoisted up the mast.

Stowing Sails

Don't stow sails for long periods in a tight sail bag. A fish-netting bag is better. I use minnow nets which I converted into a sail bag. However, no matter how they are stowed, they should still be taken out occasionally and refolded. Don't stow anything with sails, like shackles, blocks, or winch handles. Always stow sails with an accordion fold, which allows for maximum ventilation.

During the boating season, when permanently moored rather then trailered, the mainsail should be flaked down on the boom accordion fashion and loosely covered with something. You cannot leave sail, whether fiber or synthetic, exposed to the sun and the ravages of air pollution, soot and just plain dirt. Many yacht clubs and marinas in the industrial north are situated close to some electric power facility, chemical works, steel mill, foundry, coal loading dock or sewage disposal plant. I have seen many canvas convertible tops and sails ruined with a sudden shift in wind blowing ash or soot from some smoke stack—even from the stacks of a passing freighter. If dirt doesn't ruin your sails, the sun will. So keep them covered when not in use.

Cleaning Cotton Sails

You clean cotton sails just as you clean anything else made of cotton—with plain soap and water. But don't ever use bleach. Yes, it will whiten your sails beautifully, but it will also weaken the fiber. They don't tell you this on bleach labels which, after all, is used mainly to whiten handkerchiefs, T-shirts and bedsheets. But bedsheets don't have to withstand the stresses and strains of a boat sail.

There are some commercial products available for removing stains from cotton and canvas, but read the labels carefully before you buy. Some contain oxalic acid, which will damage your sails. A very weak solution of oxalic acid can be used to remove rust stains, but be sure it is diluted and don't leave it on too long. When the stain is removed, soak the sail in a large tub of water and mild detergent. With large sails, you spread them out on a lawn, hose and scrub with a brush. When thoroughly rinsed, hang up to dry by the luff. This helps the wrinkles to drop out and the sail will hold its proper shape.

If you don't care to be bothered by all this, there are sail lofts that will do this for you. They usually charge about 10 cents per square foot. Some of them even throw in some free stitching. Extensive stitching will, of course, cost extra.

Repairing Sails

Check the seams for signs of fraying and broken threads. Sails themselves, whether cotton, canvas or synthetic, always outlast their seams. A 20-year-old sail will have made at least two trips to the loft for a complete reseam job. On this point, cotton and canvas seams way outlast the seams in synthetic material where the threads are on the surface and easily chafed and broken. Canvas seam threads are deeply embedded, which protects them from chafing.

Sewing Sails

Frayed threads can be repaired easily, either by hand or a zigzag sewing machine using synthetic thread. If you sew by hand, just use the same needle holes of the original stitches. If you sew by machine, set the stitch width and length to match the original stitches.

Darning Sails

Small holes in sail can be darned in much the same manner that clothing and socks are darned. The only difference is you use a

Fig. 5-21. Here is an example of plastic tubing slit and then put over lines to prevent chafing.

synthetic thread. Small holes can also be patched temporarily with a special type of self-adhesive vinyl which comes in various sizes. The patches are placed on both sides of the hole.

However, for a permanent repair job, you can cover the hole with a patch of sail cloth material which you can stitch by hand or with your wife's zigzag sewing machine. The patch weave should run in the same direction as the sail weave. Turn the edges under before you sew.

There are special sail repair "kits" available which provide all the things needed like needles, thread, sail cloth and complete instructions. A list of suppliers will be listed at the end of this chapter.

CHAFING

Chafing is the big problem in sailing because there is just no way you can prevent it. You just live with it and improvise all sorts of devices to reduce chafe damage to a minimum. One of my favorite chafe guards is clear plastic tubing, which I always keep on hand in various diameters. Of course, you have to slit it, but this is easy if you insert a wood dowel and then cut with a razor blade. The larger diameters I use on Dacron and nylon rope; the small diameters are used on wire rope (Fig. 5-21). The plastic tubing looks neater than rubber hose material, and it doesn't blacken up your white rope.

Synthetic sails are especially vulnerable to chafing because the seam threads are on the surface where they can be easily broken by rubbing against wire rope shrouds, which have a slightly abrasive surface because of the fine strands and weave. Plastic tubing as a chafe guard merely provides a softer, less abrasive surface which lengthens the life of the seam threads. In this respect, cotton and canvas sails are better than the synthetics because the seam threads hold up much longer. The chief advantage of Dacron and nylon is that they can be stored wet in sail bags when in a hurry to hit the road, or flaked down wet on the boom and covered when tired and in a hurry to go home.

There are other advantages to Dacron, but these are important mainly in racing where sail trimming is an exact science to get the last ounce of energy from the wind. It is impossible to trim sails precisely if they shrink when wet and stretch when dry. But to the cruising sailor, who is leisurely running from point "A" to point "B" on a chart, it hardly makes any difference. The Sunday sailor, running up and down a river, or back and forth across some bay, is too contented with life to give a damn.

Sail repair kits companies include *Moody Tools Inc.*, 43 Dudley St., Providence, R.I. 02905; *Sailmakers Loft Inc.*, Box 1620, Boyton, Beach, Fla. 33435; *Sailrite Kits*, 2010 Lincoln Blvd., Venice, Calif. 90291; and *West Products Corp.*, 161 Prescott St., E. Boston, Mass. 02128.

Winch repair kit companies are *Barient Co.*, 936 Bransten Rd., San Carlos, Calif. 94070; and *Alexander-Roberts Co.*, 1851 Langley, Irvine, Calif. 92705.

Swaging tool companies are *S&F Tool Co.*, Box 1546 Costa Mesa, Calif. 92626; and *Jay Stuart Haft*, 8925 N. Tennyson Dr., Milwaukee, Wis. 53217.

Wire rope and fittings companies are *Windward Mark Inc.*, 6317 Seaview Ave., Seattle, Wash. 98107; and *Famet Marine*, 745 2nd Ave., Redwood City, Calif. 94063.

Blocks companies include *Wilcox-Crittenden,* 699 Middle St., Middletown, Conn. 06457; *Mariner Co.*, 1714 17th St., Santa Monica, Calif. 90404; and *Harken Yacht Fittings*, 1251 E. Wisconsin Ave., Pewaukee, Wisc. 53072.

Aluminum mast companies are *Dwyer Aluminum Mast Co.*, Branford, Conn. 06405; and *Zephyr Aluminum Spars*, Wareham, Mass. 02571.

Marine Power
and Propulsion Systems

There are four ways to push a boat through water: with oars, with steam/paddle wheels, with wind/sail, and with engines/propellers. The last way is the most popular. As long as the petroleum resources of the world hold up, it will probably continue to be the most used propulsion system for pleasure craft of all shapes, sizes and materials.

Steam engines we can disregard because they are strictly a novelty thing in pleasure boats—for the present at least. But who knows, if things get serious enough in the energy crisis, steam may come back in a small coal or alcohol-fired steam boiler for marine use. After all, there was once an automobile called the Stanley Steamer which utilized a small gasoline-fired boiler. But for the present, gasoline and the internal combustion engine is still the number one power source for pleasure boats.

There are two basic types of internal combustion engines in marine use, the 4-cycle and the 2-cycle. The automobile and inboard marine engines are 4-cycle. The outboard motor, and some diesel truck engines, are 2-cycle.

THE 2-CYCLE ENGINE

The basic 2-cycle engine is utter simplicity and efficiency with only three moving parts: a piston, a connecting rod, and a crankshaft. That's why they can be made so tiny for chain saws and

500-watt electric generating plants that you can hold in the palm of your hand.

The 2-cycle engine has no complicated lubricating system with pumps and a reservoir for oil. Oil is mixed with gasoline and is sucked out of the carburetor in a fine spray into the crankcase by the piston on the up compression stroke. On the down power stroke, that same piston pushes the gas/oil mixture through a port (opening) in the cylinder wall into the combustion chamber. At the same time, this incoming gas/oil pushes exhaust gas from a previous stroke out through another port on the opposite cylinder wall. The gas mixed with oil evaporates and the oil remains behind coating all surfaces.

THE 4-CYCLE ENGINE

The 4-cycle marine engine, in comparison, is a big bulky monster with timing gears, cam shafts, valve poppets, valve springs, exhaust/intake valves, distributors, intake manifolds, water-cooled exhaust manifolds, water pumps, oil pumps, crankcases, starting motors, alternators, fuel pumps, reverse gears and transmission systems with all sorts of gear ratios. Put all this in a Gray or Universal 25 horsepower marine engine, which you find in many sailing auxiliaries, and you have a hunk of iron which weighs over 600 pounds.

AUTO VERSUS MARINE ENGINES

Automobile engines are frequently converted to marine use. There are conversion "kits" you can buy for this purpose. All that can be said for these "conversions" is that they work, but not too well. I have never known anyone who had one of these conversions who was happy and who didn't soon replace it with a conventional marine engine.

The chief source of irritation with conversions is the automobile transmission. You have direct drive forward, but a 3 to 1 gear ratio in reverse. This means you have lousy brakes for docking purposes. You have to race the engine at full throttle to get any braking action. That's why boats with conversion engines are always running into docks. You would do the same thing driving into your garage if you had no brakes.

THE "REBUILT" AND "REMANUFACTURED" ENGINE

The first time I bought an inboard engine, I was confused by the terms "rebuilt" and "remanufactured." "What's the difference?" I asked Chamberlain Marine in Detroit, national distributors for Gray Marine engines. The difference is age of the serial numbers. On your "rebuilt" engines, the serial numbers may be 5, 10, or 20 years old. On your "remanufactured" engine, the serial numbers are always of current year production engines. So why are they "remanufactured?" They broke down in a new boat. These engines are all warranty returns from dealers. They probably blew a rod during the shakedown, and were replaced by the dealer with another new engine.

Warranty returns are rebuilt at the factory, but they retain their original serial numbers. For this reason they cannot be resold as new because somebody has already owned that particular serial number.

These engines are fantastic bargains and Chamberlain marine usually has a long waiting list. I have bought two and paid $500 and $600 for engines that were retailing at $1500 and $1900. Most boaters, even marine dealers, do not know that all manufacturers of marine engines have warranty returns. I always assumed that they were just fixed up, repainted and sold again as new. But it is illegal to do this, even though a "remanufactured" engine is no different from other new ones coming off the assembly line.

Why are there so many warranty returns? On the day my new yacht was first dropped in the water, the dealer himself insisted on taking the wheel for a test run out in the bay. The instant we cleared the marina, he pushed both throttles wide open and I almost fell over the transom. For 15 minutes he raced my boat at full throttle back and forth, while I got angrier every minute. Those were my engines he was abusing and I demanded to know why.

He replied: "If there's any weaknesses, any flaws in a new engine, it will show up in the first 15 minutes of hard running. So, if something's gonna give, let it give now before you take delivery."

That made sense to me, so I shut my big mouth.

The dealer told me that a surprising number of new engines broke down during shakedowns, which was good for the buyer. If you babied those engines, the way auto engines are during "break-in," a defect in a connecting rod, piston or timing gear might not show up for a long time. According to Murphy's Law, it will almost certainly show up at a time to cause you the most pain, embarrassment and expense. So always remember, when buying a new engine, auto, boat or outboard run the hell out of it the first day. That first day is when you want weaknesses to show up because the warranty signatures are still wet and the dealer will be so embarrassed he sold you a loser that he'll knock himself out to make you happy. Yet six months later that same dealer won't accept your calls from out in the boondocks where you're stranded with a broken rod. I know because I have seen it happen to a close friend.

WHY MARINE ENGINES WEAR OUT SO FAST

A quick answer to why marine engines wear out so fast is they work too hard. I wore out a brand new 100 h.p. inboard in one short summer, and I only logged 156 hours. How could this be, you ask? By underpowering. The boat I built should have been powered with 185 horsepower, a 13×13 wheel turning 3600 rpm. I installed a 100 horsepower engine, the same wheel, which never turned more than 3000 rpm. Why did I do such a dumb thing? I was very young. It was a beautiful day in May when I christened my new boat. It performed better then I expected and I was too happy to notice that the engine rpms were 600 short of design specifications. That is always the first warning of trouble, big trouble!

By haulout time my top rpm had dropped to 2400 and the engine took considerable cranking to start. When an engine cranks fast and easy, but is slow to start, that is a sure sign of bad valves. Poor compression makes the engine easy to crank, and hard to start.

When I pulled the head, I was stunned. The exhaust valves were actually flat on one edge with an opening large enough to insert a screwdriver. It amazed me that the engine ran at all; yet that same day I had taken a long last run before pulling into the Travel-lift and I could feel nothing wrong, except those 2400 rpm. In an automobile, you can always feel or sense something wrong and catch trouble before it gets too serious. Down in the bilge an engine can be sick and dying, yet it will sound good to you. This is something new boaters must learn. Out on water, everything is different and you can't trust what you hear down in the engine compartment.

What happened to my engine is not an unusual case. In fact, it's a very typical example of what happens to any internal combustion engine that is overworked. However, you will rarely see anything like this in an automobile engine because they loaf 90 percent of the time and hardly ever operate under full load conditions. If they do, it is usually only for a short time, like pulling a house trailer up a hill.

WHAT IS "FULL LOAD" OPERATION?

If the private passenger car operated under constant "full load" conditions, a Detroit engineer told me, half the cars in the United

States would be junked in six months. The other half would be in garages getting overhauled.

What is "full load?"

It is racing up a 45-degree grade in low gear at full throttle. How long do you think your automobile engine would last under those operating conditions?

Yet, a marine engine operates under these conditions all the time. A boat never coasts or freewheels. Take your foot off the gas and a car will coast a half mile. Reduce power on a boat and it stops dead in the water. A hull pushing through water is always fighting inertia and resistance. Energy is constantly being burned up to overcome that wall of resistance.

It is this 100 percent full load operation that reduces the life expectancy of your boat engine, particularly in single-screw hulls. In twin screw, one engine helps the other, reducing the load slightly. This is the biggest, most practical reason for having two engines, plus, of course, the safety factor. Two 150 horsepower engines divide the load and, one 300 horsepower carries it alone. It can only do this safely if operated at 50 percent vacuum in the intake manifold. This means reduced throttle.

HOW TO RUIN AN ENGINE

The quickest way to ruin an inboard engine, as I did, is to underpower a boat, then constantly run the engine at its full rated horsepower—which means full throttle. Rated horsepower is vastly misunderstood. You constantly hear men say: "I don't need 300 horsepower to get from one shopping center to the next." You constantly hear boaters say: "Who needs a 300 horse power gashog just to go fishing?"

They are all partly right. You don't need 300 horse power. So you don't use 300 horsepower. This is what the boaters don't understand; having 300 horsepower doesn't mean you are always using it. In fact, you never use it. A 300 horsepower engine is not really 300 horsepower until you open the throttle wide open and rev the engine up to its full design of 4400 or 4800 rpm. At 2000 rpm the engine would only be developing about 120 horsepower. Driving in traffic at 1000 rpm, it would develop about 50 horsepower. Idling at the curb, it would develop less than 25 horsepower.

The gasoline an engine burns is determined by the horsepower developed. Engineers have a rough rule of thumb way of figuring gas consumption. For every 10 horsepower an engine develops it will burn one gallon of gasoline per hour. This applies to all engines, big and small, regardless of horsepower ratings. This means that if you take a 60 horsepower engine and rev it up to develop 30 horse-power; then take a 300 horsepower engine and rev it also to develop 30 horsepower, both engines will burn the same amount of gas, which will be 3 gallons an hour.

I have tested this out on many engines in boats and cars and found it to be amazingly accurate. A 100 horsepower marine engine at ⅔ throttle will develop about 60 horsepower. And it will use exactly six gallons of gas per hour. Check it out yourself.

Let's look at this another way. To get 60 horsepower out of a small engine you would have to operate it at full throttle, or its full rated rpm. To get 60 horsepower out of a 300 horsepower engine, you only have to rev it slightly beyond a fast idle. It would burn the same amount of gas as the smaller engine, six gallons an hour to develop 60 horsepower.

One other thing. The little 60 horsepower engine would be tearing itself to pieces; the big 300 would hardly work up a good sweat.

WHY BIG ENGINES COST LESS

It is a mistake to buy a small engine because you don't need 200 or 300 horsepower or because you think it is too expensive. They are more expensive initially, but in the long run they are actually cheaper. If you only need 100 horsepower, buy 200 and then back off the throttle and just use 100. Your gas consumption will be the same as the 100 engine run at full throttle. The 100 horsepower engine will be cheaper to buy but, like mine, it won't last you more than one season at full throttle operation. You'll have an expensive valve job every year. The 200 horsepower engine, at half throttle operation, will last, well, almost forever.

EXHAUST VALVES

The weak link in the 4-cycle marine engine is the exhaust valves. They are the first thing to wear out if an engine is operated beyond what engineers call "50 percent vacuum." This is a reading taken off the intake manifold. At idling, the vacuum reading will be 100 percent. At full throttle, it will be zero. A marine engine should never be operated at zero vacuum, except for very short runs of less than five minutes.

Optimum gas economy, efficiency and long engine life is obtained when an engine is operated at 50 percent vacuum, which is usually about two thirds of an engine's design rpm. For example, if an engine develops its full horsepower at 3600 rpm, then 2400 to 2800 rpm would be the optimum cruising range. You can only get this down to a fine point with a vacuum gauge which, incidently, is a very useful accessory to have on your boat, far more so than much of the other useless junk available (Fig. 6-1). Airguide Instrument Company, 2210 Wabansia Avenue, Chicago, Illinois 60647, has a special marine vacuum gauge which is calibrated to show you in color and words where the "best," "safe," and "danger" areas are. This is one of the very few accessories that I recommend and I don't understand why the boat manufacturers themselves don't install them right along with the other instrumentation.

Many boats are improperly wheeled. The right propeller permits an engine to rev up to its full design rpm. When it doesn't, the engine can reach zero vacuum before full throttle. You can't depend on the tachometer to warn you. This is why the vacuum gauge is so important. If you are using the wrong propeller, the vacuum gauge will warn you that the danger area is approaching.

At full throttle, if an engine cannot reach full rpm, the combustion chamber is sucking in more fuel to develop less power. This builds up internal pressures and heat far beyond design limits. The exhaust gases become so hot they literally melt away one edge of the

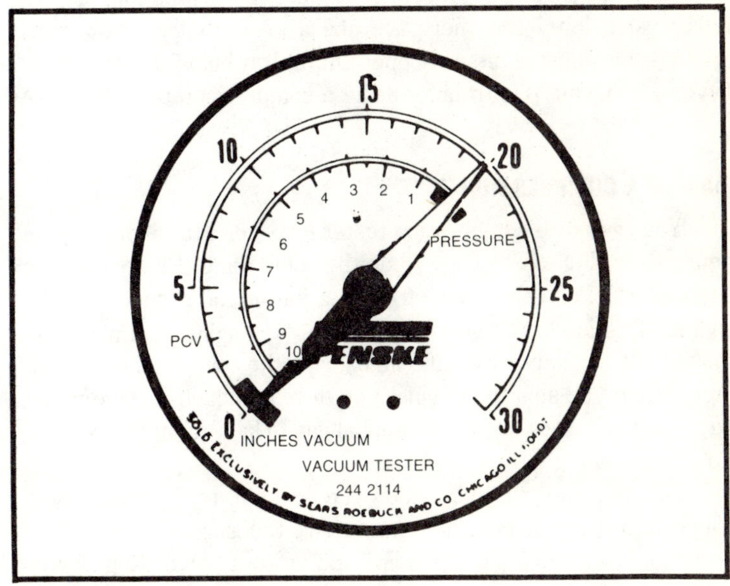

Fig. 6-1. Shown is a vacuum gauge.

exhaust valves as they leave the combustion chamber, or warp them so badly they do not seat. This causes a drastic loss of compression and power. The high internal pressure also causes excessive wear on the cylinder walls, pistons and bearings.

As a season progresses and a boat gradually loses rpm, most boatowners attribute this to moss, grass or barnacles accumulating on their bottoms. Rarely will they think of valves because they have been conditioned to believe, by advertising and planted articles in boating magazines, that "the modern marine engine has been engineered to give 2000 hours of trouble-free service." If you believe that, then you'll believe that heaven will protect the poor working girl.

Single-screw boats in the 20 to 30-foot size are most afflicted with valve troubles. Before World War II, Matthews and others were building yachts up to 50 foot with just one engine. But these were huge junks of iron developing only 60 horsepower with pistons the size of gallon oil cans. They had tremendous torque, swung big propellers on direct drive at low rpm's of 800 to 1000, and had the temperament of a St. Bernard. The modern marine engine is a low torque high rpm machine with the temperament of a French poodle. If you hit a log at 3000 rpm, all your pistons will change holes.

Today you will rarely see a new production boat down to 25 feet with just one engine. As a result, engines are lasting longer with fewer valve jobs. But there are still a lot of single-screw hulls around—and most of them are operating at way below their top rpm. If you are having this trouble, make a compression test.

MAKING A COMPRESSION TEST

You can buy a compression tester for $3 or $15, depending on your tastes (Fig. 6-2). They all do the same thing. Remove all the spark plugs. Pull center wire from distributor and ground it to the engine. This is very important. Cranking an engine with plugs removed, or distributor cap off, can damage the coil secondary windings. When you spin the engine, you develop a high voltage in the secondary windings and that potential has to have someplace to go. So you bleed it off to ground.

Set the gas throttle in wide open position, push compression gauge into a spark plug hole and crank the engine at least five seconds. Note the highest reading and write it down. Repeat this with all cylinders.

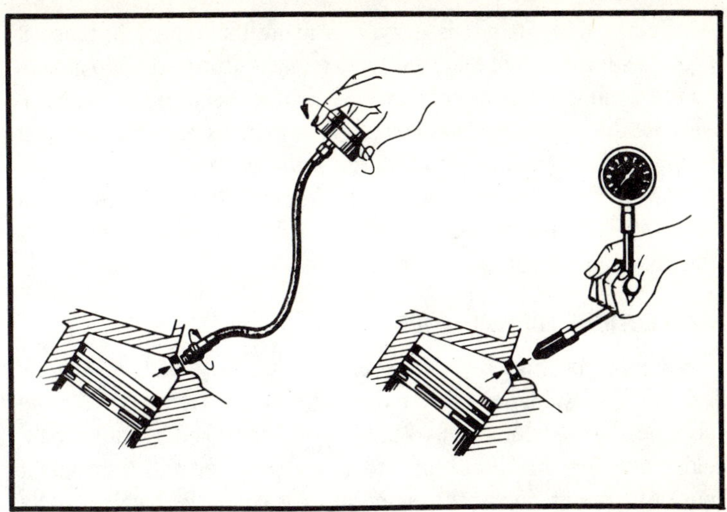

Fig. 6-2. Here are compression testers.

A new engine, or one in good condition, will have a compression reading of 120 to 150 pounds. Anything within that range can be considered satisfactory, if there is no more then a 25-pound variation between cylinder readings. A small drop in compression, like 100-110, can be considered ring wear or even a slight valve leakage. A big drop to 75-50 pounds means only one thing—burned out, warped exhaust valves.

You need a valve job now. You can have it done. You can do it yourself and save about $100.

THE VALVE OVERHAUL

Don't let yourself be intimidated by what looks like a hopelessly complex job. It isn't really. In today's age of specialization, nobody grinds valves the old-fashioned way, with physical labor and valve grinding compound. Today's garage, marina or gas station mechanic is nothing more than a disassembler and a reassembler. A mechanic just takes things apart and makes a telephone call. Some kid in a pickup comes to get your transmission, your starter, your alternator and your valve heads and takes them back to some specialty shop where the overhauling is actually done. Then it is returned by the same kid in the pickup, and the mechanic puts it all together again.

The point is, if some dumb mechanic can do this, so can you. You don't have to know how to overhaul anything today. All you have to know is how to take things apart and put them back together.

Taking things apart is easy. It's fixing that's hard because it requires special equipment, tools and endless little parts. No garage has the money to buy all the special equipment and tools needed to overhaul the many separate components in an engine. So they just let specialty shops do it. You do the same thing.

To be a take-it-apart-put-it-back-together-again "expert," all you need is a complete set of socket wrenches, and a few other tools which you should already have.

PREPARATIONS FOR VALVE JOB

Before you start the valve job, you must have on hand all new gaskets. You will need two for the valve head covers, two for the valve heads themselves, two for the water-cooled exhaust manifolds, one for the intake manifold, and one for the thermostat housing if your engine water temperature is controlled, which is only with closed cooling systems.

It is a good idea to have five or six small carton boxes to keep separate all the nuts and bolts you will remove. Also, two larger boxes will be useful for carrying and transporting the two valve heads in the trunk of your car to the machine shop because they will not send that kid in the pickup to get yours. Specialty shops don't service one-shot deals with pickup and delivery. You take it there yourself.

Drain the engine and water-cooled exhaust manifolds. There is a drain plug on each side of the block and under each exhaust manifold. This will get the water out of the area in which you will be working. Remove all hoses which connect to the exhaust manifold.

Both the exhaust and intake manifolds must be removed before you can get at the two valve heads. If the distributor is in the way, it must be removed. This is not difficult, but is ticklish. Before I do this, I always disconnect the ground clamp from the starting battery. This is merely a precautionary thing to prevent any accidents, like unintentionally cranking the engine while the distributor is out. The distributor goes back in that hole precisely as it came out. To assure this, make a reference mark on the distributor housing to line up with another mark on the block. Make a reference mark also for the rotor so it will be in the same position.

If the engine doesn't turn over, the distributor gear will mesh up in proper timing. This is the reason for disconnecting the battery ground cable. The least little bump of the starter will screw up the timing, and that's like eating worms for supper.

If the spark plug wires and distributor cap are in the way, remove, but leave the wires in the cap. Run a strip of masking tape around the distributor cap on which you can write identification numbers for each wire. You might get confused later because many of the spark plug wires are the same length and you might not know which wires goes to which plug.

With a socket wrench (you better have a set) remove all nuts, or bolts, holding down the intake manifold. It is not necessary to remove the carburetor. You may have to bang a screwdriver under one edge to get the manifold loose. Clean off all the old gasket material.

Now you can get at the valve covers. This is where it is nice to have the thin-wall sockets because on some valve covers there is little clearance around the hold-down bolts. Before you pull off the valve covers, have plenty of rags handy to clean up the mess before oil runs down into the bilge. Remove the old gasket, clean both surfaces and glue new gaskets on the covers. By the time the valves are ready, the glue will be set and that will make it easier to get the covers back on.

Use a socket wrench to remove that nut in the center of the valve rocker arm. Remove rocker arms and pull out push rods. Do not dump everything together in one box. The rocker arms and push rods must go back on exactly the same way in the same holes. You must improvise your own way of marking them because no two mechanics do it the same way. However, I'll tell you how I do it. I save the long, shallow carton box that my gaskets were shipped in. I drill 16 holes in the carton lid to fit the push rods, then number every hole. I remove the push rods in numerical order, one to 16, and put them in the numbered box holes the rocker arm end up. The rocker arms themselves I drop over the push rods. Nothing could possibly get mixed up.

Remove all valve head bolts and clean out threads carefully. Good mechanics will run a tap over the threads and oil them to eliminate friction. This is very important because dirty threads will give you a false torque reading, which could lead to disaster. Internal combustion produces high heat. Engine heads expand and contract. If head bolts are tightened slightly more on one side, expansion will crack the head. Borrow or buy a torque wrench before you get ready to reassemble (Fig. 6-3).

Remove the overhead valve heads, clean, and take them to the machine shop. They will replace all the exhaust valves, resurface the intake valves, check the springs, etc. While waiting for your heads, reach down with a magnet and remove the valve lifters for visual inspection and cleaning. Like the push rods, they go back in the same holes with the same end up. If coated with varnish, clean with a strong solvent, rub with oil and drop back in bore holes. Scrape off all the piston tops with a putty knife and vacuum out the crap. See if you can jiggle the pistons with your fingers. Feel for a ridge on the cylinder wall at the top of the piston travel. Don't be surprised to feel a sharp ridge here because a little cylinder wear is normal. That's why they put expanding rings on pistons. However, if the wear is excessive and if the piston can be easily moved back and forth, you will have a knock called "piston slap." This can be muffled with straight 40 viscosity oil, or even 50 if you live in a hot climate.

With the gasket in, drop the valve head in place. Oil all threads and finger tighten all the bolts. If you have a service manual, consult it for torque and sequence on tightening head bolts. This may seem complicated to you and it is, but head bolts must be tightened in proper sequence. If you don't have a service manual, look at Fig. 6-3 and follow the same sequence. The head must be tightened down gradually with even pressure all over. If you tighten down one side too fast, you can crack the head.

Following the sequence in Fig. 6-3 or your service manual, start off with a torque of 10 foot-pounds. Then go up in steps of 20 foot-pounds until you reach a final torque of about 100 to 110 foot-pounds for a V-8, 80 to 90 for a six, and 65 to 75 for four cylinder engines. The torque figures are only approximate because each manufacturer has different torque recommendations. But you won't be too far off using the figures.

Torque the exhaust manifold bolts to 25 foot-pounds. Same with the intake manifold. The valve covers you torque to about 5 foot-pounds.

With reference marks all lined up, drop the distributor back in the hole. Tighten the hold-down bolt. Put on the distributor cap and spark plug wires. Plug in the center wire from coil. Put the ground clamp back on the battery and crank the engine to see if all valve rocker arms are working. Start the engine and check the timing. With the hold-down bolt loosened, you turn the distributor right to advance spark, left to retard. This is fine timing and best done while actually running at high speed. With someone else at the wheel, you turn the distributor back and forth until you get maximum rpm and smoothest running. That will be your optimum timing.

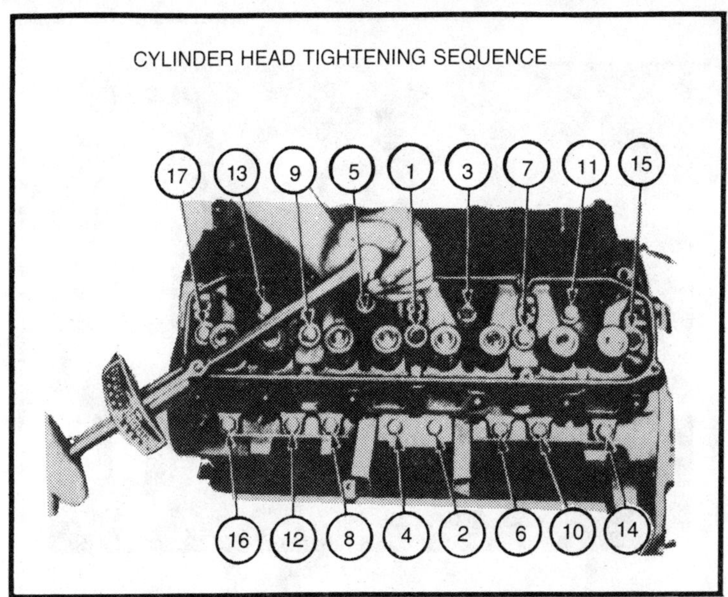

Fig. 6-3. The tightening sequence of cylinder bolts with a torque wrench.

PROPER TORQUING OF SPARK PLUGS

Having spark plugs torqued properly is far more important then realized, both by boaters and car owners. A spark plug dissipates heat to the circulating coolant through its metal-to-contact with the block. If screwed down too lightly it will not dissipate heat properly and run too hot. It may also leak and cause power loss. Too much heat erodes away the electrodes and under extreme conditions can also cause pre-ignition. Too much torque does the same thing and prevents the plug from dissipating heat properly. Too much torque can also strip threads. The only way plugs can be screwed down with precisely the right amount of metal-to-metal pressure is by measuring the turning force (torque) with a torque wrench. The right torque will depend on the plugs used and the engine. An average figure would be 20 to 25 foot-pounds. If you don't have a torque wrench, with the threads oil and finger tighten the plug as far as you can, then with a wrench go a half turn further.

HOT/COLD SPARK PLUGS

Spark plugs come in different heat ranges and this confuses many. What's the difference (Fig. 6-4)? How can you tell? By looking at the plug base, that metal just above the threads. A hot plug will

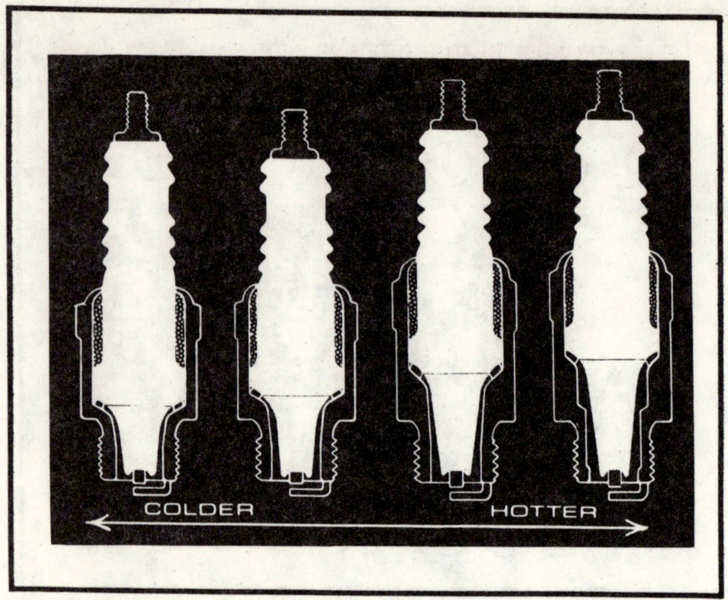

Fig. 6-4. Illustrated are spark plug heat ranges.

have a higher base and a cold plug will have a shorter base. There is more gas and more heat build-up in the higher metal base. Because of the longer travel, it dissipates more slowly to the block. The plug runs "hot" for this reason. The cold plug, with its shorter base, has less heat build-up and a shorter travel for heat dissipation. So this plug runs "cold." Other then this, "hot" and "cold" plugs are the same.

HOW TO CHOOSE THE RIGHT HEAT RANGE

The "right" plug depends on your engine's operating temperatures, and how it is used. For example, do you operate much at high speeds, like water skiing, etc. (Figs. 6-5 and 6-6)? Do you troll or operate at low speeds in cold waters? Cold operating temperatures and low speeds cause plug fouling. Load is also a factor. Pulling skiers at high speed is a load. For this type of service you want a "cold" plug. Low speed, light load and trolling in cold waters calls for a "hot" plug to prevent fouling. It's as simple as that. Why don't manufacturers install the right plugs? They don't know how you're going to use the engine, so they install plugs with "average" heat range. If you want a plug in a higher heat range, just go up in the numbers. For example, if you are using a J-11-Y and want to go up in

Fig. 6-5. Towing water skiers at high speeds is high load operation and requires a cold running plug. Low speed or light load operation, like trolling in cold water, calls for a "hot" plug to prevent fouling.

Fig. 6-6. The sailboat at the left requires a hot running plug because its auxiliary engine gets limited service. It is used mainly for docking purposes and running out channels at very slow speeds. The boat pulling the skiers is operating at top speed and full load. This calls for a "cold" running plug to prevent detonation.

heat, buy J-13-Y; if you want to go down in heat range, buy J-9-Y (Fig. 6-7).

HOW TO DETERMINE PLUG CONDITION

The general appearance of your plugs will tell you whether you need to go up or down in the heat range. Cold fouling plugs will have a black, sooty appearance caused by prolonged operation at idle or trolling speeds. A faulty choke which does not completely open can cause this by providing an over rich fuel/air mixture. One step up in heat range will cure this.

Plugs that are operating at too high a temperature will have a white or gray appearance around the insulator body, even blistered. Gap wear will be excessive around both electrodes. However, before you change this plug, bear in mind that over-advanced timing or cooling system stoppages can also cause this.

Highspeed glazing is a shiny deposit, yellow or tan in color. It usually suggests that plug temperatures have increased due to heavy loads or acceleration, as in towing skiers. For this condition, use a colder plug. Under normal operating conditions with a healthy engine, the few deposits present will be light tan or brown in color with most regular grades of gasoline.

ENGINE THERMOSTATS

In fresh water, some inboard engines with open cooling that just pumps raw water through the engines and out the exhaust run cold, very cold in the spring. The needle on my temperature gauges never moves until the first of June. Even after a hard run, my engines will be just warm to touch.

This is both good and bad. Too much heat in the engine compartment is not good. Too cold an engine is bad for operating efficiency and gas economy. According to a Pontiac Division engineer friend of mine, the internal combustion engine operates at optimum efficiency when the coolant temperature is at 212 degrees, which is the boiling point for water. However, this temperature is tough on oils. It was also impractical with alcohol-based anti-freezes which were used some years ago because alcohol boils at 167 degrees. So, 30 years ago, all cars came from the factory with 150-160 degree thermostats and car heaters produced little warmth in zero weather.

Today, with better oils and high boiling point anti-freezes, cars come from the factories with 185-195 degree thermostats and car

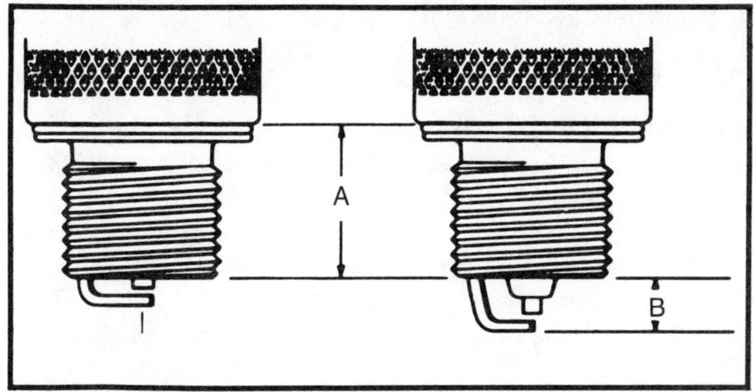

Fig. 6-7. Champion spark plugs are identified by a letter, a number and another letter. For example, in J-14-Y, the prefix letter "J" signifies reach and diameter. The "J" plug has a ⅜ reach, 13/16 hex size and 14 mm diameter. The number "14" is the heat range. The suffix letter "Y" signifies the gap style. The plug to the right is a "Y-gap" plug; the plug to the left is a "J-gap" plug.

heaters work beautifully. And engines work better and get better gas mileage. So why not put a thermostat in a marine engine?

In my owners' manual there is a specific warning about thermostats—the installation of anything in the engine cooling system which interferes with raw water circulation voids the warranty. That means no thermostats, period.

Although it wastes gas and is inefficient, there is a sound practical reason why it is best to let your engines run cold, especially in salt water. The higher the temperature, the faster salt deposits accumulate in your engine cooling water passages. In hot tropical waters, the life expectancy of an inboard engine with raw water cooling is about three or four years. In cold northern waters it is twice that time. In fresh water, high temperatures increase the rate at which silt and mud accumulate in an engine to clog up the water passages.

ENGINE OVERHEATING

You can live with a cold engine, but not with a hot one, and this is a much more common problem in today's polluted waters. Old-fasioned scooped engine water intakes have an affinity for garbage, grass, sea weeds, trash, plastic bags and the larvae of creatures that hatch in water, like mayflies and midges. A considerable amount of junk gets into engine cooling systems which clogs elbows, nipples, couplings, and oil coolers while eating up pump impellers and destroying hoses.

WATER INTAKE STRAINERS

The solution is a water intake strainer—not a filter. A "strainer" does not filter the water or "clean out the mud and silt." To do this would require a filter element as big as your engine. The strainer merely catches all the garbage and the small stuff that gets sucked in the intake. All marine type intake strainers are glass enclosed so you can see the junk accumulation and easily take apart for cleaning.

These strainers are no help with sea weeds, grass or paper bags which get sucked up over the intake and just stick there. This has happened to me twice, once with grass and once with a paper bag.

With two engines, you can always get home on one. But with single screw you stop immediately, or lose an engine.

HOW TO CLEAR A CLOGGED WATER INTAKE

Without water, an engine will freeze in less than five minutes. It can sneak up on you, unless you have idiot lights on your instrument panel. I personally don't like idiot lights, but in a case like this I can see where a bright red light would catch my attention, whereas I might not notice a temperature gauge needle climbing.

There are only two ways out of this mess: go overboard and clear the intake; or go inboard and clear the intake. I prefer the inboard method. It's easier, especially if you have a seacock on the intake.

Close the seacock and remove the hose. Then take a wire coat hanger, cut it, and bend a small "L" on one end. Drill a hole through the cork center for the wire, then insert the cork in the hose nipple over the seacock.

Open the seacock and push and probe with the coat hanger wire. There are seven long slots on the intake strainer. Work the cork around, and push the wire through all the slots. When I did it, I could see I was clearing away the obstruction because water was starting to seep in around the cork. When I momentarily removed the cork, water gushed in. So I closed the seacock. There was a piece of brown paper stuck to the wire, which is how I knew it was a paper bag. Incidently, this is why it is so important to have seacocks on all through-hull openings. It makes the clearing of that intake so much easier.

CLOSED COOLING SYSTEMS

A closed cooling system is precisely the same thing you have in your car (Fig. 6-8). You just circulate the same water/anti-freeze

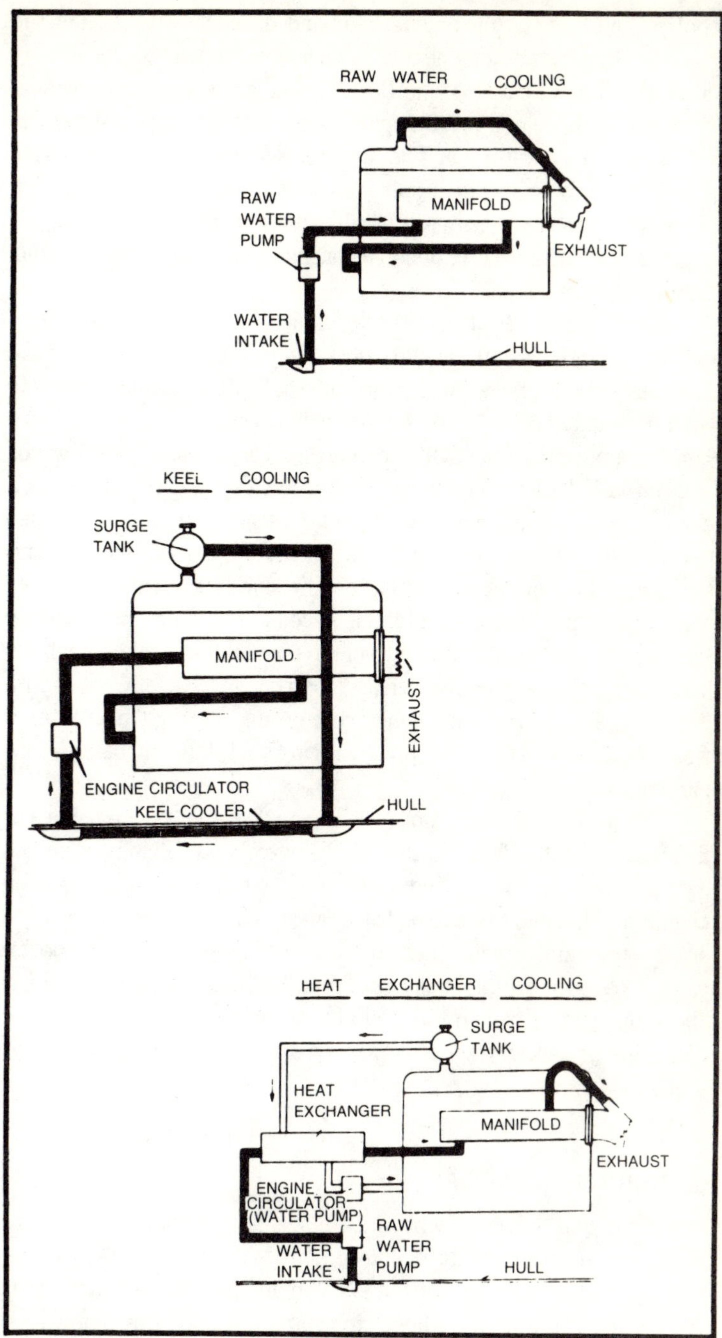

Fig. 6-8. The three types of cooling systems for marine engines.

coolant and it picks up engine heat and dissipates it through the radiator. In a marine engine a radiator is impractical. You just can't dissipate all that heat into your boat. So you dissipate it into the sea. This is how more and more engines are cooled today, especially in salt water. You will never find raw sea water cooling in a marine diesel. Nobody is going to spend all that money for an expensive diesel and then ruin it with salt water in about three years. Even gas engines are getting so expensive that you just can't afford to cool them with salt water.

Some years ago it was the fashion to put copper pipes along keels as radiotelephone ground plates. An electronics buff I know did this, but decided he wanted more use out of the copper pipe. He wanted a closed cooling system for his big yacht, so he installed two 1-inch copper pipes on each side of his keel and brazed the forwards ends into a U-turn. These two pipes became the heat exchanger for a closed engine cooling system which he installed himself. They also became the ground for his 150-watt radiotelephone. When he put that damn thing on the air I could feel the skin on my arms tingle as I walked past his boat and antenna. A coastguardsman in Sandusky told me that "when that boat in Toledo comes on the air, somebody here always falls out of bed." The closed cooling system, along with the outside plumbing, made one great ground for the transmitter. I was tempted to do the same thing with my boat, but who needs more enemies?

Closed cooling only cools the engine, not the exhaust system. Sea water must still be used to cool the exhaust. This requires an extra water pump. Closed cooling also requires an expansion chamber similar to the one on top of auto radiators. This is usually a small round tank attached near the front of the engine where coolant can back up when it expands on heating. Without this the coolant will "back up" right through the wall of your engine block. You'll make dental history when you bite off a piece of exhaust manifold with your teeth.

GETTING TOP ENGINE RPM

With your valves ground and timing set for peak rpm, if you are still below the 3600 or 4400 your engine is designed to operate at, and assuming that your bottom is clean and free of barnacles, then you are using the wrong wheel. So what do you do? Buy a new one, or repitch what you have.

If you own a big Chris Craft, and have not seen propeller prices recently, I have before me a current price schedule, 77-1, for Chris Craft and Mercruiser engine propellers. An 18-inch wheel will cost you $148. A 24-inch wheel sells for $354. A 30-inch wheel costs $563.

I presume, after careful consideration, you have decided to repitch the wheels you have. Smart move. In case you don't understand what numbers like 14×14 mean, that first figure is outside diameter and the second figure is pitch. In theory, this means that for every complete revolution, the propeller will screw itself forward 14 inches if it were turning in something semi-solid, like butter. However, in water there is many a slip with each turn of the wheel. This is why propellers are made in so many different shapes and blades. The idea is to reduce slippage, improve efficiency and increase speed. Some boaters become so wrapped up in this that they develop a paranoia about propellers. They become propeller freaks. I know one who has his garage filled with over a hundred propellers. His wife talks of having him committed.

Be warned! Propeller-psychosis is like a disease, so don't get yourself too involved. Just take your wheels to the marina and have them do what is necessary. A 1-inch change in pitch will increase rpm 250 to 300. Two inches is the maximum pitch change that can be made. It is better to have the peak rpm over than under because you don't cruise at full throttle. Always remember, a free easy turning engine is a happy engine. If you don't keep your engine happy, you'll be working on the valves again next year. So lots of luck.

LEAD-FREE GAS AND YOUR VALVES

While still on the subject of valves, unless your engine is specifically designed for them, stay away from the no-lead gasolines or you'll have another valve job even with the right propeller. If the oil companies had just gone back to making old-fashioned white marine gas, everything would have been fine. But they added phosphorous after auto manufacturers complained that the new lead-free gas was causing valve recession.

The phosphorous stopped valve recession, but created another monster which is even worse. In older engines, there are build-ups of old lead deposits. The phosphorous reacts on these lead deposits, heating them to incandescence. This causes pre-ignition, melted pistons, burned out valves and holes in pistons. New cars have no prior lead deposits. They also have special new type valve seats and hardened valves.

THE MOST IMPORTANT ENGINE WORK

There is a tendency when writing a book like this to touch all bases and cover everything on engines. I am not going to do this because there are things on your engine that you do not need to know about, and I will not waste time telling you how to fix them. For example, in my lifetime I have owned 22 automobiles, and just as many boats. I have traveled millions of miles in both. Yet I have never, never had any trouble with a fuel pump. Maybe this is a world record. Consequently, I know very little about fuel pumps. But ever since I was a kid with my first set of wheels my nose has been stuck down into a distributor. Consequently, I know a great deal about distributors. And why so much trouble with distributors? That's where all the action is.

Ignition is the most important thing you need to know about your engine. It is the most important work you will ever perform (Fig. 6-9). If you understand ignition, and learn how to work in this area, you will never have any serious problems, assuming, of course, you always remember to buy gas. That is why I am concentrating on ignition and ignoring fuel pumps, starters, crankshafts, piston rings and reverse gears.

If an engine won't start, there are just two things to check. First, you look down into the carburetor to see if it is getting gas. You do this first because it is the simplest and easiest. When you work the throttle, you can actually see gasoline squirt into the carburetor. That means everything is okay on this end, so you concentrate on ignition because that is where the trouble is.

An internal combustion engine, except diesels, will not function without a tiny electric spark. It seems like such a trivial thing, but yet even the atomic bomb had to have a catalyst. The "catalyst" that makes your engine run is a tiny spark that sets off a chain reaction of motion which is finally transmitted as torque to the propeller shaft on your boat.

One of my college professors said in a lecture on energy: "The internal combustion engine is a miracle because so much depends on so little."

And he was right. If you ever took a long good look at a distributor, you would understand what he meant. The "points" in a distributor are actually nothing but a small electric switch—and a frighteningly small one when you consider the importance of what passes through it many thousand times every minute.

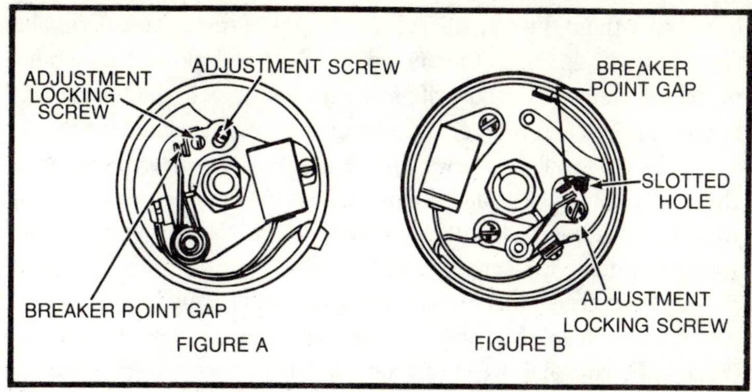

Fig. 6-9. The inside of a distributor is where all the action is. If you understand this, you can handle most of your service work and you won't be adrift at sea because you can't get the engine started. If you've got gas, and the engine won't start or run, this is almost always where the trouble is.

That insignificant little "switch" costs pennies, yet a $15,000 Cadillac is just two tons of scrap iron without it. That is what the professor was talking about. When you realize how fragile and how vulnerable to so many natural forces that switch is, you will understand what a miracle it is that the bloody thing works as well as it does.

The "gap" in the switch points when it is open is measured in thousandths of an inch. A change in the gap of only one thousandth can affect seriously the timing of an engine to such a degree that it will be hard to start. It will knock and backfire. And when you consider all the forces that are at play to change that gap, you wonder how an engine is ever kept in "tune."

Well, it isn't. To keep an engine running at peak efficiency, you would have to check and reset the points at least once a week. That is impractical. So 50 million American automobiles with old-fashioned points ignition systems are polluting the atmosphere with excessive emissions caused by untuned engines.

HOW TO GET A "HOTTER" IGNITION

There are all sorts of junk gadgets available to produce a magical "hotter" ignition for your engine. If you read the advertisements, they even convince you with words that the damn things work. But they don't. They don't really have to work because you already have a "hot" ignition. You just temporarily lost it.

So how did you lose it? The answer is in one word, resistance! This is a big word in electricity. There would be no electronic industry without the control and varied uses of resistance. A variable resistor controls the volume on your TV set and radio. A resistance produces the heat on your wife's electric range. A resistance is used in the gasoline and temperature gauges on your instrument panel.

Resistance also screws up things in your ignition system to cause a weak ignition, bad timing and even a complete breakdown. Resistance is good when used and under control. Resistance is bad when you don't want it.

And where is this "resistance" you don't want?

Everywhere! In a loose connection there is resistance! In a corroded terminal there is resistance! A much overlooked source of resistance are the battery cable terminals, with all that vile looking gook on them. Why do you suppose they put such big terminals on those cables? To provide a large surface area and a tight grip on the battery poles for good electrical contact and low resistance losses. When you only have 12 volts to begin with, you can't afford to lose any. Battery terminals become badly corroded; resistance builds up and drops voltage. A 10 percent drop in voltage to the primary side of the coil can add up to a 2,000 volt drop on the secondary side of the coil.

It all adds up. It's cumulative. A few ohms here, a few ohms there. You put in resistor spark plugs to cut down noise in your radiotelephone. You add more ohms of resistance with "interference eliminating" spark plug wires and the high tension wire from the coil to the distributor. The contacts on the distributor points become corroded and pitted because of arcing and more resistance. You add up all these ohms of resistance and suddenly you understand why it's a miracle that you have any ignition. Without that tiny spark at the end of a spark plug, all you've got in your boat is a big hunk of scrap iron for ballast.

So what do you do?

RESISTOR PLUGS AND RESISTOR SPARK PLUG WIRE

If someone at the marina store didn't tell you when you bought a new set of spark plug "noise suppressor" wire and a set of resistor plugs that you couldn't use both, then I will tell you. Get rid of either the resistor plugs or the resistance wire. You can not use both. Since you must make a choice, keep the wire and get rid of the plugs.

Automobiles come from the factory with resistance radio "noise suppressor" spark plug wires, but not resistor plugs. Spark plugs themselves cause no radio interference because they are grounded.

Conventional spark plug wire acts as an antenna to radiate high frequency oscillations which your radio picks up. If you still have noise, there are other ways to suppress it without resistor plugs. I will cover this in a later chapter on electronic gear. Resistor plugs are good for only one purpose, to throw at sea gulls that are messing up your boat and dock.

THE BATTERY TERMINALS

Study Fig. 6-10. You will note that there are two types of voltage in the ignition system, low "primary" voltage and high tension "secondary" voltage. You can have trouble on both sides Let's start at the source of all that energy, your battery terminals. If a marina mechanic installed your battery, he followed standard procedure and put some grease or vaseline on the terminals. All this does is add to the mess you eventually have to clean off. Further-

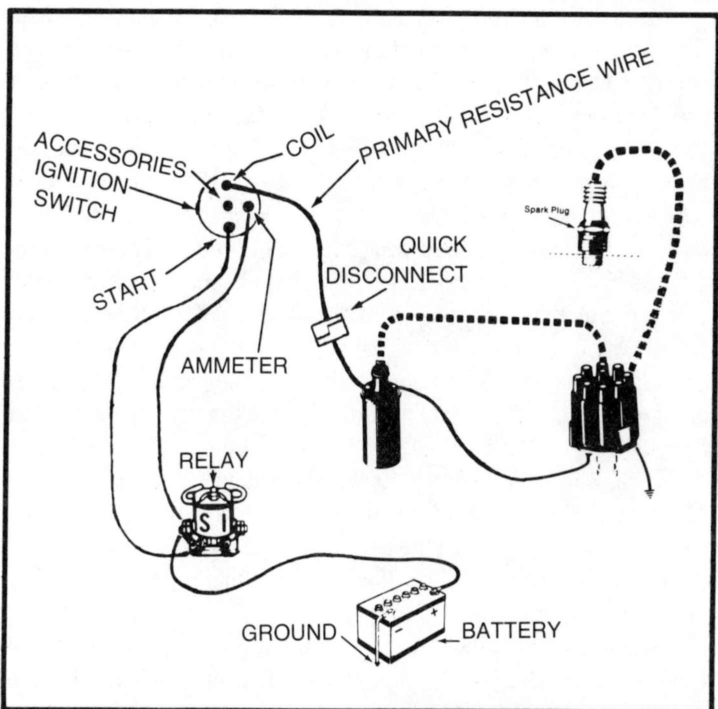

Fig. 6-10. This is where all the trouble starts. The solid lines are low voltage, which is 12 volts from the battery. The dotted lines are high voltage, up to 20,000 volts. Resistance on the low voltage side can mean a big drop on the high voltage side. Resistance, leakage, or arcing on the high voltage side can mean hard starting or no starting at all.

more, oil seeps down around the battery post. Oil is not a good electrical conductor with low voltage. I have seen resistance so high at battery terminals that the starter would not crank. It just burped when the key was turned. Yet, when the terminals and posts were cleaned and retightened, the starter worked perfectly.

BATTERY VISUAL INSPECTION

Disconnect battery cables. Clean the battery top with a solution of clean warm water and baking soda. Scrub with a stiff brush and be careful not to scatter corrosion residue. Wipe off with a cloth moistened with ammonia or baking soda. Caution: keep baking soda out of battery cells or you will weaken the electrolyte.

Check battery cables. Is the gauge heavy enough? Boat batteries are not always close to the engines. In house boats I have seen batteries installed 8 feet from the engine.

Clean battery terminals and inside surfaces of clamp terminals with a regular battery cleaning tool or emery cloth. Before connecting cable clamps to the battery, observe polarity to be doubly sure you don't put the plus (+) clamp on the negative (−) battery post. The plus battery post is always slightly larger in diameter than the negative post. Sometimes there will be a + mark stamped on top of the post. If you ever accidently cross the polarity on a battery, even for a second, it means alternator overhaul. You will burn out all the diodes. In a rectifying diode, current flows in only one direction. If you reverse that flow, you ruin the diode. Alternators generate 12-volt AC. Engines, however, run on DC. So the diodes rectify this by changing the AC to DC. Since current can only flow through them in one direction, they block out one half of the alternating current flow.

That is the reason for all the warnings about "polarity" reversal. Most marine engines, and auto as well, have negative ground. That means the ground post on the battery, the smaller one, always bolts on to the engine somewhere. If you just get this one right, you can't be wrong with the other.

Tighten battery hold-down screw nuts to three foot-pounds. Connect cable clamps to battery posts and tighten securely. The experts say you should put light mineral grease or petrolatum on all connections. Personally, I never do this because for the short time that my boat is in commission, terminal corrosion is no problem. In southern waters where boats stay in the water the whole year, I would say put on the grease.

Another reason for "weak" spark is low voltage from the battery. This can be caused by a bad cell or a battery in a low state of charge. If your batteries are at 50 percent charge, they will always

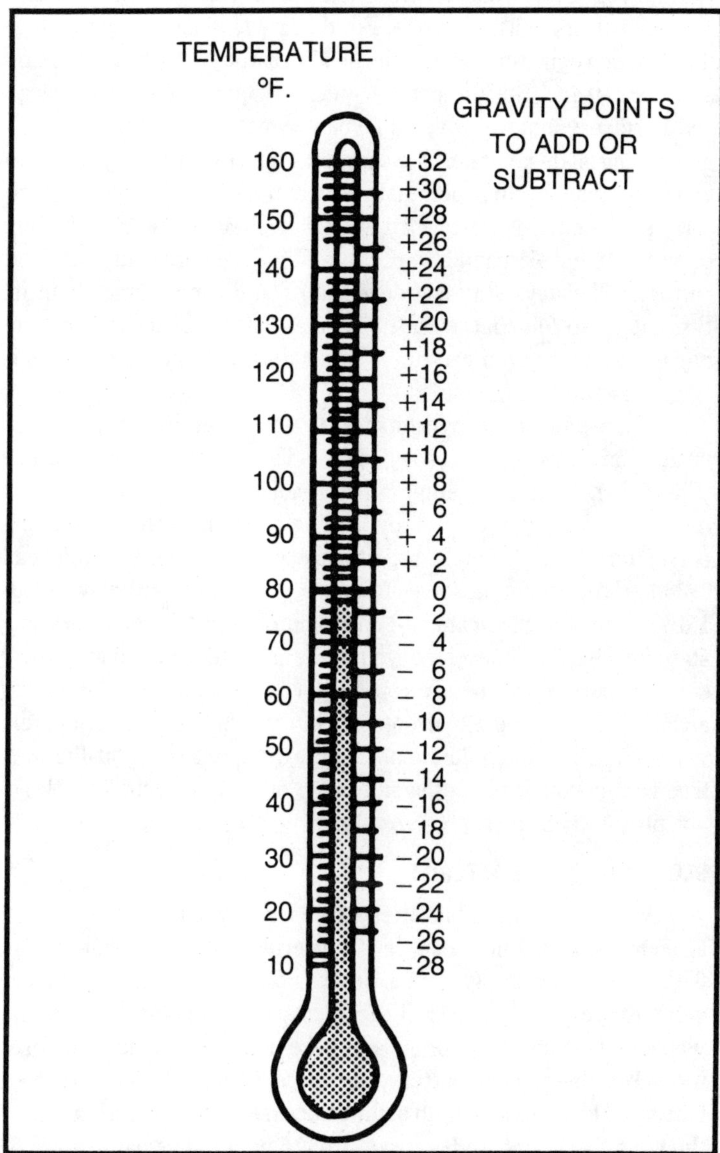

Fig. 6-11. Checking a battery with a hydrometer doesn't tell you much unless you know the temperature. The hydrometer correction chart will tell you why.

stay at 50 percent because alternators don't really charge a battery. They just hold it wherever it happens to be. A half-charged battery will always stay half-charged until you charge it up by other means. The reason your alternator won't charge up your battery is the voltage regulator won't let it. The no-load voltage test on a discharged battery will be 12 volts. For the first few minutes of running, the voltage regulator will permit the alternator to put 10 to 15 amps into the battery. But the battery quickly acquires a surface charge and surface voltage of over 14 volts. So the regulator, which is monitoring all this, cuts off the charging amps to zero and you get no more charging for your poor half-dead battery. The alternator itself carries the entire electrical load, with the voltage regulator adjusting output to meet demand and no more. As a result, your half dead battery will always stay half dead until you do something about it. Bring it up to full charge with a regular battery charger. Once an engine is started, you can run it with a dead battery. But getting it started is something else.

When you buy a hydrometer to test your battery, get the professional type which reads both specific gravity and temperature (Fig. 6-11). Without a temperature reading, the gravity reading is meaningless, as you can tell by looking at the hydrometer reading correction chart. A fully charged battery, at 80 degrees, will read 1.260. Hydrometer floats usually are not calibrated below about 1.160 and cannot indicate the condition of a battery in a very low state of charge. Therefore you may have to give your battery several hours charge before you can get a reading to see if it is taking a charge. In reading a hydrometer, the gauge barrel must be held vertically and enough fluid must be drawn up into it to lift the float free so it does not touch the sides, top or bottom of the barrel. Do not tilt the hydrometer.

SLOW CHARGING BATTERIES

Many discharged batteries can be brought to good condition again by slow charging, especially batteries that are sulphated (Fig. 6-12). Safe slow charge rate is determined by allowing one ampere per positive plate per cell. That means the safe slow charge rate would be four amperes for a 48 ampere hour battery, five amperes for a 59 ampere hour battery, six amperes for a 70 ampere hour battery. The average length of time necessary to charge a battery by the slow charge method is from 12 to 16 hours. The battery will be fully charged when it is gasing (and bubbling) freely and when there is no further rise in specific gravity.

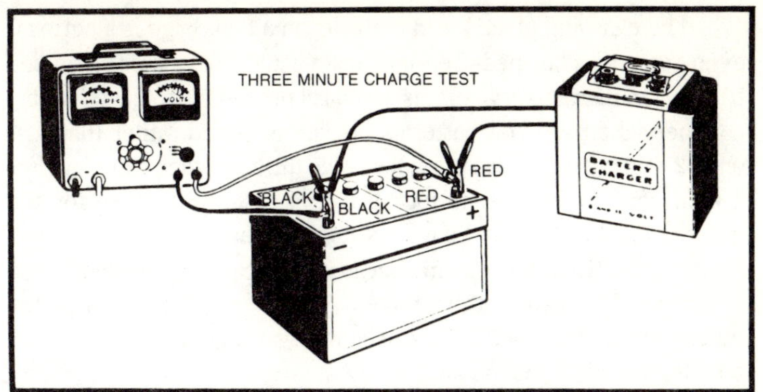

Fig. 6-12. If a battery fails to show a voltage rise after a three-minute fast charge, it is not taking a charge. If the voltage does rise, continue charging at a low rate.

Many sulphated batteries can be brought back to useful condition by slow charging at half the normal charging rate from 60 to 100 hours. This long charging cycle is necessary to reconvert crystalline lead sulphate into active materials. Batteries that are sulphated have the following characteristics: battery temperature tends to increase rapidly while charging; specific gravity increases very slowly, or not at all; battery gases excessively; and a higher than normal voltage (14 volts) is required to obtain a normal charging rate.

After the battery has been fully charged, if it fails to hold that charge, check for a cracked cell partition. Use your hydrometer bulb to blow air into each cell. If bubbles appear in an adjacent cell, you have a cracked cell. Buy a new battery.

When checking a fully charged battery with a hydrometer, if any cell has a specific gravity reading that is 25 points (.025) or more below other cells, that cell is faulty. Buy a new battery.

New batteries can be fast charged but never longer than one hour. If the battery does not show a significant rise in specific gravity after one hour of "fast" charge, the slow charge method should be used. Never permit electrolyte temperature to exceed 125 degrees during charging. Let the battery cool before continuing charge.

When batteries are being charged in the bilge of a boat, an explosive gas mixture forms beneath the cover of each cell. Do not smoke near batteries on charge or which have recently been charged. Do not break live circuits at the terminals of batteries on charge. A spark will occur where the live circuit is broken. It only takes a tiny spark that you can't even see. And lots of luck in the hospital.

The charging of lead-acid batteries in a boat bilge is a serious, even hazardous business because boats usually have more than one battery. In marine service, it is standard procedure to have two big commercial type 6-volt batteries hooked in series rather than just one 12-volt battery. This provides twice the amperage capacity. For a twin screw, this means four batteries, plus one more for the generator. On my boat I have six huge boxes of lead and I never charge more than one at a time because I'm scared to death of those monsters. My sixth battery is kept "clean" separate from all the others so it doesn't pick up a lot of ignition garbage. I use this battery only for the radio-telephone.

IGNITION SWITCH

When tuning an engine, not even the professionals think of checking that switch on your instrument panel that you turn with a key to start the engine. Yet, when everything else fails to find the source of trouble, it will be here.

The sea environment is rough on all types of electrical switching devices. If it was practical, I'd take them all home with me in the winter. I once installed a battery condition meter on a bulkhead near my wheel. By pushing buttons, it told me everything I needed to know about all six of my batteries. I was so proud of that thing. But I made the mistake of leaving it on the boat during winter layup. The next season it wasn't worth a damn. Corrosion ruined it in one winter.

If your ignition switch is making poor contact, you have high resistance. That means a drop in voltage. That means trouble like hard starting, missing, even dropping dead in the water which, according to Murphy's Law, will be at the worst possible time.

When the mechanic starts working on your engine, after you tell him what happened, he will shake his head knowlingly and mumble something about "bad points," "wet plugs," and "bad coil." This is not to suggest that he is incompetent; it's just that the symptoms are the same and it could be all those things. So rarely will the mechanics ever check the ignition switch because most marina mechanics are basically automobile mechanics who switched rather than fight. The ignition switch never causes trouble in an automobile, so they assume it will cause no trouble in a boat. Well, it does.

For one thing, auto owners aren't forever adding new accessories like extra bilge pumps, windshield wipers, horns, hailers, depth finders, remote compasses, etc. And all these things will be hooked up to the ignition switch. I have seen five and six wire terminals all piled on one screw with barely enough room for the nut. The result was a sloppy, loose connection with high resistance.

Often, with self-installed equipment, the owner will not notice those tiny letters "bat" and "ign" stamped on the back and they will hook up some accessory to the "ign" terminal. This can cause trouble because that wire marked "ign" supplies primary voltage to the coil. There is a ballast resistor in this line to drop the battery voltage down to a level where less current will flow through the primary windings. Sometimes instead of a ballast resistor, a special type of wire with built-in resistance will be used. Now all this has been computed on a precise voltage and current flow. If you add the slightest additional load or resistance to that connection on the switch, you start a snowball rolling downhill.

Check all connections on the switch for corrosion and tightness. If the switch looks bad, and you decide to replace, be sure to identify all the wires you remove so they go back on the same way.

Check the wire from "ign" to coil. There is usually a break-apart connector in this line. The ballast, if you have one, will be a ceramic-covered coil or just two coils of resistance wire. If there have been overloads, it will look burnt. Corrosion also thins out resistance wire; this further lowers primary voltage. You can lower that primary voltage just so far, then you're in trouble.

IGNITION COIL

I have never been able to learn why they call the ignition coil a "coil." It is a small transformer and nothing else. You have a primary winding. You have a soft iron core. You have a secondary winding. According to all the schematic drawings I have ever seen, that represents a transformer.

The transformer is one of the most efficient devices ever invented by man. It has no moving parts. It doesn't pollute the atmosphere. It doesn't poison cow's milk. It doesn't cause cancer in white rats. Since there is no wear or tear, they should last forever. Sometimes they don't.

Coils get blamed for a lot of things and are the favorite whipping boy for those "mechanics" you find back in the boondocks or on Route 40 gas stations west of Kansas. No matter what your trouble, if it is something not visibly apparent like a broken fan belt or if it is something that has to be diagnosed or tracked down, these "mechanics" always cop out the easy way with: "You gotta bad coil, mister."

Thousands of perfectly good coils have been removed in this manner, and then later sold to somebody else with a "bad coil."

There is no such thing as a "weak" coil or a "faulty" coil. They are not batteries that run down. A coil is either good or bad. If you are able to get home with your engine, there is nothing wrong with your coil. If there was, you would still be drifting somewhere with a dead engine waiting for the coast guard.

Under normal service, a coil will outlive you and your boat. However, coils are ruined by dumb or careless mechanics who neglect to ground the center distributor wire when cranking the engine to check dwell, or get the points in position for setting. The secondary windings are very fine wire. They can be broken by a built-up of high voltage which has no place to go if the coil is not grounded. If a strand of wire in the coil is broken, it is finished. Like Humpty Dumpty, you can never put it back together again.

High heat will damage coils by causing fine hairline cracks in the top around the terminals. High voltage will arc and leak through these cracks which you can't even see. Check the two small terminals on the low voltage side. One side goes to the switch and the other to the distributor. The third terminal is that rubber-booted tower in the center from whence comes a tiger that is always looking for a way to escape.

THE DISTRIBUTOR

Low voltage is easy to control and stays put until you close a circuit. But high voltage is a snarling tiger, ready at any instant to jump right out of the wire. That is the reason for those huge, ribbed insulators on high tension wires, and why spark plug insulators are also ribbed. High voltage will leak over the skin surface of insulators when wet or in high humidity. By putting deep ribs on the insulators, the travel distance over the skin surface is considerably lengthened and a 2-foot insulator has the surface resistance of a 4-foot insulator. This keeps the tiger in the wire where he belongs. But sometimes when potential builds up excessively high, the tiger will jump over the insulators to ground. That's what happens in a thundercloud, an over build-up of electrons arcs to ground with a loud noise, which we see and hear as lightning and thunder.

To control the tiger in ignition systems, spark plug wires are heavily insulated, distributor terminals are deeply recessed and covered with rubber boots, and still the tiger gets away sometimes through invisible holes in insulation and hairline cracks in coil covers and distributor caps. Spark plug wires should be held by harnesses and not allowed to lay on the engine.

There are many mechanics, good ones, too, who do not understand these things about high voltage. They treat it no differently than low voltage. These are the mechanics who will stick a sharp test probe into spark plug wires to see if the plugs are getting a spark. The holes left in the insulation are invisible to the eye, but not to the tiger.

HOW TO FIND HIGH TENSION LEAKS

To check spark plug wires for leaks, connect one end of a test probe to ground. Disconnect the cable at spark plug end and tie it off away from the engine. With the engine running, move the test probe along the entire length of wire. If punctures or cracks are present in the insulation, there will be a noticeable spark jump to the probe. Check all the wires, one at a time, in this manner. The secondary coil wire which goes to the center distributor terminal can also be checked in this same manner. But be sure one spark plug wire (only one) is disconnected when you make this test.

SERVICING SECONDARY CIRCUIT

All of the high tension cables must be checked for good contact at the coil, distributor and spark plugs. Wire terminals should be deeply seated. The rubber boots on both plugs and distributors should be in good condition and should fit tightly. Cable connections that are loose will corrode, increase resistance and permit water to enter the tower and cause hard-to-find ignition malfunctions that mechanics often can't locate. Rather than admit they're stumped, they say: "You gotta bad coil, mister."

To maintain the proper air seal, high tension cables should not be pulled out of the distributor or off the plugs unless absolutely necessary for replacement or because you suspect high resistance or broken insulation. When replacing cables, squeeze the air out of the rubber boots as you slide them over the distributor terminals.

CHECKING CABLE RESISTANCE

Resistance type spark plug wire will usually have some identification printed on them like "Electronic Suppression." If you own a vom (volt-ohm-meter), here's your chance to use it. Check out the actual resistance of all plug wires. Do not pull wires out of the distributor. Just remove the cap and the other end of each wire from the plug. Take resistance readings from the inside cap to the spark plug terminal. If resistance is more then 30,000 ohms, pull the wire out of cap and check it. If resistance is still more than 30,000 ohms, replace the wire. Test all wires in the same manner.

You can test distributor coil wire the same way. If combined resistance through cap and wire is more then 25,000 ohms, make another test with wire pulled out of distributor tower. If wire resistance alone is more then 15,000 ohms, replace the wire.

The purpose of all this "resistance" is to cut off the dragging tail on ignition spark, which on a oscilloscope looks like a comet. Only the forward hot end of the spark is actually needed to ignite the fuel in the combustion chamber, according to Champion Spark Plug engineers. The dragging tail creates a lot of turbulence that you pick up as noise in your radio. Resistance is supposed to cut off only the static-producing tail, which you don't need for ignition, so say the engineers. But too much resistance cuts down the forward end of the comet as well, and you have "weak spark" and missing.

HOW TO TEST DISTRIBUTOR RESISTANCE

If you bought one of those Tach-Dwell units at K-Mart or Bargain Barn for $7.95, here's your chance to use it. Checking resistance from the distributor side of the coil through the contacts (also called points) on to ground is an important test because this is where resistance causes voltage drops. The opening and closing of the contacts produces a pulsating current flow through the primary windings. This is what makes a transformer work, a pulsating or alternating current. A transformer will not work with DC. The contacts change all that and make the transformer work by interrupting the flow of DC so that it induces a rising and collapsing magnetic field in the primary windings in the same manner as AC. So the transformer works. Low 12 volts goes in, high 20,000 volts comes out—that is, if there is no voltage drop in the distributor.

To make a resistance check, proceed with a tack-dwell meter. Keep test leads apart, turn the selector switch to "Calibrate" position and adjust dwell calibration until meter needle stops on "set" line. With selector switch still in "calibrate" position, connect red lead to the distributor terminal of coil and the black lead to ground (any part of engine).

Turn ignition switch "on." The meter needle should be well within the bar marked "distributor resistance." If reading is zero or outside of bar, give engine a slight crank until meter needle moves as far right as possible. This indicates that point contacts are closed. If the needle is now within the bar, distributor resistance is normal. If it is outside the bar, there is high resistance.

Remove red test lead from distributor terminal on coil and connect it to the distributor primary terminal on the outside of the housing. Note the reading for resistance. Repeat this check to the inside terminal. Attach red terminal to each side of the points to check resistance through their contact surface. Attach red lead to distributor housing. Repeat these tests at all connections until a noticeable change occurs in the meter reading. This is how you find bad connections with high resistance. When you find one, remove the wires and clean the terminals with emery cloth.

DISTRIBUTOR CONTACTS OR "POINTS"

Pitting on "points" contact surfaces results from the transfer of metal from one surface to the other. A slight amount of pitting is normal, but when you have long sharp spikes, that is harmful and causes arcing and voltage loss. These points should be replaced.

After a few hours of operation, points will have a rough appearance, but this is normal. However, if contact surfaces are oily, mottled or dark in color, they will soon cause trouble. High primary voltage causes excessively high current flow which burns points rapidly. A bad voltage regulator can be the cause of this. So can a defective condenser or improper contact "gap" adjustment.

THE CONDENSER

When I was a kid building electronic gear, a condenser was a condenser. Today it's a capacitor. It's still the same thing, so I still call them condensers.

The condenser is connected to the "hot" side of the points and to ground where it serves the same function as a shock arrester in plumbing water lines. When you open a water faucet, then close it suddenly, pressure build-up will make your water pipes slam with an annoying sound. To stop this, you install a shock absorber in the water lines so that when high pressure water flow is suddenly stopped, that pressure buildup has someplace to go.

In electric current flow you have the same thing happen when you abruptly open and close a switch. The electric current wants to keep on flowing and in the case of points, where the gap is only a few thousandths of an inch, the current does keep on flowing by jumping the gap. This is called arcing and it is bad because unless there is a clean break in current flow, there will be a weak collapse of the magnetic field in the primary, and a corresponding weak collapse in the secondary. The result is a weak increase in voltage, or sometimes even none.

So the condenser does exactly what the shock absorber does in a water line. It absorbs the back pressure of current flow when it charges one plate of the condenser. This "charge" in one plate of the condenser passes through the condenser to ground on the next cycle. Direct current will not go through a condenser, but AC or pulsating DC will.

The condenser, by absorbing back pressure, eliminates arcing across the point gap so there is a clean break in current flow. Condensers, like coils, have no moving parts and never actually wear out. We used to make them in school with rolled up layers of tinfoil and wax paper. The wax paper insulator between the tinfoil "plates" of the condenser are called the dielectric. In a variable tuning condenser, like you have on radios, the dielectric is the air between the plates. When a condenser goes bad, it's because something went wrong with the dielectric and there is a leakage.

If you find evidences of arcing on the breaker contact surfaces, replace the condenser. It is now more or less standard procedure to do this anyway when installing new points because condensers cost so little and they do so much.

THE ROTOR

I remember an old movie where a chain gang prisoner, who as a trusty mechanic serviced all the prison cars and trucks, removed all the rotors from distributors before he escaped in a pick-up truck. It was funny watching those guards cranking away at their cars while he blithely drove away with no one in pursuit. Even if they had discovered the rotors were removed, what could they do? Where do you buy a distributor rotor on Saturday afternoon? If you do much cruising, think about that for a moment.

I had plenty of time to think one weekend in a small Canadian village on Lake Huron. I had removed my distributor cap to check the points. Putting those caps back on can be tricky with some distributors because you can get them slightly off on one side, even though the notch fits correctly. When I cranked the engine, the rotor hit one of the terminals and broke.

It was late Saturday and the closest possible source for a new rotor was Port Huron, Michigan, 75 miles away. On Monday morning I had to hire someone to drive me to Port Huron. That lousy two dollar rotor finally cost me 50 bucks. This is one of the reasons why I am such a nut today about spare parts like rotors, condensers, points, belts, plugs, propellers, shafts, etc.

I am a great believer in Murphy's Law because it has been proven to me many times. I have removed and replaced distributor caps a million times, but only once did I put one back slightly crooked. It has to be on a day when I was 75 miles away from no place at all. If you want to survive in the sea, always prepare for the worst. Then it will never happen.

Distributor rotors may look good on visual inspection, but they can have invisible aches and pains like hairline cracks. The metal surfaces which handle high voltage can pit and char. Erosion of the rotor tip increases the gap distance the voltage must jump to each plug terminal on the inside of the cap. This, in time, means trouble. When you replace rotor, keep the old one in your junk box for emergencies.

INSTALLING NEW "POINTS"

Loosen the terminal screw-nut and remove primary and condenser wires. Remove lockscrew on the stationary contact point and then take out the point. Install a new set of points. Connect primary and condenser wires. Align points. Bend the stationary arm if necessary, but never bend the movable contact.

After aligning points, adjust gap clearance according to engine manufacturer specifications with either thickness gauge or a dwell meter. The degrees of distributor dwell are the degrees through which the contact points remain closed. This is also called "dwell angle" or "cam angle." Connect dwell red lead to distributor terminal on coil and the black lead to ground. Crank engine with starter and adjust point gap until you get the proper reading for V-8, 6 or 4 cylinder engines.

IGNITION TIMING

To obtain maximum engine efficiency, the distributor must be correctly positioned on the engine to get proper timing. There are two ways to get this optimum timing. During actual operation of your boat at top speed with someone else at the wheel, you at the engine turn the distributor slowly right-left until you get maximum rpm reading on the tach. As you turn left, the engine will slow down; as you turn right, it will also slow down. Right in the middle is your best timing.

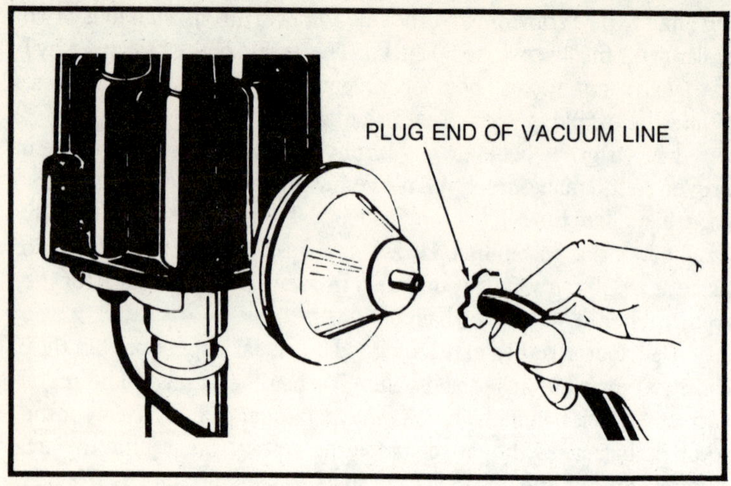

Fig. 6-13. After removing the vacuum hose, plug the end with a wad of paper.

The second way to do this is with a Timing Light, and since you bought one at K-Mart you, naturally, want to try it. Disconnect the vacuum hose at the distributor (Fig. 6-13). Connect secondary lead of timing light to No. 1 spark plug. This is the first plug on the left and front of engine. Connect the red lead to the positive terminal of the battery, black lead to negative. Start the engine and let it idle. Loosen the distributor hold-down screw just enough so you can manually turn the housing (Fg. 6-14).

Aim timing light at timing plate on flywheel (Fig. 6-15). There will be a main specification "BTC" mark, and smaller marks or

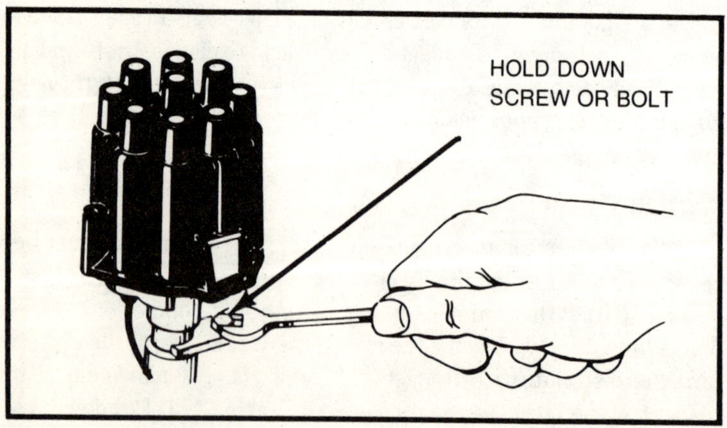

Fig. 6-14. The hold down bolt for the distributor is down on the engine block and in back.

268

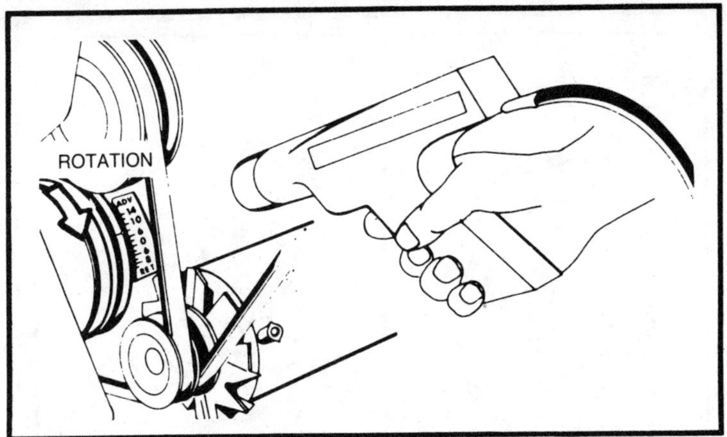

Fig. 6-15. Aim the timing light at flywheel graduation marks.

graduations on each side of it. If a light flash occurs when timing marker is past the "BTC" mark, in the direction of engine rotation, timing is retarded (Fig. 6-16). To adjust, turn the distributor housing right against the direction of rotor rotation. This advances spark.

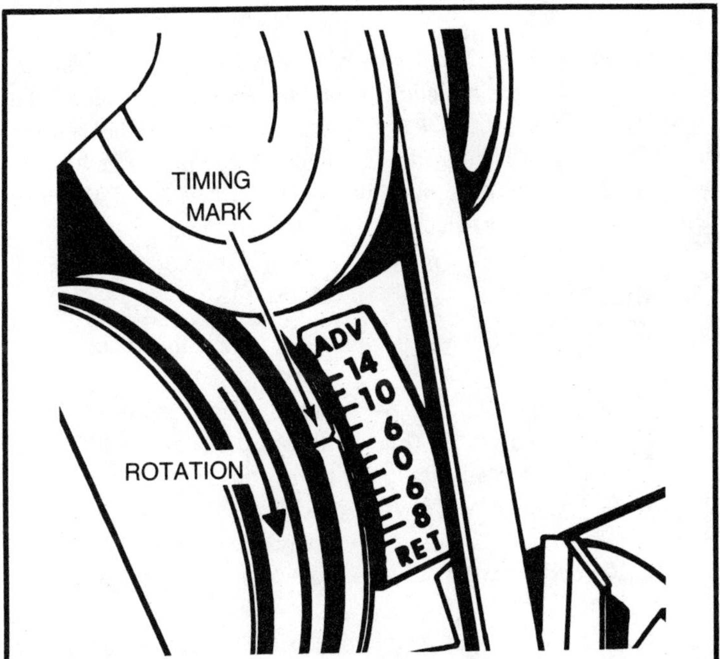

Fig. 6-16. A blinking light will show whether firing is early or late.

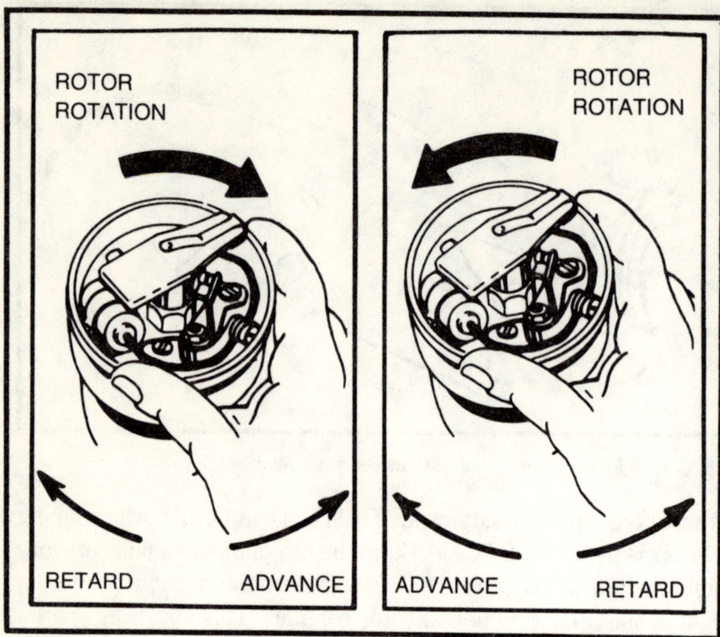

Fig. 6-17. Shown are an advancing spark and a retarding spark.

If the timing light flash occurs when the timing marker is ahead of the "BTC" mark in direction of rotation, timing is advanced. To adjust, turn the distributor left against rotor rotation. This retards spark (Fig. 6-17). Tighten the distributor hold-down screw, then recheck timing adjustment once more with the light. When timing is right, reconnect the vacuum hose to the distributor.

SOME HELPFUL HINTS

1) With big V-8 engines, remove the plugs for easier cranking.

2) When you install new points, set the "gap" on the wide side a few thousandths (Fig. 6-18). As the cam rubbing block wears, the contact surfaces will drift to the correct gap.

3) Do the same with new plugs, only set them on the narrow side to allow for gradual electrode erosion.

4) Recheck new points after 20 hours of running and reset gap.

5) If the engine idles on the rough side, first adjust the idle air mixture screws on the carburetor. If this doesn't help, try retarding the spark timing just about ⅛-inch to the left.

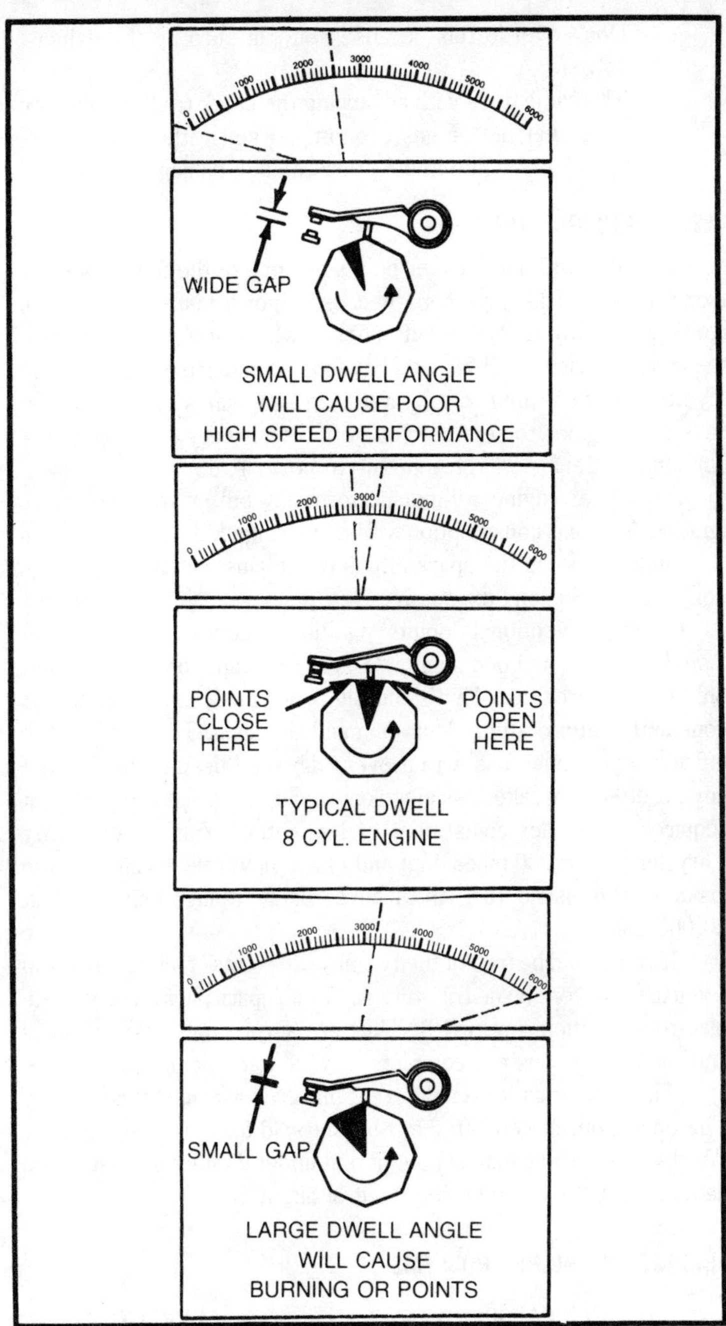

Fig. 6-18. Use this chart for setting point gap with feeler gauge or with dwell meter.

Don't overdo this because you can burn up the exhaust valves.

6) The same goes with advancing the spark (to the right) too far to get better gas economy. Even without a trace of "ping" or engine knock, you can still damage pistons.

ELECTRONIC IGNITION

Ignitions without breaker points are one of the few new electronic gadgets I like, perhaps because I got a taste of electronic ignition with my Chrysler automobile, which first started to use these new devices in 1973. So I have installed electronic ignition on my boat engines, my boat generator and my wife's car. When you have five engines to service, you get pretty weary of the constant ignition maintenance, which seems to never end.

Your boat engine will not perform any better with electronic ignition. Your gas consumption will be unchanged, but your plugs will last longer because the spark intensity remains constant and plugs don't foul up. So don't expect miracles, just less maintenance work.

When conventional "points" ignition is new and properly adjusted, it is just as good as any "Magic Box" ignition system—but only for a short time. That's the big problem. "Points" ignition is constantly deteriorating, degrading and changing. To keep it at top efficiency you must fuss with it every day, as I used to do. But not anymore. With breakerless electronic ignition, once it is installed, it requires no further adjustment or lubrication. You forget it. My Chrysler has 36,000 miles on it and I have never yet even seen the inside of the distributor. And I have changed plugs only once, at 20,000 miles.

If you would be free of the tyranny of "points" maintenance and if you hate to work on distributors and clean spark plugs, you will like electronic ignition (Fig. 6-19). They are surprisingly easy to install and the instructions are complete and easy to understand.

There are eight or ten different makes available at this writing. The ones I purchased listed at $85 but sold for $60. Montgomery Ward sells the same make I bought, but under their own house brand name and at the same selling price of about $60.

DIAGNOSING ENGINE PROBLEMS

POSSIBLE CAUSE   CORRECTION

Engine Will Not Start

Weak battery

Test battery specific gravity, recharge or replace as necessary

Corroded or loose battery connections

Clean and tighten battery connections

Moisture on igniton wires and distributor cap

Wipe wires and cap clean and dry

Faulty ignition cables

Replace any cracked or shorted cables

Faulty condenser

Replace

Corroded points

Clean with points file or replace

Incorrect spark plug gap

Clean or replace as necessary, set gap at .035

Incorrect ignition timing

Refer to igniton timing

Dirt or water in fuel line or carburetor

Clean lines

Carburetor percolating, no fuel in carburetor

Adjust bowl air vent

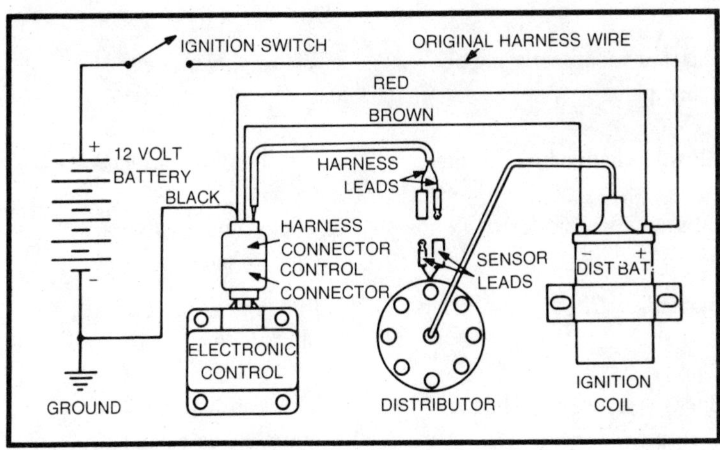

Fig. 6-19. A schematic drawing of typical electronic ignition selling for $60.

Engine Stalls

POSSIBLE CAUSE	CORRECTION
Idle speed set too low	Adjust at carburetor
Idle mixture too lean or too rich	Adjust two idle air mixture screws, left for lean, right for rich
Leak in intake manifold	Inspect intake manifold gasket, replace if necessary
Dirty, burned or incorrectly gapped points	Replace points
Worn or burned distributor rotor	Replace rotor
Faulty condenser	Replace condenser

Engine Loss of Power

POSSIBLE CAUSE	CORRECTION
Incorrect ignition timing	Refer to "ignition timing"
Worn or burned distributor rotor	Install new rotor
Dirty or incorrectly gapped spark plugs	Clean plugs, regap
Blown cylinder head gasket	Install new head gasket
Low compression	Test compression of each cylinder
Burned, warped pitted valves	Install new or regrind old valves
Back pressure in exhaust system	This can happen with some types of marine exhaust manifolds

POSSIBLE CAUSE	**CORRECTION**
Faulty ignition cables	Replace any cracked or shorted cables
Bad condenser	Replace condenser

Engine Misses On Acceleration

POSSIBLE CAUSE	**CORRECTION**
Dirty, burned or incorrectly gapped points	Replace points
Dirty or gap too wide in plugs	Clean plugs and set gap at .035
Incorrect ignition timing	Refer to "ignition timing
Burned, warped or pitted valves	Install new valves
Bad condenser	Install new condenser

Engine Misses At High Speed

POSSIBLE CAUSE	**CORRECTION**
Worn or burned distributor rotor	Replace with new rotor
Worn distributor shaft cam or excessive play in shaft	Remove and repair distributor
Dirty or incorrectly gapped points	Replace points
Gap set too wide in plugs	Clean, reset plug gaps at .035
Incorrect ignition timing	Refer to "ignition timing"
Bad condenser	Replace condenser

POSSIBLE CAUSE	CORRECTION
Dirt or water in fuel line	Clean fuel lines
Plugged element in fuel filter	Replace fuel filter element

THE OUTBOARD MOTOR

Today's big modern outboard motor is such a complex and specialized piece of machinery that it is almost completely beyond the capabilities of 99 out of 100 boat owners (Fig. 6-20). A fellow club member friend of mine at the Detroit yacht club, an engineer at GM's Chevrolet Division, has a huge black beast of a thing on his outboard which he loves to race on the Detroit River. This man has helped me better understand my own machinery, based on the Corvette block, and helped me with this book. On outboard engines he says: "You've got to own ten thousand dollars worth of highly specialized tools and equipment just to make minor repairs and adjustments. Hell, it's cheaper to just buy another engine (Fig. 6-21)."

Although I have had a lifetime love affair with outboard motors and even considered outboard power on a 23-foot cruiser I once built, I would not care to own one of today's big mills for that very reason. I would always be dependent on somebody else for service. I don't like that sort of dependency when I'm out on big water 100 miles away from my friendly dealer's "factory trained" mechanic with his "highly specialized" tools and equipment. It makes me feel insecure. I itch and scratch under the armpits when I'm insecure.

That was why I selected inboard power for the boat I was building—that and the logistics of fuel in cruiser quantities. Fuel is no problem as long as you stay close to home where big marinas have gas pumps with ready-mixed outboard fuel. But out in the boondocks they don't have special pumps for outboard gas. You mix your own. Taking on 75-100 gallons of gas and trying to get that oil in there at the same time in proper ratio is no simple task like punching holes in cans.

SELECTING THE RIGHT FRIENDLY DEALER

If you own a Johnson 85 horsepower motor, can you take it back to your Johnson dealer for service? You better not if he has just an "A" plaque over his work bench. That one "A" means he is not

Fig. 6-20. These are typical frustrations of an outboard motor owner.

Fig. 6-21. To service this "beast" requires an investment into thousands of dollars worth of specialized equipment and tools.

qualified to work on anything over 40 horsepower. A double "AA" plaque means that he has been "factory trained" to work on all motors to the top of the line, and a triple "AAA" plaque means he also has a special test tank for the big monsters, plus the latest equipment and test gear.

There is no such thing anymore as a general outboard motor repair shop. It's become specialized like medicine. You don't go to a gynecologist if you have prostate trouble. You don't go to a Mercury mechanic if your motor is an Evinrude. You go to a specialist in your particular make of motor.

PROFESSIONAL SERVICE MANUALS

If you are one of those never-give-up-do-it-yourselfers who is determined to work on his monster, don't rely on that simple little owners operation and service manual which came with the warranty papers in a plastic bag. You can buy direct from the factory their professional service manual. The Mercury Manual costs $15 and is worth it. Before you buy this, send for Mercury's "Outboard Pocket Service Guide" to get some advance warning of what you are getting into. You may change your mind when you see the mind-boggling array of strange-looking tools you will need—tools that you will never use for anything else, like fixing a lawnmower or a typewriter. The professional mechanic who earns his living with tools like these can deduct their cost and depreciation. As a pleasureboater, you can't deduct anything.

HOW TO FIND GOOD SERVICE

The biggest problem with ownership of outboard motors over 40 horsepower is finding qualified service. This is one time when price shopping for discounts is a mistake, like buying from one of those little boat liveries and fishbait operations that also has a dealer franchise for outboard motors. What kind of "special diagnostic services" will you get here?

Remember, when you invest $2000-$5000 in one of those big beasts, you aren't just buying an engine. You're also buying another wife—you're getting married to that dealer's "factory trained" mechanic. During the boating season, and after, you'll be seeing more of him than your other wife. So, before you get married again, be sure this second "wife" is qualified. A Mercury "master mechanic" must have five years experience and training on nothing else but Mercury motors.

How do you find these "master mechanics?" Look in the yellow pages of your phone book. In larger cities you will find display ads stating: "We specialize in warranty work." That is always a good sign because this dealer is able to beat the factory rate and make a profit on warranty work, so he welcomes it and even advertises for it.

To be able to beat the factory fixed rates on warranty work, and still make money, a dealer must have absolutely the best mechanics, equipment and facilities. They get the job done fast and well because their investment is too large to risk unhappy customers who will complain to the factory franchise division. They'll knock themselves out to keep you happy and coming back.

The dealer who is slow on warranty work, who doesn't want "warranty work" because "there's no money in it," is also slow in keeping up with the latest service bulletins from the factory, or in paying his mechanics a decent wage. They eventually leave him for better paying jobs. Warning! Stay away from any dealer who shuns "warranty work." The reason he shuns it is he can't do it.

RECOGNIZING PROBLEMS

Even if you can't actually work on your big outboard motor, it is helpful to at least understand what is wrong when it gives you problems so you can better communicate with your mechanic/wife and not just tell him: "The damn thing doesn't work right." There is only about ten thousand things that could cause your motor to not "work right." Give the poor guy something to look for.

Engine Misses While Idling

Possible causes include water or dirt in fuel, wrong type of plugs, spark plug gasket leaking, bad plug, ignition wire leaks, and timing off. Other possibilities are bad breaker points, a bad condenser, poor compression, carburetion (gas too lean), magneto troubles, weak magnets, and a worn adapter flange.

Engine Backfires Through Exhaust

Causes might be crossed plug wires (No. 1 wire on No. 2 plug), a defective or cracked spark plug insulator, distributor cap or magneto cracked and leaking voltage, and timing off.

Engine Backfires Through Carburetor

Problems could be bad gas, carburetor set too lean, defective reed valve, or valve not seating, bad plugs or wrong heat range, fuel/oil mixture wrong, or timing off.

Loud Noises, Engine Chatters

Troubles include flywheel tooth broken, a loose flywheel, a loose starter, broken starter, and no grease on starter mechanisms.

STERN-DRIVES

Every time I see an inboard-outboard power combination in boat magazine advertisements, I think of Centaur, the fabled half man/half horse of ancient mythology. My mind works that way, which accounts for many of my silly prejudices. I love outboards. I love inboards. I do not love the two together. Maybe it's because I keep seeing those Centaurs in a meadow playing flutes.

The inboard-outboard power combinations are mainly responsible for the huge success of houseboats, making them maneuverable and operable in shallow rivers. Houseboats, which are especially popular on big rivers, would have a devilish time in debris-cluttered rivers with conventional shaft-propeller-rudder systems. They would spend half the season out of the water having underwater gear repaired. Stern-drives kick up out of the water on hitting a submerged object.

If I owned a houseboat, I would passionately love inboards-outboards. If I owned a houseboat, I still wouldn't fool with the stern-drive unit because what I said about big monster outboard motors applies also to their lower halves. You need the same special tools and equipment, the same special service manuals, and the same special dedication of a masochist who is happy only when miserable or watching a Russian play where everybody suffers and dies at the end.

SERVICING STERN-DRIVES

These outboard drive units are most successful on trailered boats that are never left in the water (Fig. 6-22). Salt water does horrible things to stern-drives. I have taken pictures of stern-drives on trailered boats that were 10 years old, and still looked new. I have taken pictures of stern-drives on cruisers and houseboats in tropical saltwater that were only one year old, and looked ready to be melted down for scrap. Of course, the fact that the owners painted the lower units with copper bronze anti-fouling to keep off barnacles helped considerably in the fast aging process.

Another reason why trailered boat stern-drives look so good is because they are so visible, so easy to get at for regular servicing. Five days a week they rest on a trailer in the garage where they get

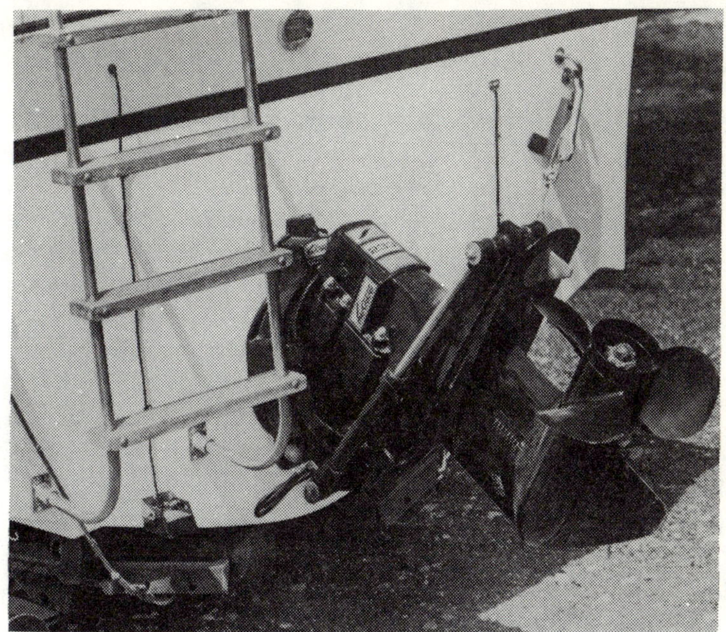

Fig. 6-22. The inboard/outboard drive lasts longer and gives better service on trailered boats. It is troublesome on boats left in the water.

love and pampering. The cruiser and houseboat stern-drive is almost totally submerged, buried in the water with only the top visible. It gets service and attention only when the boat is hauled, which is once a year in Florida for bottom scrubbing and repainting with anti-fouling.

For such a vital and complex piece of machinery, with all those gears and bearings, that just isn't enough. Marina owners have told me: "If we suggest to owners of boats with stern-drives that they haul out frequently to service them, they get resentful, even hostile. They think we're just trying to get more money out of them. Not a single boat owner has taken our advice, and I don't really give a damn anymore because they'll all be in our repairs shops soon anyway. I make more money on overhauls than haul-outs."

STERN-DRIVES AND HAUL-OUTS

There is just no way to service a stern-drive in the water. The boat must be hauled. In fresh water up north, a mid season haul-out is necessry for servicing. In warm salt water, every four months is required.

When I suggested this to a boat owner in my marina, he said: "Hell, I don't see anybody else doing it. I don't see you doing it."

There was no point in explaining to him that my boat did not have a complicated piece of machinery submerged in water. My propeller, shaft and rudder are just solid hunks of metal with nothing to grease, oil, flush out, paint, or protect against corrosion.

Here is what stern-drive manufacturers recommend. The units should be run about 15 minutes before hauling out to warm up the lubricants and get dirt and contaminants suspended so they will drain out with the oil.

Check your owner's manual for location of all drain plugs. Some stern-drives have three, some two, and some only one.

Check your manual for proper lubricant types. Some manufacturers specify SAE 90 hypoid gear oil. Some specify SAE 10W-40 motor oil. Some specify SAE 10W-30 motor oil.

Check the manual for location of sacrificial anode which is attached to the stern-drive housing to protect it from galvanic action in salt water. If it shows much corrosion, replace it even if it still looks serviceable. It's not a question of size, but how much zinc is still left that determines when to replace. The contact surfaces of the anode and aluminum are also corroding and building up resistance. If there is not good electrical contact, there will be no protection. This is why so often the anodes fail to protect.

Check the propeller for physical damage and corrosion, especially if aluminum. If stainless steel, you may have barnacles on one or two of the blades. Barnacles have a particular fondness for stainless steel. If you let your boat sit idle three or four weeks at a time, you will almost certainly have barnacles. They can throw the wheel off balance.

STERN-DRIVE PROPELLER FACTS

While on the subject of propellers, Ralph Lambrecht, a stern-drive engineering department employee says most boaters with inboards/outboards use propellers with too ittle pitch. This makes the engines rev up more. The boat takes off quickly and an illusion of great speed is created. The noise of high turning engines always does that. In fact, you are actually moving slower through the water.

Lambrecht recommends a wheel pitched to hold top rpm down to 4000, which will give top speed and better fuel consumption without overworking the engine. If your boat is in the 40-mph-plus class, Lambrecht advises you will get better performance with the stainless steel SST wheels.

PROPELLERS FOR PULLING WATER SKIERS

For pulling water skiers, you want a propeller that will get the boat moving quickly to get the skiers up out of the water. For this you need a propeller with less pitch and higher rpm. Remember, you can't have everything. Good fuel consumption, long engine life and fast take-offs are needed for water skiing.

SOME FACTS ABOUT ENGINE LIFE, FUEL ECONOMY

An OMC 235 in a typical 23-foot hull will burn 18 gallons of gasoline an hour at 4200 rpm. With the throttle backed off to 3200 rpm, fuel consumption drops to nine gallons an hour. At 50 to 75 percent throttle, engine life is several thousand hours. At full throttle, engine life is about 200 hours. This should give you something to think about.

AUXILIARY ENGINES

Engines on sailboats are called "auxiliaries." They are also called other things. The inboard auxiliary has a vile reputation and is often called the dog of marine engines. Some sailors believe that hard starting is a design feature and is built in to all auxiliaries by the manufacturers who want to discourage sailing. This is ridiculous. Auxiliary engines are hard starting dogs because they are treated like dogs by their masters.

While cruiser inboard engines are often worked to death, sailboat auxiliaries aren't worked enough, and that is what is wrong with them. The auxiliary is used mostly for docking and getting out through restricted channels to open water. Sometimes the engines don't even get warmed up because the minute the last channel marker is cleared, up goes the main sail and off goes the auxiliary.

This type of operation is very hard on engines. It reminds me of those used car ads in the classifieds that say: "A little old lady drove this one to church on Sundays. Mint condition. Low mileage."

A new car dealer service manager told me: "Never buy a used car that was driven by a little old lady who just drove it once a week to church or the grocery store. The engine never gets warmed up. The oil becomes contaminated by condensation and combustion by-products. The plugs are fouled, the ignition is corroded, the battery is almost always shot, and everything is rusty."

This is just with an automobile engine. The sailboat auxiliary is buried down in a musty bilge where it is attacked on all sides by hostile elements, like, for example, a change in temperature. Nights can be very cool in some areas; days can be very hot. Do you know what that can do to an engine buried in a tight compartment? Metal surfaces become cold at night. Air in the bilge warms up during the day and condenses on the engine. It gets drenching wet as if washed down with a hose. Engines sweat not only on the outside but also on the inside. This condensation moisture runs down into the crankcase oil, cylinder walls, carburetor, distributor and gas tank. That's how you get water in your gas.

Short runs also produce moisture through condensation. When you start up a cold engine, you generate instant heat which, in turn, produces moisture. That's why you see water dripping out the exhaust tailpipe of your car. If an engine is thoroughly warmed up and run for a while, it will dissipate this moisture. If it is not run long enough to do this, the moisture is not dissipated. Instead, sludge, harmful contaminants and acids are formed when moisture mixes with combustion by-products that get past the piston rings.

THE REASON FOR FREQUENT OIL CHANGES

What do you do about the contamination in your oil?

According to my friend, the General Motors engineer, you change the oil more often. That sounds crazy—the less you run an engine, the more often you change the oil. Unfortunately, this is the only way to get rid of the water and junk that accumulates with an engine just sitting idle in the bilge and sweating. You do, however, have an option. If you don't want to change the oil so often, then run the engine more often and longer!

HOW TO STOP SWEATING

There is a simple solution to all the sweating and condensation in your bilge. It's called an electric fan. After all, you're paying for dockside electricity, so use it.

A sailor friend of mine at the North Cape Yacht Club in Michigan keeps his bilge dry with a 100-watt light bulb and small oscillating fan. His bilge and engine is always dry and he never has trouble starting his auxiliary.

WINTER ENGINE LAYUP

There are pros and cons on how to layup marine engines with closed cooling systems (Fig. 6-23). Since the engines are filled with

Fig. 6-23. In your closed cooling systems, such as this one, there is no need to drain the engine.

permanent type anti freeze like you have in your car, why drain them and lose the rust protection? This is a good argument because rust in drained engines only hardens and builds up over the winter.

The arguments against leaving a 50/50 solution of water and anti freeze in a marine engine during a six month storage period is that ethylene glycol is an oil-based chemical. During long periods of inactivity it will separate from the water. There could be freeze damage in the lower block area.

This is no problem with an automobile engine because it is rarely idle for six months during the winter. If an engine is to be stored wet, it should be with straight undiluted anti freeze, some experts advise. Other experts disagree and claim that there is no danger of freezing with a 50/50 mixture of anti-freeze and water because the oil and water never completely separate. If there is freezing in the lower block, it will be mushy and cause no damage.

This must be true because I have never heard of an engine with closed cooling freezing up over the winter. But I have heard of engines with raw water cooling freezing because they were not completely drained.

If you don't do anything else with your engines, at least get all the water drained. This can be both an arduous and painful chore on some boats with two engines in small space. On some boats it is almost impossible for a man of average build and weight to change oil filters—and I'm talking about big name cruisers in the 30-foot class. I am often asked by friends to help them change their filters. The reason is I am so skinny I can hide behind the mast of a 30-foot sloop. I am over six feet tall and weigh 140 pounds. Two men hold me up by the legs and I can just barely squeeze down head first to reach the oil filters at the right front extreme bottom.

Getting at the water drain plugs is also a difficult job in twin screw boats, but if you have a small belly and long arms you can manage. But first, get yourself a 2×12 plank about 8 feet long. Lay this plank over your engine hatches. While laying bellydown over this plank you can reach all the drain plugs. I know because that's how I do it.

There are 8 to 13 brass drain plugs in all marine engines (Fig. 6-24). The two largest, usually 9/16, will be on each side of the block. By laying on the plank, you can just reach them with a socket wrench. It is a good idea to have two coffee cans handy in which to drop the plugs as you remove them. Leave the coffee cans on top of the engine where you can see them next spring and be reminded to replace them.

There will be one or two plugs under each exhaust manifold, the lower end for obvious reasons. Feel around for a possible third plug up around the middle. This is tight working quarters and a ratcheting box-end wrench makes the job so much easier, which is why I bought one for just this special job.

Under the waterpump housing you will find one or two plugs. There will be one or two under the oil cooler. Feel around under anything that contains water. If you feel something with a hex head, it is almost certainly a drain plug. Take it out. If it's brass, it is.

DRAINING CHECK VALVES

Many boats of recent vintage are equipped with check valves in the through-hull raw water intake. This prevents water from draining out of your intake lines everytime you stop the engines for a few minutes. When you start up again, you have instant water circulation without that worrisome time lag waiting for the pump to prime up again.

You must get the water out of the check valve or it will burst. All you need is a length of coat hanger wire. The check valve is a simple one-way-opening flap. From the outside you push that coat flap.

Fig. 6-24. There are eight to 13 brass drain plugs to remove in a marine engine such as this one.

You'll know when it's open because water will run down your arm and up your sleeve. If you're laying on your back while doing this, water will hit you right in the face as it does me every fall.

DRAINING THE OIL

There are arguments pro and con about draining the oil before winter layup. Your old oil is contaminated. I say drain it. "Draining" marine engine oil is really not the right word. You "suck" it out the dipstick tube with a pump made specially for that purpose (Fig. 6-25). Peters and Russel, Inc., Springfield, Ohio make the best because theirs fits right into the large opening of a five-gallon can. You suck the old oil out of your crankcase into the can with no dripping or mess.

If your engine is a conversion, you must use the additional sucker tube to run down the dipstick tube to the bottom of the crankcase. You can use this same pump and tube to "drain" the oil from your automobile engine, as I do. In a true marine engine, the sucker tube is not needed because the dipstick tube runs right down to the bottom of the crankcase. You just force the larger tubing over the dipstick.

PICKLING THE ENGINE

With your drain plugs all removed and oil changed, you are ready for the final step called "pickling" on the Great Lakes. To do

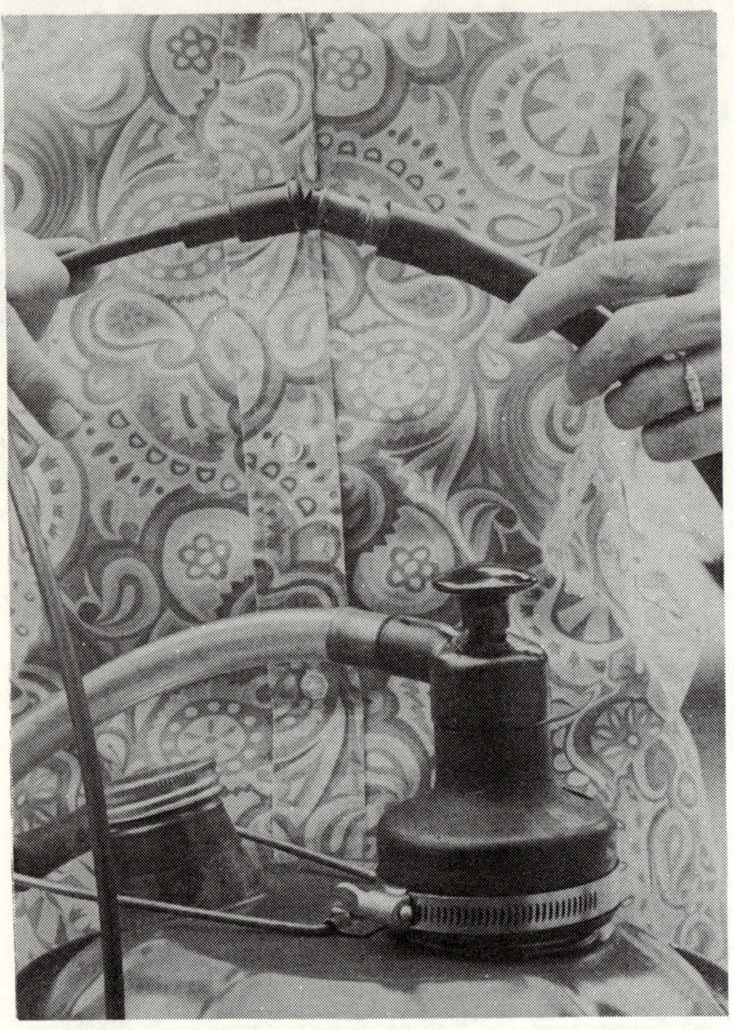

Fig. 6-25. This is the best marine type oil sump pump. The large tubing to the right fits over the engine dipstick tube. On an automobile engine, you attach the smaller sucker tubing on the left, which slides down through the dipstick tube into the crankcase.

this you will need an easy-pour container to hold a cup of engine oil. I personally use a large pump-type oil can with a long flexible pouring spout.

"Pickling" is best done in most boatyards on a Monday when there are few people around to swear at you. You will soon understand why. With the flame arrester on your carburetor removed, start the engine. With one hand on the throttle, immediately start pouring or squirting oil down the carburetor. As the engine falters, open the throttle. With a pump oil can I give 20 long squirts over a running time of about two minutes.

"Pickling" is much better than trying to pour oil into each spark plug hole because the cylinders lay at an angle and only part of them will be oiled. And there's always the risk that you might absent-mindedly put the plugs back in and crank the engine with all that oil in there. You will punch a hole in every piston. "Pickling" is better and safer because everything gets saturated with oil all the way out the exhaust system. Also, the heat produced by the short running time drys up all pockets of water which did not drain out. When you stop the engine, you will understand why Monday and a windy day is the best time to do this because the yard will suddenly look like a foggy day in London.

Marine
Electronics and Electricity

"Marine radio communications are a mess!" Those are the words of a senior officer and commander of a key Coast Guard base in the east. And I believe him because I'm a mess, too.

On December 31, 1976 I cried a little as I listened to Guy Lombardo play "Auld Lang Syne." At the stroke of midnight, my good old AM radiotelephone became an FCC outlaw (Fig. 7-1). I'm still sick about it, even though I hated the thing sometimes, especially on weekends with all that unnecessary chatter. Over a five year period, I only used it three times, and then only to request Coast Guard assistance for somebody else in trouble. But it gave me a wonderful feeling of security just knowing it was there, always ready to load 3 amps of RF current into the antenna to radiate a powerful signal from one end of Lake Erie to the other. When in Buffalo, I could talk direct with marine operators in Detroit and Lorain to check for calls.

The Coast Guard will still be monitoring the international distress frequency of 2182 because we have maritime treaties and obligations to fulfill. The Great Lakes are an international waterway and foreign vessels who have trouble in our waters will continue to use the AM radios and 2182 kHz.

I suppose in an emergency I could go on the air with my old AM station to call the Coast Guard for help. A small FCC fine would be cheaper than an investment for new VHF equipment.

Fig. 7-1. On New Year's Eve, 1977, all these radiotelephone antennas became junk.

CB OR NOT TO CB

At this writing, I don't know what to do. I am even thinking CB (citizens' band radios) because a number of manufacturers, perhaps sensing a trend, are introducing new lines of CB radios designed expressly for "marine service" (Fig. 7-2). They might be worth looking into, and waiting for, because these hard-nosed businessmen don't tool up for a new product until the slide rule boys, the consultants, the market analysts and the crystal ball gazers have all had something to say in their board rooms. Maybe they know something—like behind the scenes lobbying to change the law which now prevent the Coast Guard from even listening to CB. Changing that law would really open the flood gates. It would legitimize CB in the eyes of all old die-hard boatmen and make the equipment decent and respectable.

It is estimated that 250,000 CB radios were installed on boats in 1976. That equals ALL the vhf equipment now currently in use. And

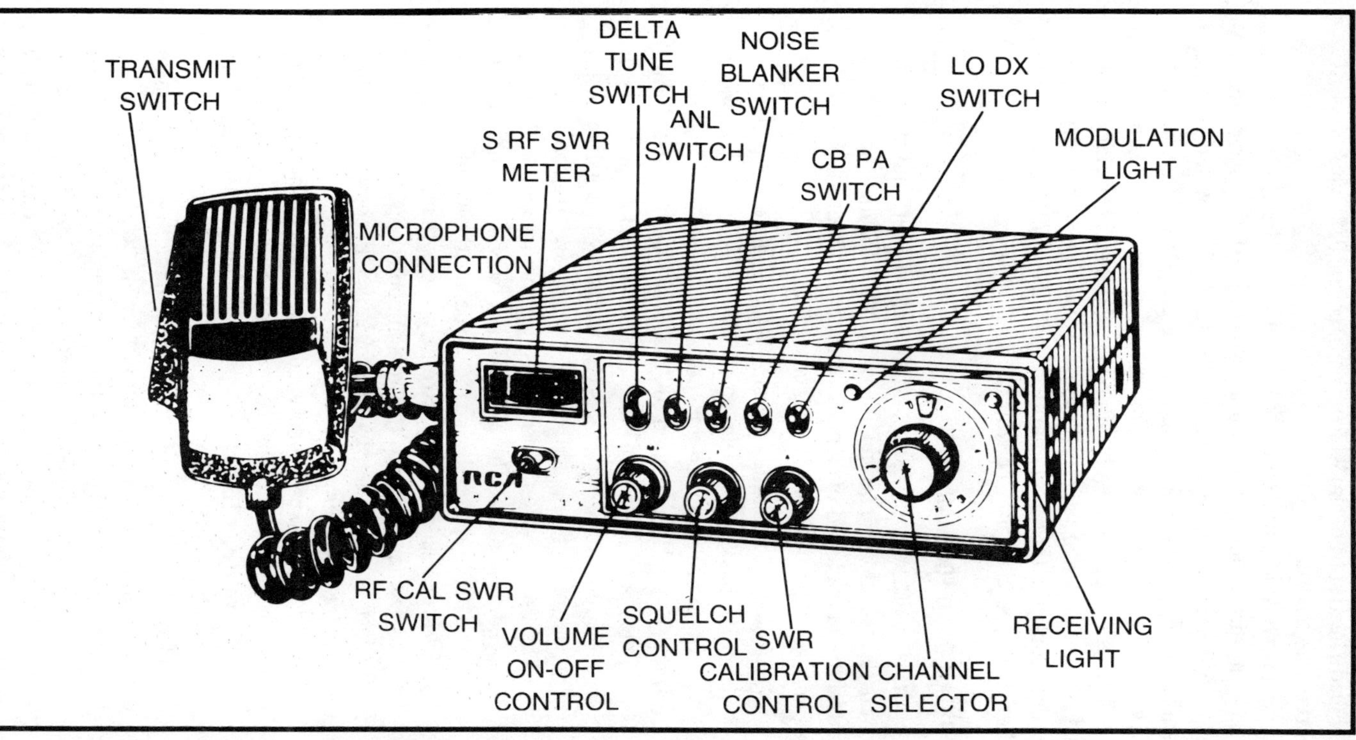

Fig. 7-2. Suddenly CB radio looks good, at least as good as VHF, and for a lot less money.

VHF had a head start of almost five years, since 1972, when the FCC decree was issued.

If CB were legitimized by the Coast Guard being required to listen to it, this would remove the last barrier and CB would descend on the boating world like a plague of locusts. They would become standard equipment on all boats, like gas gauges and tachometers. We would all be captives of CB—on water, on land and in our homes.

This is the one almost frightening difference between CB and VHF. Once you leave your boat, you are free of VHF because it can be used only in the total maritime service. With CB, on the otherhand, you can talk to anybody.

CITIZENS BAND FOR MARINERS

CB is an attractive package, with much to offer, and at a price any boater can afford. The addition of 17 more channels spread out the traffic and made CB even more attractive to boaters (Fig. 7-3). Just look at some of these advantages:

(1) You have five times as many "talk" channels to play with. VHF has 55 channels but they're not all "talk" channels. Most are reserved for special purposes.

(2) Use of VHF is limited to "essential ship business." That means no chatter. CB has no such limitations and you can talk about anything, as you can tell by just listening.

(3) Use of VHF is limited to ship-to-ship, ship-to-Coast Guard and ship-to-telephone company communications. With CB you can't talk to the Coast Guard or phone company, but you make up for it by having the rest of the world to talk to.

(4) Power hailers are an extremely useful thing to have on a boat when trying to talk to somebody approaching a gas dock, or in a nearby boat. Many CB sets have public address systems built in.

(5) There are 46 additional single-sideband channels available with CB, with none reserved for any special interests. With VHF, a 12-channel unit may leave you with only four "talk" channels.

With CBs limited range of about 10 miles, the above 40 channels are all yours when you get out on water, even including channel 19 which is completely taken over by truckers. You'll get no truck traffic out on big water. In fact, you'll get very little of anything with four watts and 10 mile range because CB antenna height is limited to 20 feet above the highest point on your boat, like cabin top and flying

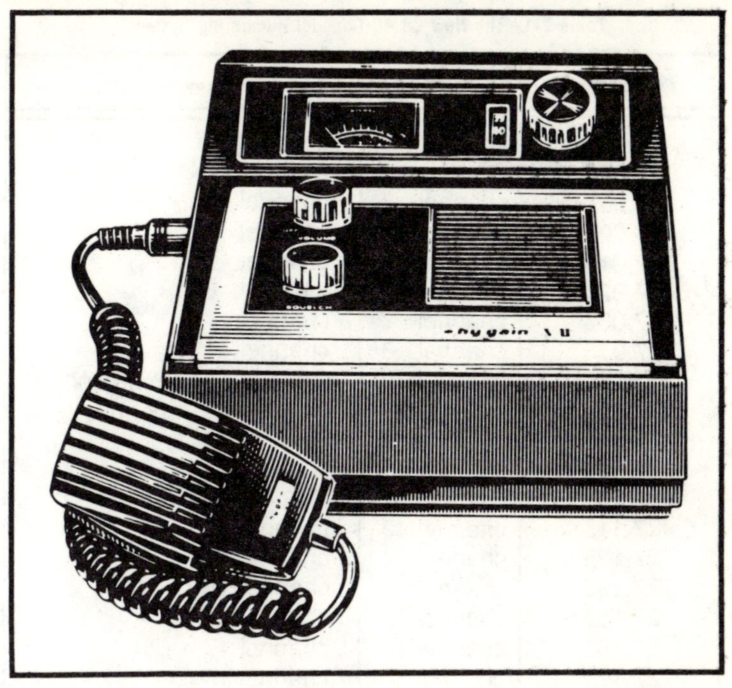

Fig. 7-3. For cruisers, the CB base stations are more suitable and more attractive.

bridge, but not masts. With VHF there is no such limit and antennas can be mounted on top of masts, which greatly increases range.

USING CB IN AN EMERGENCY

There are two emergency services you can not reach directly with CB, the Coast Guard and the marine telephone operator. You can, however, reach the Coast Guard indirectly because there is always somebody listening who will relay your call, like the state police, the various county sheriff departments and local police. All are beginning to monitor CB. Then there are volunteer monitor CB. Then there are volunteer monitoring organizations like REACT, ALERT and REST, plus yacht clubs, boatyards, commercial marinas, coast guard auxiliaries and power squadrons. If one of the above doesn't hear you, another boater, or even some trucker driving down Route 2 along the lake, will hear you and stop somewhere to phone your distress message to the Coast Guard. With CB you are never alone until you get out on big water miles from land, and then you're even alone with VHF, which doesn't have much

Table 7-1. The New CB 40-Channel Numbering System.

Frequency	Present	new
26.965	channel 1	channel 1
26.975	channel 2	channel 2
26.985	channel 3	channel 3
27.005	channel 4	channel 4
27.015	channel 5	channel 5
27.025	channel 6	channel 6
27.035	channel 7	channel 7
27.055	channel 8	channel 8
27.065	channel 9	channel 9 Emergency channel
27.075	channel 10	channel 10
27.085	channel 11	channel 11
27.105	channel 12	channel 12
27.115	channel 13	channel 13
27.125	channel 14	channel 14
27.135	channel 15	channel 15
27.155	channel 16	channel 16
27.165	channel 17	channel 17
27.175	channel 18	channel 18
27.185	channel 19	channel 19
27.205	channel 20	channel 20
27.215	channel 21	channel 21
27.225	channel 22	channel 22
27.235	new	channel (24)
27.245	new	channel (25)
27.255	channel 23	channel 23
27.265	new	channel (26)
27.275	new	channel (27)
27.285	new	channel (28)
27.295	new	channel (29)
27.305	new	channel (30)
27.315	new	channel (31)
27.325	new	channel (32)
27.335	new	channel (33)
27.345	new	channel (34)
27.355	new	channel (35)
27.365	new	channel (36)
27.375	new	channel (37)
27.385	new	channel (38)
27.395	new	channel (39)
27.405	new	channel (40)

more range than CB. Your VHF transmitting range is determined by your antenna height, not transmitter power. This is where you can save money because a 6-watt VHF with a high antenna will give you more range than 25-watts with a low antenna, and you can buy a 6-watt unit at discount for about $225, whereas the 25 watts could cost you about $800. This is something to think about. And while you are, take a look at Table 7-2 below and the transmitting range you can expect with various antenna heights.

Disregard the table, if it frightens you, and figure one mile of signal radiation for every 6 feet of antenna height above the water. With two 12-foot antennas 6 feet above the water, (one to transmit, one to receive) you have a total of 36 feet. That gives you a transmitting range of 6 miles.

I can almost hear some boater scream, "My God! I can talk that far with my power hailer."

That's almost true because I have heard the public address system in the Cleveland Lakefront Stadium when I was passing by beyond the intake crib five miles out in the lake. So, you may wonder, who needs VHF for just six miles? That's a good question. I wish I had a good answer. I have seen Lake Erie Fishermen trolling for pickerel in tiny rented rowboats 12 miles from shore. No matter which way you travel on the Great Lakes, you find yourself 40-50-75-100 miles between Coast Guard stations. There are even greater distances between marine telephone operators. On Lake Erie there are just three, in Detroit, Lorain and Buffalo, about 150 miles apart.

Table 7-2. The Chart Lists VHF Antenna Heights And Ranges.

| VHF ANTENNA HEIGHTS AND RANGE ||
Antenna height	Transmitting range
5 feet	3.2 miles (nautical)
10 feet	4.3 miles
15 feet	5.3 miles
20 feet	6.2 miles
25 feet	6.9 miles
30 feet	7.6 miles
35 feet	8.2 miles
40 feet	8.7 miles
45 feet	9.3 miles
50 feet	9.8 miles
60 feet	10.6 miles
70 feet	11.5 miles
80 feet	12.3 miles
90 feet	13.1 miles
100 feet	13.7 miles
150 feet	16.8 miles
200 feet	19.5 miles
250 feet	21.7 miles

With my old AM 100-watt transmitter, I easily reached out 300 miles on good days and sometimes at night I reached down into the Gulf of Mexico as well because I often heard some boat calling me back. And that was the reason why the FCC took away the old 2000-4000 marine band. With allowable power of up to 150 watts to the final power amplifier, the old AM units had too much range and were causing all kinds of interference problems, especially on 2182, the international distress and calling frequency. Various sections of the country had certain working frequencies allotted exclusively to them, to avoid interfering with each other, but everybody used 2182 as a common calling frequency.

VHF and CB, with their line-of-sight broadcasting range, take care of the interference problem. But it doesn't take care of the boater"s communications problem, if he wants to call the Coast Guard or marine operator just 10 miles away.

There are many questions like this on your mind, and I will answer them in a "question" and "answer" session.

HOW DO I GET MORE RANGE WITH VHF?

Buy a sailboat with a 300 foot mast (Fig. 7-4). Put your antennas on top or buy an additional SSB (single sideband) rig. This is just another reason why it is a mistake to spend a lot of money on a 25-watt VHF. Buy the cheapest VHF you can find. Your chief need for it is that you must first own a VHF before you can be legally licensed for SSB.

WHAT IS SSB?

Single sideband (SSB) operates in pretty much the same marine band as the old AM rigs which are now outlawed, but the manner in which signals are transmitted is technically different. The AM signal consisted of a "carrier" and two sidebands, one on each side of the carrier. You can actually hear the carrier on radio when nothing for a moment is being transmitted. It sounds like a distant waterfall. When voices or sound comes on, you don't hear the carrier.

The carrier serves no useful purpose, other then being a reference point, and contributes nothing to transmitting. It consumes considerable power and causes interference and inefficiency. When the unnecessary carrier is eliminated, the remaining energy is called single-sideband-suppressed carrier (SSB for short) and all transmitting power can be concentrated on one sideband to produce, in many

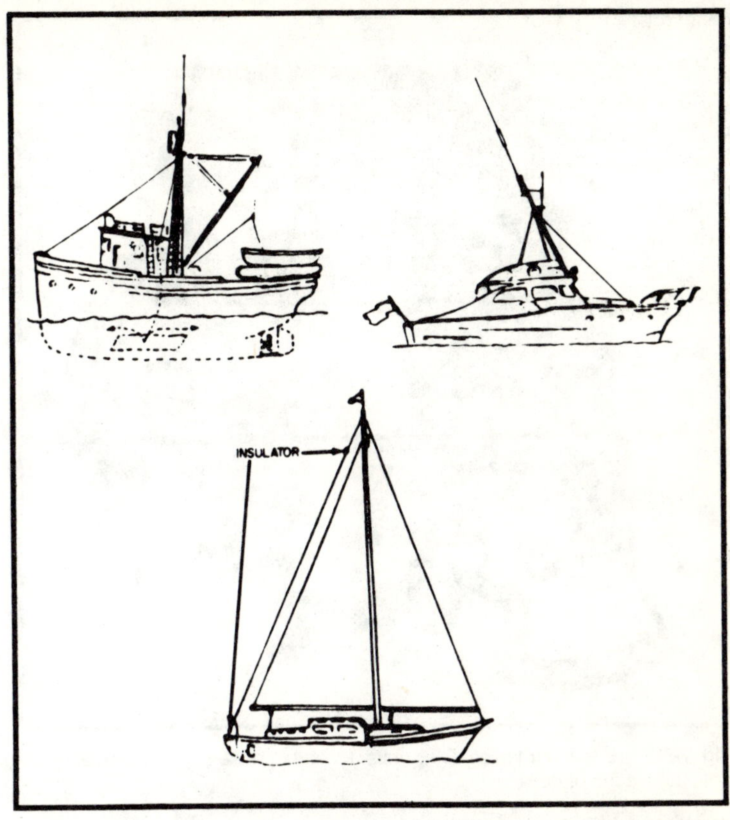

Fig. 7-4. Getting the antenna up higher is how you get more range with CB and VHF.

cases, 10 times as much talk power. On a given power output, SSB will reach farther, louder and clearer.

WHY DON'T MORE BOATS HAVE SSB?

The SSB rigs, because of more complicated circuitry, are very expensive and run from $1000 up to three times that much, plus extras (Fig. 7-5). Also, the SSB is more difficult to set up properly on wood and fiberglass boats because, like the old AM units, it requires an extensive ground system, sometimes called a "counterpoise." The antenna and ground are very critical in AM frequencies. As frequencies go higher, the water is less and less effective as a counterpoise or ground. On wooden or fiberglass boats, there must be 60 to 100 square feet of metal surface area under the SSB antenna.

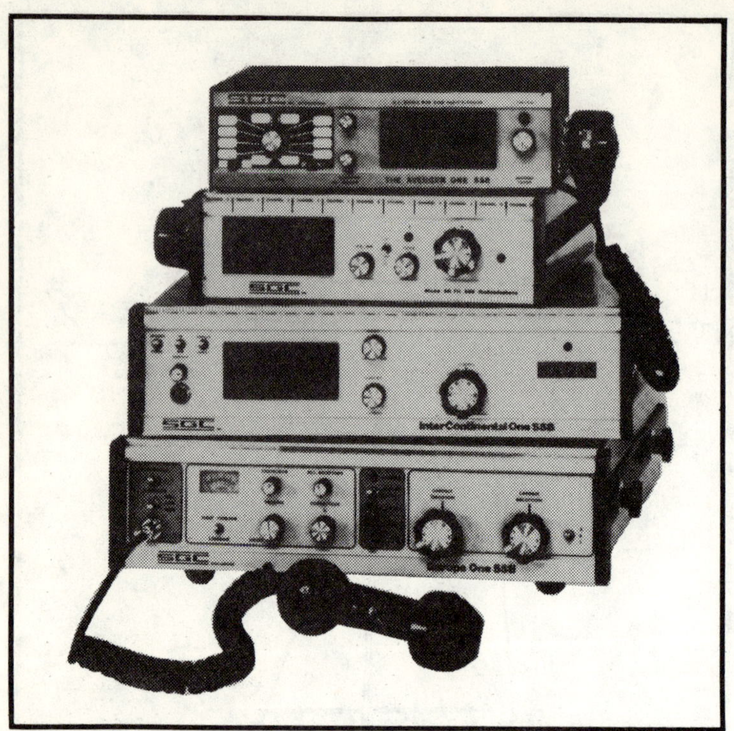

Fig. 7-5. Here are four typical SSB units. Much larger sets are available which cost thousands of dollars.

A GOOD GROUND FOR SSB

Contrary to what you may have heard, it is not necessary to put on the outside bottom of your wood boat copper sheathing to serve as a ground, even though I have done this myself in the past. I have done this other ways also with equally good results. Lining the inside bottom of the hull works just as well because when dealing with radio frequency (RF), you don't need metal-to-metal contact to transfer energy or move it from here to there. There is not any direct metal-to-metal contact in a transformer or condenser, yet RF and AC pass easily through both.

The metal that you use in lining the inside bottom of your wood boat becomes one plate of a condenser. Water outside the hull becomes another plate. The wood between them becomes the dielectric. The hull becomes a giant condenser and RF has good conductivity.

Salt water has high conductivity and in large boats with large masses of metal like water and gas tanks, two engines, AC generators, etc., it is not necessary to line the inside bottom with metal for grounding purposes. The boat's large masses of metal alone make a good ground.

This is not so with fresh water, which is a poor conductor, especially when cold. You must increase the boat's internal surface area of metal by adding more metal. Some professional marine electronics installers use copper screen material, especially in fiberglass hulls. I personally do not like copper screen because you must do a great deal of cutting and soldering. You just don't get enough surface area. Remember, when dealing with RF, metal thickness is unimportant. Only the surface area matters.

Since metal thickness is unimportant, I have used brass shim stock which you can buy in long rolls up to 12 inches wide and 25 feet long (Fig. 7-6). This brass is thinner than the paper on which this is printed. You can tack it, staple it, tape it and even glue it to any surface. On one of my boats, I ran this brass shim stock back and forth between my frames and under my engines, securing it to the bottom planking with ¼-inch bronze Arrow staples which I bought especially for this job. Overlap ends were easy to solder together because the thin metal requires so little heat.

Four 25-foot rolls of the brass shim stock gave me an additional 100 square foot of surface area. When I came to the end, I continued up the hull side with the brass and ended right under the decking where the antenna mount was located. Never use ordinary wire as a connection between your transmitter and grounding system. Wire has so little surface area. I cut a narrow 1-inch strip from shim stock, and used it as a grounding strap from the transmitter to

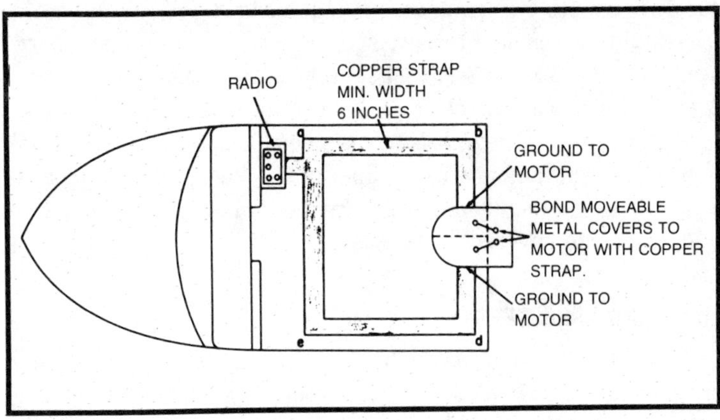

Fig. 7-6. This simple ground system for an outboard uses brass shim stock.

the ground connection under the decking. Later, on a larger transmitter, I used a 2-inch strap.

All boat machinery, gas tanks, water tanks, shafts, rudders, propellers, struts, stuffing boxes and mufflers were also tied into the grounding system to make one huge mass of metal surface. This grounding system has proven very successful for me, and I have always had one of the most powerful signals on the Great Lakes.

The performance of any SSB radio-phone will only be as good as the antenna installation. The antenna will perform only as good as the ground system lets it. All medium frequency antennas operate on the Marconi concept, like the two-wire circuit. The antenna is one wire, the ground is the other wire (Fig. 7-7). You wouldn't try to hook up the battery in your car with one heavy gauge positive cable and one thin 18-gauge ground wire. Of course not. Both wires are always the same heavy gauge. In the Marconi antenna, the ground is that same second wire that completes the circuit. It should be equal in surface area as the antenna.

I have seen boat owners go through great expense and effort to put in a good ground system, spend thousands of dollars for a radio-phone, then hook it up to the ground system with skinny 18-gauge copper wire. The finest antenna that money can buy will function only as good as that weak link you put between the ground and your transmitter.

CB GROUNDS

The body of an automobile serves as the ground, or "counterpoise," for CB radio-phones. With a steel or aluminum boat, you could use an auto-type antenna, but you shouldn't. It is always best in the marine environment to use electronic equipment designed specifically for the sea. Marine CB antennas are usually fiberglass-encased whips with corrosion-resistant fittings sealed against moisture. For wood and fiberglass boats, a counterpoise "ground plane" is built into the antenna itself. Special lay-down mounts are also available so the antenna can be dropped when going under low bridges or into covered boat wells.

LIGHTNING ARRESTERS

Where the antenna is the highest point on the boat, a lightning arrester should be added to protect your set and boat. A lightning bolt will utterly demolish the antenna, but a good marine-type arres-

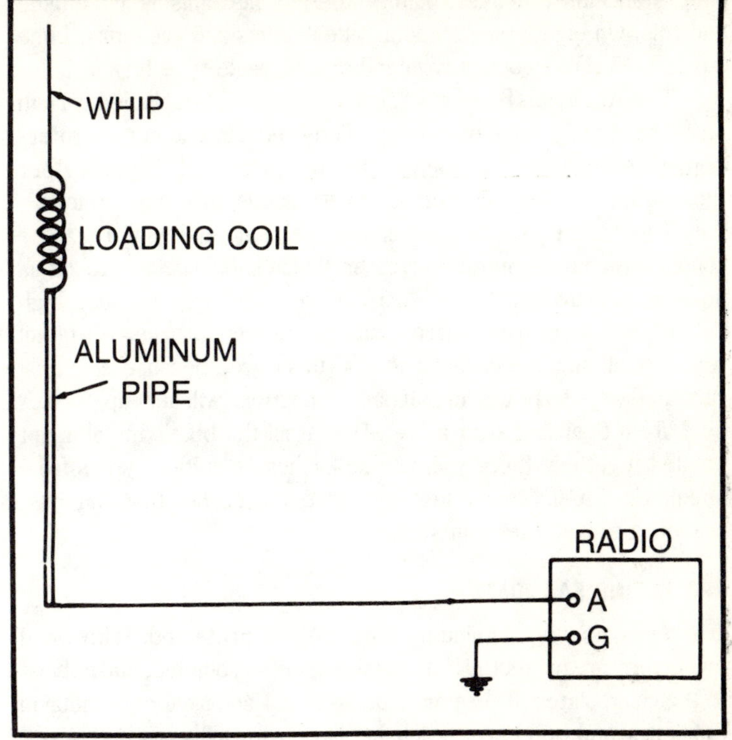

Fig. 7-7. Shown is a typical radio-phone antenna.

ter, such as available from Hy-Gain, will save your rig. Don't think it can't happen, getting hit by lightning.

I am a natural born coward who heads for the barn at sight of the first thunder cloud. Yet, I have been hit twice. Lightning out on water terrifies me. As a kid I hid under the bed during thunderstorms.

No matter how careful you are, how well you plan ahead or how much you listen to weather reports, you are inevitably going to get caught someday in a thunderstorm. When you do, you will become a good Christian and start going to church regularly, as I have. There is nothing that will teach a man how to pray faster than an electrical storm out on big water. After getting hit, I was mumbling "Hail Marys" for weeks.

Here again is where a good ground and bonding system is so important. It becomes an integral part of your boat's lightning protection. Every piece of metal on my boat is bonded together. That means all the plumbing, through-hull fittings, deck hardware, anchor, stanchions, lifelines, pulpit, steering mechanisms and engine controls. On big masses of metal, like engines and gas tanks, I use #6 and #8 AWG copper wire and special cable type terminals.

The American Boat and Yacht Council has established certain standards for lightning protection. They recommend in the protection system copper "conductors that weigh at least 50 pounds per thousand feet." That figures out as #8 gauge wire, and no less.

The radio-phone antenna is also the boat's lightning rod. The conductor from the antenna arrester device should be as straight as possible. Particularly avoid sharp 90 degree turns because high voltage will jump from sharp turns to another surface. All metal connections should be tight and resistance free because electrical current flow is so powerful that bad connections will heat up, fuse or even flash over and start a fire. Also, if all the boat's metal is not bonded together, there will be side flashes as voltage jumps from one piece of metal to another. It's these side flashes that you must prevent because they can start a fire.

PROTECTING SAILBOATS

Sailboats with aluminum masts are well protected. With wood masts they are protected if all metal rigging is grounded, and not just to the chain plates. There must be at least 1 square foot of metal in the water and tied in to the chain plates with #8 wire.

PROTECTING YOURSELF AND FAMILY

Experts say that in an electrical storm on water, the safest place to be is in the cabin, if there is one, or away from all metal objects. Keep the kids out of the head were they might touch a plumbing fixture. Running the boat could be dangerous to the skipper, like touching the reverse gear lever with one hand and a metal steering wheel with the other at the wrong time.

Sit down and ride out the storm. If you get hit, you'll just lose an antenna, but you'll gain an experience that you all can tell your friends about in church and Sunday school.

AFTER LIGHTNING STRIKES

When your eyeballs stop spinning, start checking. Lift the engine hatches and sniff. You will see smoke and smell strange odors. Never mind the smell; look for fire. If there is resistance in any of your wire terminals or bonding connections, voltage will have zapped back and forth in the bilge like a pinball. This is what causes the smoke and smells. A bad terminal connection will look like it had been welded. It will still be hot and smoking.

If there is no fire in your bilge, say two quick "Hail Marys" and then check out your radio and antenna. See if any connections fused. Finally, check your poor compass. Talk to it tenderly because it will be in a state of shock. And so will your wife. Try to get the compass card moving soon as possible, even if you have to unmount it and turn it upside down. That's what I had to do with mine.

VHF/FM ANTENNAS

At its best, VHF is a short-range communication system. With a bad antenna and lead-in hookup, you can wind up with nothing. In fact, you'll be better off with a good hailer or some pigeons. If your prime reason for buying VHF is to open up the way for an SSB license, then you won't be interested in improving your VHF transmission. You'll take whatever antenna comes with the cheapest package you can buy, install it and forget it.

FCC rules state that SSB is a high seas supplement to VHF and is to be used only when VHF range is inadequate—which is just about all the time, except when you're talking to another boat in your marina or yacht club. Some VHF sets have a "low power" switch for this very purpose, so you can cut down to just one watt for close-by talking.

This is really very funny because it suggests that VHF at full power will blast close-by receivers the way old MF used to do. I have seen some VHF installations that couldn't even get out of the marina at full power. There are marinas in California so huge that you are lucky if you can communicate from one end to the other with VHF or the new 4-watt CB. So don't be persuaded to buy a certain model of VHF just because it has that "lower power" switch. Believe me, you have enough "low power" without it.

GETTING VHF SERVICED

I mention the preceding remarks only for the ever faithful who will buy VHF and make the best of it, and this you most certainly will do because after you buy the equipment, you are on your own. There is no such thing as VHF "service." Oh sure, there are dealers who sell and so-called "technicians" who install and go through the motions of "tuning."

The almost total lack of good radio-telephone service is why I enrolled in special electronics classes so I could pass the FCC exams for a Second Class Commercial Radio-Telephone license. In almost all big boating areas, you are at the mercy of one, two, or possibly three people who have the right license to service and tune radio-telephones. In the spring they are usually swamped with work. They become bad-mannered, arrogant and will blacklist you if you are in the least bit disrespectful when they come aboard. Who needs that? So I got my own license.

KEEPING TRANSMITTERS TUNED

Radio-telephones are tough to keep tuned, especially in SSB and medium frequencies. A seagull's droppings on your antenna lead will change your plate current. If somebody spits on my dock, my antenna RF current changes.

With my old MF rig, boatmen were constantly asking me the secret of my powerful signal. It was no secret. I just kept the thing tuned. Although you are not supposed to do this without the proper license, many boaters can and do. Under the circumstances, I don't blame them. You can do it, too, if you really want to because it is not difficult. Your owner's manual will usually provide all the information you need. Tuning a radio-telephone without the proper license is technically illegal, but it is not a vile criminal act like selling dope to children.

It is also technically illegal to use profanity over the air, to hog a channel with personal chatter and refuse to get off during a Mayday. There are millions of such "technical" violations every day. I don't think the FBI will descend on you if you turn a little screw in your transmitter to adjust the plate current loading to your final PA. In any event, how will they ever know?

The poor people have their radio-phones "tuned" once in the spring, and it will cost $20 to $40, depending on how many extra crystals you installed. Before the radio man has left the marina, your transmitter is untuned when a big sailboat pulls in the slip next to you (Fig. 7-8).

It can work the other way also. You are docked between two sailboats when your transmitter is tuned. When you pull out of the slip, you are all screwed up. That's the way it was with our departed medium frequency AM rigs. It's even worse with SSB in the lower frequencies. The least bit of movement close to a boat affects them and nobody really knows why.

Radio-phone "tuners" know this and have been exploiting it for years. They just come aboard, tune your rig, and take the money and

Fig. 7-8. If your radiophone is "tuned" near something like this, you will be untuned the minute you move out of your slip.

run, as Arthur Treacher used to say. This is another reason why I took the exams and do my own tuning.

So how do you lick it? I can only tell you what I do—I never tune my rig while tied up in a dock. I do the tuning out in the lake away from all the other radio antennas, sailboat masts, rigging, electric lines, steel lamp posts, bulkheads, etc. I pick a quiet day, go out in the lake a mile, drop the lunch hook, and keep both engines running.

This is another thing commercial "tuners" neglect to do— advise you to run your engines while they work. They just tune your rig with the battery voltage. Later, when your engines are running, alternators are putting over 14 volts into your batteries and this affects current loading to the final power amplifier. With the engines running, you will be overloading to the PA. Sometimes you blow a fuse, and you wonder what the hell happened. Most of the time you don't blow a fuse, but when you go on the air, you get comments like: "I can't read you, Joe. You sound mushy." Technically, you are overmodulting.

Overloading the final PA is something all manufacturers warn technicians against because it is not only damaging, but can lead to illegal interference. But yet, only once have I ever heard a radio-phone "tuner" suggest to a boat owner that he run his engines and bring up the battery voltage before he did the final loading of plate current.

A radio-phone that is tuned out on the water somewhere with the engines running will hold that tuning reasonably well, but only when out on water. When you go back to your dock, your tuning will be way off, you will lose resonance, your plate current will be way down and you will have a weak signal. So what? So you can't blast everybody in the marina. But that's unimportant, having a good signal in a marina. The marine radio-telephone is not a toy to play with on weekends while tied up at a dock. You should get a CB for that. The important thing is your transmitters is tuned for a good signal out on the water. How often do you have a Mayday situation tied up at a dock?

If I have made you unhappy, I am sorry, but I think you have a right to at least know that when you get involved with radio-telephones on the non-commercial consumer level, you are going to get shafted many times over. This is why I cried New Year's Eve listening to Guy Lombardo. My old Sonar was all paid for. Now I've got to go out and buy a VHF just so I can legally own an expensive SSB.

Acutally VHF is good only for those big boats that never go anywhere. They spend the entire season tied up in their slips and you can hear them every weekend talking back and forth in the same marina, or to friends in another marina. With its line-of-sight range, VHF is useless once you get beyond sight of land. Don't be misled by advertised ranges of "10 to 30 miles." That is a crock of you-know-what. You will get ranges like that only if your antenna is atop a high mast 100 or 200 feet above the water. For the average American boater in his 24 to 30-footer, a high mast is just out of the question. The average range for you will be about 6 miles. And this is a very generous estimate because the average installation on small boats is inefficient. If you get a signal just out of the marina with a 5-foot 3 antenna, you will have an "average" VHF installation.

VHF ON BIG WATER

What do you do if you cruise often far beyond sight of land, which is commonplace today on the Great Lakes and coastal waters? What do you do if your engine conks half way across Lake Michigan on a cruise to Milwaukee, or half way to Biminni from Miami? If you're in the Gulf Stream off Miami, and all you've got is VHF, you will slowly starve to death, unless you can thumb a ride with a passing oil tanker or Soviet trawler on the way to the Grand Banks fishing grounds.

If you cruise any coastal waters, or if you just take your boat beyond sight of land, you should have SSB and high seas crystals.

PACKAGED VHF RADIO-PHONES

You can buy VHF in "pre-tuned" package deals which have everything you need: a transmitter-receiver, a certain number of crystals, a 5-foot 3 db (decibel) gain antenna and 15 to 20 feet of coaxial cable called RG-58U. You can get a six-watt, 12-channel package for about $225 through discount mail order sources. You can spend $800 for a fully synthesized 70-channel, 25-watt rig which will be just as useless as the one for $225. Don't waste your money. Buy the cheapest rig you can find. Don't buy without a substantial discount. Keep the box!

There are two reasons for getting a big discount, and keeping the shipping container. The discount compensates you for the "service" and "warranty protection" you will never get from the dealer. You need the box when the equipment breaks down and must be returned to the manufacturer. VHF sets are transistorized and some have potted circuitry made in Japan. You will find nobody qualified to work on this stuff, and the ones like myself who have the proper license won't touch them for less then a million dollars deposited in a Swiss bank. If you take your set back to the dealer, and since he knows less about VHF than your grandmother, it will sit on a workbench in his back shop for weeks until they can find a suitable shipping container. By returning it yourself, you will get better and faster service—usually a new rig because the so-called "manufacturer" is just an assembly operation for Japanese components. They don't "fix" anything. They replace it. They will go out of their way to keep an owner happy, but they don't give a damn about dealers.

Your "packaged" radio-phone can be easily installed by you with the antenna and lead-in cable supplied. You cannot change anything without affecting the so-called factory "pre-tuning." An FCC license is not required to install a radio-phone station, or even to work on the receiver. But you cannot legally (many do anyway) touch anything in the transmitter which will affect plate current, resonance, modulation or RF antenna current. If you add more length to the coaxial cable, you screw up the "pre-tuning." Your 25 watts become two-watts and your six-mile range becomes one mile.

You will never get six miles on a small boat with the 5-foot, 3 db gain antenna supplied with the "package." You will eventually give it the deep six and buy a 9-foot, 6 db or 21-foot, 9 db gain antenna. This, of course, changes the "pre-tuning." You can avoid this by just keeping the original 3 db antenna, but installing it atop a 10 or 12-foot extender mast, if you can reach it with the 20 feet of coaxial cable supplied. Remember, if you change the length of the cable, or change antennas, you must retune the transmitter.

ANTENNA COUPLERS

There are all sorts of electronics devices, like antenna couplers, which are supposed to automatically provide for a perfect match between transmitter and antenna/ground systems. I suppose they work, but nothing, absolutely nothing you buy or do is going to make that VHF rig reach out any further without getting the antenna up higher. That is the only way. Commercial and ocean vessels have their VHF antennas 200-300-400 feet up above the water. This is the only reason why big vessels can reach out 20, 30, and 40 miles with VHF. Yet, they use it only or short range communications, when docking, with bridge and lock tenders, tug boats and other passing ships. For long distance telephone calls, they use the high seas telephone service.

THE SSB RADIO-TELEPHONE

If you have a VHF/FM rig installed and licensed on your boat, you are eligible for an SSB license. SSB is capable of communicating hundreds, even thousands of miles from your boat. Up until recently, most SSB equipment had been designed for big ship and commercial use. Because of the extreme technical sophistication of its circuitry and its method of transmission, it had been very expensive, averaging $1,500 to $3,000, plus extras and installation. Installation was also difficult on wood and fiberglass boats.

However, with the passing of the old MF/AM radios on 2-3 MHz, and with the inadequacies and general dissatisfaction with VHF/FM, the single sideband radio-phone is the boater's only alternative if he wants to continue cruising on coastal waters beyond sight of land. New SSB equipment designed and built expressly for pleasure craft is now available at more reasonable prices, and more easily installed and tuned.

If you have had some discussions about SSB with friends you have probably heard some unfavorable comments. Most dissatisfactions are the result of poor installations or improper use of the equipment. An SSB rig must be installed right or it just will not perform as it should. Beware of "free" installations that go with sale of the equipment. I have personally made four SSB installations on boats of friends and I assure you it cannot be done "free" and done right. Expect to pay 20 to 30 percent of the equipment price for installation. And don't tell the man where and how you want the equipment installed because your wife thinks "it looks better over there."

There are certain technical guidelines the installer must follow. Sure, it may be more convenient for you if it's mounted up overhead, and the man will put it there if you insist because you're the boss and the boss is always right. But don't blame him for bad performance. Sometimes just moving the transmitter a foot to another location can make a big difference, and putting the rig up overhead in a wood or fiberglass boat can screw up everything with that long ground and antenna lead winding around corners and through holes. It's not the same as wiring up a doorbell or windshield wiper. And don't tell the man what antenna to use. Those old fiberglass whips that were so popular on old AM equipment are almost useless on SSB.

HOW TO USE SSB

Don't expect to pick up your microphone and start talking to somebody a thousand miles away. The high seas bands are far more affected by weather and propagation than the old 2-3 MHz band you are more familiar with. Most of the 2-3 MHz telephone stations around the country are not working properly, so don't hastily judge your new SSB on the basis of bad experiences with them. It's not your equipment's fault. You'll find that other owners are having the same trouble. The telephone company's equipment is highly automated, extremely complex and isn't working out the way the experts predicted. Their equipment is so sophisticated that if your transmitter is not sufficiently warmed up, you may be just enough off frequency that they won't hear you. You'll find things quite different on the high seas telephone service.

It takes time to learn all the vagaries and how to use SSB, but one thing you can depend on—high noon is the worst time for radio communications as far as distance is concerned. For example, in the early morning and late afternoon on the 8 MHz band you can reach out 1000 miles easily. But at noon your range drops down to 500 miles and less. At night your signals get lost all over the world in international interference.

You can push out 300 miles on the 4 MHz band when the sun is near the horizon, but at noon you will only reach out about 100 miles. At night you can talk to someone 600 miles away.

The frequencies above 12 MHz can cover 10,000 miles at certain times of the day, but fade considerably at night. With SSB it's all a matter of learning to adjust and schedule your transmissions (above 4 MHz) to take advantage of best atmospheric conditions. Commercial users have been doing this for years and they never miss moving their traffic. By pre-arrangement they schedule transmissions at a specific time on a specific frequency which they know, from past experience, will be best for that given time and distance. And they never miss. The ones who do miss just aren't using the equipment to best advantage.

THE ADVANTAGES OF SSB

With an SSB high seas rig installed on your boat, you will have the ultimate status symbol. And you will meet a better class of people. I know this sounds like snobbery, but it's true. If you have ever listened much to marine radio traffic on a Sunday afternoon, or to CB traffic any afternoon, I think you will understand what I mean. You don't hear inane chatter on high seas frequencies. The voices you will hear are professionals or experienced yachtsmen who know exactly what they have to say. They say it crisply, then sign off.

In the various high seas bands from, 4 MHz to 22 MHz, there is no emergency or "calling" channel like 2182 or channel 16 on VHF. So boaters can't just sit around all day monitoring their radio-phones and waiting for somebody they know to call for a signal check. That gives them an excuse to get on the air themselves for a signal check. There is no set calling procedure on high seas. You are not required by FCC rules to "monitor" anything, unless you just want to monitor one of the coast guard frequencies to hear the action, if any.

Most ship-to-ship communications are by pre-arrangement. There is no point in wasting time on the air calling from Cleveland to a friend in Ft. Lauderdale on 8281.2 in the vain hope that he might be listening on that frequency. Why should he be "listening" if he isn't expecting a call? And you don't use "channels" on high seas, just frequencies, because channel 4 is not necessarily the same frequency in all areas.

There is no idle chatter on high seas because nobody is listening or monitoring and nobody is going to answer you just for a little chit chat, as they will on VHF and CB. For this reason, you may not like

312

high seas SSB. Then again, if you hated Sunday afternoons on the old 2-3 MHz band, you will love it because you do meet a better class of people with simple names like John Jones instead of "Big Daddy." And everybody speaks English instead of jargon and numbers like 10-4. SSB is not a toy or a hobby. It is just an excellent long-range communications media for mariners, and nothing else. At least that is what it has been up until now.

HIGH SEAS TELEPHONE SERVICES

There are ship-to-shore telephone stations in virtually every country in the world. These are in addition to those you are already familiar with in 2-3 MHz and VHF. Five high seas stations are in the United States. They are "WOO," New York, N.Y.; "WOM," Ft. Lauderdale, Fla.; "KMI," Oakland, Calif.; "WLO," Mobile, Ala.; and "KQM," Honolulu, Hawaii.

You may wonder if just five telephone stations is enough for so vast an area. For SSB five is enough. For VHF a thousand wouldn't be enough.

An outstanding informational booklet called "High Seas Maritime Mobile Radio-Telephone Service" is available to you at no charge by just calling your local Bell System, or writing to American Telephone and Telegraph Company, 5 World Trade Center, New York, N.Y. 10048.

RADIO-TELEPHONE HANDBOOK

A new 72-page booklet has been published by the Radio Technical Commission for Marine Services (RTCM) to aid boatmen in the proper use of their equipment, both VHF/FM and SSB. The book is titled "How To Use Your Marine Radio-Telephone" and covers everything from obtaining a license to an appendix with listings of everything and everybody that the mariner need know about. The booklet costs $2.50 and can be purchased direct from RTCM c/o Federal Communications Commission, P.O. Box 19807, Washington, D.C. 20036.

WHY HIGH SEAS SERVICE IS BETTER

The high seas service supplied by the five phone company stations is far superior to anything now available on the 2-3 MHz and VHF bands. The reason is that these stations are staffed by highly trained technicians who really monitor the frequencies and don't depend on idiot lights to alert them to an incoming call. And these technicians have the finest electronic marvels at their disposal, like rotary beam antennas to detect and pull in very weak signals that other stations would pass off as unreadable.

They normally monitor on a non-directional antenna. When they pick you up, they will ask your location and then switch to the rotary beam antenna which will be aimed in your direction. You will have no trouble hearing them because they have 10,000 watt transmitters and directional antennas to aim their signal at you like a rifle bullet. So distance means nothing on high seas.

From the middle of Lake Huron, in the early morning or late afternoon, you can call WOM in Ft. Lauderdale on the 8 MHz bands and speak to friends by land phone. In an emergency, the coast guard station you are calling may find your signal unreadable. But the telephone stations with their vastly superior array of electronics will pick you up easily. You can call them and they will alert the coast guard or relay your call. And there is no charge for such assistance in an emergency . This is something to remember if you are ever in trouble and nobody answers.

HIGH SEAS WEATHER INFORMATION

You can also obtain up-to-date weather information from high seas shore stations. New York's WOM broadcasts Caribbean weather four times a day at 5 a.m., 11 a.m., 5 p.m. and 11 p.m.

If you keep a log, you should monitor the high seas shore stations when they make their regular hourly roll calls. The reason is you can actually hear the effects of propagation on signal strength. By keeping a record, you will know which are the best hours to transmit. This is what all experienced coastal yachtsmen have been doing for years and why they never miss with their calls.

BEFORE YOU INSTALL VHF OR SSB

A few weeks ago I was asked by a boating friend, who had just taken delivery of 36 feet of glistening fiberglass, if I would help him install a radio. I took one look at that flybridge and said: "Not even if it would help us put a manned spaceship on Pluto."

He wanted the transmitter installed way up there in the flybridge and I wanted no part of that. His new boat is a beautiful, seamless, molded, solid hunk of fiberglass. There were no openings anywhere through which a ground strap connection could be made. The battery power leads, the antenna leads and the ground connection would be interminably long. It is almost impossible to get a good installation in a flybridge, VHF or SSB. Oh, sure, the thing will work and so does a Russian flush toilet, but not too well.

With the old departed AM rigs it was easy to install radio-phones high up on flybridges—even up on those sky-high deep sea fishing towers because the higher-powered transmitters had their power packs separate from the radio itself. I had my power pack installed down in the bilge close to the battery with power leads only a foot long. I had my transmitter installed in the head where it was only 10 inches away from the antenna base and 6 inches away from a 12-inch copper ground strap. The transmitter was remotely controlled by a separate unit at the helm.

You can't do this with the new radios because they're completely self-contained and transistorized with everything in one unit. When you put these radios up in a flybridge, you've got to travel from here to hell and back with all those leads. That's why an old line marine electronics firm in New Jersey says that it is very difficult to make a good SSB installation in a wood or fiberglass boat. So many boats today have flybridges and everything has to be up there.

Another thing you must consider with flybridge installations is VD (voltage drop) with those long power leads. If you think this is trivial, put a VOM meter on your battery and have someone crank your engine. Your battery voltage will suddenly drop down to 10 volts, even less in cold weather. What many boaters do not know is that 12 volt batteries do not always deliver full voltage under load. A long lead wire to a transmitter is also part of the load. A 10 percent drop may be only 1.2 volts at the battery, but on the secondary side of a transformer putting out 650 volts, the drop in voltage becomes 65 volts.

This is another reason why radio-phones are so difficult to keep tuned. It is absolutely impossible to load the right plate current to the final power amplifier if the plate voltage is constantly changing or is too low. Equipment that is designed to operate on 12 volts must have 12 volts and not 10.5 volts—that is if you want the power you paid for.

Does your radio-phone really have to be up there in the flybridge? What's the matter with the cabin? How often do you use the phone that it must be on the flybridge at your fingertips every second? These are questions that you must answer before you buy that new phone. If you just must have the phone up in the flybridge, there is a way.

GETTING ALONG WITHOUT A GROUND SYSTEM

If you plan to incorporate the 2-3 MHz bands in your SSB, then you will need adequate grounding and must suffer all the headaches that go with trying to get connected to it from that flybridge. But, if you can get along without the 2-3 MHz bands, your installation can be considerably simplified by a new antenna, called a dipole, with its own built-in counterpoise. It is called the Melectro "SeaSpanner." This antenna is a radical departure from the Marconi antenna and it installs much in the same manner as a VHF or CB antenna with a coaxial cable lead-in. This new antenna is considerably longer, about 23 feet, but it does eliminate the biggest problem in wood and fiberglass radio installations. You can get more information on this antenna by writing to SGC, Inc., 13737 S.E. 26th Street, Bellevue, Washington 98005.

SOLVING THE POWER PROBLEM

That leaves you with just one more installation problem up in that flybridge—cutting down VD in those long battery leads. A 150-watt transmitter will consume over 30 amperes while on the air. You must increase your battery capacity or install a separate big capacity battery for the transmitter and keep it charged dockside. You must also use big fat #8 wire for leads. By using a separate battery for the phone, you will make it easier to tune the rig and keep it tuned because the operating voltage will be more steady and uniform. You will not have those high 14 plus volts when the engine is running and the alternator is charging. You will have a "clean" steady 12 volts for the radio with no garbage picked up from the engine ignition system.

THE NEW ELECTRONIC BAFFLEGAB, WITH EXPLANATIONS

If you decide to remain with some form of radio communications on your boat, then you will be hearing a lot of strange new electronic gab. Most of it is of interest only to engineers and electronic freaks. I will explain only the ones that you will frequently encounter and wonder about. For example, you probably have wondered all through this chapter just what the hell is a MHz? Things like this I will explain. However, I don't think you need an explanation for a "beat frequency oscillator," and wouldn't understand it anyway.

THE MEANING OF MHz

Once upon a time radio frequencies were called kilocycles or megacycles. Kilo is Greek and means thousand. Mega means million. For example, a 1000 kilocycles written out in numbers would be 1,000,000 cycles. One megacycle written out in numbers would be the same thing. The purpose of "kilo" and "mega" is to eliminate all the zeros.

The word "cycle" indicates one full radio wave and "frequency" is the number of those waves passing a given point in one second. A frequency of 1 megacycle means that 1000,000 waves will radiate every second. The shorter the waves the more there are to radiate in one second, which is why they are called "high frequencies" or "short waves." When you get up in the ultra-high frequencies, you start using a lot of zeros. The letter "M" eliminates six zeros. The letter "K" eliminates three zeros.

To honor Hertz, the father of modern communications, it was decided to drop "cycle" and substitute "hertz" in its place. So now we have "kilohertz" and "megahertz." This has been shortened down further to "KMz" and "MHz".

VHF/FM

The first three letters are an abbreviation for very high frequency; the second two mean frequency modulation, which is the same type of fine reception you get on commercial radio in your car. Marine VHF is in the 156 MHz band, which is close to TV channels 7 to 13. Like TV signals, VHF is strictly line-of-sight communications, which is why TV broadcasters put their transmitting antennas on top of skyscrappers or very high steel towers. And that is the reason why they can push a signal 50 and 75 miles while you can only push six miles down on the water.

FREQUENCY MODULATION

Your radio transmitter has an oscillator tube which generates a radio wave of a specific frequency. This wave becomes the radiated carrier (Fig. 7-9). It is used to literally "carry" messages, which is why it is so called. When you talk into the microphone, you create an audio wave which is imposed on the carrier by two different methods, changing its shape or altering its frequency. If you change the shape, as in Fig. 7-9, it is called "amplitude modulation." If you change the frequency, it is called "frequency modulation."

The chief advantage of FM is greater freedom from interference and static because most electrical disturbances caused by thunderstorms and automobile ignition systems are amplitude modulation in character, and are picked up as noise by all AM receivers. Your FM receiver will not pick up AM signals.

CITIZENS BAND

This is a two-way radio communications system for use by the general public that was first instituted in 1947 and called the "Citizens Radio Service." The FCC felt that the American people, who actually own all the airways, should also have some personal use of their property instead of licensing it out only to privileged groups and vested interests.

The first Citizens Radio Service was severely limited in usefulness, was very expensive, hard to get and not much better then smoke signals. So in 1958 the FCC upgraded the service with creation of the "Class-D Citizens Radio Service," which is what today we call "Citizens Band." Most CB equipment is AM modulation and is available in walkie-talkie, mobile units or cars and base stations for homes. The mobile units are tiny, very compact and operate only on 12 volts DC. Base stations are much larger, operate on 120 volts AC, but are also available to run on both 120 volts AC and 12 volts DC.

Base stations make nice installations on larger boats, especially with SSB added. The AM/SSB base station has an extra 40 channels on the lower sideband, and 40 on the upper sideband. The regular AM units are rated 4 watts output power, but the SSB is rated 12 watts PEP (peak envelope power) output. By eliminating the carrier and one sideband, you put all the transmitter power into the remaining sideband which acts to triple the power and makes SSB reach out further. The AM/SSB base station, with dual voltage, is the ideal unit for marine service, if you decide to go CB.

DOUBLE SIDEBAND

The old AM radio-telephones were double sideband. When you modulate the carrier, you get an overlap on each side. These overlaps are called the "sidebands." Both sidebands carry the same audio wave pattern, which represents the actual message, which is your voice. So transmission power is divided, or wasted, in carrying two messages. Power is also wasted in the carrier. By eliminating the carrier and one sideband, you concentrate remaining power on one

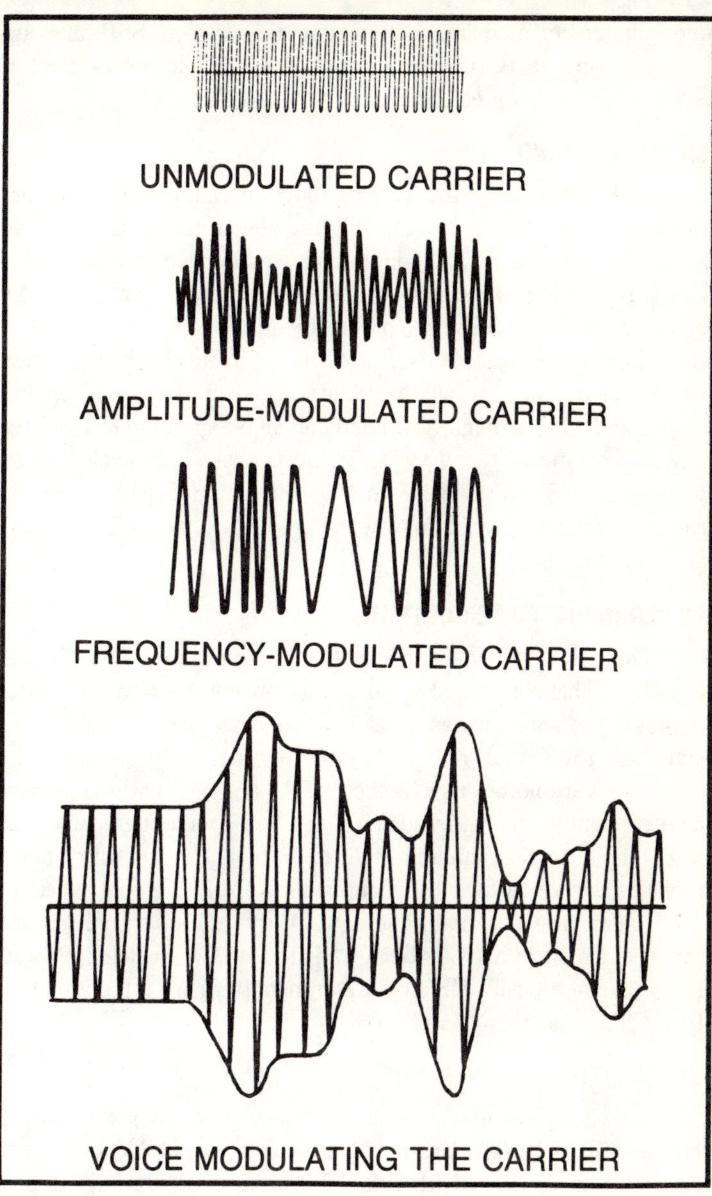

Fig. 7-9. Here is how the carrier wave is modulated.

sideband. You actually triple transmission power, which is the reason why SSB has such range.

The main reason why the old AM double sideband was eliminated was because it took up too much room with all that needless upper and lower modulation hogging up the airways. SSB takes up less space and leaves room for more channels. While you use the top sideband, somebody else can use the bottom sideband.

SINGLE SIDEBAND

This is the new wave of long-range marine communications. Actually, SSB is not new because it has been around almost as long as amplitude modulation. Radio hams have been working with it for years. But it is "new" to boaters and the general public who are now enjoying CB. Since SSB is amplitude modulation, you are subject to some interference problems. Since you are using only half the band width, you pick up only half the static and noise. When you drop that carrier and one sideband, you need only one-eighth the transmitter power. This means that 10 watts in the sideband is equivalent to 80 watts in the old AM radios. With 150 watts output in an SSB rig you can communicate almost anywhere in the world, and still have less drain on your battery.

POWER INPUT, POWER OUTPUT

The old AM radios were rated power input to the final power amplifier. This always led to some misconceptions because power output to the antenna was usually half the input. So a 60-watt rated transmitter was really only putting out 30 watts to the antenna. The antennas were notoriously inefficient. An antenna that was 30 percent efficient was considered excellent. At 30 percent efficiency, 30 watts input to the antenna ends up with only nine watts being radiated. However, very few antennas were 30 percent efficient. The majority were 20 and 10 percent. At this efficiency, only six and three watts were actually being radiated with a so-called 60-watt radio-telephone. All VHF and SSB transmitters are rated at output to the antenna.

TRANSMITTER-RECEIVER

This is a radio-phone receiver, transmitter and power pack all enclosed in one cabinet as a single unit. Some old AM radios had separate power packs with either dynamotors or vibrators to produce high plate voltages. A 150-watts unit would usually have two dynamotors, one for plate voltage, one for the modulator.

TRANSCEIVER

This is a transmitter, receiver and power pack enclosed in one cabinet but sharing many components. Since you don't transmit and receive at the same time, many components can do double duty. This is why mobile CB units are so tiny, many no bigger then a cigar box.

COAXIAL CABLE

This is a special type of low-loss antenna lead-in wire used with VHF and CB (Fig. 7-10). It can also be used with SSB and the new antenna, which has its own built-in counterpoise. Coaxial cable consists of a stranded inner core conductor wire which is surrounded by a white polyethylene dielectric. Copper braid is woven over the dielectric to form an outer conductor. A waterproof black vinyl cover is placed over the braid. The old AM radio-phones did not use coaxial cable hook-ups between transmitter and antenna, which was the reason for their poor efficiency. It was the custom at one time to use

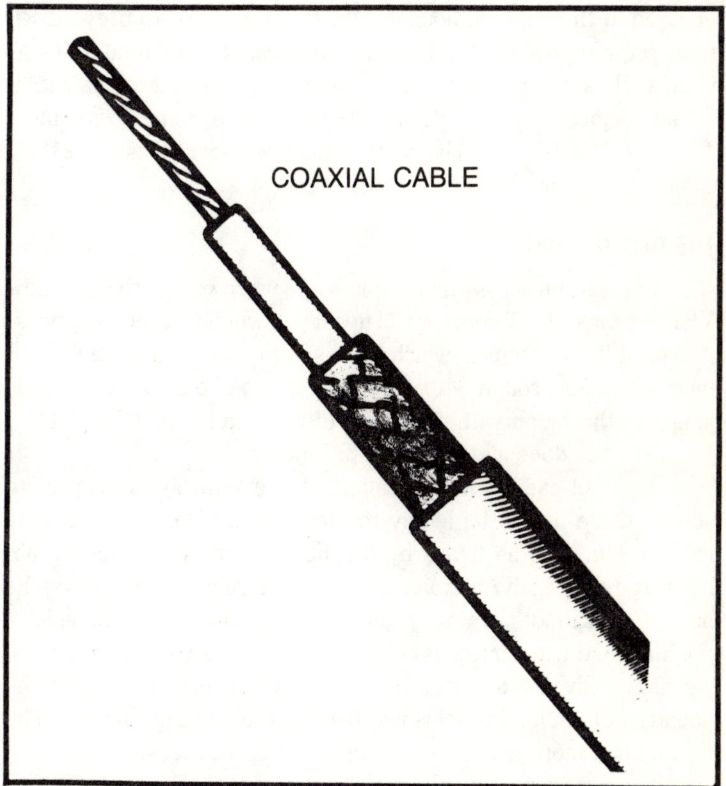

Fig. 7-10. Coaxial cable is a conductor within a conductor, but it is separated by a dielectric. The outer mesh conductor prevents radiation losses of the inner conductor.

spark plug wire because of its superior insulation. However, some spark plug wire had stainless steel wire, which is a very poor conductor, especially with RF. This contributed to even more losses and antenna inefficiency because when the lead was too long, very little RF current got to the antenna. The radio signal was radiating out of that lead-in wire instead of the antenna whip.

This is why my transmitter was installed, as one female guest later told friends: "Mr. Fenwick has his radio station installed in the toilet."

I put it there to keep the antenna and ground leads short. A remote control unit, speaker and handset were at the helm within easy reach.

With coaxial cable you don't have this problem and transmission leads can be 20 feet long without serious RF losses. The braided copper outer conductor is connected to the ground counterpoise encased in the antenna housing. It acts as a shield to prevent RF from escaping before it gets to the antenna. If you intend to install your VHF antenna atop an extension to get additional height, it would be best to discard the RG-8/U which comes with most "packaged" VHF units. Use instead the low-energy loss RG-213/U cable which is made to rigid military specifications.

THE DECIBEL (db)

You will run across this terminology when you go to buy a new VHF antenna. It will confuse and upset you when you see the prices. A typical 3 db antenna, which comes with most "packaged" VHF units, sells for around $40. A 6 db jumps to about $75 and a 9 db jumps to the moon with price tags of $150 and $250 (Fig. 7-11).

So what does all that "db" stuff mean?

Since all radio communications are eventually converted to sound, there has to be a way to measure this sound in terms of relative loudness as heard by the human ear. The decibel, (abbreviated db), is the unit used to measure relative loudness. The human ear cannot accurately detect sound values. For example, if you increase transmitter power from 100 watts to 400 watts, the signal will only sound twice as loud to the human ear. A change in the sound level of one decibel is just barely detectable by the ear. The decibel is a more accurate measurement of loudness.

The 6 db antenna will give a measured signal loudness twice what you would hear with a 3 db antenna, but it won't actually sound twice as loud to your ear. In fact, you'll hardly notice any difference

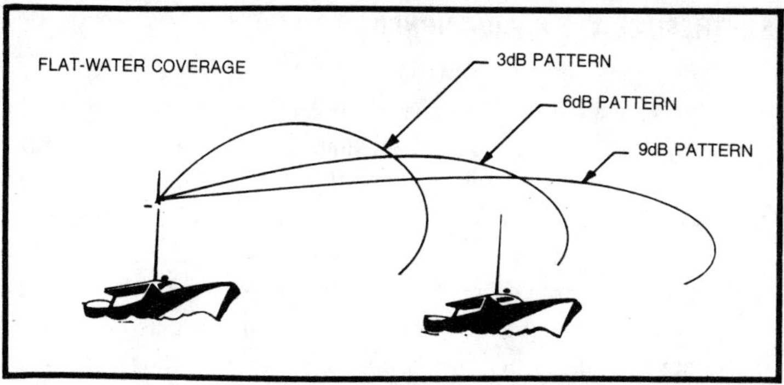

Fig. 7-11. Most packaged VHF units come with 3 dB antennas. They are also factory "tuned" to this antenna. If you substitute a different antenna, you screw up the factory "tuning."

and you'll wonder why you spent the money. Nevertheless, when you buy a packaged VHF radio, you will get a 3 db antenna. Then later when you notice that everybody else has a 6 db or 9 db, you will feel socially inferior, and proceed to upgrade your unit.

AUTOMATIC GAIN CONTROL

This is an upgrading terminology that you will find also on your TV set under a small switch with the letters AGC. It means the same thing as automatic volume control on older radios, with which you certainly are familiar. But the wording had to be changed, just like kHz for kilocycle and capacitors for condensers.

CRYSTAL CONTROL

Licensed hams in the high classes can get away without using crystals, but not you. It is required by law that all marine frequencies be controlled by crystals. These are those little metal two-pronged devices that contain a piece of quartz material which is sliced to a size where it will vibrate, or oscillate, at a certain frequency when an electric current is applied to it. If the signal that your oscillator is generating varies the slightest, up or down, it will not pass through that crystal. So the crystal acts as a policeman, keeps you honest and not wandering all over the marine band screwing up other communications.

The crystals also make it easy for you to switch channels by just turning a knob. Without them, every time you changed channels, you would have to hunt back and forth with a tuning condenser on both transmission and receiving. You'd blow your mind doing this.

SYNTHESIZED VHF RADIO-PHONES

The Japanese in 1975 introduced in this country the first synthesized VHF radio-phones which do not use a separate crystal for each channel. With a synthesized unit you can work 55 or more channels without buying any more extra crystals. This sounds terrific. But in reality it doesn't mean a thing unless you plan to embark on a world-wide cruise. The majority of boaters don't need more than 12 or 13 channels for their cruising needs.

The synthesized radio-phones have many serious drawbacks, frequency in stability being only one. With a conventional radio, if a crystal fails, you lose only one channel. With a synthesized unit if a crystal fails, you lose the whole set and you have nothing. Also, these radios draw three times as much current on standby. The least little physical shock, like riding in pounding seas, can upset the voltage-controlled oscillator and throw the set way off frequency. These radios also have a bad service record, seven times the failure rate of conventional sets.

I can personally attest to this because although I had a powerful signal, I had a lousy receiver and often couldn't hear boats that I was trying to reach. Later I learned that they had heard me, but I didn't hear them when they responded. So don't be misled into thinking that all receivers are the same.

Receiver sensitivity is measured in microvolts. A good receiver will require less signal microvolts for reception, a poor receiver will require more microvolts. A radio with a receiver rating of more than .3 microvolts should be considered a poor buy. Some of the most illustrious names in marine electronics have VHF receivers with ratings of .5 and .75 microvolts sensitivity. Some new units with unknown names measure an incredible .17 microvolts.

RECEIVER SELECTIVITY

The marine band for VHF is very narrow. If a set doesn't have good selectivity, you will be listening to taxicabs, police and fire call and FM music. The ability of a receiver to reject unwanted signals is important, especially in large metropolitan areas where there are so many powerful transmitters on high masts.

THE SINGLE CRYSTAL SETS

Most VHF units use two crystals per channel, one to transmit and one to receive. These crystals cost $10 to $12 each, or $20 to $24 per channel, plus the cost of installing and tuning by an FCC licensed technician. There are some VHF sets available now that use just one crystal per channel for both transmitting and receiving. This can represent a savings of $120 on a 12-channel set because no manufacturer gives you the crystals. Somewhere along the line you pay for them.

Crystal requirements vary from area to area. Why pay for crystals you don't need? A fisherman wants "fishing" channels, set aside by the FCC for commercial fishermen. River boaters require "lock" channels such as channel 14. Marinas use channel 9. Channels 67, 69, 71 and 72 are good for ship-to-ship between friends because these are not as busy as the more common ship-to-ship channels of 68 and 70.

INSTALLATION OF VHF

The factory pre-tuned VHF packages are so easy to install that a French poodle can do it. All it takes is a few screws to mount the unit on a bulkhead. The power cord supplied is hooked up to a 12-volt battery. The coaxial cable is fitted with the supplied connectors and plugged into the back of the radio. And how will it work? Just like a Russian toilet. It flushes, but not too well.

Production line mass tuning techniques have proven to be less than satisfactory. They meet FCC regulations which require that crystals be tuned to within 1500 cycles (Hz) of the assigned frequency. This satisfies the FCC but it shouldn't satisfy you because the crystals can be tuned to within 10 cycles (Hz) of the assigned frequency, which will give you greater range and sharper communications. Why be satisfied with anything less?

THE MEANING OF "SWR"

The three letters "SWR" mean standing wave ratio and are used to rate antenna efficiency. If the amount of RF energy transmitted by the antenna equals the amount received through the coaxial cable from the radio, this would be a standing wave ratio (SWR) of 1:1, which is perfect—so perfect it is never achieved because, for practical reasons, it is impossible.

The best that can be hoped for or worked for is an SWR of 1.5:1. This means that some of your signal is lost between the transmitter and antenna. This is considered acceptable, but not all antennas have such an acceptable loss ratio. Many have an SWR of 2.5:1 and even 3:1. How can you tell? You can't. All antennas look alike. What do you do? Look around and ask questions. Time and tide has a way of separating chafe from wheat. In a big marina you will note that certain types of gear and antennas will always predominate. There is a reason. That particular gear or antenna has survived through trial and error. It is a fundamental law of nature. Only the best survive. In this instance, follow the crowd. Go out into the electronic jungle on your own and you will get screwed four different ways.

"SIMPLEX" AND "DUPLEX" COMMUNICATIONS

When you start investigating SSB, you will note that some are available with 12 "simplex" plus 12 "duplex" channels. You will wonder what the devil it all menas.

With conventional radio-phones, you push the microphone button to talk; when finished you say "over" and release the button to listen. In other words, you can't both talk and listen at the same time as you do over your home telephone. Conventional radio-phones are one frequency "simplex" operations.

In duplex operations you can both talk and listen at the same time, which can be a wonderful convenience for some people who just never get the hang of push-the-button-to-talk, release-the-button-to-listen. I know people who have been boating for 20 years and still don't know how to talk over the radio-phone. Some sort of nervous reflex action makes them push that microphone button before you finish a sentence. As a result, they miss the last few words of your transmission, you miss the first few of theirs, and you have nothing but confusion and a constant repeating of "I don't read you! I don't read you!"

It can be even worse when you make a telephone call through a shore station with your mother-in-law in South Bend, Indiana who is taking care of the kids while you and the wife take a second honeymoon cruise alone. You try to explain to her that she must listen while you are talking, but this is something you will never get across to a mother-in-law who has three kids at her elbow waiting to talk. You will run up $65 in toll charges for the call and get nothing but heartburn.

For the cruising boater who must maintain daily shore contact with a business, duplex radio communications is almost a necessity, if for no other reason than health. In 15 minutes of ship-to-shore talk on important business, a man's blood pressure can jump from 140 over 90 to 190 over 120.

Non-boaters just don't understand one-way marine radio communications, or they forget, and conversations rarely go well.

Mostly they are disasters. This is why I absolutely loathe ship-to-shore telephone calls and will make them only when a gun is pointed at my head. On ocean passenger vessels, all ship-to-shore radio communications are of the two frequency type or "duplex," which is the more common term.

SAVING DROWNED ELECTRONICS

If you hang around boats long enough, you will inevitably get wet, according to the mathematical law of probabilities. You will get caught in a squall, the wind will rip off your canvas top, and you won't

Fig. 7-12. When you live with things like this, as I do, you acquire much experience in saving drowned possessions.

even care because you'll be laying on the deck in the cockpit praying. Squalls pass just as quick as they come. If you ever get caught in one, you will know why old boatmen are rarely non-believers.

After the squall passes, the sun will come out and you will survey the damage. You will find not 1 inch of dry space on your boat. Everything will be drowned; including the hi-fi and your new VHX which you just installed. And you will wonder how all that water got in the cabin because even the curtains will be wet and dripping. Getting caught in a squall is like driving your car through one of those new car washes where water hits you from all directions. If you leave a window open, the inside of your car will also be washed.

And yet you will be lucky because squalls drench you with clean, soft, sweet fresh water. If you're going to get drenched, it's nice when the water is clean and drinkable. But I know of a dozen perfectly natural acts of God in nature that can drown your boat in filth, mud and polluted water. Every year thousands of boats get sunk right at their slips during high winds which back in Kansas would only stir up some dust. But where there is water, high winds move that water, either away from you or to you. When the water is blown away, your boat lays in the mud. Sometimes it will sit right on top of a broken, jagged cement building block which will rip a hole in your bottom planking. When the water returns, as it always does, your boat will stay on the bottom.

There are dozens of other ways this can happen, and they are all called "Acts of God," like hurricanes and tornados. In the midwest where I live, it is a dull week when we don't have at least one "tornado watch."

On the subject of restoring and reviving drowned electrical equipment, I have had much experience. I have twice looked at 2 feet of Lake Erie in my living room and seen a pool table and TV set floating in the basement (Fig. 7-12). I have seen one of my boats wrecked and laying on the bottom in 8 feet of water. And I have cried a lot and I have cursed the sea. But I have never lost a home, a boat, a motor, an engine or a radio. And yet all my neighbors had to replace everything that was run by electricity. And you will, too, if you do what they did—turn the equipment on TOO SOON.

Everyone does this in the mistaken belief that getting the thing running soon as possible will prevent rust and water damage. They think that heat from a running motor will help dry it out.

Don't worry about rust, especially in your engine (Fig. 7-13). The existing coat of oil on all internal surfaces will protect your

Fig. 7-13. Don't panic. Don't worry about rust in an engine. This outboard motor was submerged for two days; yet I restored it and it is in service today.

engine from rust for a few days, so don't panic and imagine your engine being eaten up by rust with every minute of delay. I once saw a disassembled marine engine in the open cockpit of a workboat that lay exposed to the weather for two months, and nothing rusted.

The most important thing you must remember is don't run anything that is electrical. In other words, don't connect it to a power source. Don't even think electricity, for a while at least. First comes clean-up.

Take home with you everything that is removable (Fig. 7-14). With a radio, get the chassis out of the cabinet. Pull all the crystals. All the mud, silt, and particularly salt water, must be flushed out thoroughly. A fine hose spray is good, but not too strong. Do not use a brush, just water spray. Flush with the water spray from all directions and in all crevices and holes, especially the prong holes of the crystals.

Now drain thoroughly, turning in all directions. Do not wipe off with a rag; do not even touch anything. If possible, set it up in the sun to drain and dry while you go on to the next piece of equipment. When everything is washed and drained, you proceed to the next step.

For this you need a good vacuum cleaner, the type where you can switch the hose to the exhaust side and use as a blower. Alll shop-vacs are of this type. You must first empty the vac tank and remove the dirty paper bag filter over the motor. It will be covered with a thick layer of dirt, which greatly reduces suction. Under the paper bag will be an additional flannel bag filter. You can leave the paper bag off temporarily because you will not be sucking any dirt into the vac. You want all the air movement you can get.

I used a reducing adapter which enabled me to use household type accessories, namely the small hose and crevice tool. By reducing down, you get more air pressure. You can even get more pressue by taping over half the crevice tool opening.

Let the shop-vac run for a few minutes. As the motor warms up, you will get warm and then hot air under high pressure, which is perfect for blowing out all your electrical gear. Give each piece at least five minutes of blowing from all directions. Then go back and do it all over again.

This will dry out and remove about 95 percent of the moisture. It's that last five percent that you have to worry about. For example, when you pulled the crystals, the socket holes will still contain moisture. There are endless little openings and crevices where moisture will lurk and not be blown out.

If you're not in a hurry, time will take care of that last five percent of moisture. If you're in a hurry, put each piece in the kitchen oven for a slow bake at low temperatures of about 170 degrees. Check oven temperature with a separate thermometer. Don't be impatient. On a typical radio chassis, it will take about two to three hours. On a typical ¼ horsepower induction type motor, it will take three to five hours.

Let the equipment cool down completely over-night. Put the chassis back in its cabinet and you're ready for a trial run.

I have had good success drying out all types of 120-volt AC motors by applying low DC voltage directly to the windings. Coils have a reactance to AC, but not to DC. There is just enough resistance in the windings to produce heat when you apply 12 volts and low amperage to the motor electrical connections. Do not use a 12 volt battery with all that uncontrollable amperage because you will literally melt the windings. I always use my battery charger which has adjustable current output. It only takes six amperes.

The motor will get uncomfortably warm after a few hours, but no more so than it does under normal service. It will take eight to 16 hours to dry out a motor in this manner. I have done this to at least a dozen motors and restored every one to full service.

Fig. 7-14. This is a typical Sunday afternoon on the Detroit River. Although everything on this boat was soaked, everything could be saved, and was.

Table 7-3.   VHF Channel Listings.

VHF CHANNEL LISTINGS			
Channel	transmit	Receive	Intended Service
6	156.300	156.300	This channel mandatory for all VHF/FM equipped vessels. Intended for intership safety use only.
7A	156350	156.350	Working channel for commercial vessels.
8	156.400	156.400	Same as above.
9	156.450	156.450	Ship-to-shore and ship-to-ship for all vessels.
10	156.500	156.500	Same as channel 7A
11	156.550	156.550	Same as channel 7A
12	156.600	156.600	Ship-to-ship, ship-to-shore, also port operations for commercial.
81A	157.075	157.075	U.S Government use only.
82A	157.125	157.125	U.S. Government use only.
83A	157.175	157.175	U.S. Government use only.
84	157.225	161.825	Public use, ship-to-shore, same as channel 24.
85	157.275	161.875	Same as Channel 24.
86	157.325	161.925	Same as Channel 24.
87	157.375	161.975	Same as channel 24.
88A	157.425	157.425	This is the commercial fishing channel.
WX1	-------	162.550	For receiving weather reports only from Department of Commerce and National Oceanic & Atmospheric Administration.
WX2	------	162.400	Same as WX1.
WX3	------	162.475	Same as WX1.

One last thing, with a capacitor start motor you will either have to by-pass the capacitor with a jumper wire, or remove it. You'll have to do this eventually because dunked capacitors work for a while and then fail.

HIGH SEAS CHANNELIZING

A typical lower priced SSB High Seas unit will have these High Seas Channels: ship-to-shore (telephone), 4 MHz band; U.S. Coast Guard, 4 MHz band; ship-to-ship, 4 MHz band; U.S. Coast Guard, 6 MHz band; ship-to-ship, 6 MHz band; ship-to-shore (telephone), 8 MHz band; U.S. Coast Guard, 8 MHz band; ship-to-ship, 8 MHz band; and time & weather, 10 MHz band.

Few SSB radios offer all-band range because the price would be staggering, like $10,000-$20,000 and more. Most radios will include the 2-MHz coastal bands and the 4 and 6-MHz high seas bands. When you go up a little higher in price, you get the 8 and 12-MHz bands. A little more money and you get 16 and 22-MHz. Radios with these bands will often cost more than your boat.

A boater in Florida and east coast waters will usually have these channels:

Channels 3 and 4 in the Miami area are usually allocated to special crystals in the 2-MHz band for contacting the Miami and Nassau Marine operator.

Table 7-4. This Table Gives Channels For Boaters In Florida And East Coast Waters.

Channel	Frequency	Intended Use
1A	2182	International Distress and Calling.
2A	2630	Ship-to-Ship
2B	2670	Coast Guard working frequency.
5A	4094.8	Coast Guard
6A	4123.6	High-Seas phone operator (WOM)

Table 7-5. Popular High Seas Frequencies And Their Users (continued on page 335).

POPULAR HIGH SEAS FREQUENCIES		
Transmit	**Receive**	**Use**
4094.8	4393.4	U.S. Coast Guard
6207.2	6521.8	U.S. Coast Guard
8226.8	8760.8	U.S. Coast Guard
4136.3	4136.3	International Ship/ship
4139.5	4139.5	International Ship/ship
4434.9	4434.9	International Ship/ship
6210.4	6210.4	International Ship/ship
6213.5	6213.5	International Ship/ship
6518.6	6518.6	International Ship/ship
8281.2	8281.2	International Ship/ship
8284.4	8284.4	International Ship/ship
12421.0	12421.0	International Ship/ship
12428.0	12428.0	International Ship/ship
12424.5	12424.5	International Ship/ship
16565.0	16565.0	International Ship/ship
16572.0	16572.0	International Ship/ship
16568.5	16568.5	International Ship/ship
4072.4	4371.0	Oakland (KMI) telephone
4101.2	4399.8	Oakland (KMI) telephone

Table 7-5. continued from page 334.

POPULAR HIGH SEAS FREQUENCIES		
Transmit	**Receive**	**Use**
4126.8	4425.4	Oakland (KMI) telephone
8204.4	8738.4	Oakland (KMI) telephone
8201.2	8735.2	Oakland (KMI) telephone
8214.0	8748.0	Oakland (KMI) telephone
12382.5	13161.5	Oakland (KMI) telephone
12372.0	13151.0	Oakland (KMI) telephone
16512.5	17307.5	Oakland (KMI) telephone
16509.0	17304.0	Oakland (KMI) telephone
4091.6	4390.2	New York (WOO) telephone
4104.4	4403.0	New York (WOO) telephone
4126.8	4425.0	New York (WOO) telephone
8223.6	8757.6	New York (WOO) telephone
8220.4	8754.4	New York (WOO) telephone
12396.5	13175.5	New York (WOO) telephone
12393.0	13172.0	New York (WOO) telephone
16321.5	17321.5	New York (WOO) telephone
16523.0	17318.0	New York (WOO) telephone
4123.6	4422.2	Ft. Lauderdale (WOM) telephone
4130.0	4428.6	Ft. Lauderdale (WOM) telephone
4117.2	4415.8	Ft. Lauderdale (WOM) telephone

POPULAR HIGH SEAS FREQUENCIES		
Transmit	**Receive**	**Use**
8262.0	8796.0	Ft. Lauderdale (WOM) telephone
8258.8	8792.8	Ft. Lauderdale (WOM) telephone
8271.6	8805.6	Ft. Lauderdale (WOM) telephone
8274.8	8808.8	Ft. Lauderdale (WOM) telephone
12361.5	13140.5	Ft. Lauderdale (WOM) telephone
12358.0	13137.0	Ft. Lauderdale (WOM) telephone
12407.0	13186.0	Ft. Lauderdale (WOM) telephone
16491.5	17286.5	Ft. Lauderdale (WOM) telephone
16530.0	17325.0	Ft. Lauderdale (WOM) telelphone
16474.0	17269.0	Ft. Lauderdale (WOM) telephone
16544.0	17339.0	Ft. Lauderdale (WOM) telephone
		FOR CRUISING THE CARIBBEAN
4123.6	4422.2	Bermuda Radio (VRT) telephone
8255.6	8789.6	Bermuda Radio (VRT) telephone
12340.5	13119.5	Bermuda Radio (VRT) telephone
16495.0	17290.0	Bermuda Radio (VRT) telephone
		ANTILLES...
4136.3	4409.4	Curacao (PJC) telephone
8268.4	8770.4	Curacao (PJC) telephone
12403.5	13154.5	Curacao (PJC) telephone
16533.5	17300.5	Curacao (PJC) telephone

Transmit	Receive	Use
POPULAR HIGH SEAS FREQUENCIES		
		MARTINIQUE
4085.2	4383.8	Fort de France (FFP) telephone
8217.2	8751.2	Fort de France (FFP) telephone
		BARBADOS
4098.0	4396.6	Barbados Radio (8PO) telephone
8210.8	8744.8	Barbados Radio (8PO) telephone
		FOR CRUISING THE PACIFIC
4117.2	4415.8	Honolulu (KOM) telephone
8217.2	8751.2	Honolulu (KQM) telephone
12375.5	13154.5	Honolulu (KQM) telephone
16477.5	17272.5	Honolulu (KQM) telephone
		TAHITI
4085.2	4383.8	Mahina Radio (FJA) telephone
8230.0	8764.0	Mahina Radio (FJA) telephone
		FIJI
4078.8	4377.4	Suva Radio (3DP) telephone
8262.0	8796.0	Suva Radio (3DP) telephone
		AMERICAN SAMOA
4098.0	4396.6	Pago Pago (KUQ) telephone
8249.2	8783.2	Pago Pago (KUQ) telephone
		SOLOMON ISLANDS
12368.5	13147.5	Honiara Radio (VQJ) telephone
8204.4	8738.4	Honiara Radio (VQJ) telephone

Table 7-5. continued from page 337.

POPULAR HIGH SEAS FREQUENCIES		
Transmit	**Receive**	**Use**
		FRENCH POLYNESIA
4085.2	4383.8	Noumea (FJP) telephone
8230.0	8764.0	Noumea (FJP) telephone
		AUSTRALIA
4072.4	4371.0	Sydney Radio (VIS) telephone
8223.6	8757.6	Sydney Radio (VIS) telephone
12333.5	13112.5	Sydney Radio (VIS) telephone
16470.5	17265.5	Sydney Radio (VIS) telephone
		NEW ZEALAND
4110.8	4409.4	Wellington Radio (ZLW)
8236.4	8770.4	Wellington Radio (ZLW)
12389.5	13168.5	Wellington Radio (ZLW)
16498.5	17293.5	Wellington Radio (ZLW)
		SINGAPORE
4078.8	4377.4	Singapore Radio (9VG)
8223.6	8757.6	Singapore Radio (9VG)
12333.5	13112.5	Singapore Radio (9VG)
16498.5	17293.5	Singapore Radio (9VG)
6204.0	6204.0	**SOUTH PACIFIC EMERGENCY**

Table 7-6. More VHF Channel Listings. (continued on page 340)

	VHF CHANNEL LISTINGS		
Channel	Transmit	Receive	Intended Service
13	156.650	156.650	This is the primary channel used at bridges and locks. Call signs can be omitted and one watts maximum power must be used.
14	156.700	156.700	Same as channel 12
15		156.750	No transmit on this channel. This is a receive only channel for weather, time signals, notices to mariners, etc.
16	156.800	156.800	This channel is mandatory on all vessels. It is your distress, safety and calling channel. It must be monitored at all times.
17	156.850	156.850	Available for vessels to communicate with state and local agencies.
18A	156.900	156.900	Same as channel 7A
19A	156.950	156.950	Same as channel 7A
20	157.000	161.600	Traffic directing channel in ports.
21A	157.050	157.050	U.S. Government use only.
22A	157.100	157.100	For communicating with Coast Guard after making contact on channel 16. This is a must channel.
23A	157.150	157.150	U.S. Government only.
24	157.200	161.800	Ship-to-shore for general public communications. Every boat with limited channels should have this.
25	157.250	161.850	Same as channel 24.

			VHF CHANNEL LISTINGS
Channel	**Transmit**	**Receive**	**Intended Service**
26	157.300	161.900	Same as channel 24.
27	157.350	161.950	Same as channel 24.
28	157.400	162.000	Same as channel 24.
65A	156.275	156.275	Same as channel 12
66A	156.325	156.325	Same as channel 12
67	156.375	156.375	Same as channel 7A, except limited to ship-to-ship communications.
68	156.425	156.425	This is a good all-purpose working channel for pleasure boats and, next to channel 70, is the most popular and first choice for boats with limited channel capacity.
69	156.475	156.475	Same as channel 68.
70	156.525	156.525	Same as channel 68, but limited to ship-to-ship use.
71	156.575	156.575	Same as channel 68.
72	156.625	156.625	Same as channel 68, but limited to ship-to-ship use.
73	156.675	156.675	Same as channel 12.
74	156.725	156.725	Same as channel 12
77	156.875	156.875	Same as channel 7A, but limited to ship-to-ship use.
78A	156.925	156.925	Same as channel 68.
79A	156.975	156.975	Same as channel 7A.
80A	157.025	157.025	Same as channel 7A.

Table 7-7. CB Radio Manufacturers.

MANUFACTURERS OF CB RADIOS

Cobra, 1801 W. Belleplaine, Chicago, Ill. 60613

Lafayette Radio, Ill Jericho Turnpike, Syosset, N.Y. 11791

Midland International Corp., Box 19032, Kansas City, Mo. 64141

Motorola, Inc., 1301 E. Algonquin Rd., Schamburg, Ill. 60172

Radio Shack, Ft. Worth, Tex. 76107

RCA, Cherry Hills Offices, Camden, N.J. 08101

Royce Electronics Corp., 1746 Levee Rd., N. Kansas City,

Mo. 64116

SBE Inc., 220 Airport Blvd., Watsonville, Calif. 95076

Table 7-8. Listed Are Manufacturers Of SSB (Single Sideband) Radiotelephones.

MANUFACTURERS OF SSB (Single Sideband) RADIOTELEPHONES

Decca Marine Inc., 40 W. 57 St., New York N.Y. 10019

General Aviation Electronics Inc., 4141 Kingman Dr., Indianapolis, Ind. 46226

Kaar Electronics Corp., 232 Westcott Dr., Rahway, N.J. 07065

Konel Corp., 271 Harbor Way, S. San Francisco, Calif. 94080

Micro Instruments Co., 580 Opper St., Escondido, Calif. 92025

Motorola, 2100 N. Meacham Rd., Schaumburg, Ill. 60196

Northern Radio Co., 4027 21st Ave., W. Seattle, Wash. 98199

RF Communications Co., 1680 University Ave., Rochester, N.Y. 14610

Raytheon Marine Co., 676 Island Pond Rd., Manchester, N.H. 03103

SGC Inc., 13737 S.E. 26th St., Bellevue, Wash. 98005

Side-Band Associates Inc., 1133 Old Bayshore Highway, San Jose,

Calif. 95112

Table 7-9. Manufacturers Of VHF/FM Radiotelephones.

MANUFACTURERS OF VHF/FM RADIOTELEPHONES

Apelco Marine Electronics, 676 Island Pond Rd., Manchester, N.H. 03103

Brisson Development Inc., 27203 Harper Ave., St. Clair Shores, Mich. 48081

Bristol Electronics Inc., 651 Orchard St., New Bedford, Mass. 02744

Brocks Electronics Corp., 12 Blanchard Rd., Burlington, Mass. 01803

Comdel Inc., Beverly Airport, Beverly, Mass. 01915

Decca Marine Inc., 40 W. 57 St., New York, N.Y. 10019

Emergency Beacon Corp., 15 River St., New Rochelle, N.Y. 10801

Gem Marine, 3565 S. Blvd., Lake City S.C. 29560

General Aviation Electronics Corp., 41441 Kingman Dr., Indianapolis, Ind. 46226

Hy-Gain Electronics Corp., 8601 N.W. Hwy 6, Lincoln, Neb. 68505

ICOM-EAST, 3331 Towerwood, Dallas, Tex. 75234

ICOM-WEST, 13256 Northrup Way, Bellevue, Wash. 98005

INTECH INC., 282 Brokaw Rd., Santa Clara, Calif. 95050

Konel Corp., 271 Harbor Way, S. San Francisco, Calif. 94080

Modar Electronics Inc., 2100 Meacham Rd., Schaumburg, Ill. 60172

Motorola, 2100 N. Meacham Rd., Schaumburg, Ill. 60172

Pathcom Inc., 24049 S. Frampton Ave., Harbor City, Calif. 90710

Pearce-Simpson, Box 800, Biscayne Annex, Miami, Fla. 3315

RF Communications Div., 1680 University Ave., Rochester N.Y. 14610

Ray Jefferson, Main & Cotton Sts., Philadelphia, Pa. 19103

Raytheon Marine Co., 676 Island Pond Rd., Manchester, N.H. 03103

Shakespeare Co., Box 246 Columbia S.C. 29202

Ski-Way Communications, 10833 E. Jefferson, Detroit, Mich. 48214

Skytronics Inc., 227 Oregon St., El Segundo, Calif. 90245

Table 7-10.

Manufacturers Of Marine Antennas And Radiotelephone Grounding Systems.

**MANUFACTURERS OF MARINE ANTENNAS
AND RADIOTELEPHONE GROUNDING SYSTEMS**

**Marine Antennas
Radiotelephone Grounding Systems**

Hy-Gain Electronics Corp., 8601 Northeast Highway 6, Lincoln, Neb. 68505

Hummel MFG Co., 164 95th St., Howard Beach, N.Y. 11414

Melectro Products Inc., 19919 144th St., N.E. Woodinville, Wash. 98072

Morad Electronics Corp., 1125 N.W. 46th St., Seattle, Wash. 98012

Shakespeare Antenna Group, Box 246, Columbia, S.C. 29202

Phelps Dodge Communications Co., Rt. 79, Marlboro, N.J. 07746

Antenna Specialists Co., 12435 Euclid Ave., Cleveland, Ohio 44106

Aquadynamics Inc., 6940 Farmdale Ave., N. Hollywood, Calif. 91605

Boat Electrical Systems

Electricity is a mystery to most boatmen. It's even a mystery to many people who live and work with it every day. Steinmetz, the electrical wizard of General Electric, was once asked by a woman: "What is electricity?"

When Steinmetz started to explain at great length in words she had never heard before, the woman interrupted with a question, "Can't you explain it in words I can understand?"

Steinmetz pondered a moment, then said: "Electrons in motion. That's three simple words. They tell you everything you need to know about electricity."

He was right. Electrons in motion is energy, the power source we call "electricity." In the atom are two very minute particles called protons and electrons. They are in all matter, even living matter. For every proton there is an electron, and they have a strong magnetic attraction to each other. Move a proton and a electron reacts by also moving. And the instant you force an electron to move, you create energy.

How does electricity move through a solid piece of copper? It doesn't. Well, it doesn't move like water flowing through a pipe. You must remember, copper wire is also made up of electrons and protons. Electrical energy is already there. Make one electron move and they all move.

To illustrate, think of a long row of bowling balls filling up a rack to the very end. What happens if you force one more bowling ball on the rack? All the balls will move. And that is how electricity "moves" through a copper wire.

In each atom there is an equal number of protons and electrons. Because of the strong attraction they have for each other, they resist any effort to break up their equal numbers. If some outside physical action breaks up their equal number, and there are more electrons than protons in an atom, then that atom immediately is charged and driven to do something to get things equal again. This urge to do something is also called "potential," another word for voltage, which is analogous to water pressure in a pipe.

The greater the disparity in numbers of protons and electrons, the greater the potential, until finally something happens. When this happens in the atmosphere, the electrons leap from the sky to the earth. We call this lightning. That flash you see in the sky is electrons in motion, fighting to get back with their brother protons.

On a smaller scale, this is what happens when you get out of your car on a dry winter day, touch the door handle and get a jolt as a spark arcs off your fingertips. When you turned in your seat, your wool coat rubbed against the plastic seatcovers and altered the equal arrangement of protons and electrons. You yourself developed a potential of charged energy. When you touched the grounded door handle, the excess of electrons in you moved to get back with the protons.

You now know the basics of electricity, even what it looks like. That blue streak of light jumping off your fingertips was electrons in motion. And as Steinmetz said, you don't really have to know anymore, unless you are involved in engineering or research.

Back to electricity on boats. Once upon a time it was very simple. Lead acid batteries in six, 12 or 32 volts supplied all the electrical energy necessary for boats, even up to millionaire yachts. There were no 115-volt shore power outlets to plug into at the dock. Why not? It just wasn't necessary. Who needed it? Everybody used ice. The word "electronics" hadn't even been coined as yet and boatmen, surprisingly, managed to go to sea and come back with only a magnetic compass to guide them. Nobody got lost, ran out of gas, hung up on a mudbank or hit a red channel marker. In fact, it was considered a black day of shame for a boatman to run aground in his own home waters. But the ultimate disgrace was to hit a red channel marker. It was like hitting your mother in church while she was on her knees praying.

These boatmen never heard of depth sounders, radar, loran or microwave ovens. But they knew all about charts, used them religiously, and for things other than calculating how far it was to the next yacht club bar.

The cruising boat today, 25 feet and up, has an exceedingly complicated wiring system. When you buy a fancy offshore fishing yacht today, you get with it enough copper wire to rewire half the homes in Tupelo, Mississippi. I was told by a marine electrician for the Matthews Boat Company that just the electrical wiring alone in one of their yachts cost over $10,000.

I tell you this in the hope that it will make you think before you start making plans to install an electric hot water heater, air conditioning, a heat pump, or a 3,000-watt Onan AC generator. You very likely have forgotten that you already have an electric range/oven, refrigerator and hi-fi. That little old 3,000 watt Onan just won't do the job. See how easy it is to get into trouble?

WHAT IS GROUND?

You've got to understand the language and not be mystified like the high school gym teacher who couldn't understand why her headlights burned bright for a while, then dim, then bright again. When the mechanic told her they were poorly grounded, she said: "What on earth is ground?"

This puzzles many people. And the reason that it puzzles is that an automobile is insulated from the ground by its rubber tires. A boat floats on water, many feet from the bottom. An airplane can be flying thousands of feet above ground. A television set or radio can be sitting on a wood table, using its metal chassis as a "ground." None of the above are in actual direct contact with the earth, which is true ground.

The word "ground," as so freely used by mechanics, electricians and television repair men, means different things to each. To the mechanic, ground means the engine, frame or body of an automobile because it is the second wire, the negative wire of the automobile DC electrical system. I use the term "wire" when conductor would be better. The total automobile itself serves as the negative conductor. The positive conductor is the "hot" wire. When a spark plug or light bulb is secured to the engine or body, it becomes negative polarity. The single "hot" wire completes the circuit. The metal chassis of a TV set serves the same purpose. It is a common connecting point for all wires of the same negative polarity.

True ground is the earth itself. All alternating electricity is tied to the earth by the white grounded conductor in your house wiring.

This wire is usually clamped to a water pipe in your basement. Although in alternating current the polarity (negative/positive) is constantly switching back and forth between the two conductors, (black/white) the white conductor always remains at ground potential. Voltage between the two conductors may change, but voltage between the white conductor and ground never changes.

In television sets, the white conductor is secured to the chassis. So even though the television set is sitting on a wood table in a wood house, it still is in contact with true ground.

There is enough conduction in water to give a boat contact with ground. Warm salt water has excellent conductivity, which is why radiotelephones radiate stronger signals in tropical waters.

WHAT IS POLARITY?

This is the difference between those two cables secured to your boat batteries. One cable is negative (−), the other cable is positive (+). Owner manuals that come with new cars usually warn you never to cross the polarity by switching the battery cables around. If you do, you'll burn out all six diodes in the alternator. Just remember that the negative cable, in 99 out of 100 installations, always goes directly to the engine block. If you can just remember this, you can't go wrong with the other cable.

WHAT IS A CONDUCTOR?

A conductor is any length of copper wire that is used to connect an accessory to a live electric outlet.

WHAT IS DIRECT CURRENT?

The energy from a lead acid battery is the truest, purest "direct current," also called DC. It is a steady flow of current, like water out of a hose, directly from and back to the battery. One wire is always positive. One wire is always negative.

There are other forms of DC, also called pulsating direct current. This is usually alternating current which has been changed (rectified) with one half of the alternation blocked out. The result is a stop-and-go flow of current in one direction. Automobile and marine engines operate on DC. The alternator, however, produces 12 volts AC. This is the reason for those six diodes. Current flows through a diode only in one direction, where its volume is controlled. But when you reverse the polarity, there is no control on the volume of amperage. The flood gates are open and a huge mass of current hits the diodes, burning them out instantly.

WHAT IS ALTERNATING CURRENT?

The invention of alternating current, and the transformer, is what made America a great industrial giant. When Thomas Edison lit up the streets of New York with the first electric lights, he took only the first small step toward the electrification of America. Edison produced the electricity for those lights with DC dynamos, which produced voltage at the exact potential needed. To light up the entire city of New York would have required more dynamos every few blocks all over the city.

The big drawback to DC is that you can't mass produce it in large volume, then ship it to where it is needed. It would require the movement of astronomical volumes of current just to meet the needs of one small city. And it would require copper conductors as big in diameter as telephone poles. There just isn't enough copper in the world to move even a fraction of the energy this country uses in one day if it were to be generated and transported in direct current.

Alternating current and the transformer changed all that by making it possible to generate large volumes of electricity in a single central location, and then transport it long distances in small wire no thicker then a lead pencil. It was the transformer, one of the most efficient and useful devices ever invented, that made this possible. Direct current will not work in a transformer. But alternating current will—in fact, AC and the transformer were literally made for each other. And together they made America a great industrial power because AC powered motors turn all the wheels.

To transport electricity long distances, actually hundreds of miles, it must be generated in very high voltages and low amperage. High voltage does not require heavy conductors, but high amperage does. So the trick of moving large volumes of electricity is to do it at extremely high voltages, like 500,000 volts, and low amperage. When this high voltage reaches its destination, perhaps in some neighbor state, it goes to those small substations enclosed by barbed wire fences with signs reading "Danger! High voltage!"

Transformers in this substation reduce the voltage and feed it out to dozens of other transformers until finally it reaches that last small transformer on a utility pole near your home. Here it is dropped down to 230 volts, and then delivered to your home.

Each decrease in voltage produces an equal increase in amperage. You put in 500,000 volts and 1,000 amps at the power plant; out of transformers at the other end comes 115 volts and enough amperage to take care of a small town.

Ampere

Ampere means the amount of current flowing at a given time. If electricity was water, you would call it gallons-per-hour.

Ampacity

The current carrying capacity of a wire or conductor is ampacity, which you can compare to the water moving capacity of a pipe. The bigger the wire, the more amperage it can handle without heating up, and the less is lost through excess resistance, which increases with heat.

Gauge

This is a word with more than one meaning. But to a electrician it means the diameter of a copper conductor. The higher the number, the smaller diameter the wire. Expensive battery jumper cables will be 4 ga. (gauge). Cheap ones will be 10 ga. Rubber insulated household extension cords are usually 18 ga.

Alternator

This mechanical device generates alternating current without brushes or commutator.

Generator

This mechanical device generates direct current, but uses brushes and a commutator.

Dynamo

This device uses mechanical energy to produce electrical energy.

Dynamotor

This is a dynamo and an electric motor using the same shaft. These were much used in the power packs of medium frequency radiotelephones that required high plate voltages to the final power amplifier. The little 12 volt DC motor spun the dynamo which, in turn, generated 400/800 volts which went directly to the final PA tube.

Induction Motor

A motor that runs on AC without brushes or commutator is an induction motor.

Universal Motor

This motor that runs on both AC and DC. Most power tools, like electric drills, are of this type.

Hot

The "hot" wire is not at ground potential. In three wire 115-volt wiring, it is the black wire that is often referred to as "hot." In four wire 115/230 volt wiring, both the black and red wires are "hot."

Insulator

An insulator is anything that doesn't conduct electricity. Glass and ceramics are among the best and most used.

Rectifier

A device which changes AC to DC is a rectifier. It was once the biggest glass tube in a radio or television. Now tiny transistors or diodes do the same job. Battery charges are also sometimes referred to as rectifiers.

Relay

Relay is a switch operated electrically when current passing through a coil creates a magnetic force which activates a electrical contact.

Resistance

Anything which restricts the flow of current is resistance. This restriction, or resistance, is measured in ohms.

Short Circuit

A disruption of the flow of current from a power source to a light bulb or other device is called a short circuit. This happens when the two wires accidently come together. It always trips a circuit breaker or blows a fuse. Bringing two wires together, with no load between them, opens the flood gates for a massive flow of current—in fact, all the 500 amps in a lead-acid battery. If the circuit is not fused, 10 ga. solid copper wire will instantly glow red hot and even melt. That's how boat fires sometimes start.

Watt

Electrical energy is measured in watts. If you have an appliance which is rated at 10 amps, multiply the amperage by the volts. Thus

$115 \times 10 = 1150$ watts. If you know the wattage and want the amperage, divide 1150 watts by 115 volts and you get 10 amps.

Power Source

This can be a battery, a generator, a transformer or main switch box—anything from where the juice comes.

Commutator

The commutator is the copper rotor on the shaft end of a electric motor or generator. It is segmented, causing a stop-go-stop flow of current from the carbon "brushes" like that produced by the points in an auto distributor.

Transformer

A transformer is a remarkably simple, useful and efficient device with no moving parts to wear out. It consists of two coils (primary, secondary) and an iron core magnet. The number of windings on the coils is determined by how much the voltage is to be increased or decreased. For example, if there are ten times as many windings in the secondary coil as in the primary, output voltage will increase ten times. This works the same in reverse, with voltage decreased ten times.

A question perhaps now arising in your mind is how does an automobile coil (same as a transformer), work with DC since, as previously mentioned, a transformer will not work with DC. It will if you change it to pulsating current. That is what the points and distributor do in an automobile. Points are nothing more than an electric switch which interrupt the flow of current so that it creates a rising-collapsing magnetic field in the coil windings. This makes a transformer work. This is what alternating current does when it stops 60 times a second to reverse flow. The direction of flow means nothing. It's the stop-go-stop flow of current that makes the transformer work.

DOCKSIDE AC WIRING

Only 10 years ago, dockside wiring at many big city yacht clubs and marinas was crude and makeshift, often just two wires strung between 2×4 extensions nailed on pilings. If it was this bad at the big rich yacht clubs, it was still good compared to what you found on many rivers and canals, especially the Erie/New York Canal system to the Hudson River. It was here that I burned out the motor in my refrigeration compressor because of excessively low voltage. I got a VOM reading of 96 volts in one small town, which I will not identify because I had such a wonderful visit there.

You find real peace and contentment, in the small river and canal communities where everybody says hello, where the mayor or chief of police helps you tie up for the night, then offers to buy you a drink. But you also find damn few conveniences in these wonderful places.

In the big conglomerate-owned marinas of Florida and California you get conveniences, dockside service, telephones, garbage pick up and television hook ups. You also get shafted if you carelessly bend over to cleat a bow line. But things are getting better all the time on the rivers, and you can thank us old pioneers with converted ice boxes and wood boats because we helped get the names and locations of these little places listed in Waterway Cruise Directories. They are now shaping up to take advantage of the increased boating traffic. I am both pleased and unhappy about this. I'm going to miss those free drinks with the mayor.

NEW MARINE WIRING STANDARDS

If you've been around boats very long, then you are irritated by the confusion and lack of standards in equipment designed to bring that wonderful new energy from the nuclear power plant across the bay into our boats. After all, how can we run our air conditioners and microwave ovens? How can we get hot water for our showers? How can we relax on Sundays after a hard week of scratching for money, stalling off bill collectors and writing letters to our congressmen to complain about that damn nuclear power plant across the bay?

The 115-volt and 230-volt AC receptacles at big marina docks today use the same electrical wiring system that is standard throughout the U.S. This is a 4-wire system and the wires are coded. The black wire is hot and ungrounded, carrying 115 volts AC above earth ground. The red wire is also hot and ungrounded, carrying 115 volts above earth ground. The white wire is neutral. It is a current carrying conductor which is grounded to earth. The green, sometimes bare wire, does not conduct current. It is a safety shock-preventing device maintained at ground potential and secured to metal electrical boxes, equipment frames, metal power tools, and anything which can be touched by human hands. The black and white wires will give you 115 volts. The red and white wires also will give you 115 volts. The black and red wires will give you 115 volts. The black and red wires will give you 230 volts. And don't ever forget that.

Home wiring systems are split into two separate 115 volt circuits, and one or two 230-volt circuits. One circuit will feed off the black and white wires. A second will feed off the red and white wires. The purpose of this is to balance the current draw on the main feeder line. There will be additional circuits drawing 230 volts off the red and black wires for electric ranges, clothes dryers, air conditioners and hot water heaters.

SHORE POWER RECEPTACLES

Modern marinas today supply both 115 volts and 230 volts, but not out of the same receptacle. All Americans are equal before the law, but not all boats are equal. Some are old. Some are new. Some are big. Some are small. The big, newer boats will be wired just like your home so you can have all the Greek tycoon goodies like air conditioning, his and hers heads and even a bidet for the lady. That's right, bidet! I saw my first one in this country last summer on an old Matthews. The owner's wife was fascinated when she saw her first bidet during a European vacation. So they bought one and had it shipped direct to their marina back home, where it was later installed.

Configuration of the receptacles for various phases of just 115 volt service are different, as you can see in Figure 8-1. The 15-amp female receptacle on the left is the familiar one that you have in your home. Note how the black wire slot is slightly smaller. Most television sets made today have power cords made for this socket, to prevent you from crossing polarity by getting the white wire into the black hole.

Figure 8-1 shows the various approved female receptacles for 115-volt service. Under the National Electrical Code, "receptacles for boat shore power shall be of the locking type and grounded. They must be rated at a minimum of 20 amps, calculated on a basis of 25 watts per foot of dock length."

CHANGING OLD BOAT WIRING

Twist lock male plugs and female receptacles are standard on all new boats built today. If you own, or have recently purchased, an older boat (of which there are millions still afloat), you can update your wiring. In fact, you have to, unless you want to explain to your wife why she can't bring aboard her electric skillet, coffee maker,

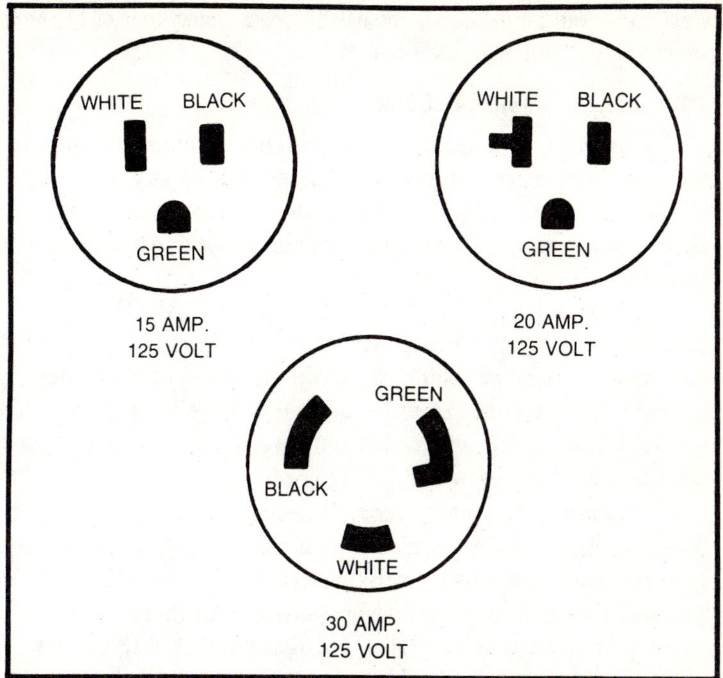

Fig. 8-1. These are the three approved female receptacles that you will be seeing in marinas and yacht clubs all over the country. You must carry with you a shore power cord, with the proper male plug, to fit these receptacles. Don't panic! You can always carry adapters. This is the least of your troubles.

toaster, deep fryer, steam iron and hair dryer. Remember the sales talk you gave her, to get that second mortgage on the house so you could buy the boat, where she would have all the conveniences of home? To avoid trouble, you better just fix the wiring.

You don't have to live with old fashioned two-wire non-grounded electrical wiring just because your boat is old. But you better change it because every time you bring that hot black wire, and that white grounded wire, aboard your boat without that green wire, you are playing Russian roulette without a gun.

Try to remember that there is a big difference between 2-wire electricity in a home and on a boat. Your home is dry, the interior is wood. Your boat is always wet, and you are never more than a few inches away from something that is ground potential. In a sense, you are always sitting in a bathtub filled with water, and a radio playing beside you. Fool around with that radio and you're dead.

This is the reason why I bought the first cordless electric power drill to hit the consumer market back about 1962. It is battered and worn today but I still keep it aboard. I have a deadly fear of 115-volt shore power on a boat, especially when working with power tools.

YOUR BOAT'S UMBILICAL CORD

No matter how much the yacht club and marinas modernize their electrical service, it means nothing to you unless you can safely use it. You do this through your boat's umbilical cord, that very special heavy duty cable with the very special locking receptacles at both ends.

In their Safety Standards for Small Craft, the ABYC, or American Boat and Yacht Council, states: "Shore power cable should match the shore power outlet. Cable should be of sufficient length to extend a minimum of 10 feet beyond the bow or stern. Type ST3 conductor cable is recommended and wire gauge should be slightly heavier than the boat wiring."

This means if your boat wiring is 12 gauge, get a 10 gauge shore power cable. It will be as thick as your thumb. If you buy one at a marina store already fitted with the connectors, you'll choke when you hear the price. If you cry easily, perhaps it might be better to do as I did. Make up your own cable. I bought 100 feet of 12 gauge wire away from marine outlets. I did the same with the connectors. I made up two separate 50-foot cables. One is usually all I need at yacht clubs and marinas. But you will occasionally find need for just a little more reach to get to that juice.

The quickest way to ruin a vacation, and a marriage, is to plan on having fried chicken, beans and cold beer after a hot six-hour run. Then you find yourself standing on the river bank with the shore power cable in your sweaty hands, the plug still 10 feet short of reaching the shore receptacle. Your family is tired, hot, hungry and irritable. When your wife calls you a dummy for not having enough wire, you blow up. This is how fights start. Remember Murphy's Law. Don't let things screw up.

AC WIRING STANDARDS FOR BOATS

Wiring for old boats that had six, 12 or 32 volt DC battery power was simple, just two wires. There is no shock hazard with low voltage battery electricity. A green grounding wire is unnecessary.

But when you bring 115 volts AC aboard ship, you are confronted with the latest edition of the National Electric Code. I have tried to read this book, but it is so big and heavy I can't even lift it. In this First Testament of the Holy Writ of Electricity, it says thousands of words which I have slightly condensed to three major points of interest for boatmen. On board AC electrical service must present an absolute minimum shock hazard. Boat AC electrical systems must not be the cause of any electrolytic corrosion to host or neighboring boats. Boat AC electricity must have a minimum voltage drop between the shore receptacle and the equipment aboard ship that are being operated.

The ABYC, which publishes the Second Testament of the Holy Writ, recommends installation of a "system voltmeter to monitor input voltage from shore outlets, and to check on voltage from on-board AC generators, such as the ones in Fig. 8-2. They also state that the boat's system must be so designed that shore power and on-board generators don't feed the same circuit simultaneously.

ON-BOARD AC GENERATORS

If you are considering the purchase of an AC generator, such as the Onan and Kohler in Fig. 8-2, here is an imporatant piece of advice. Don't buy a generator with an engine that runs at 3600 rpm. And why not? Because you don't have to put up with all that damn noise from a high winding mill. Generators are available with engines that only turn 1800 rpm. The difference will amaze you.

You can demonstrate this to yourself next time you cut the grass. Open the throttle on your mower. Then cut it down to a fast idle. Note the difference in sound and noise. At 3600 rpm your mower will have all the cats in the neighborhood hiding under cars. At 1800 rpm you can actually talk without raising your voice.

Another important point is the AC generators with 3600 rpm engines are usually rated for "intermittent service." This means you can't tie up to a mooring off shore and then let the generator run continuously day and night. They aren't designed for that type of heavy duty service. A steady six to eight hour run is about the maximum before you must stop the engine and let it rest while you check the oil. And that is the reason they are rated at "intermittent service." They run out of oil! Or rather, they will run out of oil if you don't stop running them and check.

Heavy duty continuous service generators, the type installed on larger boats over 45 feet, have slow, 1800 rpm turning engines. They also have an automatic oil replenishing system which maintains a proper level of oil in the engine crankcase. The separate oil reservoir can be serviced and refilled without stopping the engine. So long as the engine has oil and fuel, it can run forever. Boats with this type of electrical power never bother with shore power, except at their home ports where the right type of service is available.

The high rpm engines also burn up oil at a prodigious rate, making it necessary to stop them often for an oil check. It would be dangerous to let such a generator run for long periods unattended.

I have lost many hours of sleep tied up next to boats with noisy generators. I have been around many boats that I didn't even know had a generator. They were so quiet.

The 1800 rpm generators will cost more, in fact, considerably more. But if you can afford a boat big enough to need a generator, you can afford to live with less noise pollution. If you can't, drink King George IV instead of Chivas Regal for one boating season. If you have to please and impress important clients, pour the King George into empty Chivas Regal bottles. Your clients will never know the difference.

The chairman of the board of a big national food servicing organization told me this. Feeding and boozing people is his business. He is so rich he bought a 60-foot Chris Craft Connie over the telephone and never even asked how much it cost. Yet he serves King George on his boat in plain glass decanters, and all his guests think they are drinking Chivas Regal. He told me the money he has saved doing this helped to pay for his yacht.

The ABYC insists that a boat's entire AC electrical system be so constructed and secured that it will withstand the shocks and strains of a rough sea passage. What they're trying to say is that when you get caught in a wallowing beam sea for about four hours, with your lifelines dipping into solid water on every roll, you better make sure your AC generator won't break loose and make funny noises down below. One of life's hairy experiences at sea is when something that is supposed to be secured portside suddenly starts banging and rolling around starboard.

The ABYC further insists that the AC electrical system be so constructed as to provide maximum shock protection for guests aboard, for swimmers in the water, for guests transferring from a dinghy to the boat, from the boat to shore, or in any situation where a guest might have one hand on the boat and a foot in the water.

WHY GENERATORS ABOARD INCREASE YOUR LIABILITY

Putting an AC generator on your boat involves more than just writing out a check. It also involves your personal responsibilities and liabilities. Think about this before you spend all that money.

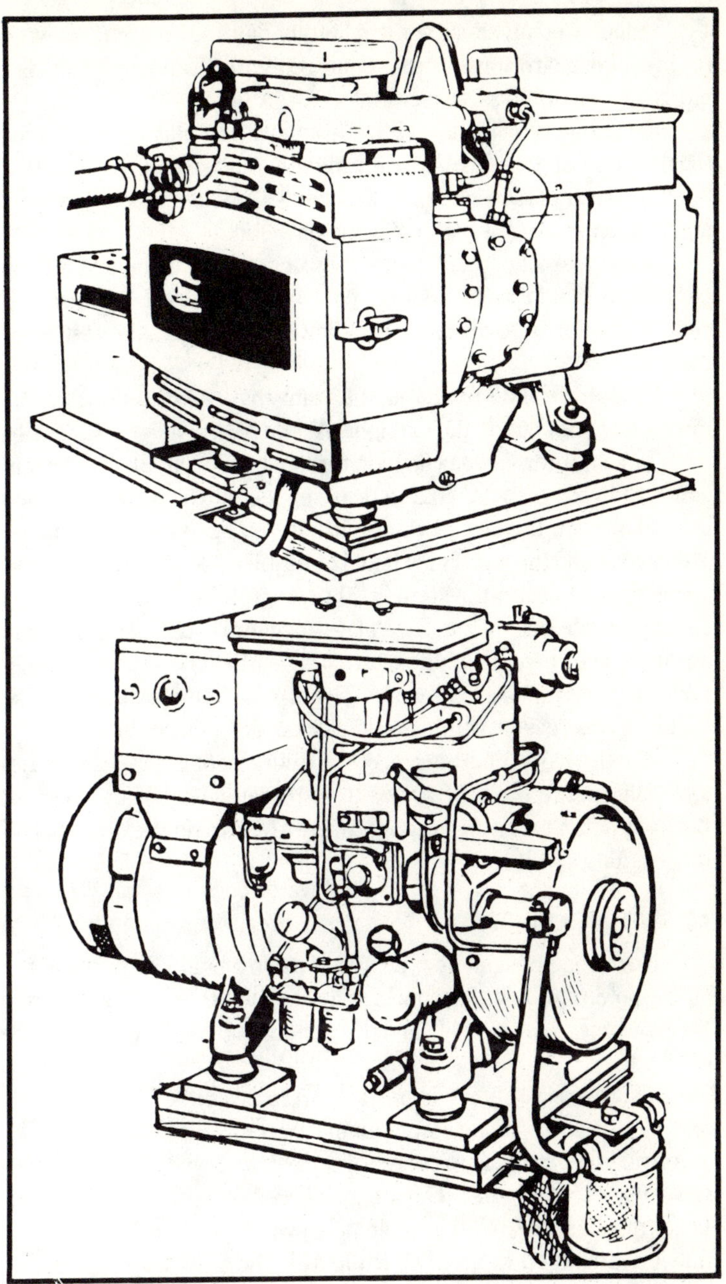

Fig. 8-2. There is an important difference in the boat AC generators illustrated. One is of the "intermittent service" type. The other is heavy duty "continuous service." This is a very important consideration when buying one, but salesmen rarely mention it.

You're anchored off shore some quiet hot day and your guests want to dive overboard for a swim. Your generator is running to make more ice cubes for all those drinks.

Preparing to climb up the transom swim ladder, a guest's foot touches one of your boat's twin rudders. And suddenly a beautiful Sunday afternoon becomes a disaster. Your insurance company must defend you in a big negligence law suit.

A fact many boatmen do not fully understand is the instant any person, or child, puts a foot on your boat, you as the owner and captain are fully responsible for their well being and safety, with no reservations.

If, after reading this, you still want that AC generator, by all means buy one, but do the job right. As the ABYC suggests, install a system voltmeter so you can monitor inputs and outputs, both from shore and your own AC source. It is suggested you mark lower and upper limits on the fact of your voltmeter. The low limit should be 103.5 volts and the high limit should be 126.5 volts. The frequency of an alternating current system is 60 cycles (60 Hz). You will always see this mentioned on the name plates of motors, television sets and appliances. It means that the alternating current reverses its direction of flow 60 times each second. The precise non-variation in these cycles is the reason why electric clocks are so accurate.

Half the world operates on 60 cycle alternating current electricity. Half operates on 50 cycle. If you ever go to Bridgetown or Barbados, don't plug into shore power. They are in the other half of the world.

AC SWITCHES ON BOATS

Never use household type switches on a boat. They are of the single-pole type and disconnect only the black conductor. Marine type switches are two pole and disconnect both the black and white conductors.

There are two very important reasons for this. When marina shore outlets are wired, often an inexperienced or careless workman will unintentionally reverse the black and white conductors in the female shore outlet. Even experienced electricians sometimes make this mistake. With a single pole switch you would be opening only the grounded white wire, but leaving the black wire closed. In a boat this is dangerous, very dangerous!

Another reason for the two-pole switch is there are many marinas that purposely use reversed polarity, with the black wire the

grounded conductor. And you will never see any warnings posted.
When cruising in strange country, never take anything for granted.
Never assume that the electrical outlet on that piling near your dock
will automatically match up with your boat's wiring.

THE 115-VOLT WIRING SYSTEM FOR BOATS

There are two standard 115 volt AC wiring systems in use
today on all manufactured boats. The most common one is the

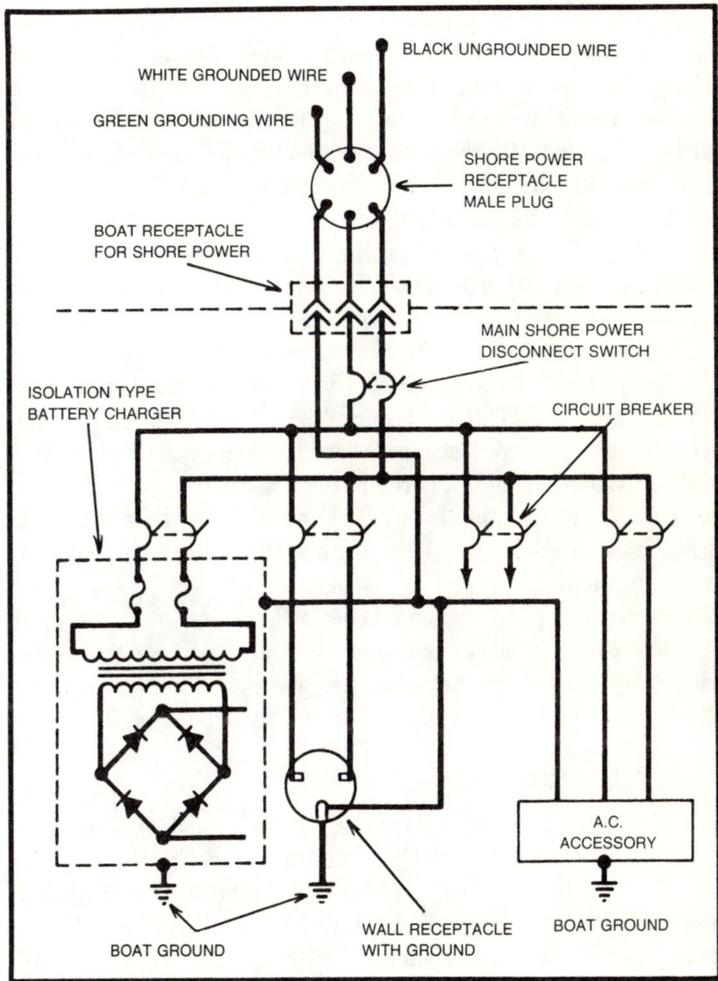

Fig. 8-3. This is the basic wiring, or starting point, for all AC wired boats built
today. Only one wall receptacle is shown for brevity. You just make more tap-ins
for more outlets.

three-wire 115-volt AC system with a marine battery charger. Larger boats and yachts with factory installed AC generators, air conditioning and major appliances, will have a four-wire 115/230-volt wiring system.

In Fig. 8-3, note how the shore power disconnect switch opens black and white conductors simultaneously. All load circuit breakers do the same thing. Note how the green grounding conductor is connected to the metal frame, case, etc., of all electrical devices on the boat.

The shore power receptacle, which is usually on a cabin side or deck, must be the reverse service self-locking type with water tight self-closing caps. When you buy a new cruiser today, this is usually provided as standard equipment—but not everything. Some builders provide you with the proper connectors for each end of your shore power cable. But you buy the wire yourself.

In Fig. 8-4, the addition of that fourth red wire changes things considerably. This is the kind of wiring you get on larger boats with factory-installed AC generators for air conditioning and electric ranges. The main disconnect switch is in both the black and red conductors, but not the white neutral wire.

In the boat's 115-volt circuits you will note that single pole switches are used. This is permitted only in 115/230 volt wiring because here the red, black and white wires are not tied in to the boat's grounding system. Therefore the white wire is never dangerous once the red and black wires are disconnected by a switch or circuit breaker. All grounding in this system is done only with the green conductor.

There is never any switch or overload protection in the green conductor. Its continuity must never be violated because that green wire is all that stands between you and possible electrocution. Respect it. The lives of you and your family depend on it.

FUSES FOR AC CIRCUITS

A boat's AC wiring is completely separate and different from the boat's DC wiring. So don't be misled or confused by that long row of little glass fuses in the head back of the helm. These are the fuses only for the DC side of your boat's electrical system. The AC fuses will generally be in a different location, usually in the main AC switchboard or panel, which is always close to the shore power receptacle. There will be a multi-pole switch here which shuts off all current, but does not disconnect the green grounding conductor.

The most common type of fuse you will find in today's manufactured boats is the trip-free circuit breaker. These are designed to prevent you from trying to physically over-ride the open circuit by holding it down manually. There are two types of trip-free circuit breakers, thermal and magnetic. I personally do not like the thermal type. It's fine in a home, but not in a boat. Boat interiors, like an automobile, can get awfully hot in the summer sun. This does not contribute to thermal circuit breaker honesty or dependability.

The ABYC requires that all current carrying conductors be protected by a fuse or circuit breaker with a rating of no more than

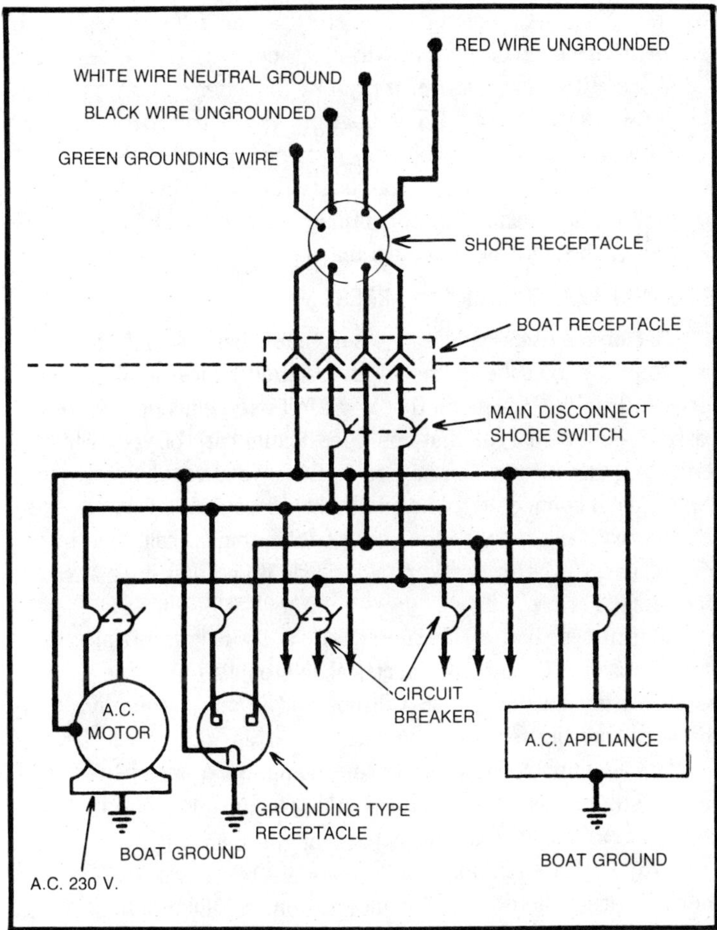

Fig. 8-4. This is the basis for all wiring on larger boats with 115/230 volt shore cables. Note how all switches on 230-volt circuits, and the main shore disconnect switch, open both the black and red conductors.

125 percent of total capacity. This means on a 20-ampere circuit you would have a 25-ampere fuse. Any circuit supplying power to an AC motor must also be protected by a fuse of the same rating of 125 percent. All load carrying circuits and conductors in branch outlets must also be protected.

PROTECTING METAL BOATS FROM AC ELECTRICITY

Metal boats require additional protection from AC shore power, which can cause electrolytic corrosion. This is achieved by the installation of an isolation transformer between the boat and shore electricity. This is a 1:1 transformer, which means 115 volts in, 115 volts out. If you examine the schematic drawing in Fig. 8-5, you can see that there is no direct metal-to-metal contact between the boat and shore. Electricity is transmitted by induction in that magnetic field between the two coils. The boat draws electricity from shore. Yet at the same time it is completely isolated from shore. You get the power without the problems. Your boat is theoretically suspended in air, isolated from land. If you continue to have problems with AC electricity, they are of your own making.

ISOLATION TYPE BATTERY CHARGERS

Battery charges, which are a permanent part of a boat's electrical system, should be of the type designed expressly for marine service. This doesn't mean that you can't use your dependable old Sears Roebuck charger that has been taking care of your car batteries for years. Sure, continue to use it on your boat batteries, but don't leave it connected to the battery when you are away, not even if it automatically reduces the charge down to a so-called harmless trickle charge. Battery makers like Exide do not consider a trickle charge as "harmless."

Marine type battery chargers, like the one in Fig. 8-6, are a part of the boat's AC and DC electrical systems. The price is high because they do things you will not find in any automotive type charger. One big feature is the isolation transformer which is an absolute essential for any charger permanently left in a boat's electrical system. It assures you that nothing from shore power AC will get into your boat's DC wiring.

Why is this so important? For one thing it protects you from shock hazard while down in the bilge servicing something, anything that is metal. It greatly reduces the possibility that your boat's AC system will cause galvanic corrosion, especially if your boat is steel or aluminum.

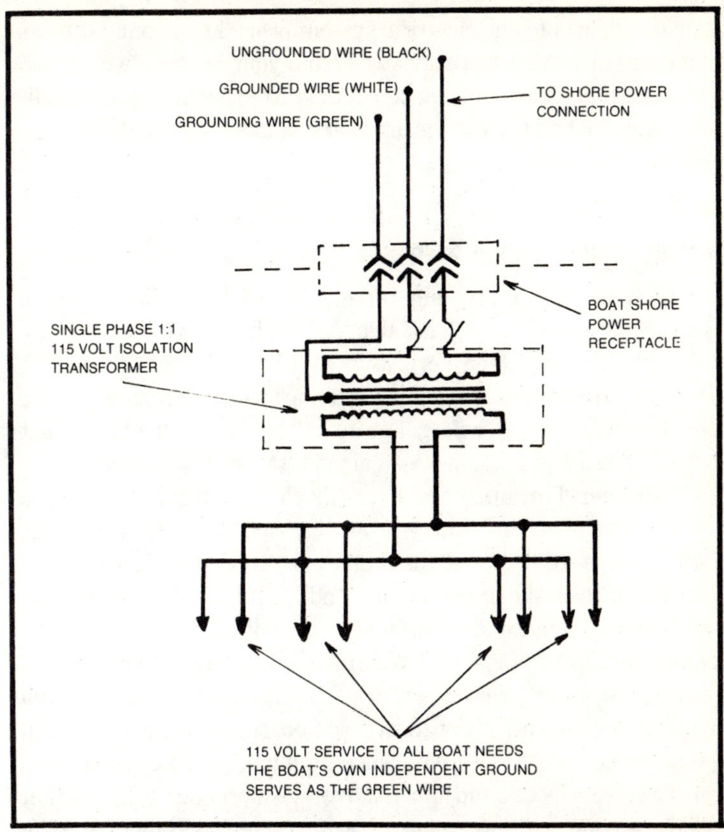

Fig. 8-5. The single phase 1:1 isolation transformer is the recommended way to protect metal boats, along with steel and aluminum ones, from galvanic corrosion problems with AC 115-volt electrical systems.

Shore AC current passes only through the primary windings. The secondary windings receive electricity by induction through the magnetic field and not by direct metal-to-metal contact. This enables the boat's current carrying conductors to float free of ground, making them literally dead wires.

Another important feature of marine chargers like the Constavolt and Sentry is low AC ripple. With auto chargers a high percentage of the AC wave pattern gets superimposed on the boat's DC after is it rectified. In an automobile this is unimportant. On a boat when AC ripple gets too high, it causes hum in radios and interference on television and other electronic equipment.

Marine chargers use full wave rectification plus filters to eliminate the AC ripple. Expensive chargers, like the Constavolt, are a permanent part of your electrical system. They keep your batteries fully charged even if you stay away from your boat for weeks and your bilge pumps are running constantly. They switch on automatically when the battery voltage drops and switch off when the battery reaches full voltage.

GROUND FAULT INTERRUPTER

High voltage alternating current electricity on small boats, especially at sea, is more risk than I think it is worth. I got along without it for years, and very well. And I often wonder why it is necessary to have a damn generator eating up my expensive gas on a 50-mile run just so my wife can make coffee. The coffee tasted just as good when she made it on an alcohol stove.

However, I'm human and just as much a victim of advertising as the next boatman. So I worry about that tiger I live with. Electric shock on a boat, especially a metal one, has considerably more wallop to it then shock in a home. And it's a lot easier to get that wallop on a boat because when at sea, even on calm days, boats are always wet from flying spray. Water spray is always coming at you, even when you hit small 1-foot waves. Hit bigger waves and you drown under the spray. For this reason boats are always wet, damp and never completely dry out. Since I am a born professional worrier, I was a perfect set-up for a relatively new product on the market called a ground fault interrupter. It is marketed by Hubbell Pass & Seymour, Inc. So I investigated.

This device, which protects against electrical shock, is installed in the AC power system, along with its own built receptacles. Any accidental contact between a conductor and ground energizes the device, which instantly shuts off the power. Wonderful! But how does it work in actual practice? It doesn't.

The ground fault interrupter is so sensitive that a fault current of 5/1000ths of an ampere will activate it and cause it to shut off the power. This may work out in a home, but not on a boat. There is so much moisture and dampness on a boat that small leaks of current from appliances are inevitable. And these small leaks always exceed the tiny 5/1000ths of an amp it takes to activate the interrupter. If you try to correct this by increasing the leak level response of the interrupter, you lower its level of protection to the point where it becomes useless as protection against shock. So forget about ground fault interrupters for your boat.

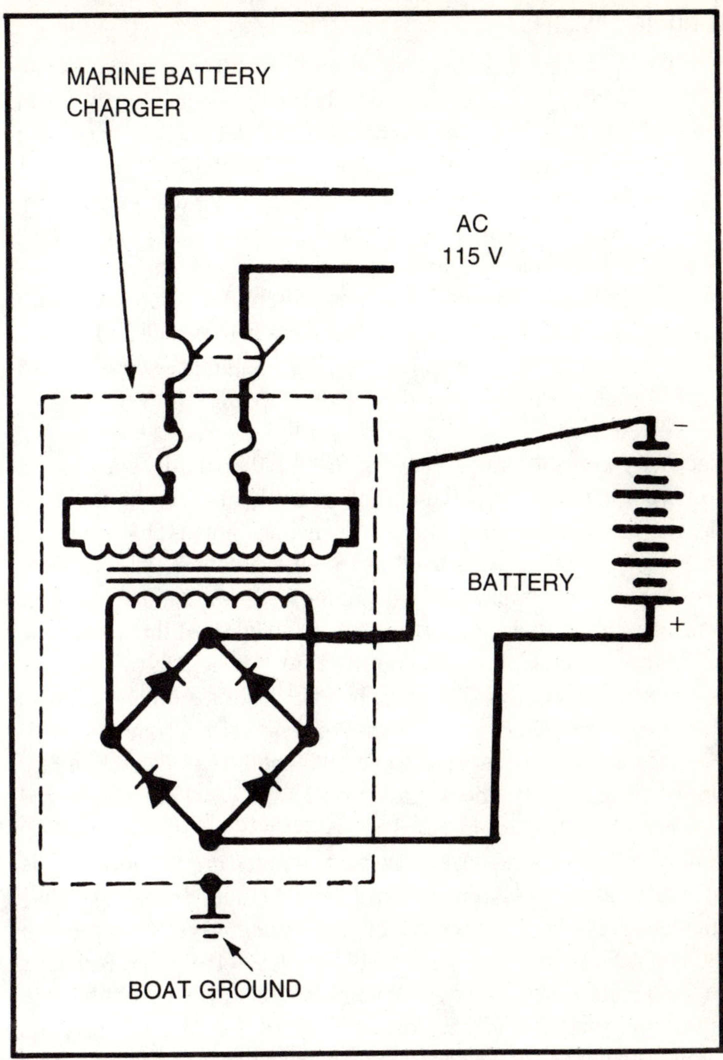

Fig. 8-6. Marine battery chargers are a permanent part of a boat's electrical system, which is why the isolation transformer is so important. Without this isolation, you might someday be electrocuted while servicing your engine.

The only protection you have against that tiger on your boat is your own maintenance work and vigilance. Nobody else really gives a damn about you and your family, to be realistically brutal. As Voltaire said: "Every man has a right to go to hell in his own fashion." But you don't have to go there. So take a long look at the AC wiring on your boat.

BONDING SYSTEMS

If you own an older boat, or recently bought one, and it has an AC generator, check to see if it has a bonding system like the one in Fig. 8-7. If it doesn't, do something, or get rid of that damn generator. Why didn't previous owners do something? They didn't because the original "previous" owner didn't have that generator.

You will find some strange electrical wiring on boats over 20 years of age. There are millions of them still afloat. Some were originally built with six-volt DC engines, then later re-powered with 12-volt engines. On some really old cruisers you will still find 32-volt DC systems and one huge engine that can weigh three tons. These fine old yachts are still around.

When marinas and yacht clubs started to make 115-volt dock electricity available, the owners of these old boats did some quick do-it-yourself wiring so they could avail themselves of this free electricity. Yes, dock electricity was free, and not just too long ago. The electrical receptacles used were the old vintage type with just two slots. There was no round grounding hole. So boat owners, naturally, wired their boats the same way and used the same type 2-wire receptacles. They had no need for a bonding system.

You will rarely find electrical bonding systems on older boats. However, when AC comes aboard, you must have a common bonding system to which every piece of metal is tied, as shown in Fig. 8-7. On my boat even the deck hardware, bits, cleats, stanchions and bow pulpit are tied to the bonding strap.

Wide copper strap makes the best common ground because it is so much easier to fasten terminals to it without soldering. I use stainless steel ⅜-inch sheetmetal screws and drive them through the copper into the inner keel. This not only secures the terminal, but also holds down the strap. With heavy cable you almost have to tap on to it with a soldered connection, and that means a propane torch. And I get very nervous using a torch down in the bilges. Strap and terminal screws are so much easier and safer.

If you have just bought an old cruiser (they'll still be around another 50 years), make a careful survey of the wiring before you take your family on a vacation cruise. If you have just purchased a used boat of fairly recent manufacture, and you want to add an AC generator, stick to 115 volts. Your boat will have the standard three-wire AC system, and this will be compatible with a straight 115-volt generator. You will encounter no difficulties hooking it up to your wiring.

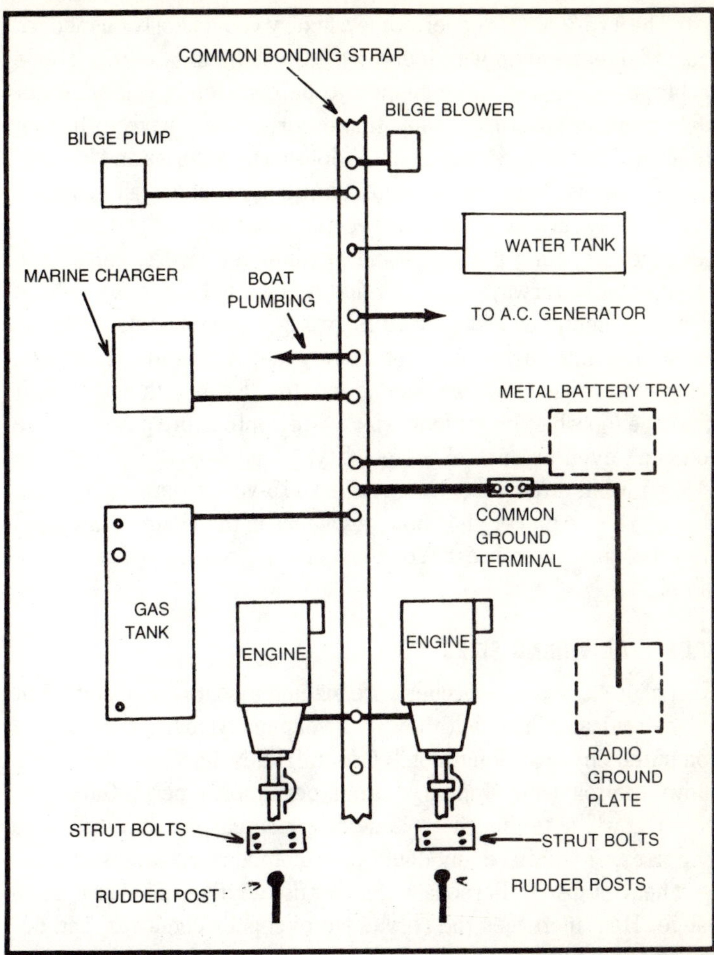

Fig. 8-7. The bonding strap here is 6-inch wide copper flashing material which is sweat soldered together. The strap should run the full length of the boat over the inner keel, bent over frames. In place of strap, four or six gauge copper cable can be used.

But if you get big ideas and, without consulting anybody, order a 115/230 volt generator, you will have fits. You will develop an eye twitch and start talking to yourself. The 115/230 volt generator is designed for a four-wire AC system. And your boat has the standard three-wire system. In this system, the white conductor is a grounded conductor. This, in turn, is compatible with about 99 percent of shore power receptacles. But in the four-wire system, the white wire is not a grounded conductor. Neither is the black or red wires. All grounding is done with only the green wire.

The 115/230 volt generator is a luxury you find only on modern yachts 50 feet and up with four-wire AC electrical systems. These yachts are designed and equipped to be completely self sufficient while cruising away from their home ports. They have to be self sufficient, unless they cruise only in Southern California and Florida. In these areas, big conglomerate-owned marinas are all equipped with the latest in four-wire shore receptacles. But once you get away from these boating paradises and get into the rivers, canals and intracoastal waterways, you will find nothing but three-wire shore power—sometimes just two wires strung between 2×4s. In these areas, the big yachts are completely dependent on their own generating capacity for weeks and months. Even with adapters, it would be foolish to plug a four-wire system into shore power where you can't even be sure of the polarity.

With the three-wire system and a 115-volt generator, you can plug into shore power just about anywhere in the United States and give your generator a rest. You must give it a rest so you can check the oil.

PROPER AC WIRING SIZES

With high AC voltage, proper wire size on a boat is important, but not as critical as it is with low DC voltage. Amperage drops are computed on a wire length of 100 feet. The National Electric Code allows the following amperage drops per ampere per 100 feet.

You will note that the voltage drop decreases as the wire size increases. If you have any doubts about wire size, always use the next heavier gauge. Personally, I never use anything smaller than 10 gauge. Heat increases the resistance of copper conductor and decreases the durability of the insulation. In areas where the wire is exposed to heat from the sun, under hot cabins and decks, I prefer 8 gauge wire.

Table 8-1. AC Wiring Sizes And Voltage Drops

GAUGE	AMPACITY	VOLTAGE DROP
14	15	.48
12	20	.31
10	30	.20
8	40	.13
6	55	.08

Standardization in electrical fixtures at marinas is coming along at about the same breakneck snail's pace as our national conversion to metrics. Except in those boating heavens on the west coast and Florida, you are still going to find old fashioned two-hole receptacles back in the boondocks with uncertain polarities. With these old receptacles, you can't tell by sight alone which hole is the black and which is the grounded white.

If you look closely at a standard grounded receptacle, like the ones in your home, you will note that one of the slots is slightly smaller. This is always the black wire. Television sets today have power cords where one blade on the male plug is slightly larger. This is to prevent you from inserting the plug wrong and crossing the polarity.

Just 10 years ago, television set owners were being electrocuted when they put the plug in wrong. This is back when many table model television sets had metal cabinets. When you crossed the polarity in these sets, the chassis became hot instead of negative ground. And if there was leakage, the metal cabinet also became hot. If the set was in a room near a heat radiator or on a kitchen counter near the sink, it was dangerous. If a woman were to touch the cabinet and a water faucet at the same time, she was dead.

I personally owned such a set, sold by a big mail order house, and I checked it once with my VOM meter. By simply turning the power plug around, I could put 115 volts into the metal cabinet.

When the accidental electrocutions attributed to metal TV cabinets hit the news columns with alarming frequency, manufacturers were forced to come out with statements like there was no shock hazard with metal television cabinets because the chassis was insulated in complete electrical isolation from the cabinet. What this means is that wherever the chassis was secured to the cabinet, it was sitting on a insulator. But when television repair men pulled that chassis for service, the insulation was often broken. And there went the "isolation."

It wasn't too long after those electrocutions that metal television cabinets disappeared from the market place to be replaced by plastic cabinets. Also, power cords had the type of male plug that could not be reversed.

You have the same situation on a boat. Technically, a boat's bonding system and the AC ground are supposed to be "isolated" from each other. Even with crossed polarity in the AC system, there should be no shock hazard. But I wouldn't care to bet my life on this, even on my own boat. There are just too many imponderables, too many things that can screw up the best laid plans of mice and men.

There are two things in this world I will never trust or be completely comfortable with. One of them is high voltage electricity. The other is high voltage used car dealers.

I sincerely hope you have been impressed with all this—the deadly seriousness of electrical polarity on a boat. If it hasn't, let me put it another way. Think of your boat as a bathtub filled with water and you sitting in it with a radio playing beside you while you shave with an electric shaver. This is an American version of Russian roulette. Does that impress you? Have I got your attention now?

HOW TO CHECK POLARITY

So how do you cope with polarity? The same way I do—make a polarity check before you insert your shore power cord. It's really very simple.

To be able to use those old fashioned two hole receptacles, you need an adapter. You probably already own a few because they come with many power tools that have three pronged power cords. The manufacturer supplies you with the adapter so you can use his tool with older ungrounded receptacles. All such adapters have a length of loose wire attached, which is used for externally grounding the tool to a screw on the receptacle box. In fact, the manufacturers protect themselves by warning you to do this. Okay. But what good is that advice if the receptacle box itself isn't grounded? This is common with two hole receptacles out in the boondocks.

So what do you do?

First you find the black conductor in that receptacle. Then you find another external ground. There are two easy ways to do this. Buy an inexpensive circuit tester, the type with two wires and a small neon light. Or make a test light. This is just an ordinary light bulb in a weathrproof rubber light socket with two extending wires, bare on the ends.

To find the black wire, insert the bare end of one tester wire into one of the receptacle holes. The other wire you touch to ground, usually a water pipe. If nothing happens, then you have touched the white, the grounded conductor. Now reinsert the test wire into the other hole. This time the light will come on. And that hole is the black conductor.

When you insert your shore cable, just be sure that the black side of your male plug goes into the black side of the female receptacle. If you are uncertain about this, go back to Fig. 8-1 and note the 15-amp receptacle. The smaller slot is the black wire. If you are the forgetful type, why not mark the hot prong with a piece of red tape for future reference?

There is still the loose wire of the adapter which must be separately secured to ground, preferably a water pipe if there is one. There is always a waterpipe somewhere around the docking area. It's just that you may occasionally have to travel some distance to reach it. For this reason, do as I do, always carry spare lengths of grounding wire, up to 50 feet, all with small battery charger type spring clamps attached. This is a quick easy way to make that temporary overnight ground hook-up.

WIRING NEW APPLIANCES ON A BOAT

I have never met or heard of a man who bought a boat, and was completely satisfied with everything on it. That man just doesn't exist—well, not in boating. The sea and boats attract a special breed of man, but damn few women. It is the nature of women to hate boats. But women love their men. So women put up with boats and even pretend to like them. Some of them even sand and paint bottoms. An unforgettable sight is to watch a woman laying on her back sanding a bottom with all that copper paint falling on her face. That woman loves her man because a woman will do this most wretched of human labors only for a man she loves.

And men know this. So we men knock ourselves out trying to make it up to them. We keep improving and updating our boats by installing all sorts of kitchen appliances. I have seen 30-foot cruisers so loaded down with women-type appliances that you couldn't find work space in the galley to slice bread for sandwiches. The boats were so gutted with "labor saving" junk, which are also space hogs, that they had become all but unlivable. There was no room in the galley cupboards to store food. Limited space under the sink was taken up by a huge soundproofed garbage disposal. Other limited space was monopolized by a dishwasher, toasters, mixers, blenders, wiener cookers, hamburger fryers, electric frypans, rotisserie, coffee maker, deep fryer, broiler and pressure cooker. This is just a partial list for small cruisers, 30 feet and under. On larger boats I have seen automatic washers, electric dryers and microwave ovens. I met a boatman from Buffalo who has a real pipe organ on his boat.

I was tied up next to him one summer in the Georgian Bay when that damn thing awakened me about ten in the morning with Wagner's Twilight of the Gods. It was the man's wife playing the organ. It was the only way he could keep her happy and get her on that boat. There is no limit to what a man will do to keep his boat and his wife.

This means you will be installing many new electrical appliances on your boat, maybe even a pipe organ. You will also be installing some gadgets for yourself, like a new searchlight, power haler, anchor winch and radar. Here is what you must do.

The outside metal structure or frame of refrigerators, air conditioners, space heaters, dishwashers and garbage disposals should be connected to the boat's common ground bonding system with copper #8 gauge wire, or heavier. All appliances, especially refrigerators, should be physically bolted down so they do not shift when the boat rolls or pitches in heavy weather. Refrigerators, and all electric motors, must have ventilation. They have heat to dissipate, which has to go somewhere. Refrigerators, in particular, must be able to dissipate heat or they will cycle excessively long, which only creates more heat.

Unlike your home, your boat has two kinds of electrical energy. Always consult the name plate on the equipment to determine voltage required, whether AC or DC. Always use the wire size specified, or even one gauge heavier. If #10 is specified, use #8.

For equipment that will operate on the boat's DC power, put a switch and fuse only in the hot (ungrounded) wire.

For equipment that operates off the boat's AC system, put a switch and fuse in both conductor wires, the black and white.

On AC equipment, be sure to tie the green ground wire to the frame or chassis. This is in addition to that heavy wire (#4 gauge) to the boat's bonding system.

All fuses, AC and DC, should be of a protective rating not exceeding appliance demand by more than 125 percent. This means if the appliance uses eight amps, you protect it with a 10-amp fuse or trip-free circuit breaker. And this fuse protects only that one piece of equipment.

BOAT DIRECT CURRENT SYSTEMS

We now enter a different world of electrical energy, the low voltage direct current world. This is a comfortable, safe world that I know and love. Death does not stalk you here, hiding behind some wet equipment. The worst that can happen here is an occasional

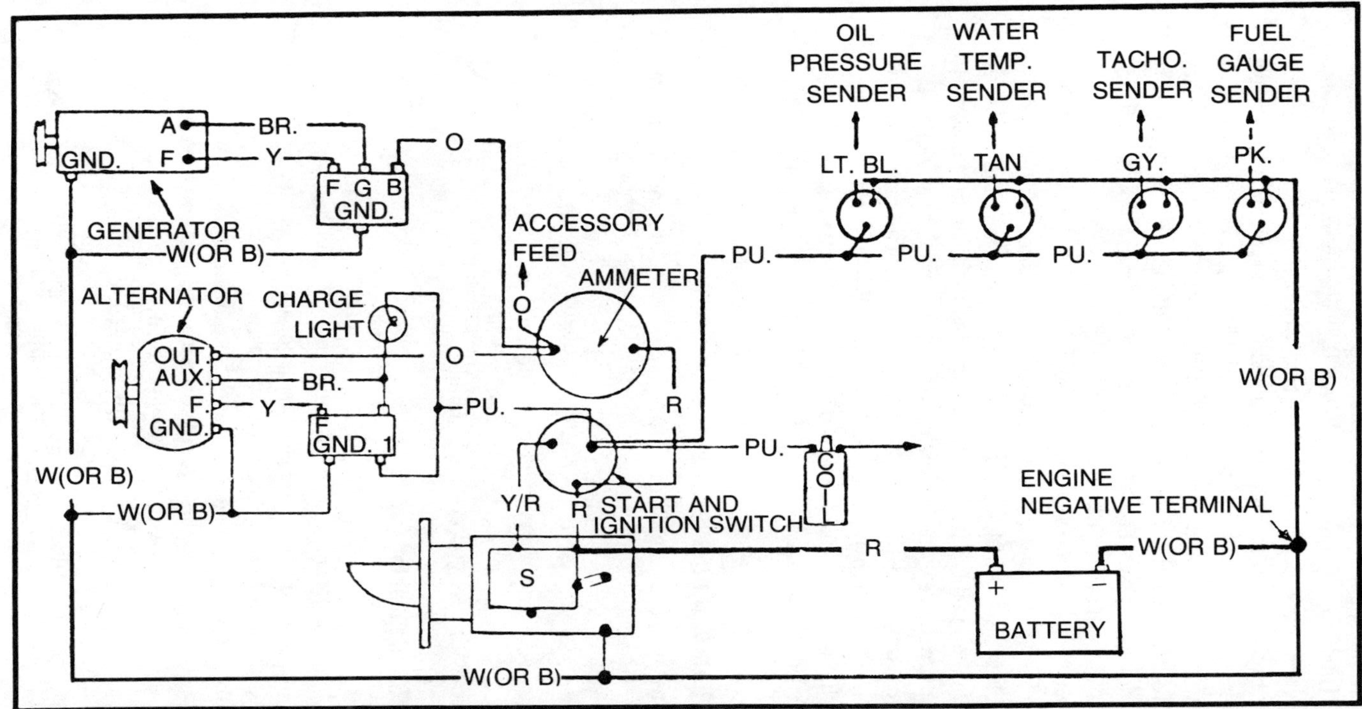

Fig. 8-8. The nice thing about DC wiring is that it is color coded. Once you become familiar with the code, you can get by without a schematic drawing.

short circuit, a spark, some smoke, and a blown fuse or burned out diode. But you personally are always safe in this world—until you bring shore power aboard, mixing two worlds.

In Fig. 8-8 you see the wiring diagram of a typical DC electrical system, showing both an old fashioned DC generator and newer alternator. The reason for this is that there are still many old boats around with Gray and Chris Craft six-cylinder up-draft engines and DC generators. Newer boats, of course, will have down-draft engines and alernators. Except for the generators and voltage regulators, the wiring for both is the same.

In Fig. 8-9 you see how two batteries are hooked up in parallel to handle heavy DC electrical requirements. Hooking the batteries parallel gives you the same voltage but double the ampere hours. It is so much easier on your back to install two 100-ampere-hour batteries in parallel than one 200-ampere-hour. The big single battery will often weigh over a hundred pounds. Why risk a hernia trying to get that massive box of lead into your boat? If you need even more ampere hours, install a third or fourth battery, keeping them all in parallel.

THE GROUND IN DC SYSTEMS

The word "ground" may still confuse you, but don't feel retarded. It confuses me too sometimes. But some wise man once said, "When confused, mumble." So I mumble a lot. On an automobile, the car itself is the grounded conductor. Every piece of metal on your car is a current-carrying conductor. It is the second wire in a 2-wire DC system. I used automobiles as an illustration because with this you are more familiar.

Grounding Conductor

Look at these words carefully, "grounded" and "grounding." If you read through this quickly, you miss the "ed" and "ing" on the end of "ground." That's how you get confused, and in trouble. There is a big difference between those two words.

The "grounding conductor" does not, under normal conditions, carry current. This is that third extra wire that you don't even have on an automobile. So why is it on your boat, since the engine DC is similar to an automobile? Your cruiser has two electrical systems, one like you have at home and one like in your car. The primary purpose of that third wire is to ground any stray current and prevent shock.

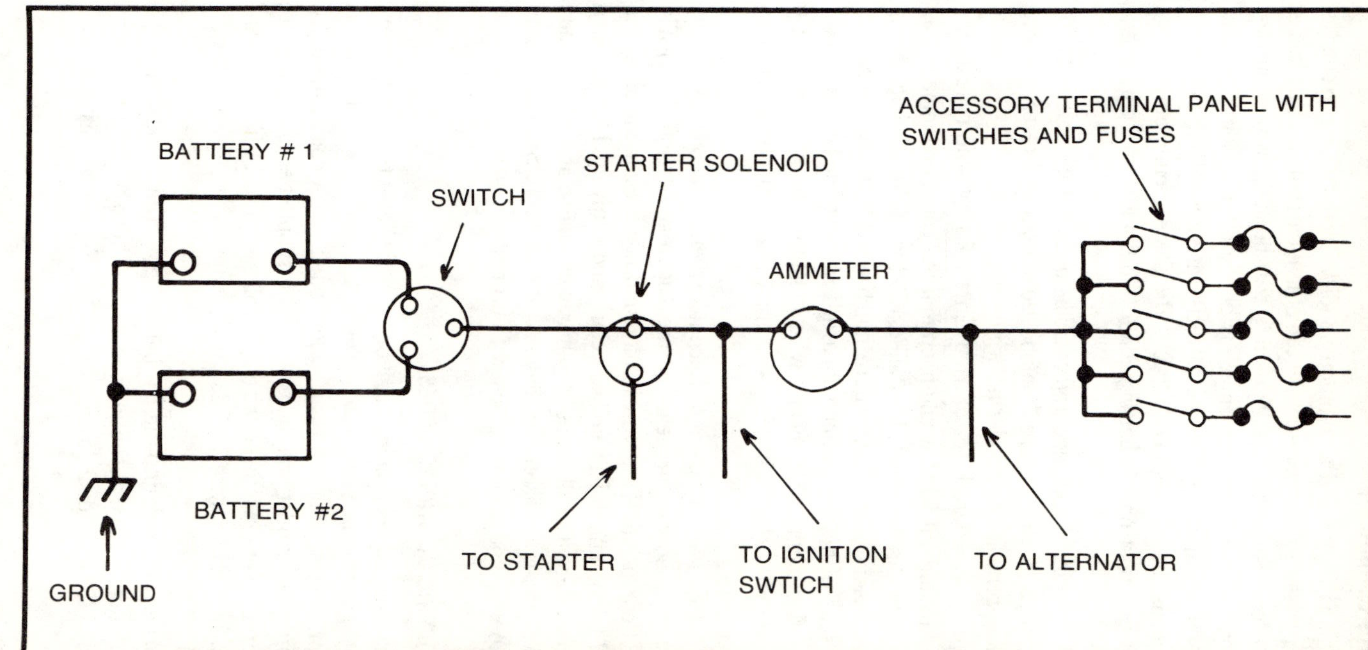

Fig. 8-9. Amperage capacity on a boat can easily be increased with extra batteries installed parallel in this manner. You can add as many as you need. This extra capacity also helps to maintain a steady voltage, so necessary in keeping electronic gear operating at peak output.

BONDING CONDUCTOR

This is also called a common bonding ground. This ground is also supposed to be a non-conductor of live current. I know this is going to confuse you when you study that bonding system in Fig. 8-7. You will see where the engine is tied into the bonding system. Then you will also see that the batteries are tied into the engines. This means that the bonding strap is the same ground potential as that ground post on the battery itself. True and very confusing, I know.

The common bonding strap could be used to carry current and, in fact, often is. But you aren't supposed to do that. I can sense you becoming rebellious, wondering why.

Well, I wondered, too. Strictly in a spirit of true research, I decided to find out what would happen if the common binding strap was used to carry current. I installed a Peters & Russel bilge pump at the transom of my boat where much water always collected in heavy seas with spray coming aboard. I ran just one red wire (hot) back to this pump. The second wire I clamped to a rudder post 6 inches away. My boat's bonding system was now carrying current to that pump.

That was four years ago. Each fall when I haul out, I carefully inspect my underwater gear for the slightest sign of electrically induced corrosion. To date I have found none. So what does this prove? I don't know. I am still searching and studying. I have a deep personal interest in all forms of galvanic corrosion aboard ship, and what I do is for a reason. You have no such reason. So according to the experts, you aren't supposed to do that.

IDENTIFYING DC WIRING CODES

Electric codes require that you be visibly able to identify every fixed conductor in your boat's electrical system. This is why all current carrying conductors are color coded. Color coding in the AC system of your boat, and home, is quite simple because there are just three colors in a three-wire 115-volt system—black, white and green. In the four wire 115/230 volt system a fourth color, red, is added.

When you look into the DC battery powered circuits on boats, that is when you see all the colored wires. There are ten basic colors specified for individual circuits by the ABYC's new wiring code.

Black

This color is the ungrounded conductor, the plus (+) side of your battery.

Red

Like black, this wire is also a power feed, and the lead to the water temperature transmitter. It is also the main lead from battery to starter, then to the starter ignition switch and to the ammeter.

Green

All bonding conductors must be colored green. The only exception is when bare wire is used. Bare wire can be used ONLY for bonding, which makes identification obvious.

Blue

This is the lead from the ignition coil to the switch. It is also used for instrument and cabin lights. Light blue wiring is used from the oil pressure transmitter to the oil pressure gauge.

Dark Gray

This is the color code for wires from a tachometer sender to the tachometer itself. It is also used for navigation lights, between the fuse, switch and lights.

Brown

Leads from fuses or switches to bilge pumps are brown. So are leads from a generator armature to the ground terminal of the voltage regulator. It is also the lead from the alternator auxiliary terminal to the "idiot light," and then to the voltage regulator.

Orange

This is the feed line for various accessories coming off the ammeter to a fuse or switch panel. It is also the lead from the ammeter to a generator or alternator output terminal.

Purple

Two purple wires run from the ignition switch. One goes to the coil and one runs to the distribution panel for various instruments. A third wire will run from the panel to the instruments.

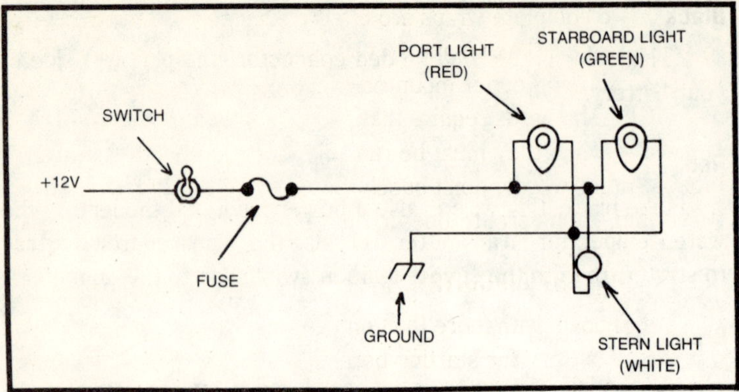

Fig. 8-10. The smallest of powerdriven boats will have some measure of DC wiring, even if it serves nothing more than as navigation lights, as shown in the this illustration.

Tan

This is the color coded wire running from the water temperature transmitter to the gauge.

Pink

This is the lead from the fuel tank transmitter to its gauge on the instrument panel.

If you buy a recently manufactured boat, its DC wiring will follow this color code. The ABYC feels that it is not necessary for the builder to supply the buyer with a wiring diagram, or schematic drawing when wiring is color coded. However, the builder must supply you with some form of color code identification.

Manufacturers of boats all use the same colors in their wiring, but not necessarily the same way. For example, one builder may use a black lead to the oil pressure, red to the water transmitter. Another builder may use blue for the oil and tan for the water. This is unimportant if the builder supplies you with color identification. Each builder can use the colors any way he wishes.

COLOR CODING YOUR OWN BOAT WIRING

The ABYC feels that it is proper under the color code to use a single color for all wiring if an identifying colored sleeve or tag is attached to wires at both terminals. This is the way you color code the wiring in an older boat.

The best and easiest way to do this is with Scotch brand or Mystick tape, which is available in dozens of colors. You should make at least two complete wraps around the wire near the terminal that the wire serves. Then make up your own color identification reference record and keep it mounted on a bulkhead near the engines. The ABYC standards require that AC wiring be kept separate from DC wiring when they must be run together in a common trough or tube. In other words, don't bunch them all together tightly. If there isn't room, then reroute one or the other.

DIRECT CURRENT CIRCUITRY

On all boats with more than one engine, it is not recommended to use one battery for starting both engines with a second battery used for accessories, lights, etc. Each engine should have its own battery for starting and nothing else. Additional batteries, in parallel if needed, should be used for accessories, lights, pumps, radiotelephone, electronic equipment, etc. On a single engine boat, there should be one battery for the engine alone and additional batteries for accessories. This assures utmost reliability at sea and fewer distress calls to the Coast Guard for a tow because of a dead engine.

All DC circuts, other than the engine itself, must be of the 2-wire type (Figs. 8-10 and 8-11). This is where boats differ from an

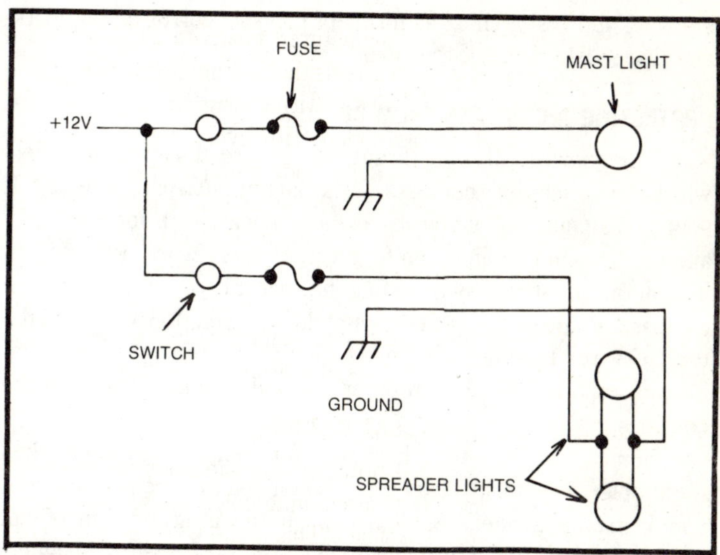

Fig. 8-11. This illustration shows how the DC wiring starts to grow with a small sailboat which, in addition to navigation lights, must also have mast and spreader lights.

automobile, which has one-wire circuitry. As previously mentioned, the automobile itself serves as the second wire.

In marine service, you run two wires to everything. This even excludes common rail conductors which serve as a connecting point for a number of accessories like lights, compass, windshield wipers, horn, bilge pump and bilge blowers. When you have a number of accessories tied together at a common grounding point, you have an overload situation on the single wire which runs from the common rail conductor to ground itself. You have six or 10 hot feeder conductors running to all those accessories, but only one grounding conductor. Even if it is #10 gauge wire, it can't handle the current load of all those accessories. In an automobile, that huge mass of metal, the car itself, is the return wire and there is just no way you will ever overload that return wire.

On a boat, you must have two wires running to every piece of equipment, accessory, light, etc. The "hot" wire will be color coded for the equipment served. For example, cabin lights are served by a color coded blue wire. So your "hot" wire is blue and the return conductor is yellow. To a bilge pump it will be brown and yellow. You must never substitute the green wire for the return conductor.

You can find these things violated on half the boats afloat. I myself have violated them, but I knew what I was doing. I have been studying and researching all forms of galvanic corrosion on boats, and that is why I break the rules.

PROTECTING A COMPASS FROM DC

Direct current flowing through a wire creates a magnetic field which plays tricks on a compass. It also affects auto-pilot accuracy. If someone suggests that you shield your compass with some material like lead, thank him and then forget it. It won't work. I tried it. In fact, nothing works. Try rerouting the wires. If you can't, move the compass. If you can't, as a last act of desperation, twist-wind all the the DC wires together. The magnetic field from twist-wound conductors tend to cancel each other out and minimize affect on the compass.

Sometimes DC wiring is blamed for compass deviation when the problem is actually elsewhere. When you look behind or under your instrument panel, see all that spaghetti wiring and think of that before you start trying to untangle the mess. Look for iron, magnets and beer cans. Yes, beer cans throw off more compasses than DC wiring.

A big news story last year was about a wealthy industrialist who ran his company's $300,000 yacht right up on a rock-covered beach. He had been making a high speed night run from Put-In-Bay to La Salle, Michigan. When asked how he got so far off course as to run up on that beach, he replied: "I put a beer can down next to my compass. It pulled me off course about six degrees."

Transistor radios and all radios, including the receiver on radiotelephones, have powerful magnets in their speakers. Worm gears in steering mechanisms are often right under the area where a compass is mounted. If the compass is mounted on top of a decking area forward of the helm, look under that deck. Often this area will be either a head or large closet. Look for metal towel rods, clothes hangers and hooks. Are you sure the towel rods and hooks are brass? I had to replace all these things in my boat because they were not brass.

If your compass deviates more than two degrees, DC wiring is not the blame. You can make a positive check. If there is no current flow in DC wiring, there is no magnetic field. Right? So disconnect the battery that supplies the current for all those DC wires. Then check your compass. If the compass remains steady on the same heading, you have your proof. Obviously, this is a check that must be made tied up in your slip, and on a quiet day when your boat is not swinging and fighting the lines.

RECEPTACLES FOR DC

Wall outlets for DC should be highly recognizable and physically different from outlets for 115-volt AC. If you ever plug a 12-volt light into a 115-volt socket, you'll discover why. There are special marine receptacles made expressly for boat DC electrical systems. If you can't find them locally, buy yourself a Manhattan Marine & Electric Co. catalog for one buck. It's worth the price just as a reference. The address is 116 Chambers Street, New York City, N.Y. 10007

DANGERS OF SPARK-MAKING EQUIPMENT

Any motor, generator, switch, or other spark-making device should be kept out of that low area of the bilge where water settles when the boat is at rest. Gasoline fumes, being heavier than air, also settle here along with the bilge water you want to pump overboard. This is no place for anything that makes sparks.

Peters & Russel of Springfield, Ohio manufacture a fine pump that can be mounted up high out of the bilge area (Fig. 8-12). A

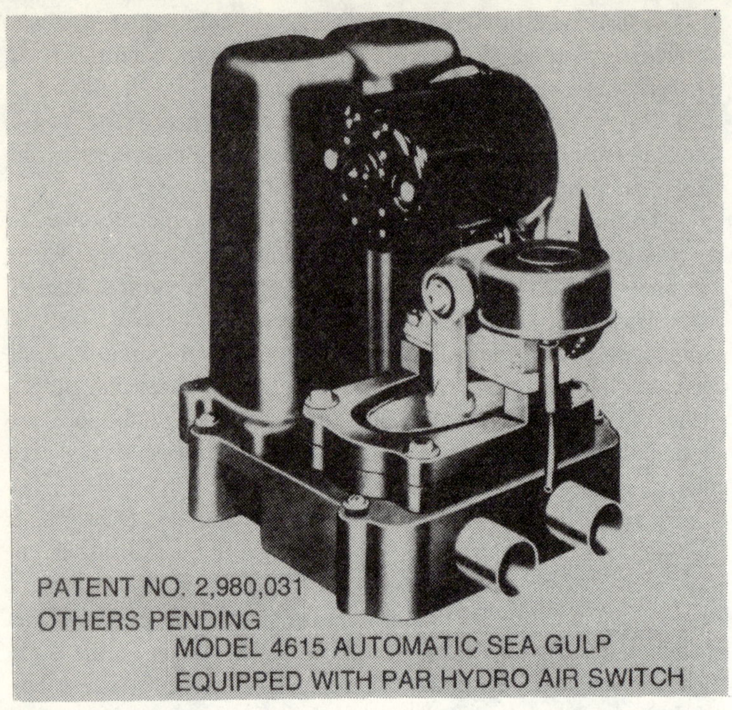

Fig. 8-12. This is one of the best boat pumps made. It does more than one pumping job and does it safely out of the dangerous bilge area.

suction hose and pick-up mount run down to the bilge water. This pump has a dry lift up to 16 feet from the intake. With 2-way "Y" valves, it can be used for many purposes, as shown in Fig. 8-13. I have this pump on my boat. When I change engine oil, I pump it out through the bilge discharge outlet where it drops into a square plastic bucket which I have hanging over the side and laying up against the hull. This way no dirty engine oil ever is spilled into my bilge and no drippings ever soil my teak.

The ABYC specifies that switchboards and DC distribution panels should not be located in the bilge or engine compartment, or close to fuel tanks, but up above decks in an easily accessible location that is well ventilated and protected from the weather. This means rain, salt spray and drippings from up above. If DC distribution circuits are located at the helm, out in an open cockpit, they should be well protected from spray, especially salt spray, which is devastating on electrical circuitry.

Musty, damp panels and switchboards tend to become conductive, which leads to stray currents leaking all over the place which, in turn, leads to corrosion, and more leakage. It starts slow and then snowballs. What may seem like endless nit-picking to a land person is quite serious to a sea person.

I can't repeat this often enough. The land and the sea are two different environments. Nowhere is this more quickly apparent than when you bring electricity aboard ship. Electrical circuit panels in a home can survive for 20 to 50 years, and when opened they look as clean as the day the home was built. But one year on a boat and everything will be coated and corroded. In five years it will look like something recovered from the sunken wreck of a Spanish Galleon.

The sea is impersonal and democratic. It destroys everything with equal ferocity. But sometimes I suspect the sea does have a special fondness for electrical circuitry.

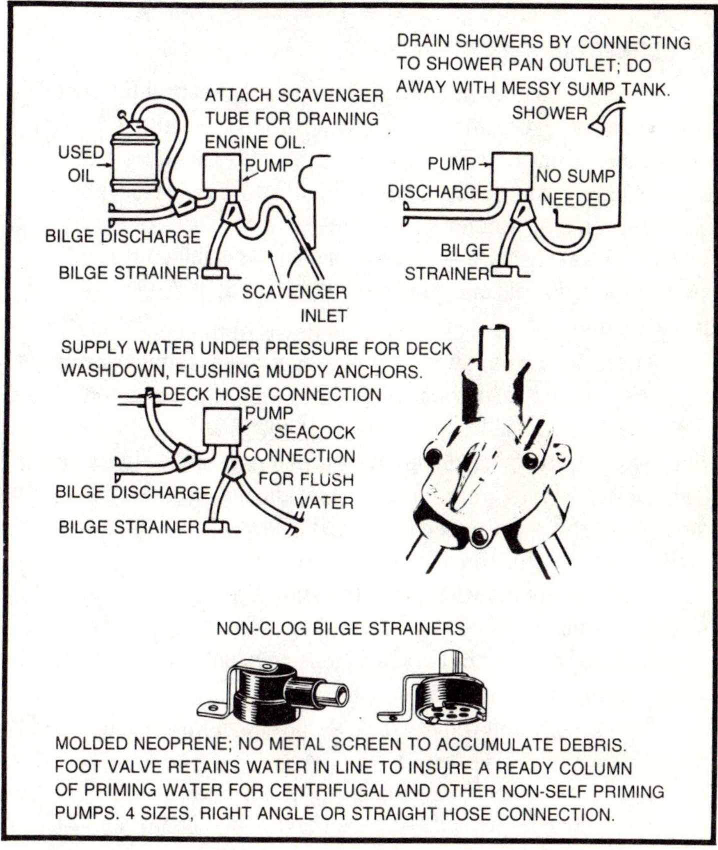

Fig. 8-13. The Peters and Russel pump is mounted out of the bilge and, with the use of 2-way "Y" valves, is utilized for many different jobs.

Residential type enclosed switchboxes and distribution panels are fine for homes. They are not fine for boats, even though they are extensively used, and by builders who should know better. They corrode. They rust badly, and rust holds moisture, which is plentiful on boats. The end result is something even cockroaches shun.

The ideal enclosed switchboard is stainless steel or Monel. They meet the most rigid safety requirements. They are highly corrosion-resistant. They look so neat and shipshape that I love them. I wish I could afford them.

The ABYC recommends metal, but wood enclosure boxes are acceptable, provided all terminal strips, fuse blocks, switches and circuit breakers are mounted on a high dielectric insulating material. This material must also be non-moisture-absorbing and non-combustible.

DC CONNECTIONS AND TERMINALS

Here is a boat-buying tip. If you are in the market for your first boat, new or used, make it a point to examine the DC wiring, especially the main switchbox and distribution panel. I can tell far more about a boat's quality from this than by a visual inspection of the bottom or sniffing around in the bilge, poking in dark corners with an ice pick. A top quality boat, built by a quality manufacturer, will have switchboxes, panels and distribution centers that are joyous things to gaze upon.

There will be neat wires, evenly spaced on terminal strips with ring type (not forked) terminals that are crimped and sleeved on each wire. Each wire will be properly color coded and additionally identified on the terminal strip by words that say "bilge blower," "windshield wipers," etc. This control panel will be easy to get at; yet it will be well protected from the weather. It will have adequate space open for the addition of more accessories.

Just looking at such a panel tells you that a builder who will do such an excellent job on something that is not readily visible, and is often ignored by most buyers, has done an equally fine craftsmanlike job on the rest of the boat.

However, when you see main switchboard wiring that looks like a pack rat communal nesting ground, you can walk away assured that the rest of that boat is not much better. Externally, the boat will bedazzle the eye with "Alabama Flash" and gimmickry—things which don't mean a damn when your guts are being shaken loose in a heavy chop. This is when you begin to see behind the window dressing and understand the Biblical words: "Vanity of vanities; all is vanity." Remember this when you go shopping for a boat and forget about the ice pick.

Terminals, splices, connections and plugs are where electrical troubles start in boat wiring. This is where corrosion does its evil work. Always use corrosion-resistant studs, nuts, washers and terminals, which you will not find at your local hardware store. You will have to pay premium prices to those who serve the marine trade.

Although fork-type terminals are much used, the ring-end terminals are better, especially where you have more than one wire attached to a terminal stud. It gets pretty crowded around some connections, like the ignition switch.

I have seen eight wires, with fork terminals, connected to the ignition switch stud. If you sneezed while working in this area, two or three wires would fall off. This is the reason for the ring terminals. Even if the nut works loose, no wires will fall off.

A maximum of four wires is allowable at one terminal stud. If more is required, use a jumper wire to another stud alongside, where you can attach four more conductors. Crimp type terminals are fine. These are available with insulating sleeves in various colors, useful in color coded wiring.

Multi-wire plug connectors are acceptable, but here you must have soldered connections for low resistance. All the wires must be clamped or supported in some way to prevent strain on any individual wire. The plugs must be sealed and water-resistant at least. Each wire must be sleeved to insulate it from all the other pins. The plug connectors must be of the lock-in type so they can withstand vibration without coming apart.

When doing any soldering, always use resin core radio-type solder. Acid core solder is absolutely unsuitable because it causes instant corrosion in a salt water environment and can ruin a circuit in a very short time.

Splices are something to avoid like a cold shower early in the morning. Splices always look untidy and are a mark of the amateur. If you must splice, at least do it right. Then hide it. Even good splices are ugly, an offense to the eye. When you cut the wire for a splice, stagger the cuts about 2 inches so if the two soldered wires become bare, a short circuit will not occur. Tape each soldered splice separately. Then tape them together. There is no way this can be done to look inoffensive with plastic tape, which itself is an abomination to be avoided. You never make splices where they will be highly visible.

Table 8-2. Total Amperages For Six-Volt Circuits With A 3 Percent Voltage Drop.

	TOTAL AMPERAGE IN 6-VOLT CIRCUITS										
	10	15	20	25	30	35	40	45	50	55	60
(6 volts——3% voltage drop wire sizes)											
5'	12	10	8	8	6	6					
10'	8	6	6	5	4	3					
15'	6	6	5	3	2	2					
20'	6	4	3	2	1	1					
25'	5	3	2	1	0	0					
(12 volts——3% voltage drop wire sizes)											
5'	14	12	12	10	10	8	8	8	8	8	6
10'	12	10	8	8	6	6	6	5	5	5	4
15'	10	8	6	6	5	5	4	4	3	3	2
20'	8	6	6	5	4	3	2	2	2	2	1
25'	8	6	5	4	3	3	2	1	1	1	0
(32-volts——3% voltage drop wire sizes)											
5'	18	16	16	14	14	14	12	12	12	12	10
10'	16	14	12	12	10	10	10	10	8	8	8
15'	14	12	10	10	10	8	8	8	6	6	6
20'	12	10	10	8	8	8	6	6	6	6	5
25'	12	12	8	8	6	6	6	6	5	5	4

While inspecting the engine compartment of a $25,000 cabin cruiser recently, I saw a cluster of wires from a multi-wire plug connection running a length of 8 feet, hanging loose in the air like a bath-room clothesline in a sorority house. The builder of this boat once had a big name in the industry. You could see their four-color ads in all the boating publications. For years this builder ignored the pleas of dealers for better quality control. Today that big name builder is out of business. Show me a badly wired boat. I'll show you a badly built boat.

PREVENTING VOLTAGE DROP

The more current you put into six and 12-volt wiring, the more important wire size becomes. This you can see for yourself by studying Table 8-2.

The wire sizes provide for an acceptable 3 percent voltage drop. Note as you go up in voltage, wire sizes get smaller. The old six-volt system, even at distances of only ten feet, called for #8 wire on only a 10-amp circuit. On a 35-amp circuit you were using #3 wire, which is battery cable size for 12-volt cars.

On your 12-volt systems, wire size gets smaller, and #12 wire is acceptable on a 10-foot run. On a 32-volt system you can use #16 wire.

If a 10% voltage drop is acceptable, you can drop down considerably in wire sizes. This was one of the main reasons auto manufacturers switched from six to 12 volt systems. Of course, they gave other reasons. A 12-volt starting motor has more muscle to crank big engines. An alternator requires less service and puts out more amperage. But the real reason was money. They cut costs by millions with smaller gauge wire which uses up less copper.

Table 8-3 is for a voltage drop of 10 percent. This may be acceptable for cabin lights, compass light and running lights. It is not acceptable for DC motors, electronic gear and especially radiotelephones.

With your 32-volt system you have an additional 5 feet added on to maximum wire lengths. This is why you will find 32-volt systems on almost all big cruisers over 30 years old because it made for more efficient use of battery power without resorting to excessively heavy copper cables strung all over the boat.

A 10 percent voltage drop does no harm to a light bulb. It just slightly reduces the amount of light. In fact, voltage drop is good for

Table 8-3. Total Amperages For Six-Volt Circuits With A 10 Percent Voltage Drop.

	TOTAL AMPERAGE IN 6-VOLT CIRCUITS										
	10	15	20	25	30	35	40	45	50	55	60
(6-volts——10% voltage drop wire sizes.)											
5'	14	14	14	12	12	12					
10'	14	12	10	10	8	8					
15'	12	10	8	8	8	6					
20'	10	8	8	8	6	6					
25'	10	8	6	6	4	4					
(12-volts——10% voltage drop wire sizes.)											
5'	14	14	14	14	14	14	14	14	12	12	12
10'	14	14	14	12	12	12	10	10	10	10	8
15'	14	14	12	10	10	10	8	8	8	8	8
20'	12	12	10	10	8	8	8	6	6	6	6
25'	10	10	10	8	8	8	6	6	6	6	4
(32-volts——10% voltage drop wire sizes.)											
5'	14	14	14	14	14	14	14	14	14	14	14
10'	14	14	14	14	14	14	14	14	14	14	14
15'	14	14	14	14	14	14	14	12	12	12	12
20'	14	14	14	14	14	12	12	12	10	10	10
25'	14	14	14	12	12	12	10	10	10	10	10
30'	14	14	14	12	12	10	10	10	10	8	8

light bulbs and makes them last longer. Voltage drop is harmful to motors of all types because it increases current draw in equal ratio to the drop in voltage. It's like being on a see-saw. When one end goes down, the other end goes up. Motors have wire windings to handle a specific current draw. If they draw too much current, the windings get warm. They can even get very hot and burn off the insulation. This causes an even increased overload and a burned out motor.

Voltage is an especially serious matter with radiotelephones. You have little enough radiated power with today's lousy new equipment. With low voltage you have even less, unless you just enjoy gabbing with other boats around the marina or club.

I have always wired my radiotelephones directly to the battery with #2 wire. Back in the days when I had a 6-volt Gray engine, I used 6-volt battery cables which are as thick as a man's index finger. If you read the owner's manual that comes with your radiotelephone, you will find that it particularly stresses proper wire size for the battery leads.

HOW TO DETERMINE EXACT VOLTAGE DROP

Determining the exact voltage drop at your radio, or some other accessory, requires a volt meter, preferably one with various scales. The shorter the volt range, the more accurate your test. A 15-volt range is ideal. Select some accessory with a high current draw, or even your radiotelephone. Let both the radio and transmitter warm up thoroughly. A radiotelephone has its biggest current draw when actually transmitting, that is with the microphone button pushed in. With the transmitter on the air, check voltage at the battery terminals. Then quickly check the voltage again at power terminals in back of the radio.

A fully charged battery will deliver 12 volts under load. But you rarely will ever get a full 12 volts at a heavy draw accessory or radiotelephone. What you don't get is your percentage of loss. For example, when you activate the starting motor on your boat engine, and then check its voltage, you will get a reading of about 10 volts with a good battery.

This represents a voltage drop just under 17 percent. However, this is acceptable with an engine starting motor because they are designed and heavily wired for massive amperage draws. In subzero weather, auto starting motors will draw 400-500 amps in short spurts.

With a radiotelephone, even 3 percent is undesirable because what may seem like a trivial loss at 12 volts becomes a considerable loss after it goes through a transformer and is stepped up about 50 times to produce high plate voltages. What started out as only a trivial half-a-volt voltage drop suddenly becomes a 50-volt drop in plate voltage to the final power amplifier tube. The transformer is a marvelously efficient device, but you only get out of it what you put in. Less voltage in results in less voltage out. So voltage drops becomes a serious matter with any kind of equipment that has transformers—and radiotelephones sure do have transformers in profusion.

To keep your losses at 3 percent, use wire sizes recommended by the ABYC in the tables. If you can tolerate losses of 10 percent, use the smaller gauge wires. If you can tolerate no voltage drop, increase your battery capacity with additional batteries in parallel, or use copper wires big as your index finger.

ALTERNATORS

Once upon a time, and not too long ago, all automobiles had DC generators. They had a limited output, usually about 15 amps. But to get 15 amps you had to race hell out of the engine or drive 35-40 miles an hour. At slow traffic city speeds, they only put out about two amps. With an engine idling, they put out nothing. As a result, if you had your heater and radio on while just driving around town, your battery would run down. If you also were using your headlights, your battery would quickly get so low you might not get your car started the next morning.

With more and more accessories being added to automobiles, something had to be done. The alternator was the answer. It produces 30 to 75 amps, depending upon size. It produces a high amperage output at low engine speeds. This was an immediate boon to police cars that cruise about cities at slow speeds, yet require high amperage for their radiotelephones.

Why is the alternator able to produce high output at slow engine speeds? Actually, it isn't able to do this any better than the old DC generators. It's just that the alternator isn't really turning all that slow.

Old DC generators were geared by a belt pulley to turn the same speed as the engine crankshaft. The alternator, however, is geared up to turn two and three times as fast as the engine. That means, with an engine idling at 500 rpm, the alternator can be turning 1500 rpm. At top speeds, alternators will rev up to 12,000 rpm. This is why the alternator is able to produce high amperage at low engine speeds.

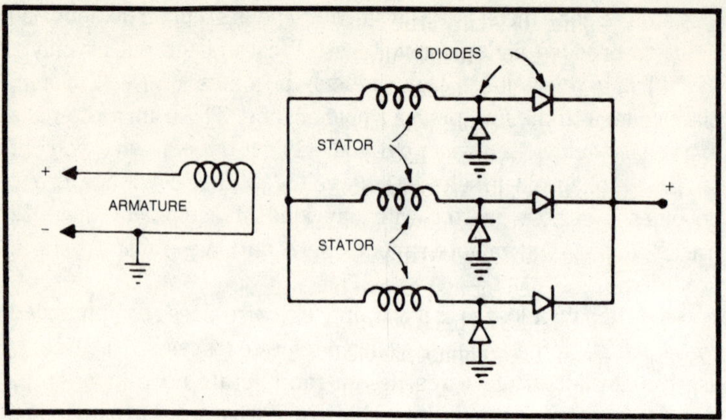

Fig. 8-14. The six diodes in an alternator act like a check valve in a water line, which lets water flow in only one direction.

Perhaps you are wondering why this couldn't have been done with the old DC generators. There is a good reason. Their armatures were so big and heavy that they could never be revved up to the same high rpm ratio as the alternator rotor, which is small and light. The DC armatures at 12,000 rpm would literally fly apart.

The alternator has other advantages. It does not have brushes or a commutator, which were a source of trouble and maintenance with old cars. The brushes, actually pieces of square carbon which touched and rubbed against the commutator, would wear down, had to be adjusted and then replaced. And the commutators, with all that rubbing and friction, would also wear down and build up resistance. This meant an overhaul job. Alternators, on the other hand, often outlast the car itself.

The armature in the alternator is stationary. It is called the stator. It is three sets of windings, terminating in three sets of diodes, as you can see in Fig. 8-14. The rotating part of the alternator is sometimes called an armature, but a more proper name is rotor, since it turns.

The rotor windings are excited by a tiny current from the battery. Without this little push, the alternator just won't work. This is the alternator's one big weakness; it will not charge a dead battery. Unless there is that tiny feedback to excite the rotor field windings, you get nothing. There is a way out of this predicament in an emergency, if you just happen to have two six-volt lantern batteries available. Hook them up in series, then run leads as shown in Fig. 8-15. The positive goes to the rotor, the negative to the alternator frame. This tiny little current is all the push needed to get an alternator putting out full output into the dead battery.

The alternator is efficient, quietly does its job and rarely causes trouble. There are people who have been driving cars for 20 years and never even knew they had an alternator. But it is not entirely trouble-free. Most alternator troubles are the result of goofs when installing and hooking up a new battery. It's an easy mistake to make, even for people who know what they are doing. Switch the polarity of those battery cables for just an eye blink, and all six diodes will burn out. The diode is like a check water valve which only lets water flow in one direction. They cannot handle a reverse flow of current, which is what happens when you cross or switch the cables around.

THE VOLTAGE REGULATOR

The alternator is the beginning and the end of the DC electrical system. But there is still the policeman who regulates traffic flow from the alternator. If left uncontrolled, the alternator would quickly ruin a battery by over-charging it to death. This is the reason for that little black metal box called the voltage regulator.

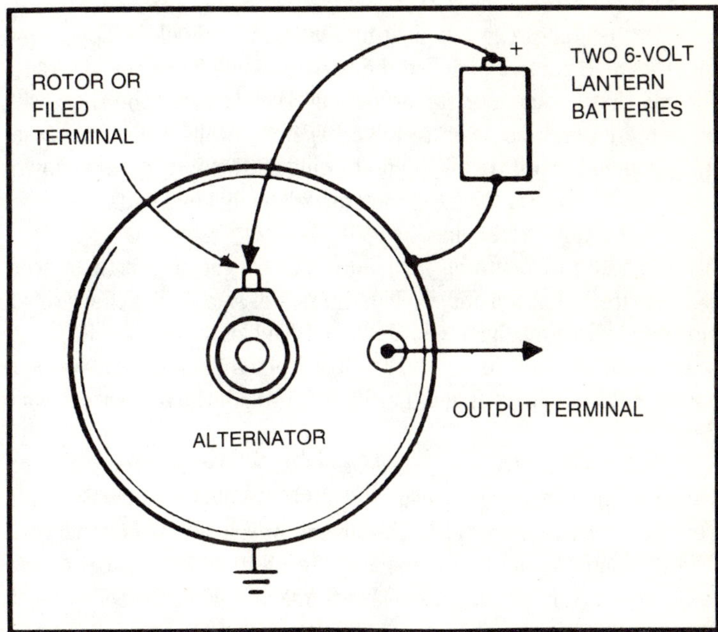

Fig. 8-15. The current required to energize, or "excite" the armature windings (also called rotor) is so small that a lantern battery, or even a half dozen flashlight batteries in series, will do the job.

Voltage regulators are usually set to maintain a system charging at 14 volts. If a battery is fully charged, they will maintain a residual charging rate of three or four amps, which will not harm a battery. When a battery is approaching discharge, its voltage drops. Rotor circuit resistance also drops and maximum current flows through the rotor coil. The rotor's magnetic field strength is high and the alternator's output reaches its maximum point for a given rpm.

The voltage regulator tries to maintain voltage at a precise and constant level, increasing the charging rate when battery voltage is low, decreasing it when it rises. There is one drawback, however. The alternator will not bring up to full charge a completely discharged battery. In other words, the alternator does not do quite the same job as a battery charger.

If you put a fully charged battery on your boat, the alternator will keep it fully charged. However, if your battery becomes 50 percent discharged after a week of operating bilge pumps while you are away, the alternator will bring it up slightly, then maintain it at that level, which is still only about 50 percent. No matter how much you run the engine, the battery level will not go up or down.

ALTERNATORS ARE NOT BATTERY CHARGERS

This is something few boatmen know, but should. They know that the bilge pump has pulled the battery down, but they naturally assume that a four hour run across the lake or down the river will bring the battery up again to full charge. So each week, the same thing happens, with the bilge pump bringing the battery level down lower and lower. Finally the cumulative effect leaves a battery so low it will not crank the engine.

This is how boatmen frequently get caught out on the water with a battery that will not crank their engine. And always they are so surprised when this happens. They tell the Coast Guard, who must make a report on all distress calls, "I just bought a new battery and I use my boat every weekend. I can't understand why the battery was dead."

Men who go to sea should never take anything for granted. Never assume that just because you use your boat every Sunday, your battery is fully charged. The alternator is not a battery charger. The alternator is a battery maintainer. It will maintain your battery at full charge if it is at full charge. It will maintain your battery at half charge if it is at half charge.

Although alternators are supposed to maintain a residual charging rate of three or four amps, even with a fully charged battery, they don't really do that. If they did, they would eventually bring up to full charge a completely dead battery.

Alternators do maintain voltage at a constant rate, which is usually 14 volts. But a battery can quickly reach a surface voltage of 14 volts after only a short charge and still be in a 50 percent rate of discharge. When voltage reaches 14 volts, the regulator decreases charging current flow until it reaches point zero on your ammeter. So your battery stays at 50 percent.

Perhaps now you get the message. Perhaps now you understand why seasoned boatmen do not depend on their alternators to keep their batteries at full capacity. They use marine type chargers which do the job safely, efficiently and automatically.

I have never known an experienced boatman who was not afraid of big water. Personally, I reach a state approaching panic when I see the Gulf Stream off Miami. Just thinking of what might happen if both my engines stopped in the Gulf Stream makes my heart pound and my body wet with cold sweat. I'm scared to death of big water. Yet I can't stay away because I love it.

TROUBLESHOOTING YOUR ELECTRIC MOTORS

With all the electric motors aboard even the smallest of cruisers, there will inevitably come a time when one of them will just buzz, hum and heat up when you push the button.

Don't get excited! Don't go looking for the marina electrician because you'll never find him. In fact, it's actually easier to find a plumber on Sunday. Do a little troubleshooting on your own first before you look for help.

Feel the motor. Is it warm? Is it cold? This is important. If warm, it is getting juice. If cold, it is not. Always check the fuse first on a cold motor.

If the motor just hums but won't turn over, it may be the starter windings. All AC motors have an extra "motor" inside with more muscle to overcome inertia and give it that extra push to get it rolling. Sometimes you can give a belt or pulley a push manually to get a motor started. This is proof positive that the trouble is in the starter windings. This is not a do-it-yourself repair job. But you can remove the motor, take it to a specialty shop that repairs and rebuilds electric motors. They'll do the job faster, better and cheaper than the marina. You can have your motor back in two or three days. Take it to the marina electrician and you'll be lucky to get it back in two or three months. You might not even get it back at all.

Overheating does not always mean starter problems. Dry, sticky bearings will do the same thing. Don't you ever believe those mystic words "requires no lubrication," or "lubricated for life." I have disassembled new motors that were "lubricated for life" and found dry dust in the bearings. You'll be pleasantly surprised to learn what a little oil and grease can do for a motor that hums and gets warm.

Another cause of overheating is overload. Try taking the load off the motor to see how it operates. If the motor winds up faster with the load removed, it is overloaded.

This is a common problem with windshield wiper motors. I have burned out six in six years—and four of them were rated as "Heavy Duty Marine" windshield wipers. They weren't. Today everything made is "heavy duty," which is just a cover-up for price increases.

Boat windshield wipers work under different conditions than the automobile type, which are used only when it rains, or when the windshield is dirty. A cleaning agent is squirted on the glass. The wiper blade cleans it off.

Boat wipers are used mostly when it is not raining to clear off occasional spray. Spray hitting a boat windshield is not a steady thing like rain. The glass is intermittently wet and dry, but most of the time it is dry. This is what increases the load on windshield wiper motors, swinging that rubber blade on dry glass and causing the motor to overheat and burn out.

I have been fighting this problem for years and have come up with a solution which seems to be working. Try using smaller wiper blades and less spring tension on the wiper arm. This reduces the load.

Windshield wiper motors give no warning of trouble. They just stop working. You throw them away. But some motors give warnings of impending trouble. They cycle on and off. They have thermal circuit breakers which reset themselves after cooling. This saves the motor. It also warns you. So find out why the motor overheats.

Overload is not the only thing which makes motors overheat. High voltage does the same thing. Now there is another paradox for you, and to confuse you. Low voltage also causes motors to overheat.

As previously stated, alternators are set to generate 14 volts. However, they often put out more. I have checked out 16 volts on some alternators, with 15 volts being quite common. With your engine running, your entire DC system voltage is 15 or 16 volts.

Tied up at the dock, or anchored, your system voltage drops down to 12 volts under load. Notice how your cabin lights brighten when your engine is running and how your searchlight throws a more powerful beam.

You can easily check your alternator voltage with a VOM meter. If it is over 14 volts, this could be the cause of your motor overheating. This is also the cause of fuses blowing in radiotelephones. What to do about it?

If it is causing you too much trouble, especially with your electronic gear, pull the alternator and buy a rebuilt exchange. You can do this yourself in one afternoon. And rebuilts on an exchange basis don't cost too much.

But have somebody else do it and you will be hung up at the dock for three months. You'll have to sell one of your kids to pay the bill.

If a DC or universal motor is making funny noises and causing interference in your television, open it up and check the brushes and commutator. If worn, replace the brushes. You must order these yourself direct from the manufacturer because marinas don't like to be bothered with "nickle and dime stuff" requiring paperwork and correspondence. Before putting in the new brushes, clean off the commutator with extra fine sandpaper.

If your AC motor won't start, even after you give it a good manual spin, it could be the starting capacitor—if it is a capacitor-start motor. This is a cylindrical object usually mounted on the motor somewhere. Remove the capacitor and check it with your VOM. The instruction book that comes with all VOMs will tell you how to check out a capacitor, or condenser, which is what it really is. If you don't have a meter, and are in a hurry, replace the capacitor. They only cost a few bucks.

Noisy motors are a nuisance because the sound gets telegraphed through the boat. Check the motor mountings because this is the source of most motor noise. Try remounting the motor on rubber pads. You'll be surprised what a little black sponge rubber can do.

I have yet to encounter a problem, electrical or mechanical, that couldn't be handled by prayer, patience and a little work. I have yet to encounter a problem that was handled on Sunday by the marina electrician—that most elusive of living creatures who is harder to find on Sunday then the abominable snowman.

I know of nothing that can make a boat owner stop believing in God faster than trying to find a marine electrician on Sunday.

Index